T0213840

Lecture Notes in Artificial Intelligence 9422

Subseries of Lecture Notes in Computer Science

More information about this series at http://www.springer.com/series/1244

José M. Puerta · José A. Gámez
Bernabé Dorronsoro · Edurne Barrenechea
Alicia Troncoso · Bruno Baruque
Mikel Galar (Eds.)

Advances in Artificial Intelligence

16th Conference of the Spanish Association
for Artificial Intelligence, CAEPIA 2015
Albacete, Spain, November 9–12, 2015
Proceedings

Springer

Editors

José M. Puerta
University of Castilla-La Mancha
Albacete
Spain

José A. Gámez
University of Castilla-La Mancha
Albacete
Spain

Bernabé Dorronsoro
University of Cadiz
Cadiz
Spain

Edurne Barrenechea
Public University of Navarre
Pamplona
Spain

Alicia Troncoso
Pablo de Olavide University
Sevilla
Spain

Bruno Baruque
University of Burgos
Burgos
Spain

Mikel Galar
Public University of Navarre
Pamplona
Spain

ISSN 0302-9743 ISSN 1611-3349 (electronic)
Lecture Notes in Artificial Intelligence
ISBN 978-3-319-24597-3 ISBN 978-3-319-24598-0 (eBook)
DOI 10.1007/978-3-319-24598-0

Library of Congress Control Number: 2015949405

LNCS Sublibrary: SL7 – Artificial Intelligence

Springer Cham Heidelberg New York Dordrecht London

Printed on acid-free paper

Springer International Publishing AG Switzerland is part of Springer Science+Business Media
(www.springer.com)

Preface

This volume contains a selection of the papers accepted for oral presentation at the 16th Conference of the Spanish Association for Artificial Intelligence (CAEPIA 2015), held in Albacete (Spain), during November 9–12, 2015. This was the 16th biennial conference in the CAEPIA series, which was started in 1985. Previous editions took place in Madrid, Alicante, Málaga, Murcia, Gijón, Donostia, Santiago de Compostela, Salamanca, Seville, La Laguna, and Madrid.

This time, CAEPIA was coordinated with various symposia, each one corresponding to a main track in Artificial Intelligence (AI) research: II Symposium on Evolutionary Algorithms and Metaheuristics (JAEM), II Symposium on Information Fusion and Ensembles (FINO), V Symposium of Fuzzy Logic and Soft Computing (LODISCO), VII Symposium of Theory and Applications of Data Mining (TAMIDA) and the Symposium on Artificial Intelligence Technology Transfer (TTIA). Furthermore, five workshops devoted to specific topics in AI research were associated with CAEPIA 2015: First Workshop in Big Data and Scalable Data Analytics (BIGDADE), Workshop on Social Robotics and Human–Robot Interaction (RSIM), Workshop on Intelligent Systems and Environment (SIMAB), Workshop on Linked Data Usage in Spanish: Present and Future (UDEEPF), and the Third Workshop on Intelligent Metaheuristics on Logistics Planning (MILP). We would like to highlight that two of these events (LODISCO and BIGDADE) could not have been organized without the collaboration of two thematic research networks funded by the Spanish Government (MINECO): the Network on Fuzzy Logic and Soft Computing (Red Temática en Lógica Difusa y Soft Computing), LODISCO (TIN2014-56381-REDT) and the Network on Big Data and Scalable Data Analysis (Red Temática en Big Data y Análisis de Datos Escalables), BIGDADE (TIN2014-56425-REDT).

CAEPIA is a forum open to worldwide researchers to present and discuss their last scientific and technological advances in AI. Its main aims are to facilitate the dissemination of new ideas and experiences, to strengthen the links among the different research groups, and to help spread new developments to society. All perspectives — theory, methodology, and applications — are welcome. Apart from the presentation of technical full papers, the scientific program of CAEPIA 2015 included three invited lectures, a Doctoral Consortium and, as a follow-up to the success achieved with CAEPIA 2013, a special session on outstanding recent papers (Key Works) already published in renowned journals or forums.

With the aim of maintaining CAEPIA as a high-quality conference, and following the model of current demanding AI conferences, the CAEPIA review process runs under the double-blind model. The number of submissions received by CAEPIA and associated tracks was 175; however, in order to produce a high-quality volume with selected papers, the authors were requested to mark their paper as candidate to be published in the LNAI volume. This decision, made by the authors, plays an important role as quality filter, and thus only 49 of the 175 submissions attained this mark.

These 49 papers were carefully peer-reviewed by three members of the CAEPIA Program Committee with the help of additional reviewers from the associated symposia and workshops. The reviewers judged the overall quality of the submitted papers, together with their originality and novelty, technical correctness, awareness of related work, and quality of presentation. The reviewers stated their confidence in the subject area in addition to detailed written comments. On the basis of the reviews, the program chairs made the final decisions. After the review process, 31 out of the 49 marked papers were accepted for oral presentation and publication in this volume. This selection contains papers from the CAEPIA main track, LODISCO, JAEM, TAMIDA, FINO, SIMAB, BIGDADE, UDEEPF and RSIM.

The three distinguished invited speakers at CAEPIA 2015 were Pedro Meseguer (CSIC, Spain), Nuria Oliver (Telefónica I+D, Spain) and Manuela Veloso (Carnegie Mellon University, USA). They presented three very interesting topics on current AI research: "Constraint Programming: A Powerful Technology for AI" (Meseguer), "Towards Data-Driven Models of Human Behavior" (Oliver) and "Human–Robot Interaction in Symbiotic Autonomous Mobile Service Robots" (Veloso).

The Doctoral Consortium (DC) was specially designed for the interaction between PhD students and senior researchers. AEPIA and the organization of CAEPIA will recognize the best PhD work submitted to the DC with a prize, as well as the best student and conference paper presented at CAEPIA 2015. Furthermore, for the first time, and with the aim of promoting the presence of women in AI research, a new prize was set at CAEPIA 2015: the *Frances Allen* award, which is devoted to the two best AI PhD Thesis presented by a woman during the last two years.

The editors would like to thank everyone who contributed to CAEPIA 2015 and associated events: the authors of the papers, the members of the Scientific Committees, additional reviewers, the invited speakers, etc. Thanks are also due to Jacinto Arias and Javier Cózar, who designed the website of the CAEPIA conference, managed it, and compiled the proceedings. Final thanks go to the Organizing Committee, our local sponsors (UCLM, DSI, ESII and I3A), the EasyChair and Springer teams, and AEPIA for their support.

July 2015

José M. Puerta
José A. Gámez
Bernabé Dorronsoro
Edurne Barrenechea
Alicia Troncoso
Bruno Baruque
Mikel Galar

Organization

General Chairs

José A. Gámez   Universidad de Castilla-La Mancha, Spain
José M. Puerta   Universidad de Castilla-La Mancha, Spain

Program Chairs

Pedro Aguilera-Aguilera (SIMAB)
Enrique Alba (JAEM)
Amparo Alonso-Betanzos (BIGDADE)
Ramón Álvarez-Valdés (MIPL)
Edurne Barrenechea (LODISCO)
Bruno Baruque (FINO)
Pablo Bustos (RSIM)
Miguel A. Cazorla (RSIM)
Emilio Corchado (FINO)
María J. Del Jesús (BIGDADE)
Bernabé Dorronsoro (JAEM)
Mikel Galar (FINO)
José A. Gámez (CAEPIA)
Raul García-Castro (UDEPF)

Ismael García-Varea (RSIM)
Francisco Herrera (BIGDADE)
Luis Martínez (LODISCO)
Jesús Martínez-Gómez (RSIM)
José L. Molina (SIMAB)
Francisco Parreño (MIPL)
José M. Puerta (CAEPIA)
Mariano Rico (UDEEPF)
José C. Riquelme (TAMIDA)
Rafael Rumí-Rodríguez (SIMAB)
Emilio Soria (TTIA)
Alicia Troncoso (TAMIDA)
Boris Villazón-Terrazas (UDEEPF)

Program Committee

Jesús Aguilar, Spain
Pedro Aguilera-Aguilera, Spain
Enrique Alba, Spain
Jesus Alcalá, Spain
Rafael Alcalá, Spain
Amparo Alonso-Betanzos, Spain
Ada Álvarez, Spain
Ramón Álvarez-Valdés, Spain
Carlos Ansótegui, Spain
Alessandro Antonucci, Switzerland
Lourdes Araujo, Spain
Marta Arias, Spain
Gualberto Asencio-Cortés, Spain
Ghislain Atemezing, France

Jaume Bacardit, UK
Emili Balaguer, UK
Edurne Barrenechea, Spain
Bruno Baruque, Spain
Benjamín Bedregal, Spain
José M. Benítez, Spain
Pablo Bermejo, Spain
Concha Bielza, Spain
Christian Blum, Spain
Daniel Borrajo, Spain
Juan Botía, UK
Alberto Bugarín, Spain
Humberto Bustince, Spain
Pablo Bustos, Spain

Serafín Moral, Spain
J. Marcos Moreno, Spain
José A. Moreno, Spain
Juan A. Nepomuceno, Spain
Hermann Ney, The Netherlands
Thomas D. Nielsen, Denmark
Manuel Ojeda-Aciego, Spain
José A. Olivas, Spain
Eugénio Oliveira, Portugal
Eva Onaindia, Spain
Sascha Ossowski, Spain
Francisco Parreño, Spain
Juan Pavón, Spain
Antonio Peregrín, Spain
José M. Peña, Sweden
Rafael Peñaloza, Italy
Filiberto Plá, Spain
Héctor Pomares, Spain
José M. Puerta, Spain
Javier Pérez-Florido, Spain
Helena Ramalhinho Lourenco, Spain
M.J. Ramírez, Spain
Mariano Rico, Spain
Juan Pedro Rigol, Spain
José C. Riquelme, Spain
Ramón Rizo, Spain
Juan J. Rodríguez, Spain
Emma Rollón, Spain
Jesús Ángel Román Gallego, Spain

Michael Rovatsos, UK
Rafael Rumí-Rodríguez, Spain
Jorge Sales, Spain
Antonio Salmerón, Spain
Roberto Santana, Spain
José A. Sanz, Spain
Ángel Sappa, Spain
Cristina Sarasua, Spain
Eduardo Segredo, Spain
Carles Sierra, Spain
Emilio Soria, Spain
Thomas Stützle, Switzerland
Luis Enrique Sucar, Mexico
Luciano Sánchez, Spain
M. Inés Torres, Spain
Alicia Troncoso, Spain
Laura Uusitalo, Finland
M. Belen Vaquerizo, Spain
Sebastián Ventura, Spain
José Luís Verdegay, Spain
Joan Vila Francés, Spain
José Ramón Villar, Spain
Pedro Villar, Spain
Mateu Villaret, Spain
Jordi Vitria, Spain
Amelia Zafra, Spain
Marta Zorrilla, Spain
Pedro Zorrilla, Spain

Organizing Committee

José Antonio Gámez, UCLM (Chair)
José Miguel Puerta, UCLM (Chair)
Juan Ángel Aledo, UCLM
Juan Ignacio Alonso, UCLM
María Teresa Alonso, UCLM
Jacinto Arias, UCLM
Pablo Bermejo, UCLM
Javier Cózar, UCLM
María Julia Flores, UCLM
Ismael García-Varea, UCLM
Jesús Martínez-Gómez, UCLM
Luis de la Ossa, UCLM

Francisco Parreño, UCLM
Luis Rodríguez-Ruiz, UCLM
Cristina Romero, UCLM
Gonzalo Vergara, UCLM

Sponsors

- Asociación Española de Inteligencia Artificial (AEPIA)
- Universidad de Castilla-La Mancha (UCLM)

Contents

Knowledge Representation, Reasoning and Logic

Intelligent Systems and Environment

Intelligent Web and Recommender Systems

Machine Learning and Data Mining

Metaheuristics and Evolutionary Computation

Social Robotics

Bayesian Networks and Uncertainty Modeling

A Novel Weakly Supervised Problem: Learning from Positive-Unlabeled Proportions

Jerónimo Hernández-González[✉], Iñaki Inza, and Jose A. Lozano

Intelligent Systems Group, University of the Basque Country UPV/EHU,
Donostia - San Sebastián, Spain
{jeronimo.hernandez,inaki.inza,ja.lozano}@ehu.eus

Abstract. Standard supervised classification learns a classifier from a set of labeled examples. Alternatively, in the field of weakly supervised classification different frameworks have been presented where the training data cannot be certainly labeled. In this paper, the novel problem of learning from positive-unlabeled proportions is presented. The provided examples are unlabeled and the only class information available consists of the *proportions* of positive and unlabeled examples in different subsets of the training dataset. An expectation-maximization method that learns Bayesian network classifiers from this kind of data is proposed. A set of experiments has been designed with the objective of shedding light on the capability of learning from this kind of data throughout different scenarios of increasing complexity.

Keywords: Positive-unlabeled learning · Label proportions · Weakly supervised classification · Structural EM method · Bayesian network models

1 Introduction

In standard supervised classification, the categorizing behavior of a problem of interest is reproduced by a classifier. Learning techniques infer the categorizing behavior from a given set of *certainly* labeled (categorized) problem examples. The objective is to, given a new unlabeled example, accurately predict its category (class label).

Other classification frameworks which do not provide such a *certainly* labeled dataset for training a classifier have received considerable attention in the related literature. Specific techniques have recently been proposed for learning accurate classifiers from weakly labeled datasets. In the popular semi-supervised learning [4,21], for instance, only a subset of the training examples are labeled. In positive-unlabeled learning (PU) [3], a binary classification problem is solved by learning a classifier from a training dataset with only a subset of positive examples. A limited labeling process only allows us to identify a subset of positive examples, whereas the rest remains unlabeled (both positive or negative examples compose the unlabeled subset). The class information is provided in a completely different way in the learning from label proportions (LLP) [16,18] problem. In this case,

© Springer International Publishing Switzerland 2015
J.M. Puerta et al. (Eds.): CAEPIA 2015, LNAI 9422, pp. 3–13, 2015.
DOI: 10.1007/978-3-319-24598-0_1

although the training examples are provided individually unlabeled, the dataset is organized in groups of examples (named as *bags* in the related literature); for each bag, the proportion of examples that belong to each class is available.

A novel weakly supervised classification problem, which is halfway between the exposed positive-unlabeled and the label proportions frameworks, has been abstracted from a real application. The problem consists of identifying early-stage embryos that will succeed in reaching advanced developmental stages with the objective of selecting the most promising embryos to use in procedures of assisted reproduction [7,13,17]. The problem examples describe embryos in an early stage and a binary class variable represents the achievement of an advanced embryo development. An embryo with developmental capability is correlated with the success of assisted reproductive technologies (ARTs) [7] (i.e., inducing a pregnancy). However, the training dataset is composed of embryos used in previous ART procedures and the nature of the problem makes the labeling process unfeasible. On the one hand, in an ART cycle where three embryos are transferred to a woman and only one implants (success), it is impossible to state which one of the three transferred embryos implanted and which failed [17]. On the other hand, as there are several causes for implantation failure [1], it cannot be claimed that an embryo that failed to implant was unable to develop. Thus, the resulting training dataset is composed of a set of unlabeled examples that are provided grouped in subsets and, for each of subset, the proportion of positive (and unlabeled) examples is provided. From LLP [16,18], this problem borrows the dataset divided in subsets and the grouped information of supervision provided by means of proportions. Its similarity with PU [3] consists in the fact of being based on binary classification problems where only information about the presence of positive examples is provided (no information is provided about the class of the other *unlabeled* examples). This is also the main difference with LLP, where the proportions of examples assigned to each class label are explicitly known for each subset of examples.

Do not confuse this problem with some kind of generalized multiple instance learning (G-)MIL framework [20]. In MIL, each bag represents a single example (with multiple descriptions) which is labeled. In fact, the objective of the problem is to build a classifier of bags. On the contrary, in our problem the nature of bags is completely different: they do not represent examples and, accordingly, labeling a bag is senseless. In this novel problem, instances are examples and, therefore, learning techniques produce classifiers of single instances. In fact, our kind of bags is the product of an unfeasible labeling process that is only able to globally provide partial class information for the examples in the group (bag). In this paper we show that learning accurate classifiers from this kind of weakly supervised data is possible and can be efficiently performed.

The rest of the paper is organized as follows. In the next section, a formal definition of the problem is presented. Then, we present an Expectation-Maximization (EM) method for learning Bayesian network classifiers from this kind of data. Next, a set of experiments that simulate different problem scenarios of increasing difficulty is set up to show the limits in the learning ability of our method. The paper finishes with some conclusions and future work.

2 Learning from Positive and Unlabeled Proportions

In this paper, the presented problem receives the name of learning from positive and unlabeled proportions (PUP) due to its similarity with both learning from label proportions and positive-unlabeled learning paradigms. Like the standard supervised learning paradigm [15], the problem is described by a set of n predictive variables $(X_1, \ldots, X_n)$ and a class variable C. Moreover, $\mathcal{X}$ denotes the instance space (all the possible value assignments to the n predictive variables) and, given the binary nature of the problem, the label space (the set of all possible class labels) is $\mathcal{C} = \{-, +\}$. Accordingly, a problem example $(\mathbf{x}, c)$ is a $(n + 1)$-tuple that assigns a value to each variable and is supposed to be i.i.d. sampled from some underlying probability distribution.

In this novel weakly supervised paradigm, the examples of the available training dataset D are provided grouped in b bags $D = \mathbf{B}_1 \cup \mathbf{B}_2 \cup \cdots \cup \mathbf{B}_b$, where $\mathbf{B}_i \cap \mathbf{B}_j = \emptyset, \forall i \neq j$. Each bag $\mathbf{B}_i = \{\mathbf{x}_1, \mathbf{x}_2, \ldots, \mathbf{x}_{m_i}\}$ groups m_i examples and the associated m_{i+} value ($m_{i+} \leq m_i$) indicates the *minimum* number of positive examples in $\mathbf{B}_i$. Other ($m_i - m_{i+}$) examples in $\mathbf{B}_i$ are unlabeled and nothing is known about their class label. In this paper, the problem of partial observability is restricted to the class variable: It is assumed that the predictive variables are fully observed. As a standard supervised classification problem, the objective is to learn a classifier that infers the label of new unseen examples.

Note that in a bag $\mathbf{B}_i$ with $m_{i+} = m_i$ there is no uncertainty about the label of its examples: all of them are positive. In this paper, the term *consistent completion* of a bag $\mathbf{B}_i$ is used to refer to any m_i-tuple that assigns a label to the examples in $\mathbf{B}_i$ fulfilling m_{i+}; i.e., the number of positive labels in a consistent completion of $\mathbf{B}_i$ is, at least, m_{i+}.

3 A SEM Method for Learning Bayesian Network Classifiers from Positive and Unlabeled Proportions

We propose a learning algorithm based on the Structural Expectation-Maximization (SEM) strategy [8], which iteratively alternates the estimation of the most probable labeling for the examples of each bag (according to m_{i+}) and the improvement of the learnt model. In this analysis, three kinds of Bayesian network models have been used as probabilistic classifiers: naive Bayes (NB) [11], tree augmented naive Bayes (TAN) [9] and K-dependence Bayesian network (KDB) [19]. A Bayesian network, represented by a pair $(G, \boldsymbol{\theta})$, is a probabilistic graphical model that encodes the conditional dependencies between a set of random variables $\mathcal{V}$ using a directed acyclic graph (DAG). The graph structure, $G = (\mathcal{V}, \mathcal{R})$, codifies the arcs $\mathcal{R}$ (conditional dependencies) between nodes $\mathcal{V} = (X_1, \ldots, X_n, C)$ (random variables), and $\boldsymbol{\theta}$ is the set of parameters of the conditional probability functions of each variable given its parents in the graph. Our choice has been motivated by the notable interpretability of the BN models: influences and dependencies among variables can be induced from the explicit probability relationships. The general classification rule of the considered BNCs is:

$$\hat{c} = h(\mathbf{x}) = \underset{c}{\operatorname{argmax}} \, p(C = c) \prod_{v=1}^{n} p(X_v = x_v | PA(X_v) = pa(x_v), C = c)$$

where $pa(x_v)$ is the vector of values assigned in the example $\mathbf{x}$ to the predictive variables which are parents of X_v —$PA(X_v)$— in the network structure.

Based on the assumption of conditional independence between the predictive variables given the class variable, naive Bayes presents the simplest network structure among the considered BNCs. TAN and KDB are the next step forward in terms of network structure complexity and allow models to capture some conditional dependencies between predictive variables. Friedman [9] and Sahami [19] proposed a method for learning, respectively, TAN and KDB structures from complete datasets. NB, given its fixed structure, does not require structural learning. All model parameters can be estimated, in case of complete data, with maximum likelihood estimates by means of frequency counts [12].

The Structural EM strategy (SEM) provides a suitable framework to infer both the graph structure and the model parameters of BNCs from weakly labeled data. The EM strategy, proposed by Dempster et al. [6], is used in our framework to obtain the maximum likelihood parameters from this kind of weakly supervised data. Iteratively, the method calculates the probabilities of the different label assignments for each example given the current fit of the model, and re-estimates the model parameters. Under fairly general conditions, the iterative increment of the likelihood has been proved to converge to a stationary value (most of the times, a local maximum) [14]. Additionally, the SEM strategy incorporates an outer loop to the parametric-convergence loop of the classical EM, and iteratively improves an initially-proposed structure.

In Algorithm 1, a pseudo-code of the SEM method developed in this paper is shown. In the initialization, the dataset is completed labeling the examples of each bag according to a randomly selected consistent completion (line 2 in Algorithm 1). Then, the complete dataset is used to estimate an initial fit of the model by means of the previously exposed classical techniques (line 3). At each iteration, model parameters are estimated by frequency counts, as usual, from the recently estimated complete dataset (line 7). The estimator implements the Laplacian correction in order to avoid zero counts. In line 9, the neighborhood of structures is composed by all those structures that can be reached from the current structure by means of a single change (reverse and deletion/inclusion). Only those candidate structures that fulfill the constraints of the selected type of BNC are considered. Candidate changes are evaluated using the log K2 score [5] and that which improves the score of the current structure most is chosen. As the log K2 score is decomposable, the arc inclusion/deletion can be evaluated by only taking into account the arc-destination variable and its parents. The inner-loop E-step (line 6) is the key point of our proposal, where the current fit of the model is used to estimate the completion of the training examples.

Algorithm 1. Pseudo-code of our Structural EM method.

```
 1: procedure STRUCTURALEM(D, maxIt, ε)              ▷ D: PUP dataset
 2:      D̂₀ ← initialLabeling(D)            ▷ maxIt: max. number of iterations
 3:      M ≡ (G₀, θ₀) ← standardLearning(D̂₀)      ▷ ε: threshold (stop condition)
 4:      repeat
 5:          repeat
 6:              D̂ⱼ ← completionEstimating(D, M ≡ (Gᵢ, θⱼ₋₁))
 7:              θⱼ ← parametricLearning(D̂ⱼ, Gᵢ)
 8:          until (diff(θⱼ, θⱼ₋₁) < ε) Or (j = maxIt)
 9:          Gᵢ ← findMaxNeighborStructure(D̂ⱼ, Gᵢ₋₁)
10:      until (Gᵢ = Gᵢ₋₁) Or (i = maxIt)
11:      return M ≡ (Gᵢ, θⱼ)
12: end procedure
```

3.1 A Probabilistic Completion for the Training Examples

The procedure in Line 6 of Algorithm 1 calculates, for each bag $\mathbf{B}_i$, a reliable joint labeling for the examples of the bag using the probabilistic predictions of the current fit of the model and fulfilling the *minimum* number of positive examples (m_{i+}). As m_{i+} tends to m_i, the PUP class information allows us to discard an increasing number of label assignments to the examples of a bag $\mathbf{B}_i$. In a scenario without any class information, the number of possible label assignments for a group of m_i examples is $|\mathcal{C}|^{m_i}$ (in this binary problem, $|\mathcal{C}| = 2$). If this group of m_i examples form a bag $\mathbf{B}_i$ with certain m_{i+}, the number of possible label assignments is reduced to:

$$2^{m_i} - \sum_{h=0}^{m_{i+}-1} \binom{m_i}{h}$$

This reduction implies the consideration of joint label assignments to all the examples of the bag. The set of considered joint assignments is composed of all the consistent completions for $\mathbf{B}_i$. A consistent completion is represented by a tuple of labels, $\mathbf{e} = (e_1, e_2, \ldots, e_{m_i})$, where each e_j is the class value assigned to the jth instance of $\mathbf{B}_i$ and fulfills the minimum number of positive labels (at least m_{i+} labels $e_j \in \mathbf{e}$ are positive). Consequently, the probability of assigning a label c to an example $\mathbf{x}_j \in \mathbf{B}_i$ has to be jointly calculated together with the rest of examples in $\mathbf{B}_i$. According to the assumption of i.i.d. sampling, the joint probability of a class assignment $\mathbf{e}$ for the examples of a bag $\mathbf{B}_i$ can be calculated as the product of the conditional probabilities of each class label e_j given its respective example $\mathbf{x}_j \in \mathbf{B}_i$:

$$p(\mathbf{e}|\mathbf{B}_i) = \prod_{j=1}^{m_i} p(C = e_j | X_1 = x_{j1}, \ldots, X_n = x_{jn}) \tag{1}$$

Our method builds a *probabilistic* consistent completion $\mathbf{E}$ for each bag (line 6 in Algorithm 1). A probabilistic consistent completion $\mathbf{E}$ assigns example $\mathbf{x}_j$ to class label c with probability E_{jc}, where $\sum_{c \in \{-,+\}} E_{jc} = 1$ and

$E_{jc} \geq 0, \forall \mathbf{x}_j \in \mathbf{B}_i$ and $\forall c \in \{-, +\}$ such that $\sum_{j=1}^{m_i} E_{j+} \geq m_{i+}$. For each bag $\mathbf{B}_i$, our method obtains the joint probability of each non-probabilistic consistent completion $\mathbf{e}$ according to Eq. 1. Then, probability E_{jc} is calculated as the normalized summation of the joint probability of all the consistent completions that assign label c to example $\mathbf{x}_j$:

$$E_{jc} = \frac{\sum_{\mathbf{e}|e_j = c} p(\mathbf{e}|\mathbf{B}_i)}{\sum_{\mathbf{e}} p(\mathbf{e}|\mathbf{B}_i)} \tag{2}$$

The resulting probabilistic consistent completion is used to label the examples of $\mathbf{B}_i$.

Due to the exponential increase in the number of consistent completions, this approach becomes unfeasible as m_i grows and m_{i+} decreases. For unfeasible bags, an approximate solution with almost invariant time requirements is proposed. This alternative procedure also carries out a probabilistic completion, but using a Markov Chain Monte Carlo (MCMC) approximation [14]. MCMC [2,10] approximates a probability distribution of interest by means of Markov chains and estimates the expected value using samples drawn from the Markov chain.

The stage involving the first bi samples is not considered to calculate the expected value (probabilistic consistent completion, $\mathbf{E}$). This stage, known as $burn$-in [2], is assumed to be the interval required to reach the stationary distribution that simulates the probability distribution of interest. Other s completions are sampled to estimate the probabilistic consistent completion. At each step, a new sample $\mathbf{e}_{t+1}$ is randomly selected from the neighborhood of $\mathbf{e}_t$, which is composed of any consistent completion obtained by (1) changing the sign of a label e_{tj} (if m_{i+} remains fulfilled) or (2) swapping two labels e_{tj} and $e_{tj'}$ with different signs. A rejection MCMC procedure [10] has been implemented, where the new sample $\mathbf{e}_{t+1}$ is rejected with probability $max(0, p(\mathbf{e}_t|\mathbf{B}_i) - p(\mathbf{e}_{t+1}|\mathbf{B}_i))$. In case of rejection, the previous sample $\mathbf{e}_t$ is duplicated. It can be easily shown that this proposal fulfills the conditions that guarantee sequence convergence. The final completion $\mathbf{E}$ is estimated as the proportion of samples that assign each $\mathbf{x}_j \in \mathbf{B}_i$ to each $c \in \{-, +\}$:

$$E_{jc} = \frac{1}{s} \sum_{t=bi+1}^{bi+s} 1_{[e_{tj}=c]}$$

In the final method, this approximate MCMC-based approach is carried out for those bags with a number of consistent completions larger than $bi + s$. For the rest of bags, the previously exposed exact procedure is used.

4   Experiments

The main objective of this set of experiments is to evaluate our proposal when dealing with different experimental conditions of increasing class uncertainty.

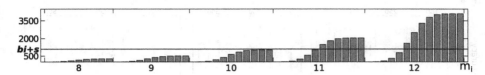

Fig. 1. Graphical summary of the number of consistent completions of a bag as its size (m_i) increases and the *minimum* number of positive examples decreases ($m_{i+} = \{m_i, m_i - 1, \ldots, 0\}$). The horizontal black line marks the threshold (in this paper, $bi + s = 1100$) for applying a MCMC approximation to estimate the labeling.

Due to the lack of publicly available real PUP datasets, artificially generated data has been used to evaluate our proposal. Fully labeled datasets are sampled and, subsequently, these are transformed to PUP datasets with different bag sizes (m_i) and *minimum* numbers of positive examples (m_{i+}). First of all, our procedure for aggregating a PUP dataset from a fully labeled dataset uses a parameter to indicate the *global proportion of positive examples* whose labels are removed (r_+). A dataset of positive and unlabeled examples is obtained and all the examples are distributed in *bags of size* m_i (second parameter). In order to generate scenarios of different complexity, a third parameter, h, indicates the *distribution of the positive examples throughout the bags*. When $h = 0$, all the positive examples are grouped in the minimum possible number of bags. This scenario promotes the arrangement of bags with $m_{i+} = m_i$, i.e., certainly labeled examples are available. At the opposite extreme, when $h = 1$, the positive examples are homogeneously distributed throughout the bags. That is, the bags reach their averaged maximum complexity.

Experimental Setting. In order to sample the synthetic datasets, 9 generative models are randomly generated, three models for each BNC type (NB, TAN and 2DB). All of them involve 10 binary predictive variables and one binary class variable. TAN and 2DB structures have been randomly generated. Their model parameters have been obtained randomly by sampling a Dirichlet distribution with all the hyper-parameters equal to 1. Three sample sizes (100, 250 and 500) have been considered. From each generative model and for each sample size, 10 datasets have been sampled. To sum up, 90 fully labeled datasets have been sampled (9 generative models × 10 repetitions) for each sample size (3).

In order to aggregate scenarios of different class uncertainty, the three parameters involved are assigned a range of values: $m_i = \{3, 6, 9, 15, 21\}$, $r_+ = \{0.0, 0.25, 0.5, 0.75\}$ and $h = \{0.0, 0.25, 0.5, 0.75\}$. The set of values has been selected to explore the whole spectrum of class uncertainty scenarios. It can be appreciated in Fig. 1 that, as bag size m_i exceeds 10, the probability of aggregating bags for which the approximate MCMC procedure has to be employed rises. For each fully labeled dataset and configuration of these three parameters, 10 different aggregations are randomly generated.

From the resulting dataset of each aggregated scenario the exposed three types of Bayesian network classifiers (NB, TAN and 2DB) are learnt. That is,

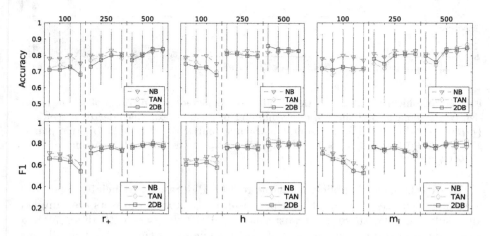

Fig. 2. Results of the three considered types of classifiers (NB, TAN and 2DB) learnt in a variety of scenarios of different uncertainty. In these figures, average accuracy (top row) and F1 (bottom row), and their associated standard deviation values are shown. Vertical divisions of the figures separate experiments performed with different sample sizes $m = \{100, 250, 500\}$. In each column, one of the three parameters is studied and used to simulate different scenarios. Each line links the results of a type of classifier in different scenarios aggregated by fixing the other two parameters and increasing only the studied one: in the first column $r_+ = \{0.0, 0.25, 0.5, 0.75\}$, in the second column $h = \{0.0, 0.25, 0.5, 0.75\}$ and in the last column $m_i = \{3, 6, 9, 15, 21\}$.

we have evaluated the proposed method learning 3 types of Bayesian network classifiers from 270 synthetic datasets (9 models × 3 sample sizes × 10 repetitions), each of them aggregated 10 times in 80 different scenarios (4 h × 4 r_+ × 5 m_i). All the experiments are evaluated in a 10 × 5-fold cross validation process. Bags are aggregated first and the CV folds are then built such that the division in bags of the PUP dataset is respected.

The Structural EM method uses two parameters: the threshold that indicates parametric convergence is set to 0.1 %, and the maximum number of iterations for both structural and parametric convergence is fixed to 200 iterations. The parameters of the MCMC procedure are set to $bi = 100$ samples of burn-in and $s = 1000$ samples to estimate the completion.

Results. In order to test the influence of the global number of labeled (positive) examples r_+, our method is evaluated in scenarios aggregated with increasing r_+ values, whereas both of the other parameters are fixed ($m_i = 9$ and $h = 0.5$) with the objective of attenuating their impact in the results. Both illustrations in the first column of Fig. 2 represent the obtained results in terms of accuracy and F1 metrics, respectively. Similarly, the influence of the distribution of the labeled (positive) examples among the aggregated bags h is shown by evaluating our method in scenarios generated with different h values and fixed $m_i = 9$ and $r_+ = 0.5$. Both illustrations of the second column of Fig. 2 represent the obtained results in terms of accuracy and F1 metrics. The corresponding results are graphically presented in the second column of Fig. 2. Finally, the influence of the bag size m_i is tested. The results are shown in the third column of Fig. 2 and, following the same strategy, both of the other parameters are fixed ($r_+ = 0.5$ and $h = 0.5$) whereas the m_i parameter is assigned different values to aggregate a range of PUP scenarios.

Discussion. A set of considerations can be highlighted from the experimental results of the proposed method:

- Both r_+ and h parameters affect the average number of consistent completions of the aggregated bags (i.e., the class uncertainty of the overall dataset) and, probably, the complexity of the inferred PUP scenario. In fact, r_+ directly reduces the number of labeled (positive) examples. However, in practice, both r_+ and h seem to have a similar limited influence in the performance of the learnt classifiers. Only in the experiments where the sample size is small ($m = 100$) and when a large value is assigned to any of the parameters (the difficulty to identify the real label of the examples increases) a reduced performance of the classifiers is appreciated. This shows the stability of our method when enough examples are provided.
- Our approximate MCMC procedure successfully deals with large bag sizes $m_i = \{15, 21\}$. Beyond the expected downward trend of the results as m_i increases, the use of this approximate approach does not produce any exceptional drop in performance of the method. Moreover, as the size of the dataset rises, learnt classifiers show an enhanced performance independently of the procedure (exact or approximate) used for estimating the probabilistic consistent completion. To sum up, the reliability of the MCMC procedure is shown by means of the stable and competent results obtained when an approximation has been carried out.
- Among the selected types of BNCs, the NB classifiers show the best performance (in terms of both accuracy and F1 metrics) when few training examples are available. As the sample size grows, TAN and 2DB classifiers, with a more intricate network structure, seems to fit better the generative probability distribution. The performance of all the types of BNCs is enhanced with larger datasets, but the results (in terms of both accuracy and F1) reflects that the improvement is stronger for TAN and 2DB classifiers. Regarding the variation of the value of other parameters, all the classifiers consistently show a similar response. In conclusion, NB is the most robust type of BNC in these experiments, while in case of high sample sizes, TAN and 2DB classifiers outperform NBs.

5 Conclusions

In this paper, a novel weakly supervised classification problem has been described, learning from positive-unlabeled proportions. We propose an EM method to learn

BNCs from proportions of positive and unlabeled examples. The proposed methodology deals with the uncertainty that characterizes this kind of data and is able to adapt automatically to the specific challenges that are issued in different problem scenarios of increasing class uncertainty.

The use of artificially generated data in the experimental setting of this work has allowed us to calculate performance metrics for this problem. In a real scenario, this would have been impossible: evaluation and other procedures need to be adapted to the use of this kind of weakly labeled data. Therefore, further research is required for developing all these procedures that will eventually allow us to test the proposed methodology in a real PUP scenario. More easily achievable, the use of standard (fully labeled) real datasets should be considered. Although they also require the synthetical generation of the bag/labeling structure, it would provide an initial evaluation of the behavior of our methodology in real data. Moving to a different issue, it could be interesting to explore the possibility of adjusting the MCMC parameters (bi and s) independently for each single bag depending on its level of class uncertainty. This will surely have certain implications on the behavior of our method, as it uses $(bi + s)$ as threshold for applying the MCMC approximation to estimate the probabilistic consistent completion. Consequently, the use of other thresholds independent of the MCMC parameters should be studied. Finally, it would be interesting to study the relationship among this and the positive-unlabeled learning paradigms.

Acknowledgments. This work has been partially supported by the Basque Government (IT609-13) and the Spanish Ministry of Economy and Competitiveness MINECO (TIN2013-41272-P). Jerónimo Hernández-González holds a grant (FPU) from the Spanish Ministry of Education, Culture and Sports.

References

1. Achache, H., Revel, A.: Endometrial receptivity markers, the journey to successful embryo implantation. Hum. Reprod. Update **12**(6), 731–746 (2006)
2. Brooks, S.P.: Markov chain monte carlo method and its application. J. R. Stat. Soc. Ser. D-Statist. **47**(1), 69–100 (1998)
3. Calvo, B., Larrañaga, P., Lozano, J.A.: Learning Bayesian classifiers from positive and unlabeled examples. Pattern Recogn. Lett. **28**(16), 2375–2384 (2007)
4. Chapelle, O., Schölkopf, B., Zien, A.: Semi-Supervised Learning. The MIT Press, Cambridge (2006)
5. Cooper, G.F., Herskovits, E.: A Bayesian method for the induction of probabilistic networks from data. Mach. Learn. **9**(4), 309–347 (1992)
6. Dempster, A.P., Laird, N.M., Rubin, D.B.: Maximum likelihood from incomplete data via the EM algorithm. J. R. Stat. Soc. Ser. B-Stat. Methodol. **39**(1), 1–38 (1977)
7. Ebner, T., Moser, M., Sommergruber, M., Tews, G.: Selection based on morphological assessment of oocytes and embryos at different stages of preimplantation development: a review. Hum. Reprod. Update **9**(3), 251–262 (2003)
8. Friedman, N.: Learning belief networks in the presence of missing values and hidden variables. In: Proceedings of the 14th ICML, pp. 125–133 (1997)

9. Friedman, N., Geiger, D., Goldszmidt, M.: Bayesian network classifiers. Mach. Learn. **29**(2–3), 131–163 (1997)
10. Gilks, W.R., Richardson, S., Spiegelhalter, D.J.: Markov Chain Monte Carlo in Practice. Chapman & Hall, London (1996)
11. Hand, D.J., Yu, K.: Idiot's Bayes–not so stupid after all? Int. Stat. Rev. **69**(3), 385–398 (2001)
12. Heckerman, D.: A tutorial on learning with bayesian networks. Technical report MSR-TR-95-06, Learning in Graphical Models (1995)
13. Hernández-González, J., Inza, I., Crisol-Ortíz, L., Guembe, M.A., Iñarra, M.J., Lozano, J.A.: Novel weakly supervised classification techniques for human assisted reproduction: a case study. Stat. Med. (2015, Submitted)
14. McLachlan, G.J., Krishnan, T.: The EM Algorithm and Extensions. (Wiley Series in Probability and Statistics). Wiley-Interscience, New York (1997)
15. Mitchell, T.: Machine Learning. McGraw Hill, New York (1997)
16. Musicant, D.R., Christensen, J.M., Olson, J.F.: Supervised learning by training on aggregate outputs. In: Proceedings of the 7th IEEE International Conference on Data Mining (ICDM 2007), pp. 252–261 (2007)
17. Patrizi, G., Manna, C., Moscatelli, C., Nieddu, L.: Pattern recognition methods in human-assisted reproduction. Int. Trans. Oper. Res. **11**(4), 365–379 (2004)
18. Quadrianto, N., Smola, A.J., Caetano, T.S., Le, Q.V.: Estimating labels from label proportions. J. Mach. Learn. Res. **10**, 2349–2374 (2009)
19. Sahami, M.: Learning limited dependence Bayesian classifiers. In: Proceedings of the 2nd International Conference on Knowledge Discovery and Data Mining (KDD 1996), pp. 335–338 (1996)
20. Weidmann, N., Frank, E., Pfahringer, B.: A two-level learning method for generalized multi-instance problems. In: Lavrač, N., Gamberger, D., Todorovski, L., Blockeel, H. (eds.) ECML 2003. LNCS (LNAI), vol. 2837, pp. 468–479. Springer, Heidelberg (2003)
21. Zhu, X., Goldberg, A.B.: Introduction to Semi-Supervised Learning. Synthesis Lectures on Artificial Intelligence and Machine Learning. Morgan & Claypool Publishers, San Rafael (2009)

Parallelisation of the PC Algorithm

Anders L. Madsen[1,2]([✉]), Frank Jensen[1], Antonio Salmerón[3], Helge Langseth[4], and Thomas D. Nielsen[2]

[1] HUGIN EXPERT A/S, Aalborg, Denmark
anders@hugin.com
[2] Department of Computer Science, Aalborg University, Aalborg, Denmark
[3] Department of Mathematics, University of Almería, Almería, Spain
[4] Department of Computer and Information Science, Norwegian University of Science and Technology, Trondheim, Norway

Abstract. This paper describes a parallel version of the PC algorithm for learning the structure of a Bayesian network from data. The PC algorithm is a constraint-based algorithm consisting of five steps where the first step is to perform a set of (conditional) independence tests while the remaining four steps relate to identifying the structure of the Bayesian network using the results of the (conditional) independence tests. In this paper, we describe a new approach to parallelisation of the (conditional) independence testing as experiments illustrate that this is by far the most time consuming step. The proposed parallel PC algorithm is evaluated on data sets generated at random from five different real-world Bayesian networks. The results demonstrate that significant time performance improvements are possible using the proposed algorithm.

Keywords: Bayesian network · PC algorithm · Parallelisation

1 Introduction

A *Bayesian network* (BN) [9,11] is a powerful model for probabilistic inference. It consists of two main parts: a graphical structure specifying a set of dependence and independence relations between its variables and a set of conditional probability distributions quantifying the strengths of the dependence relations. The graphical nature of a Bayesian network makes it well-suited for representing complex problems, where the interactions between entities, represented as variables, are described using *conditional probability distributions* (CPDs). Both parts can be elicited from experts or learnt from data, or a combination. Here we focus on learning the graphical structure from data using the PC algorithm [17] exploiting parallel computations.

Large data sets both in terms of variables and cases may challenge the efficiency of pure sequential algorithms for learning the structure of a Bayesian network from data. Since the computational power of computers is ever increasing and access to computers supporting parallel processing is improving, it is natural to consider exploiting parallel computations to improve performance of learning

© Springer International Publishing Switzerland 2015
J.M. Puerta et al. (Eds.): CAEPIA 2015, LNAI 9422, pp. 14–24, 2015.
DOI: 10.1007/978-3-319-24598-0_2

algorithms. In [7] the authors describe a MapReduce-based method for learning Bayesian networks from massive data using a search & score algorithm while [5] describes a MapReduce-based method for machine learning on multicore computers. Also, [16] presents the R package **bnlearn** which provides implementations of some structure learning algorithms including support for parallel computing. [3] introduces a method for accelerating Bayesian network parameter learning using Hadoop and MapReduce. Other relevant work on parallelisation of learning Bayesian network from data include [4,6,7,10,14]. In this paper, we describe a parallel version of the PC algorithm for learning the structure of a Bayesian network from large data sets on a shared memory computer using threads. The proposed parallel PC algorithm is inspired by the work of [13] on vertical parallization of TAN learning using Balanced Incomplete Block (BIB) designs [18]. The results of an empirical evaluation shows a significant improvement in time performance over a purely sequential implementation.

2 Preliminaries and Notation

2.1 Bayesian Networks

A BN $\mathcal{N} = (\mathcal{X}, G, \mathcal{P})$ over the set of random variables $\mathcal{X} = \{X_1, \ldots, X_n\}$ consists of an acyclic directed graph (DAG) $G = (V, E)$ with vertices V and edges E and a set of CPDs $\mathcal{P} = \{P(X \mid \mathrm{pa}(X)) : X \in \mathcal{X}\}$, where $\mathrm{pa}(X)$ denotes the parents of X in G. The BN $\mathcal{N}$ specifies a joint probability distribution over $\mathcal{X}$

$$P(\mathcal{X}) = \prod_{i=1}^{n} P(X_i \mid \mathrm{pa}(X_i)).$$

We use upper case letters, e.g., X_i and Y, to denote variables while sets of variables are denoted using calligraphy letters, e.g., $\mathcal{X}$ and $\mathcal{S}$. If the Bayesian network contains continuous variables that are not discretized, then we assume these to have a Conditional Linear Gaussian distribution.

We let $\mathcal{D} = (c_1, \ldots, c_N)$ denote a data set of N complete cases over variables $\mathcal{X} = \{X_1, \ldots, X_n\}$ and we let $I(X, Y; \mathcal{S})$ denote conditional independence between X and Y given $\mathcal{S}$. When learning the structure of a DAG G from data, we use a test statistic to test the hypothesis $I(X, Y; \mathcal{S})$ using $\mathcal{D}$.

2.2 PC Algorithm

The task of learning the structure of a Bayesian network from $\mathcal{D}$ amounts to determining the structure G. The PC algorithm of [17] is basically:

1. Determine pairwise (conditional) independence $I(X, Y; \mathcal{S})$.
2. Identify skeleton of G.
3. Identify v-structures in G.
4. Identify derived directions in G.
5. Complete orientation of G making it a DAG.

Step 1 is performed such that tests for marginal independence (i.e., $S = \emptyset$) are performed first followed by conditional independence tests where the size of S iterates over $1, 2, 3, \ldots$ taking the adjacency of vertices into consideration. That is, in the process of determining the set of conditional independence statements $I(X, Y; S)$, the results produced earlier are exploited to reduce the number of tests. This means, that we stop testing conditional independence of X and Y once a subset S has been identified such that the independence hypothesis is not rejected. When testing the conditional independence hypothesis $I(X, Y; S)$, the conditioning set S is restricted, e.g., to contain only potential neighbours of either X or Y, i.e., a variable Z is excluded from S, if the independence test between X (or Y) and Z was previously not rejected. This is referred to as the PC* algorithm by [17], but we will refer to it as the PC algorithm.

Steps 2 to 5 use the results of Step 1 to determine the DAG G. We will not consider Steps 2 to 5 further in this paper as experiments demonstrate that the combined time cost of these steps is negligible compared to the time cost of Step 1. The reader is referred to, e.g., [17] for more details.

2.3   Balanced Incomplete Block Designs

[13] describes how BIB designs can be applied to learn the structure of a TAN model from data by parallelisation using processes on a distributed memory system. Here, we will use BIB designs to control the process of testing for marginal independence on a shared memory computer using threads.

This section provides the necessary background information on BIB designs to follow the presentation of the method proposed. A design is defined as:

Definition 1. (Design [18]) *A design is a pair (X, A) s.t. the following properties are satisfied:*

1. *X is a set of elements called points, and*
2. *A is a collection of nonempty subsets of X called blocks.*

In this paper, we only consider cases where each block is a set (and not a multiset). A BIB design is defined as:

Definition 2. (BIB design [18]) *Let v, k and λ be positive integers s.t. $v > k \geq 2$. A (v, k, λ)-BIB design is a design (X, A) s.t. the following properties are satisfied:*

1. $|X| = v$,
2. *each block contains exactly k points, and*
3. *every pair of distinct points is contained in exactly λ blocks.*

The number of blocks in a design is denoted by b and r denotes the *replication number*, i.e., how often each point appears in a block. Property 3 in the definition is the *balance* property that we need. We want to test each pair exactly once and therefore require $\lambda = 1$. A BIB design is *symmetric* when the number of blocks equals the number of points. This will not be the case in general.

Example 1. Consider the $(7, 3, 1)$-BIB design. The blocks are (one out of a number of possibilities):

$$\{123\}, \{145\}, \{167\}, \{246\}, \{257\}, \{347\}, \{356\}, \tag{1}$$

where $\{abc\}$ is shorthand notation for $\{a, b, c\}$. This BIB design is symmetric.

There is no single method to construct all BIB designs. However, a difference set can be used to generate some symmetric BIB designs.

Definition 3. (Difference Set [18]) *Assume $(G, +)$ is a finite group of order v in which the identity element is 0. Let k and λ be positive integers such that $2 \leq k < v$. A (v, k, λ)-difference set in $(G, +)$ is a subset $D \subseteq G$ that satisfies the following properties:*

1. $|D| = k$,
2. *the multiset $[x + y : x, y \in D, x \neq y]$ contains every element in $G \setminus \{0\}$ exactly λ times.*

In our case, we are restricted to using $(\mathbb{Z}_v, +)$, the integers modulo v. If $D \subseteq \mathbb{Z}_v$ is a difference set in group $(G, +)$, then $D + g = \{x + g | x \in D\}$ is a translate of D for any $g \in G$. The multiset of all v translates of D is denoted $Dev(D)$ and called the development of D [18, page 42]. It is important to know that BIB designs do not exist for all possible combinations of v, k, and λ.

The concept of a difference set can be generalized to a *difference family*. A difference family is a set of base blocks. A difference family can be used to generate a BIB design similarly to how difference sets are used to generate BIB designs. Table 1 shows a set of difference families for BIB designs on the form $(q, 6, 1)$, which we will use later.

Table 1. Examples of difference families for a set of $(q, 6, 1)$ BIB designs.

BIB design	Difference family	#(base blocks)	$b = v \cdot$ #(base blocks)
(31,6,1)	$\{(1, 2, 7, 19, 23, 30)\}$	1	31
(91,6,1)	$\{(0,1,3,7,25,38),$ $(0,5,20,32,46,75),$ $(0,8,17,47,57,80)\}$	3	273
(151,6,1)	$\{(1, 32, 118, 7, 73, 71), \ldots\}$	5	755
(211,6,1)	$\{(0, 1, 107, 55, 188, 71), \ldots\}$	7	1477
(271,6,1)	$\{(1, 242, 28, 9, 10, 232), \ldots\}$	9	2439

The base blocks in Table 1 have been generated using SageMath[1]. The value $q = 6$ is chosen for practical reasons as difference families for generating the blocks need to be known to exist and we need to be able to store the corresponding count tables in memory.

---

[1] http://www.sagemath.org.

3   Parallelisation of PC Structure Learning

Improving the performance of the PC algorithm on large data sets can be achieved in a number of ways, see, for instance, [10,14,16]. Here we consider an approach where the tests for (conditional) independence are performed in parallel. We use two different approaches based on threads. When testing for marginal independence the set of tests to be performed are known in advance and we use BIB designs to obtain parallization by threads. For the higher order tests we create an edge index array, which the threads iterate over to select the next edge to evaluate for each iteration. The edge index array contains all edges that has not been removed at an earlier step and it is sorted in decreasing order of the test score. Step 1 of the PC algorithm is implemented as three steps:

1. Test all pairs X and Y for marginal independence.
2. Perform the most promising higher-order conditional independence tests.
3. Test of conditional independence $(X, Y; \mathcal{S})$ where $|\mathcal{S}| = 1, 2, 3$.

In [17] bounding the order of the conditional independence relations is suggested as a natural heuristic to reduce the number of tests. Experiments show that by far the most edges are removed for low order tests and statistical tests become increasingly unreliable as the size of the conditioning set increases. For these reasons, the size of the conditioning set is limited to three in the implementation. In Step 3 of the process of testing for conditional independence between X and Y given $\mathcal{S}$, we select $\mathcal{S}$ as a subset of the potential neighbours of X (except Y).

3.1   Test for Marginal Independence

The tests for pairwise marginal independence $I(X, Y; \emptyset)$ for all pairs X, Y should be divided into tasks of equal size such that we test exactly all pairs X, Y for marginal independence. This is achieved using BIB designs on the form $(q, 6, 1)$ where q is at least the number of variables. The blocks of the BIB design are generated using a difference family (e.g., Table 1). Blocks are assigned to threads using the unique rank of each thread. A thread with rank r iterates over the block array and considers only blocks where the array index modulus t equals r

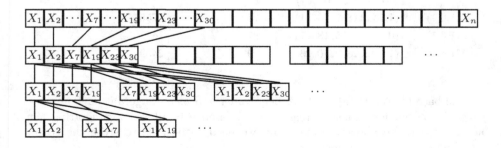

Fig. 1. Example illustrating the use of $(q, 6, 1)$ and $(3, 2, 1)$ designs.

where t is the number of threads (the uniqueness means that there is no need for synchronization). When a thread has selected a block, it performs all pairwise independence tests using a $(3, 2, 1)$ BIB design (all pairs) where the 6-block is marginalized to three blocks with four variables each (in this case each point corresponds to two variables). The table of four variables are marginalized down to all pairs for testing where the first pair is ignored producing a total of $\binom{6}{2} = 15$ tests. Figure 1 illustrates this principle. Notice that $q = 6$ represents 15 pairs and we should, in principle, obtain a speed-up of a factor 15 compared to just computing all pairs individually.

3.2 Extra Heuristics

Once the testing for marginal independence is completed, a new step compared to the traditional PC algorithm is performed. This step performs for each edge a set of the most promising tests, i.e., tests with high likelihood of not rejecting the independence hypothesis. At this and the following steps of the conditional independence testing we do not know in advance which tests we are going to perform (since we are using previous results to reduce the number of tests performed).

For each edge (X, Y) the set of *best candidate variables* to include in the conditioning set $\mathcal{S}$ are identified using the weight of a candidate variable Z. The *weight* $w(Z \,|\, (X, Y))$ is equal to the sum of the test scores for (X, Z) and (Y, Z). We create an array of best candidates. This array contains up to five variables, which are all neighbours of X (or Y), i.e., the independence hypothesis has been rejected so far. The main reason for limiting the size to five variables is to make sure that the count table fits in memory. If variables have many states, then the number of candidates is reduced. This array is sorted by the sum of the edge weights. The threads iterate over the sorted edge index array. A thread performs all tests for a selected edge (with the size of $\mathcal{S}$ running from one to three) from the table of up to seven variables. For the table of counts all possible tests are performed generating subsets using the combinatorial number system [12].

The extra heuristics step is responsible for finding a significant number of the independence relations. In combination marginal independence testing and the extra heuristics step usually find by far the highest number of independence relations meaning that higher order tests mainly ensure that no further independence relations can be found. The tests performed for each edge are stored.

3.3 Higher Order Testing

Once testing for marginal independence and the testing based on extra heuristics are completed, the remaining higher order tests for each edge are performed (unless independence has been established at a previous step). The algorithm iterates over $|\mathcal{S}|$ from one to three stopping when an independence hypothesis $I(X, Y; \mathcal{S})$ is not rejected. The threads iterate over the sorted edge index array. Candidate variables to be included in the conditioning set $\mathcal{S}$ are determined as potential neighbours of either X or Y. This list of edges (the candidate and its potential neighbour X or Y) is sorted as described above and all possible subsets are generated again using the combinatorial number system in order to perform the most promising tests first.

In an iteration, each thread selects an edge and performs all conditional independence test for $|\mathcal{S}| = i$ and writes the result to the edge index array. There is only synchronization on the edge index array when a thread decides which edge to test and when writing to the array as we need to ensure that two threads do not select the same edge to test and that a thread does not try to read the array when another thread is writing its results to the array. This synchronization is also performed in the previous step.

Table 2. Networks from which data sets used in the experiments are generated.

Data set	$|\mathcal{X}|$	Total CPT size
Ship-Ship [15]	50	130,478
Munin1 [1]	189	19,466
Diabetes [2]	413	461,069
Munin2 [1]	1,003	83,920
Sacso [8]	2,371	44,274

4   Empirical Evaluation

Random samples of data have been generated from the five networks of different size listed in Table 2. Three data sets are generated at random for each network with 100,000, 250,000, and 500,000 cases. All data sets used in the empirical evaluation are complete, i.e., there are no missing values in the data. The empirical evaluation is performed on a Linux computer running Red Hat Enterprise Linux 7 with a six-core Intel (TM) i7-5820 K 3.3 GHz processor and 64 GB RAM. The computer has six physical cores and twelve logical cores. The parallel PC algorithm is implemented employing a shared memory multicore architecture. All data is loaded into the main shared memory of the computer where the process of the program is responsible for creating a set of POSIX threads to achieve parallelisation. In the experiments, the number of threads used by the program is in the set $\{1, 2, 3, 4, 6, 8, 10, 12\}$ where the case of one thread is considered the baseline and corresponds to a sequential program.

The average computation time is calculated over five runs with the same data set. The computation time is measured as the elapsed (wall-clock) time of the different steps of the parallel PC algorithm. We measure the computation time of the entire algorithm in addition to the time for identifying the skeleton (Step 2), identifying v-structures (Step 3) as well as identifying derived directions (Step 4) and completing the orientation of edges (Step 5) combined.

Figure 2 (left) shows the average run time in seconds (left axis) and speed-up factor (right axis) for ship-ship using 500,000 cases. Notice that the computation time is low for the ship-ship network even with one thread meaning that the

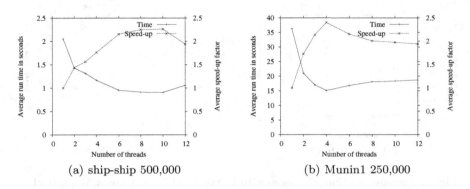

(a) ship-ship 500,000   (b) Munin1 250,000

Fig. 2. Average run times for ship-ship with 500,000 cases and Munin1 250,000 cases.

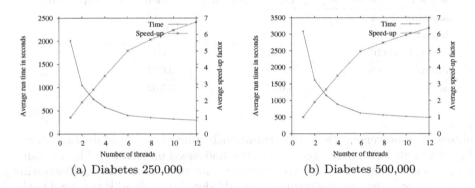

(a) Diabetes 250,000   (b) Diabetes 500,000

Fig. 3. Average run times for Diabetes with 250,000 and 500,000 cases, respectively.

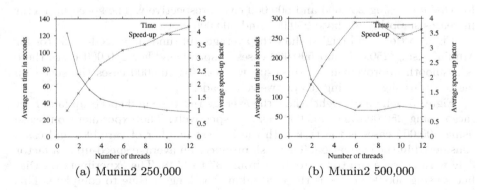

(a) Munin2 250,000   (b) Munin2 500,000

Fig. 4. Average run times for Munin2 with 250,000 and 500,000 cases, respectively.

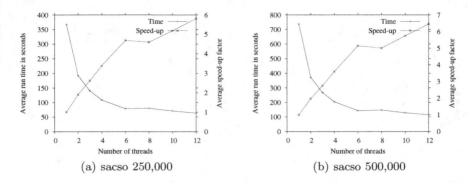

(a) sacso 250,000   (b) sacso 500,000

Fig. 5. Average run times for sacso with 250,000 and 500,000 cases, respectively.

Table 3. Average run times in seconds for Steps 2 to 5.

Data set	Skeleton (Step 2)	v-structures (Step 3)	Orientation (Steps 4 and 5)
Ship-Ship	0	0	0
Munin1	0.005	0	0.001
Diabetes	0.001	0.004	0.002
Munin2	0.006	0.002	0.034
Sacso	0.051	5.692	0.502

potential improvement from parallelisation is limited as the evaluation shows. Figure 2 (right) shows the average run time and speed-up factor for Munin1 using 250,000 cases where the speed up deteriorates for six or more threads illustrating the principle of diminishing returns. The additional threads adds overhead to the process and we expect that the increase in time cost is due to the synchronisation on the edge index array.

Figure 3 (left) and (right) show the average run time and speed-up factor for Diabetes using 250,000 and 500,000 cases, respectively. The speed up factor increases smoothly for both 250,000 and 500,000 cases.

Figure 4 (left) and (right) show the average run time and speed-up factor for Munin2 using 250,000 and 500,000 cases, respectively. For 250,000 cases there is a smooth improvement in speed-up whereas for 500,000 cases the speed up factor drops slightly using ten or twelve threads.

Figure 5 (left) and (right) show the average run time and speed-up factor for sacso using 250,000 and 500,000 cases, respectively. The experiment on sacso using 500,000 cases is the task with the highest number of variables and cases considered in the evaluation. This task produces an average speed-up of a factor 6.46 with average run time dropping from 737 to 114 s. The experiment on Diabetes using 500,000 cases is the task taking the longest time to complete. This task produces an average speed-up of a factor 6.36 with average run time dropping from 3084.65 to 484.65 s. Table 3 shows the average time cost of identifying the skeleton (Step 2), identifying the v-structures (Step 4), identifying derived directions (Step 4) and completing the orientation to obtain a DAG (Step 5). It is clear from Table 3 that the costs of Steps 2 to 5 are negligible compared to the total cost.

5 Discussion

This paper introduces a new approach to parallelisation of learning the structure of a Bayesian network from data using the PC algorithm. The approach is based on the use of threads with all data cases stored in shared memory. The PC algorithm consists of five main steps where the focus of this paper has been on performing the independence tests in parallel as the results in Sect. 4 clearly demonstrate that the total time cost of Steps 2 to 5 are negligible compared to the time cost of Step 1.

Step 1 of the PC algorithm consists, as presented in this paper, of three steps. In the first step the tests for marginal independence are performed. Parallelisation of this step is based on the use of difference sets and families where the tests to be performed are known in advance as all pairs are to be tested for marginal independence. In the second step a set of the most promising higher order tests are performed whereas in the third step tests for conditional independence are performed using conditioning sets of size one, two and three, respectively.

The edge index array is the central bottleneck of the approach as it is the only element that requires synchronization. Synchronization is limited to selecting which edge to test and does not include synchronization of the counting and testing. The counting usually being the most time consuming element of testing for conditional pairwise independence.

The PC algorithm is known to be sensitive to the order in which the conditional independence tests are performed. This means that the number of threads used by the algorithm may impact the result as the order of tests is not invariant under the number of threads used. This is a topic of future research.

The results of the empirical evaluation of the proposed method on a Linux server with six physical cores and twelve logical cores show a significant time performance improvement over the pure sequential method. For most cases considered there is a point where using additional threads does not improve performance illustrating the principle of diminishing returns. In a few cases, where the number of variables is low, the number of cases is low, or both increasing the number of threads used may increase time costs.

There is some variance in the run time measured. This should also be expected as the evaluation is performed on systems serving other users, i.e., the experiments have not been performed on an isolated system.

References

1. Andreassen, S., Jensen, F.V., Andersen, S.K., Falck, B., Kjærulff, U., Woldbye, M., Sørensen, A.R., Rosenfalck, A., Jensen, F.: MUNIN – an expert EMG assistant. In: Computer-Aided Electromyography and Expert Systems, Chapter 21. Elsevier Science (1989)
2. Andreassen, S., Hovorka, R., Benn, J., Olesen, K.G., Carson, E.R.: A model-based approach to insulin adjustment. In: Stefanelli, S., Hasman, A., Fieschi, M., Talmon, J. (eds.) Proceedings of the Third Conference on Artificial Intelligence in Medicine. Lecture Notes in Medical Informatics, pp. 239–248. Springer, Heidelberg (1991)
3. Basak, A., Brinster, I., Ma, X., Mengshoel, O.J.: Accelerating Bayesian network parameter learning using hadoop and MapReduce. In: Proceedings of the 1st International Workshop on Big Data, Streams a nd Heterogeneous Source Mining: Algorithms, Systems, Programming Models and Applications, pp. 101–108 (2012)
4. Chen, W., Zong, L., Huang, W., Ou, G., Wang, Y., Yang, D.: An empirical study of massively parallel Bayesian networks learning for sentiment extraction from unstructured text. In: Du, X., Fan, W., Wang, J., Peng, Z., Sharaf, M.A. (eds.) APWeb 2011. LNCS, vol. 6612, pp. 424–435. Springer, Heidelberg (2011)
5. Chu, C.-T., Kim, S.K., Lin, Y.-A., Yu, Y., Bradski, G., Ng, A.Y., Olukotun, K.: Map-reduce for machine learning on multicore. In: NIPS, pp. 281–288 (2006)
6. de Jongh, M.: Algorithms for constraint-based learning of Bayesian network structures with large numbers of variables. Ph.D. thesis, Uniòf Pittsburgh (2014)
7. Fang, Q., Yue, K., Fu, X., Wu, H., Liu, W.: A MapReduce-based method for learning Bayesian network from massive data. In: Ishikawa, Y., Li, J., Wang, W., Zhang, R., Zhang, W. (eds.) APWeb 2013. LNCS, vol. 7808, pp. 697–708. Springer, Heidelberg (2013)
8. Jensen, F.V., Skaanning, C., Kjærulff, U.: The SACSO system for troubleshooting of printing systems. In: Proceedings of the Seventh Scandinavian Conference on Artificial Intelligence (2001)
9. Jensen, F.V., Nielsen, T.D.: Bayesian Networks and Decision Graphs, 2nd edn. Springer, New York (2007)
10. Kalisch, M., Buhlmann, P.: Estimating high-dimensional directed acyclic graphs with the PC-algorithm. J. Mach. Learn. Res. **8**, 613–636 (2008)
11. Kjærulff, U.B., Madsen, A.L.: Bayesian Networks and Influence Diagrams: A Guide to Construction and Analysis, 2nd edn. Springer, New York (2013)
12. Knuth, D.E.: The Art of Computer Programming, Volume 4, Fascicle 3. Addison-Wesley, Reading (2005)
13. Madsen, A.L., Jensen, F., Salmeron, A., Karlsen, M., Langseth, H., Nielsen, T.D.: A new method for vertical parallelisation of tan learning based on balanced incomplete block designs. In: Proceedings of PGM, pp. 302–317 (2014)
14. Nikolova, O., Aluru, S.: Parallel discovery of direct causal relations and Markov boundaries with applications to gene networks. In: 2011 International Conference IEEE Parallel Processing (ICPP), pp. 512–521 (2011)
15. Papanikolaou, A.: Presents Modern Risk-based Methods and Applications to Ship Design, Operation, and Regulations. Springer, Heidelberg (2009)
16. Scutari, M.: Learning Bayesian Networks with the bnlearn R Package. J. Stat. Softw. **35**(3), 1–22 (2010)
17. Spirtes, P., Glymour, C., Scheines, R.: Causation, Prediction, and Search. Adaptive Computation and Machine Learning, 2nd edn. MIT Press, Cambridge (2000)
18. Stinson, D.: Combinatorial Designs - Constructions and Analysis. Springer, New York (2003)

Regularized Multivariate von Mises Distribution

Luis Rodriguez-Lujan[✉], Concha Bielza, and Pedro Larrañaga

Departamento de Inteligencia Artificial, Universidad Politécnica de Madrid,
Campus de Montegancedo, 28660 Boadilla del Monte, Madrid, Spain
luis.rodriguezl@alumnos.upm.es
{mcbielza,pedro.larranaga}@fi.upm.es
http://cig.fi.upm.es

Abstract. Regularization is necessary to avoid overfitting when the number of data samples is low compared to the number of parameters of the model. In this paper, we introduce a flexible L_1 regularization for the multivariate von Mises distribution. We also propose a circular distance that can be used to estimate the Kullback-Leibler divergence between two circular distributions by means of sampling, and also serves as goodness-of-fit measure. We compare the models on synthetic data and real morphological data from human neurons and show that the regularized model achieves better results than non regularized von Mises model.

Keywords: von Mises distribution · Directional distributions · Circular distance · Machine learning

1 Introduction

Directional data is ubiquitous in science, from the direction of the wind to the branching angles of the trees. However, directional data has been traditionally treated as regular linear data despite of its different nature. Directional statistics [4] provides specific tools for modelling directional data. If the normal distribution is the most famous distribution for linear data, the von Mises distribution [6] is its analogue for directional data.

If we extend the von Mises as a multivariate distribution [3], we face the problem that no closed formulation is known for the normalization term when the number of variables is greater than two, and, therefore it cannot be easily fitted nor compared to other distributions. We introduce a computationally optimized version of the full pseudo-likelihood as well as a circular distance to address these problems.

Another problem in some application areas, like neuroscience, is that data is scarce and expensive. In these situations regularization is needed to prevent overfitting. We propose a L_1 regularization for the multivariate von Mises distribution that allows us to introduce prior beliefs on the relation between the variables.

© Springer International Publishing Switzerland 2015
J.M. Puerta et al. (Eds.): CAEPIA 2015, LNAI 9422, pp. 25–35, 2015.
DOI: 10.1007/978-3-319-24598-0_3

This paper is organized as follows. Section 2 reviews the univariate and multivariate von Mises distributions. In Sect. 3 we propose a circular distance that is applied to estimate the KL divergence between two distributions. Then, in Sect. 4 we compare the von Mises distribution to the Gaussian distribution over synthetic data using the approximated KL divergence as the evaluation metric. We repeat the same process on real data from human neurons in Sect. 5, this time using the approximated KL-divergence as a two-sample test, and show that the regularized multivariate von Mises distribution always achieves better results. We conclude the paper in Sect. 6 with a final discussion and some proposals for future work.

2   The Multivariate von Mises Distribution

Directional statistics is a field within statistics that deals with angles, or equivalently, directions in space. Among the variety of directional distributions, the von Mises distribution is particularly noteworthy since it is considered the circular analogue of the normal distribution but having better mathematical properties than the wrapped-normal distribution [3,5,8].

The univariate von Mises distribution belongs to the exponential family and its density function is given by:

$$f_{VM}(\theta; \mu, \kappa) = \frac{1}{2\pi I_0(\kappa)} \exp\left\{\kappa \cos\left(\theta - \mu\right)\right\} \tag{1}$$

where μ is the mean angle and κ the concentration parameter, i.e. the inverse of the variance, and I_0 is the modified Bessel function of order 0.

Based on its exponential definition, we can define a multivariate von Mises distribution [3] analogous to the multivariate normal distribution. For $\boldsymbol{\theta} = (\theta_1, ..., \theta_p)$ the density function is defined as:

$$f_{MVM}(\boldsymbol{\theta}; \boldsymbol{\mu}, \boldsymbol{\kappa}, \boldsymbol{\Lambda}) = \frac{1}{Z(\boldsymbol{\kappa}, \boldsymbol{\Lambda})} \exp\left\{\boldsymbol{\kappa}\cos(\boldsymbol{\theta} - \boldsymbol{\mu})^T + \frac{1}{2}\sin(\boldsymbol{\theta} - \boldsymbol{\mu})\boldsymbol{\Lambda}\sin(\boldsymbol{\theta} - \boldsymbol{\mu})^T\right\} \tag{2}$$

where $\boldsymbol{\mu} = (\mu_1, ..., \mu_p)$ and $\boldsymbol{\kappa} = (\kappa_1, ..., \kappa_p)$ are the multidimensional equivalents of μ and κ in the univariate von Mises respectively, and $\boldsymbol{\Lambda} = (\lambda_{ij})$ is a $p \times p$ symmetric matrix with $\lambda_{ii} = 0$ and $\lambda_{ij} \geq 0$.

Unfortunately, the normalization term $Z(\boldsymbol{\kappa}, \boldsymbol{\Lambda})$ does not have a known closed-form formula for any p greater than two, so it has to be approximated numerically, making the calculation of the density function intractable computationally.

2.1   Pseudo-Likelihood

Due to the complexity of computing the normalization term in the density function of Eq. (2) it is not practical to use the likelihood as the target function to fit the multivariate von Mises distribution given a set of data samples [3]. In this same article, the authors propose to use the pseudo-likelihood as a consistent approximation of the likelihood term. Since each marginal conditional term for the multivariate von Mises is a univariate von Mises, the full pseudo-likelihood for a p-dimensional $\boldsymbol{\theta} = (\theta_{i,j})$ that contains N independent samples can be expressed as:

$$PL(\boldsymbol{\theta}|\boldsymbol{\mu}, \boldsymbol{\kappa}, \boldsymbol{\Lambda}) = (2\pi)^{-Np} \prod_{i=1}^{N} \prod_{j=1}^{p} \frac{1}{I_0(\kappa_j^i)} \exp\left\{\kappa_j^i \cos(\theta_{i,j} - \mu_j^i)\right\} \qquad (3)$$

where μ_j^i and κ_j^i are, respectively, the j-th marginal mean and concentration given the i-th data sample:

$$\mu_j^i = \mu_j + \arctan\left(\frac{\sum_{l \neq j} \lambda_{j,l} \sin(\theta_{i,l} - \mu_l)}{\kappa_j}\right) \qquad (4)$$

$$\kappa_j^i = \sqrt{\kappa_j^2 + \left(\sum_{l \neq j} \lambda_{j,l} \sin(\theta_{i,l} - \mu_l)\right)^2} \qquad (5)$$

2.2 Optimization

Given a set of samples, to compute the parameters of the multivariate von Mises distribution that maximize the pseudo-likelihood we define a minimization problem where the loss function is minus the natural logarithm of the pseudo-likelihood defined in (3). This loss function can be written as:

$$L(\boldsymbol{\theta}|\boldsymbol{\mu}, \boldsymbol{\kappa}, \boldsymbol{\Lambda}) = (pN)\log(2\pi) + \sum_{i=1}^{N} \sum_{j=1}^{p} \left\{\log(I_0(\kappa_j^i)) - \kappa_j^i \cos(\theta_{i,j} - \mu_j^i)\right\} \qquad (6)$$

We simplified the loss function (6) to reduce its complexity (from a computational point of view) by expressing sums as matrix products and by applying trigonometric properties to reduce the number of operations to be computed, specifically, to avoid the computation of the tangent inverse function. To do so, the first step is to define the $N \times p$ matrix $\boldsymbol{\Phi}$ as:

$$\boldsymbol{\Phi} = \sin(\boldsymbol{\theta} - \boldsymbol{\mu})\boldsymbol{\Lambda}$$

Then, we can reduce the second term in the sum using some simple trigonometric identities:

$$\kappa_j^i \cos(\theta_{i,j} - \mu_j^i) = \kappa_j^i(\cos(\theta_{i,j})\cos(\mu_j^i) + \sin(\theta_{i,j})\sin(\mu_j^i))$$

$$= \kappa_j^i \left(\frac{\cos(\theta_{i,j} - \mu_j)\kappa_j}{\kappa_j^i} + \frac{\sin(\theta_{i,j} - \mu_j)\phi_{i,j}}{\kappa_j^i}\right)$$

As result we obtain a more compact version of the loss function, that do not require to compute the tangent inverse:

$$L_c(\boldsymbol{\theta}|\boldsymbol{\mu}, \boldsymbol{\kappa}, \boldsymbol{\Lambda}) = \sum_{i=1}^{N} \sum_{j=1}^{p} \left[\log(I_0(\kappa_j^i)) - \cos(\theta_{i,j} - \mu_j)\kappa_j - \sin(\theta_{i,j} - \mu_j)\phi_{i,j}\right] \qquad (7)$$

To find the minima for function (7) we will use the quasi-newton L-BFGS-B algorithm [10] which is an extension of the well-known L-BFGS method that supports simple constraints such as $\kappa_j > 0$. This method only requires to evaluate the loss function and its partial derivatives. Since the optimal μ parameter is the vector formed by the marginal means, only partial derivatives with respect to κ and Λ need to be computed in order to use this method. Please note that A_0 stands for $\frac{I_1}{I_0}$ where I_1 is the modified Bessel function of order 1.

$$\frac{\partial L_c}{\partial \kappa_j} = \sum_{i=1}^{N} \left[A_0(\kappa_j^i) \frac{\kappa_j}{\kappa_j^i} - \cos(\theta_{i,j} - \mu_j) \right] \tag{8}$$

$$\frac{\partial L_c}{\partial \lambda_{j,k}} = \sum_{i=1}^{N} \left[\sin(\theta_{i,k} - \mu_k) \left(\frac{A_0(\kappa_j^i)}{\kappa_j^i} \phi_{j,k} - \sin(\theta_{i,j} - \mu_j) \right) \right] \tag{9}$$

A comparison of the fitting execution time between the regular loss function provided by [8] based on the Eq. (6) and the optimized version in (7) was performed for a 5-dimensional von Mises distribution. Both methods were implemented in *ANSI C* and executed in similar conditions. The results in Fig. 1 show that the optimized version is significantly faster as the number of samples increase.

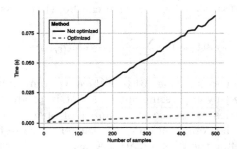

Fig. 1. Mean fitting time per number of samples of a 5-dimensional von Mises function. Each execution was repeated 100 times with 2 additional warm-up iterations.

2.3 Regularization

The regularized learning of the multivariate von Mises distribution has already been proposed by other authors [8]. However, from a Bayesian point of view, if we penalize equally all components in matrix Λ as it is done in the standard L_1 regularization, we are adding the prior belief that all components $\lambda_{i,j}$ are similar (in scale terms) which may not correspond with our previous knowledge of the problem as it is studied in [9] for the multivariate normal distribution.

To add prior knowledge about the structure we propose a generalized version of the L_1 penalization for the multivariate von Mises distribution where each component $\lambda_{i,j}$ is individually weighted. To do so, a symmetric penalization matrix $\mathbf{\Psi}$ is defined with the only restriction that all elements should be positive. Then, the function to minimize is:

$$g(\boldsymbol{\theta}|\boldsymbol{\mu}, \boldsymbol{\kappa}, \boldsymbol{\Lambda}) = L_c(\boldsymbol{\theta}|\boldsymbol{\mu}, \boldsymbol{\kappa}, \boldsymbol{\Lambda}) + \sum_{j=1}^{p} \sum_{k \neq j} |\lambda_{j,k}| \psi_{j,k} \qquad (10)$$

Although the absolute value of $\lambda_{i,j}$ is not a differentiable at 0, we can find a differentiable function that approximates the absolute value with arbitrary precision. Bearing in mind that the number of real values that can be represented in a computer is finite, i.e. the minimum distance between real values is given by what is known as the machine epsilon, we can treat the absolute value function as if it was differentiable at any point. Then we just need to add a new term to the partial derivative with respect to $\lambda_{j,k}$:

$$\frac{\partial g}{\partial \lambda_{j,k}} = \frac{\partial L_c}{\partial \lambda_{j,k}} + sgn(\lambda_{j,k}) \psi_{j,k} \qquad (11)$$

where sgn is the sign function that evaluates $sgn(0) = 0$.

3   Evaluation

The impossibility to express the normalization term of the multivariate von Mises distribution (12) as a closed formula for any p restrains the use of typical measures of divergence between distributions such as the Kullback-Leibler divergence since we cannot evaluate the density function in any point, which also impedes the use more powerful goodness of fit tests.

Other authors have used the angle between original and fitted parameters [8] or the pseudo-likelihood value [3] as evaluation metrics, but these approaches are either only applicable to synthetic data from a known distribution or rely on the approximated likelihood.

To overcome these drawbacks, we propose to use the approximation of the KL divergence for multivariate distributions [7] as evaluation measure. This approach takes two sets of samples as input (one from each distribution or one from the real data and the other sampled from the learned model) and uses the distance to the k-th nearest neighbor to approximate the KL divergence. Given two sets of samples $\{X_i\}_{i=1}^{n}$ and $\{Y_i\}_{i=1}^{m}$ from two p-dimensional distributions P and Q, the approximated KL divergence [7] between P and Q is computed as:

$$\hat{D}_k(P\|Q) = \frac{p}{n} \sum_{i=1}^{n} \left[\log \left(\frac{r_k(\mathbf{x_i})}{s_k(\mathbf{x_i})} \right) \right] + \log \frac{m}{n-1} \qquad (12)$$

where $r_k(\mathbf{x_i})$ and $s_k(\mathbf{x_i})$ are the distance to the k-th nearest neighbour of $\mathbf{x_i}$ in $\mathbf{X} \setminus \mathbf{x_i}$ and $\mathbf{Y}$ respectively.

To generate samples from the multivariate von Mises distribution we can either use a rejection sampling algorithm [5] for small or moderate p or use a

Gibbs sampler for higher p [8]. However, we still need to define a distance that computes the distance between two multivariate circular points. We defined a distance between two points $a, b \in [0, 2\pi)^p$ in Eq. (13) that takes into account the periodicity of circular data.

$$d(a, b) = ||a - b^*||_2$$

where:

$$b^* = (b_i^*)_{i=1}^p = \begin{cases} b_i & \text{if } |a_i - b_i| \leq \pi \\ b_i + 2\pi & \text{if } |a_i - b_i| > \pi \text{ and } a_i > \pi \\ b_i - 2\pi & \text{if } |a_i - b_i| > \pi \text{ and } a_i \leq \pi \end{cases} \qquad (13)$$

4   Multivariate von Mises vs. Multivariate Gaussian

For high values of the concentration parameter, the univariate von Mises distribution approximates a normal distribution on the circumference. This behaviour extends to the multivariate case. However, it is not clear yet how this behaviour is affected either by the Λ parameter or the dimension p [8].

We used the empiric KL divergence defined in [7] along with the distance proposed in Sect. 3 to design a set of experiments with the aim of studying the behaviour of the multivariate normal and von Mises distribution when fitting circular data with different configurations. In addition, a regularized von Mises distribution is included in the comparison with penalization matrix $\Psi = (\psi_{i,j}) = |i - j|$, which is similar to the Λ band matrix configuration in the experiments, and it also matches the penalization used in Sect. 5.

We generated random samples from different configurations of parameters, varying: (a) The number of variables from 4 to 50; (b) the number of samples from 10 to 500 in the simplest case (4 variables) and from 50 to 1000 in the most complex (50 variables); (c) the concentration vector κ from a vector where all values were equal to 0.1 to a vector where all values were 7.0; and (d) the Λ matrix from a very sparse configuration where all elements were equal to zero to a dense configuration where all elements were distinct of zero. For all configurations and variables the mean value μ was fixed at π.

The procedure below is repeated for each combination of parameters 20 times to compute the approximate KL divergence as the average of all 20 results:

1. A set of N p-dimensional samples are generated from a multivariate von Mises distribution with parameters μ_0, κ_0 and Λ_0
2. Multivariate normal and von Mises (regularized and non-regularized) distributions parameters are fitted from the N samples
3. Another set of m p-dimensional samples are generated from both original distribution and learned ones. Please note that m can be different from N. Then, the empiric approximation of the KL divergence is computed using these m samples

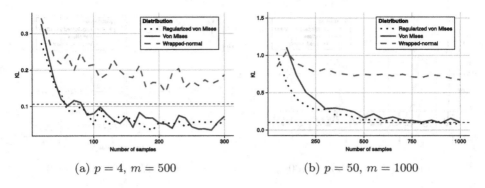

(a) $p = 4$, $m = 500$ (b) $p = 50$, $m = 1000$

Fig. 2. Approximated KL divergence for low concentration κ and very sparse $\boldsymbol{\Lambda}$.

The results for a sparse $\boldsymbol{\Lambda}$ matrix with low concentration κ can be seen in Fig. 2. Both von Mises distributions obtain better results than the multivariate normal distribution. If the number of samples is high enough, the regularized and non regularized von Mises perform similarly. As expected, the number of samples needed to obtain the same fit in both regularized and non regularized distributions is higher as the number of variables increases.

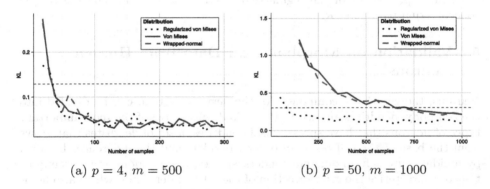

(a) $p = 4$, $m = 500$ (b) $p = 50$, $m = 1000$

Fig. 3. Approximated KL divergence for high concentration κ and dense $\boldsymbol{\Lambda}$.

In Fig. 3 we can see the results for the opposite case, high concentration κ and dense $\boldsymbol{\Lambda}$ matrix. In this case with high concentration the multivariate normal distribution obtains similar or better results than the von Mises distribution. It is important to note that although the penalization matrix does not exactly match the real Λ_0 matrix structure, i.e. we do not have a perfect prior, the regularized version still performs equally or better than the non regularized one. In all cases we observe that the regularized von Mises distribution produces a better fit when the number of samples is low.

Plots in Fig. 4 depict how the variation of the concentration parameter affects each of the distributions under evaluation for a fairly high number of samples

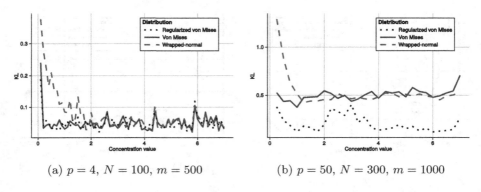

(a) $p = 4$, $N = 100$, $m = 500$ (b) $p = 50$, $N = 300$, $m = 1000$

Fig. 4. Approximated KL divergence for concentration κ varying and banded Λ.

($N = 100$ and $N = 300$ respectively). In Fig. 4a we observe that both versions of the multivariate von Mises obtain similar results, independently of the concentration, due to the high number of samples with respect to the number of variables. It is also interesting to note that as the concentration parameter increases, the normal distribution approaches the von Mises, getting similar KL values for $\kappa > 2.0$ in both Fig. 4a and b. From Fig. 4b we can preliminarily say that the improvement of the regularized distribution it is not affected by the concentration parameter κ.

5 Validation on Morphological Data from Human Neurons

Neurons, the very basic component of the nervous system, can be divided into the cell body, dendrites and axon. Pyramidal cells is one of the most important types of neurons that have special basal dendrites, a set of dendrites that grows from the base of the cell body. In order to understand the differences between pyramidal neurons from different genders, species, brain regions, etc. it is important to characterize the grow direction of these basal dendrites, which also helps to simulate and understand the functionality of these neurons.

We downloaded a set of 3D reconstructions of human pyramidal neurons [2] from NeuroMorpho.Org [1], a public repository of neural reconstructions. The data includes gender and age, as well as other metadata related to the brain region or the reconstruction method. We restricted our selection to reconstructions from adults and with neurons belonging to the occipital lobe or the frontal lobe.

The original data in plain text format was parsed and the angles between dendrites were measured. To establish a criteria on variable ordering, the longest dendrite was taken as the principal and angles where numbered following a counter-clockwise ordering as depicted in Fig. 5. It is noteworthy that for a neuron with p dendrites, we have $p - 1$ angles since the last one is completely determined by the rest.

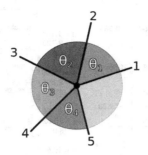

Fig. 5. Inter-dendrite angles.

We fitted a von Mises regularized distribution with a penalization matrix that grows with respect to the distance between angles. e.g. in Fig. 5 the value of $\psi_{1,4}$ is 2 (the shortest path between angles 1 and 4 is 1-5-4). We performed repeated train and test validation with 100 repetitions and use the empiric approximation KL divergence defined in Sect. 3 as evaluation metric. In each repetition, a 75 % of the original samples were selected at random as training set, leaving the remaining portion as the test set. In addition we also fitted a regular von Mises distribution for comparison purposes. Results are displayed in Table 1. In every case the regularized distribution obtains similar or better results.

Table 1. KL - divergence results for inter-dendrite angles.

Dendrites ($p+1$)	Gender	Brain Region	Samples (N)	vM	vM Regularized
5	Male	Occipital lobe	19	0.95	0.80
5	Female	Occipital lobe	28	0.76	0.74
5	All	Occipital lobe	47	0.58	0.57
5	Male	Frontal lobe	21	0.86	0.76
5	Female	Frontal lobe	21	0.81	0.65
5	All	Frontal lobe	42	0.50	0.49
6	Male	Frontal lobe	16	1.28	1.17
6	Female	Frontal lobe	12	1.41	1.33
6	All	Frontal lobe	28	1.13	0.96

A summary of the multivariate von Mises function fitted is shown in Fig. 6. The rose plots in the diagonal depict the marginal distributions in the original data, the numbers in the upper triangle are the $\lambda_{i,j}$ parameters of the multivariate von Mises while the values in the first column correspond to the mean and concentration parameters.

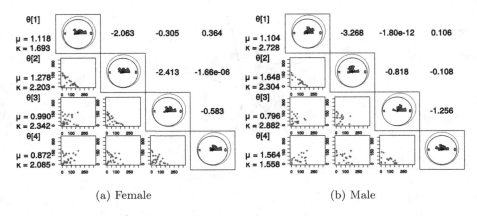

(a) Female   (b) Male

Fig. 6. Angles between dendrites from adult occipital lobe neurons with 5 basal dendrites (Color figure online).

6   Conclusion and Future Work

This paper introduces a computationally optimized formulation of the pseudo-likelihood for the multivariate von Mises distribution that reduces fitting time and provides better scalability. We also propose a multivariate circular distance that can be used to compute an empirical approximation of the Kullback-Leibler divergence. We have studied the behaviour of normal and von Mises distributions using this approximated measure as reference.

Also, a generalized L_1-penalization for the multivariate von Mises distribution has been proposed and tested in cases where the number of samples is low. We applied the regularized model to the angles between basal dendrites of human pyramidal cells. A thorough study of the penalization matrix needs to be done in order to clarify the parameter scale and the impact in the final result.

All methods described in this paper will be published in an R package that will support sampling and fitting of the multivariate von Mises distribution as well as multivariate circular plots and statistics.

Acknowledgements. This work has been partially supported by the Spanish Ministry of Economy and Competitiveness through the Cajal Blue Brain (C080020-09; the Spanish partner of the Blue Brain initiative from EPFL) and TIN2013-41592-P projects, by the Regional Government of Madrid through the S2013/ICE-2845-CASI-CAM-CM project, and by the European Union's Seventh Framework Programme (FP7/2007-2013) under grant agreement no. 604102 (Human Brain Project).

References

1. Ascoli, G.A., Donohue, D.E., Halavi, M.: Neuromorpho.org: a central resource for neuronal morphologies. J. Neurosci. **27**(35), 9247–9251 (2007)

2. Jacobs, B., Schall, M., Prather, M., Kapler, E., Driscoll, L., Baca, S., Jacobs, J., Ford, K., Wainwright, M., Treml, M.: Regional dendritic and spine variation in human cerebral cortex: a quantitative Golgi study. Cereb. Cortex **11**(6), 558–571 (2001)
3. Mardia, K.V., Hughes, G., Taylor, C.C., Singh, H.: A multivariate von Mises distribution with applications to bioinformatics. Can. J. Stat. **36**(1), 99–109 (2008)
4. Mardia, K.V., Jupp, P.E.: Directional Statistics, vol. 494. Wiley, New York (2009)
5. Mardia, K.V., Voss, J.: Some fundamental properties of a multivariate von Mises distribution. Commun. Stat-Theor. M. **43**(6), 1132–1144 (2014)
6. Mardia, K., Zemroch, P.: Algorithm as 86: the von Mises distribution function. Appl. Stat. **24**, 268–272 (1975)
7. Pérez-Cruz, F.: Kullback-Leibler divergence estimation of continuous distributions. In: IEEE International Symposium on Information Theory, pp. 1666–1670. IEEE (2008)
8. Razavian, N., Kamisetty, H., Langmead, C.J.: The von Mises graphical model: Regularized structure and parameter learning. Technical report CMU-CS-11-108, Carnegie Mellon University, Department of Computer Science (2011)
9. Tan, K.M., London, P., Mohan, K., Lee, S.I., Fazel, M., Witten, D.: Learning graphical models with hubs. J. Mach. Learn. Res. **15**(1), 3297–3331 (2014)
10. Zhu, C., Byrd, R.H., Lu, P., Nocedal, J.: Algorithm 778: L-BFGS-B: Fortran subroutines for large-scale bound-constrained optimization. ACM T. Math. Softw. **23**(4), 550–560 (1997)

Parallel Importance Sampling in Conditional Linear Gaussian Networks

Antonio Salmerón[1](✉), Darío Ramos-López[1], Hanen Borchani[4],
Ana M. Martínez[4], Andrés R. Masegosa[2], Antonio Fernández[1],
Helge Langseth[2], Anders L. Madsen[3,4], and Thomas D. Nielsen[4]

[1] University of Almería, 04120 Almería, Spain
{antonio.salmeron,drl102,afalvarez}@ual.es
[2] Norwegian University of Science and Technology, 7491 Trondheim, Norway
{andres.masegosa,helgel}@idi.ntnu.no
[3] Hugin Expert A/S, 9000 Aalborg, Denmark
anders@hugin.com
[4] Aalborg University, 9220 Aalborg, Denmark
{hanen,ana,tdn}@cs.aau.dk
http://www.amidst.eu

Abstract. In this paper we analyse the problem of probabilistic inference in CLG networks when evidence comes in streams. In such situations, fast and scalable algorithms, able to provide accurate responses in a short time are required. We consider the instantiation of variational inference and importance sampling, two well known tools for probabilistic inference, to the CLG case. The experimental results over synthetic networks show how a parallel version importance sampling, and more precisely evidence weighting, is a promising scheme, as it is accurate and scales up with respect to available computing resources.

Keywords: Importance sampling · Variational message passing · Conditional linear Gaussian networks · Hybrid Bayesian networks

1 Introduction

Today, omnipresent sensors are continuously providing streaming data on the environments in which they operate. For instance, a typical monitoring and analysis system may use streaming data generated by sensors to monitor the status of a particular device and to make predictions about its future behaviour, or diagnostically infer the most likely system configuration that has produced the observed data. Sources of streaming data with even a modest updating frequency can produce extremely large volumes of data, thereby making efficient and accurate data analysis and prediction difficult. One of the main challenges is related to handling uncertainty in data, where principled methods and algorithms for dealing with uncertainty in massive data applications are required. Probabilistic graphical models (PGMs) provide a well-founded and principled approach

© Springer International Publishing Switzerland 2015
J.M. Puerta et al. (Eds.): CAEPIA 2015, LNAI 9422, pp. 36–46, 2015.
DOI: 10.1007/978-3-319-24598-0_4

for performing inference and belief updating in complex domains endowed with uncertainty.

In this paper, we are interested in a particular type of PGMs, the so-called Bayesian networks [13], and more precisely, *hybrid* Bayesian networks, where discrete and continuous variables coexist. Our goal is to analyse the performance of probabilistic inference in hybrid Bayesian networks in scenarios where data come in streams at high speed, and therefore a quick response is required. Because of that, we will focus our analysis on conditional linear Gaussian (CLG) models [10,11], instead of more expressive alternatives such as mixtures of exponentials [12], mixtures of polynomials [18] and mixtures of truncated basis functions in general [9], as inference in the latter models is in general more time consuming [15].

The remainder of the paper is organised as follows. Section 2 establishes the necessary background and contains the problem formulation. Section 3 describes the algorithms we consider in this paper. The core of the contributions is in Sect. 3.2, where we develop a parallel algorithm based on importance sampling for CLG networks. Its performance is tested in Sect. 4 and the paper ends with the conclusion in Sect. 5.

2 Preliminaries

Bayesian networks (BNs) [3,8,13] are a particular type of PGM that has enjoyed widespread attention in the last two decades. Attached to each node, there is a conditional probability distribution given its parents in the network, so that in general, for a BN with N variables $\mathbf{X} = \{X_1, \ldots, X_N\}$, the joint distribution factorizes as $p(\mathbf{X}) = \prod_{i=1}^{N} p_i(X_i|Pa(X_i))$, where $Pa(X_i)$ denotes the set of parents of X_i in the network. A BN is called *hybrid* if some of its variables are discrete while some others are continuous.

We will use lowercase letters to refer to values or configurations of values, so that x denotes a value of X and boldface $\mathbf{x}$ is a configuration of the variables in $\mathbf{X}$. Given a set of observed variables $\mathbf{X}_E \subset \mathbf{X}$ and a set of variables of interest $\mathbf{X}_I \subset \mathbf{X} \setminus \mathbf{X}_E$, *probabilistic inference* consists of computing the posterior distribution $p(x_i|\mathbf{x}_E)$ for each $i \in I$, where X_i can be either discrete or continuous. If we denote by $\mathbf{X}_C$ and $\mathbf{X}_D$ the set of continuous and discrete variables not in $\{\mathbf{X}_i\} \cup \mathbf{X}_E$, and by $\mathbf{X}_{C_i}$ and $\mathbf{X}_{D_i}$ the set of continuous and discrete variables not in $\mathbf{X}_E$, the goal of inference can be formulated as computing

$$p(x_i|\mathbf{x}_E) = \frac{p(x_i, \mathbf{x}_E)}{p(\mathbf{x}_E)} = \frac{\displaystyle\sum_{\mathbf{x}_D \in \Omega_{\mathbf{x}_D}} \int_{\mathbf{x}_C \in \Omega_{\mathbf{x}_C}} p(\mathbf{x}; \mathbf{x}_E) \mathrm{d}\mathbf{x}_C}{\displaystyle\sum_{\mathbf{x}_{D_i} \in \Omega_{\mathbf{x}_{D_i}}} \int_{\mathbf{x}_{C_i} \in \Omega_{\mathbf{x}_{C_i}}} p(\mathbf{x}; \mathbf{x}_E) \mathrm{d}\mathbf{x}_{C_i}}, \tag{1}$$

where $\Omega_{\mathbf{X}}$ is the set of possible values of a set of variables $\mathbf{X}$ and $p(\mathbf{x}; \mathbf{x}_E)$ is the joint distribution in the BN instantiated according to the observed values $\mathbf{x}_E$.

Often, one is not interested in the full posterior distribution of X_i, but rather in the probability of the variable taking values on a given interval (a, b), which amounts to computing

$$p(a < X_i < b|\mathbf{x}_E) = \frac{\int_a^b \left(\sum_{\mathbf{x}_D \in \Omega_{\mathbf{x}_D}} \int_{\mathbf{x}_C \in \Omega_{\mathbf{x}_C}} p(\mathbf{x}; \mathbf{x}_E) d\mathbf{x}_C \right) d x_i}{\sum_{\mathbf{x}_{D_i} \in \Omega_{\mathbf{x}_{D_i}}} \int_{\mathbf{x}_{C_i} \in \Omega_{\mathbf{x}_{C_i}}} p(\mathbf{x}; \mathbf{x}_E) d\mathbf{x}_{C_i}}, \qquad (2)$$

if X_i is continuous. If it is discrete, instead of the variable taking values on an interval, we are interested in one of its possible values, i.e.

$$p(X_i = x_i|\mathbf{x}_E) = \frac{\sum_{\mathbf{x}_D \in \Omega_{\mathbf{x}_D}} \int_{\mathbf{x}_C \in \Omega_{\mathbf{x}_C}} p^{R(X_i = x_i)}(\mathbf{x}; \mathbf{x}_E) d\mathbf{x}_C}{\sum_{\mathbf{x}_{D_i} \in \Omega_{\mathbf{x}_{D_i}}} \int_{\mathbf{x}_{C_i} \in \Omega_{\mathbf{x}_{C_i}}} p(\mathbf{x}; \mathbf{x}_E) d\mathbf{x}_{C_i}}, \qquad (3)$$

where $p^{R(X_i = x_i)}(\mathbf{x}; \mathbf{x}_E)$ denotes the restriction of function $p(\mathbf{x}; \mathbf{x}_E)$ to the value x_i of variable X_i, if X_i is discrete. We call the probabilistic inference tasks described in Eqs. (2) and (3) a *query*.

2.1 Conditional Linear Gaussian Networks

A *Conditional Linear Gaussian Network* is a hybrid Bayesian network where the joint distribution is a conditional linear Gaussian (CLG) [11]. In the CLG model, the conditional distribution of each discrete variable $X_D \in \mathbf{X}$ given its parents is a multinomial, whilst the conditional distribution of each continuous variable $Z \in \mathbf{X}$ with discrete parents $\mathbf{X}_D \subseteq \mathbf{X}$ and continuous parents $\mathbf{X}_C \subseteq \mathbf{X}$, is given as a normal density by

$$p(z|\mathbf{X}_D = \mathbf{x}_D, \mathbf{X}_C = \mathbf{x}_C) = \mathcal{N}(z; \alpha_{\mathbf{x}_D} + \boldsymbol{\beta}_{\mathbf{x}_D}^{\mathsf{T}} \mathbf{x}_C, \sigma_{\mathbf{x}_D}) \qquad (4)$$

for all $\mathbf{x}_D \in \Omega_{\mathbf{X}_D}$ and $\mathbf{x}_C \in \Omega_{\mathbf{X}_C}$, where α and β are the coefficients of a linear regression model of Z given its continuous parents; this model can differ for each configuration of the discrete variables $\mathbf{X}_D$. Therefore, the conditional mean of Z is a linear model on its continuous parents, while its standard deviation, σ_D, only depends on the discrete ones.

After fixing any configuration of the discrete variables, the joint distribution of any subset $\mathbf{X}_C \subseteq \mathbf{X}$ of continuous variables is a multivariate Gaussian whose parameters can be obtained from the ones in the CLG representation. For a set of M continuous variables $Z_1, \ldots, Z_M$ with a conditionally specified joint density $p(z_1, \ldots, z_M) = \prod_{k=1}^{M} p(z_k|z_{k+1}, \ldots, z_M)$, where the k-th factor, $1 \le k \le M$, is such that

$$p(z_k|z_{k+1}, \ldots, z_M) = \mathcal{N}(z_k; \mu_{z_k|z_{k+1}, \ldots, z_M}, \sigma_{z_k}),$$

it holds that the joint is $p(z_1, \ldots, z_M) = \mathcal{N}(z_1, \ldots, z_M; \boldsymbol{\mu}, \boldsymbol{\Sigma})$, where $\boldsymbol{\mu}$ is the n-dimensional vector of means and $\boldsymbol{\Sigma}$ is the covariance matrix of the multivariate distribution over random variables $Z_1, \ldots, Z_M$ and both $\boldsymbol{\mu}$ and $\boldsymbol{\Sigma}$ are derived from the parameters in Eq. (4) [17].

3 Approximate Inference in CLG Networks

Exact inference in CLG networks is a computationally expensive task that requires the construction of a *strong* junction tree in order to guarantee that the continuous variables are marginalised out first [10]. Hence, in scenarios as stream processing, where quick responses are required, the use of approximate algorithms becomes necessary. In this section we analyse two approaches to approximate inference in CLG networks. Both are based on general techniques for probabilistic inference able to provide quick answers to queries, namely *variational inference* [1] and *importance sampling* [6].

3.1 Variational Inference

Variational inference is a deterministic approximate inference technique, where we seek to iteratively optimise a variational approximation to the posterior distribution of interest [1]. Let $\mathcal{Q}$ be the set of possible approximations; then the variational approximation to a posterior distribution $p(\mathbf{x}_I | \mathbf{X}_E = \mathbf{x}_E)$ is defined as

$$q^*_{\mathbf{x}_E}(\mathbf{x}_I) = \arg \min_{q \in \mathcal{Q}} D(q(\mathbf{x}_I) \| p(\mathbf{x}_I | \mathbf{X}_E = \mathbf{x}_E)),$$

where $D(q\|p)$ is the KL divergence between q and p.

A common approach is to employ a *variational mean-field* approximation of the posterior distribution, so that the approximation factorises over the individual variables involved, i.e.,

$$q^*_{\mathbf{x}_E}(\mathbf{x}_I) = \prod_{i \in I} q^*_{\mathbf{x}_E}(x_i). \tag{5}$$

During the optimisation of the variational mean-field one performs a coordinate ascent, where we iteratively update the individual variational distributions while holding the others fixed [7]. Updating a variational distribution essentially involves calculating the variational expectation of the logarithm of the original conditional distributions of the model. This can be done efficiently and in closed form when the distributions involved are conjugate-exponential [2]. A general architecture for supporting *variational message passing* (VMP) in graphical models is presented in [20], highlighting how distributions that are conjugate-exponential families can be utilised to efficiently represent the messages by the expected natural statistics. In this paper, we consider the application of VMP to CLG networks, and therefore the posterior distribution of the variables in the network will be the factors in Eq. (5), represented as normal densities for continuous variables and as multinomials for the discrete ones.

3.2   Importance Sampling

Importance sampling [6] is a versatile simulation technique that in the case of inference in BNs amounts to transforming the numerator in Eq. (2) by multiplying and dividing by a distribution p^* that, unlike $p(\mathbf{x}, \mathbf{x}_E)$, is easy to handle and, more precisely, from which samples can easily be drawn.

Let θ denote the numerator of Eq. (2), i.e. $\theta = \int_a^b h(x_i) dx_i$ with

$$h(x_i) = \sum_{\mathbf{x}_D \in \Omega_{\mathbf{x}_D}} \int_{\mathbf{x}_C \in \Omega_{\mathbf{x}_C}} p(\mathbf{x}; \mathbf{x}_E) d\mathbf{x}_C.$$

Then, we can write θ as

$$\theta = \int_a^b h(x_i) dx_i = \int_a^b \frac{h(x_i)}{p^*(x_i)} p^*(x_i) dx_i = E_{p^*}\left[\frac{h(X_i^*)}{p^*(X_i^*)}\right], \qquad (6)$$

where p^* is a probability density function on (a, b) called the *sampling distribution*, and X_i^* is a random variable with density p^*. Let $X_i^{*(1)}, \ldots, X_i^{*(m)}$ be a sample drawn from p^*. Then it is easy to prove that

$$\hat{\theta}_1 = \frac{1}{m} \sum_{j=1}^m \frac{h(X_i^{*(j)})}{p^*(X_i^{*(j)})} \qquad (7)$$

is an unbiased estimator of θ.

As $\hat{\theta}_1$ is unbiased, the error of the estimation is determined by its variance, which is

$$\text{Var}(\hat{\theta}_1) = \text{Var}\left(\frac{1}{m} \sum_{j=1}^m \frac{h(X_i^{*(j)})}{p^*(X_i^{*(j)})}\right) = \frac{1}{m^2} \sum_{j=1}^m \text{Var}\left(\frac{h(X_i^{*(j)})}{p^*(X_i^{*(j)})}\right)$$

$$= \frac{1}{m^2} m \text{Var}\left(\frac{h(X_i^*)}{p^*(X_i^*)}\right) = \frac{1}{m} \text{Var}\left(\frac{h(X_i^*)}{p^*(X_i^*)}\right). \qquad (8)$$

The key point in importance sampling is the selection of the sampling distribution since, according to Eq. (8), it determines the accuracy of the estimation. The rule is that the closer p^* is to h, the lower the variance is [4].

A simple procedure for selecting the sampling distribution is the so-called *evidence weighting* (EW) [5]. In EW, each variable is sampled from a conditional density given its parents in the network. The sampling order is therefore from parents to children. The observed variables are not sampled, but instead they are instantiated to the observed value. A version of this algorithm in which the conditional densities are dynamically updated during the simulation procedure was introduced in [19]. In this paper we will only use static sampling distributions, as that is the fastest alternative.

Hence, adopting EW means that h involves the product of all the conditional distributions in the Bayesian network, while p^* involves the same conditional distributions except those ones corresponding to observed variables.

Note that the denominator in Eq. (2) is just the probability of evidence, which has to be estimated as well in order to have an answer to a query (recall that $\hat{\theta}_1$ is just an estimator of the numerator). It was shown in [4] that numerator and denominator can be estimated using the same sample. To achieve this, instead of taking a sampling distribution defined on (a, b) it must be defined on the entire range of X_i. In such case, the estimator in Eq. (7) becomes an estimator of the denominator (probability of evidence) and the same estimator, evaluated only in the points in the sample that fall inside (a, b), is an estimator of θ.

Function EW($\mathbf{X}$,P,$\mathbf{x}_E$,X,a,b,M)
Input: The set of variables in the network, $\mathbf{X} = \{X_1, \ldots, X_N\}$, in topological order.
  The distributions in the network $P = \{p_1, \ldots, p_N\}$. Evidence $\mathbf{X}_E = \mathbf{x}_E$. The
  target variable X. Sample size M.
Output: An estimation of $P(a < X < b | \mathbf{X}_E = \mathbf{x}_E)$
begin
  | **Initialization:**
  | $s_1 \leftarrow 0$; $s_2 \leftarrow 0$.
  | **for** $j \leftarrow 1$ **to** M **do**
    | **Sample generation:**
    | $w_1 \leftarrow 1$; $w_2 \leftarrow 1$.
    | **for** $i \leftarrow 1$ **to** N **do**
      | **if** $X_i \notin \mathbf{X}_E$ **then**
        | Simulate a value $x_i^{(j)}$ for X_i using $p_i(x_i | Pa(x_i))$.
        | $w_2 \leftarrow w_2 * p_i(x_i^{(j)} | Pa(x_i))$.
      | **end**
      | **else**
        | Let $x_i^{(j)}$ be the value of X_i in $\mathbf{X}_E$.
      | **end**
      | $w_1 \leftarrow w_1 * p_i(x_i^{(j)} | Pa(x_i))$.
    | **end**
    | **if** $w_1 \neq 0$ **then**
      | Let $x^{(j)}$ be the value of X in the simulated configuration $x_1^{(j)}, \ldots, x_N^{(j)}$.
      | **if** $x^{(j)} \in (a, b)$ **then**
        | $s_1 \leftarrow s_1 + w_1/w_2$
      | **end**
      | $s_2 \leftarrow s_2 + w_1/w_2$
    | **end**
  | **end**
  | **return** s_1/s_2.
end

Algorithm 1. The EW algorithm for answering a probabilistic query.

The details of the inference procedure are given in Algorithm 1. In the For loop devoted to sample generation, w_1 and w_2 represent, respectively, the values of h and p^* for the simulated configurations. Each variable is simulated using its conditional distribution. In fact, we can only simulate from marginals rather than conditional distributions. That's why EW starts simulating from root nodes, where marginal distributions are attached to them. Once root nodes are simulated (i.e. we have a value for them), their children are simulated by first instantiating their conditional distributions to the simulated values for the roots, obtaining, therefore marginal densities. As we are operating with CLG networks, the marginal distribution for each discrete variable is a multinomial while it is a normal for each continuous variable. In both cases, simulating values from them is straightforward [14].

Some configurations can be useless for the estimation procedure. That is the case in which w_1 becomes zero which happens when a simulated configuration is incompatible with the observations. As an example, consider a BN with two binary variables X and Y, where $P(X = 0) = 0.9$, $P(Y = 0|X = 0) = 0$ and $P(Y = 0|X = 1) = 0.5$. It means that, approximately, 90 % of the times the value simulated for X will be 0. Assume that we have observed $Y = 0$. As $P(Y = 0|X = 0) = 0$, 90 % of the times the simulated configuration will be discarded. This problem only arises when simulating discrete variables, as the normal density for a continuous variable is never equal to 0.

In regards of scalability, it is worth pointing out that the iterations in the For loop for sample generation can be executed in parallel. This is due to the fact that the items in the sample are independent of each other. As that loop constitutes the fundamental workload of the algorithm, the scalability is potentially high, using, for instance, a multi-threaded implementation. Our proposal for scaling up the algorithm consists of using parallelisation in the above mentioned For loop. We have used Java 8 streams in our implementation.

Even though all the discussions above were focused on queries involving a continuous variable, similar arguments can be developed for discrete queries, where instead of an interval, we seek the probability of a variable taking on a fixed value. For the sake of simplicity, we omit here the details for the discrete case.

4　Experimental Evaluation

In order to test the accuracy and scalability of EW with respect to available computing resources, we conducted an experiment over two randomly generated CLG networks with 10 and 500 variables respectively, half of them continuous and the rest binary discrete variables. The aim of this choice is to test the behaviour of the algorithm when dealing with small as well as with large models. The number of links was set to double the number of variables. We have not considered any parallelisation issue for VMP, but we have included it in the experimental analysis as a bench mark.

For each network, we randomly generated a set of observations for 5 % of the variables. Queries were also selected at random, by choosing a variable and

Table 1. Error and run times for VMP.

	10 vars	500 vars
Run time (seconds)	0.0739	9.6917
Error	0.4657	2.2759

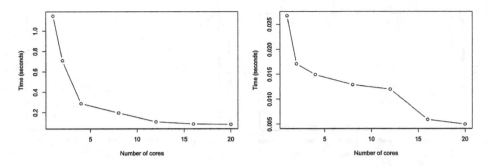

Fig. 1. Run time as a function of the number of cores for EW over a randomly generated CLG network with 500 variables (left) and 10 variables (right).

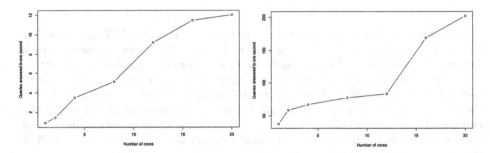

Fig. 2. Number of queries answered per second as a function of the number of cores for EW over a randomly generated CLG network with 500 variables (left) and 10 variables (right).

generating a number α from a standard normal distribution and taking the interval (a, b) with $a = \alpha - 0.5$ and $b = \alpha + 0.5$. Each query was answered using VMP and EW, the latter with samples of size 1000, 5000 and 10000. Each experiment was replicated for an increasing number of cores ranging from 1 to 20. The experiments were run on a dual-processor AMD Opteron 2.8 GHz server with 32 cores and 64 GB of RAM, running Linux Ubuntu 14.04.1 LTS.

Each run was repeated 10 times and the run time and error of the estimations were averaged over the 10 runs. The error of the estimations was computed using the χ^2 divergence. Let p_i, $i = 1, \ldots, 10$ be the exact probability corresponding to the query in run i, and let q_i be the estimated value. The χ^2 divergence is computed as

$$\chi^2 = \frac{1}{10} \sum_{i=1}^{10} \frac{(q_i - p_i)^2}{p_i}.$$

The χ^2 divergence is specially appropriate for measuring errors in probability estimations, as it is measured taking into account the magnitude of the value to estimate, and not simply the absolute or square deviation.

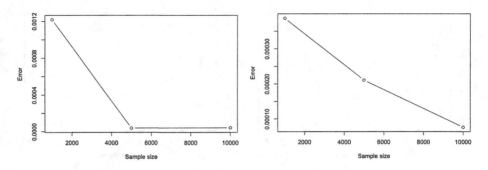

Fig. 3. Error attained by EW as a function of the sample size for a network with 10 variables (left) and with 500 variables (right).

The results of the experiments in terms of run time for EW are shown in Fig. 1. The results for VMP are given in Table 1. The plots correspond to a sample of size 1000 for EW, and show the evolution of the run time as a function of the number of cores used during the computation. It can be seen how in both networks EW scales up with respect to the number of cores. we conjecture that the jump in the curve at 12 cores is probably due to the small magnitude of the run time (of the order of miliseconds) and hence, any small variation due to any issue external to the algorithm can cause it, specially taking into account that the server where the experiments were run was shared with other users.

The ability of the algorithm for processing streams is illustrated in Fig. 2, where the number of queries answered per second is given as a function of the number of cores. It can be seen that the algorithm is able to process up to 12 queries in a second for the 500 variable network, and over 200 per second for the 10 variable network, when using 20 cores.

There is a big difference in favour of EW with respect to VMP in what concerns computing time, according to Table 1. For instance, when using 20 cores, EW gives an answer in less than 0.1 s, while VMP takes around 9, in the large network. In the small network, with only 10 variables, the results are similar, resulting EW as a much faster procedure, reaching response times for 20 cores below 0.005 s. It means that the method is able to answer around 200 queries in 1 s, which is of special interest when processing queries coming in streams.

The behaviour of the EW algorithm in terms of error is summarised in the plots in Fig. 3, where the χ^2 divergence is represented versus the sample size. As expected, the error goes down as the sample size increases. Even with the lowest sample size considered (1000), the errors are fairly low for the large and small networks. The errors reported by VMP are considerably higher, as reported in Table 1.

5 Conclusion

In this paper we have analysed the problem of approximate inference in CLG networks with special interest in parallelisation issues. We have tested the behaviour of two general approaches to probabilistic inference when applied to CLG networks. Importance sampling, and more precisely EW, has shown to be preferable to VMP both in terms of speed and accuracy. The quick responses provided by EW suggest that it is potentially an appropriate inference method for answering queries when evidence comes in form of a stream.

Though the experimental results are promising, they are still limited. We intend to study the inference problems in more complex settings, involving networks with more variables and more links. Also, the randomly generated networks did not include a high concentration of extreme probabilities for the discrete variables, i.e. zeros in the probability tables. In scenarios of extreme probabilities, EW is known to be not so accurate [16], and therefore more sophisticated methods as the ones proposed in [4] for mixtures of truncated exponentials, are to be developed.

Acknowledgments. This work was performed as part of the AMIDST project. AMIDST has received funding from the European Union's Seventh Framework Programme for research, technological development and demonstration under grant agreement no 619209.

References

1. Attias, H.: A variational Bayesian framework for graphical models. In: Advances in neural information processing systems, pp. 209–215 (2000)
2. Beal, M.J.: Variational algorithms for approximate Bayesian inference. Ph.D. thesis, Gatsby Computational Neuroscience Unit, University College London (2003)
3. Cowell, R.G., Dawid, A.P., Lauritzen, S.L., Spiegelhalter, D.J.: Probabilistic Networks and Expert Systems. Statistics for Engineering and Information Science. Springer (1999). ISBN 0-387-98767-3
4. Fernández, A., Rumí, R., Salmerón, A.: Answering queries in hybrid Bayesian networks using importance sampling. Decis. Support Syst. **53**, 580–590 (2012)
5. Fung, R., Chang, K.C.: Weighting and integrating evidence for stochastic simulation in Bayesian networks. In: Henrion, M., Shachter, R.D., Kanal, L.N., Lemmer, J.F. (eds.) Uncertainty in Artificial Intelligence, vol. 5, pp. 209–220. North-Holland, Amsterdam (1990)
6. Hammersley, J.M., Handscomb, D.C.: Monte Carlo Methods. Chapman & Hall, London (1964)
7. Jaakkola, T.S., Qi, Y.: Parameter expanded variational Bayesian methods. In: Advances in Neural Information Processing Systems, pp. 1097–1104 (2006)
8. Koller, D., Friedman, N.: Probabilistic Graphical Models: Principles and Techniques. MIT Press, Cambridge (2009)
9. Langseth, H., Nielsen, T.D., Rumí, R., Salmerón, A.: Mixtures of truncated basis functions. Int. J. Approximate Reasoning **53**(2), 212–227 (2012)

10. Lauritzen, S.L., Jensen, F.: Stable local computation with conditional Gaussian distributions. Stat. Comput. **11**(2), 191–203 (2001)

11. Lauritzen, S.L., Wermuth, N.: Graphical models for associations between variables, some of which are qualitative and some quantitative. Ann. Stat. **17**, 31–57 (1989)

12. Moral, S., Rumí, R., Salmerón, A.: Mixtures of truncated exponentials in hybrid Bayesian networks. In: Benferhat, S., Besnard, P. (eds.) ECSQARU 2001. LNCS (LNAI), vol. 2143, p. 156. Springer, Heidelberg (2001)

13. Pearl, J.: Probabilistic Reasoning in Intelligent Systems: Networks of Plausible Inference. Morgan Kaufmann Publishers Inc., San Mateo (1988)

14. Rubinstein, R.Y.: Simulation and the Monte Carlo Method. Wiley, New York (1981)

15. Rumí, R., Salmerón, A.: Approximate probability propagation with mixtures of truncated exponentials. Int. J. Approximate Reasoning **45**, 191–210 (2007)

16. Salmerón, A., Cano, A., Moral, S.: Importance sampling in Bayesian networks using probability trees. Comput. Stat. Data Anal. **34**, 387–413 (2000)

17. Shachter, R.D., Kenley, C.: Gaussian influence diagrams. Manage. Sci. **35**, 527–550 (1989)

18. Shenoy, P.P., West, J.C.: Inference in hybrid Bayesian networks using mixtures of polynomials. Int. J. Approximate Reasoning **52**, 641–657 (2011)

19. Sun, W., Chang, K.C.: Probabilistic inference using linear Gaussian importance sampling for hybrid Bayesian networks. In: Signal Processing, Sensor Fusion, and Target Recognition XIV. Proceedings of SPIE, vol. 5809, pp. 322–329 (2005)

20. Winn, J.M., Bishop, C.M.: Variational message passing. J. Mach. Learn. Res. **6**, 661–694 (2005)

Fuzzy Logic and Soft Computing

Glaucoma Diagnosis: A Soft Set Based Decision Making Procedure

José Carlos R. Alcantud[1], Gustavo Santos-García[1(✉)],
and Emiliano Hernández-Galilea[2]

[1] Facultad de Economía y Empresa and Multidisciplinary Institute of Enterprise
(IME), Universidad de Salamanca, 37007 Salamanca, Spain
{jcr,santos}@usal.es
http://diarium.usal.es/jcr
[2] Facultad de Medicina, Head of Ophthalmology Service of Hospital Clínico
Universitario de Salamanca, Universidad de Salamanca, 37007 Salamanca, Spain
egalilea@usal.es
http://diarium.usal.es/santos

Abstract. Glaucoma is one of the main causes of blindness in the world.
Until it reaches an advanced stage, Glaucoma is asymptomatic, and an
early diagnosis improves the quality of life of patients developing this
illness.

In this paper we put forward an algorithmic solution for the diagnosis
of Glaucoma. We approach the problem through a hybrid model of fuzzy
and soft set based decision making techniques. Automated combination
and analysis of information from structural and functional diagnostic
techniques are used in order to obtain an enhanced Glaucoma detection
in the clinic.

Keywords: Soft set · Fuzzy set · Soft expert system · Glaucoma ·
Diagnosis

1 Introduction

In this paper we take advantage of the theory of soft sets and fuzzy sets in order
to design a procedure to diagnose Glaucoma risk.

Imprecise or uncertain data require the use of mathematical principles
designed to capture these characteristics. The most successful approach in this
regard is fuzzy set theory, which allows partial membership. In this position a
property can be gradually verified and it can define sets in a non-traditional way.
Fuzzy sets have been applied to many branches of science and technology since
Zadeh's seminal paper [42].

In a different vein, the theory of soft sets was initiated by Molodtsov [22].
Not only did he provide fundamental results, but he also proved that soft set
theory was applicable to many fields. In particular, Molodtsov showed that soft
set models encompass the fuzzy sets models.[1] Other references worth mentioning

---

[1] The manuscript Alcantud [2] proves other relationships among these and related
concepts.

© Springer International Publishing Switzerland 2015
J.M. Puerta et al. (Eds.): CAEPIA 2015, LNAI 9422, pp. 49–60, 2015.
DOI: 10.1007/978-3-319-24598-0_5

are Maji *et al.* [21], Aktaş and Çağman [1] and Maji, Biswas and Roy [19]. In the case of incomplete information, standard references that propose decision making criteria include Han *et al.* [15], Qin *et al.* [26] and Zou and Xiao [44].[2]

The aim of this paper is to provide an application of fuzzy and soft set theory in ophthalmology which continues the research conducted by Hernández Galilea *et al.* [17]. Data from clinical examinations, standard perimetry and analysis of the nerve fibers of the retina with scanning laser polarimetry (NFAII;GDx) are combined to design an expert system that can be of avail to diagnose Glaucoma.

1.1   Glaucoma Diagnosis

Glaucoma is responsible for 20 % of blindness in Europe. It represents a public health problem all over the world (cf., [10]). It is an asymptomatic disease and early diagnosis represents an important objective. Glaucoma is an optic neuropathy characterized by progressive loss of retinal ganglion cells and by changes in the optic nerve head. It is associated with visual field loss. There are various risk factors of Glaucoma, the most important being intraocular pressure (IOP). Older patients who have a larger cup-disc ratio, greater elevation of IOP, or thinner corneas appear to be more likely to develop Glaucoma [13]. Pressure-independent factors that may predict the onset of Glaucoma or ocular hypertension may include genetic predisposition, altered optic-nerve microcirculation, systemic hypotension, race, or myopia (cf., [14]).

A number of studies show that structural and functional techniques often identify Glaucoma patients when Glaucoma severity is not too advanced (v. [5,43]). A combination of both techniques can improve Glaucoma detection (v. [28,34]).

The functional studies performed today in clinical practice with conventional computerized perimetry (static, threshold, white stimulus on white background), do not appear to be optimal and sensitive to detect early functional damage in many individuals. A significant number of patients with ocular hypertense and suspect of Glaucoma with normal standard visual fields present deficits of the visual function in other tests [31].

The single most effective method of Glaucoma diagnosis is direct examination of the optic nerve fibers, although essential in the diagnosis of Glaucoma, it is a non sensitive technique. In addition, normal eyes may have an optic nerve indistinguishable from incipient Glaucomatous eyes. The structural changes in the fiber layer of the retina and neuroretinal ring of the optic disk may occur before a deficit is determined in the visual field. Damage in the retinal nerve fibers layer (RNFL) or in the optic disk allows the identification of Glaucoma in the most incipient phase of clinical evolution even in absence of any kind of deficit in the visual field (cf., [39]).

The most universally accepted criterion to establish a definitive diagnosis of Glaucoma has usually been the loss of the visual field. Now it is commonly

---

[2] The manuscript Alcantud and Santos-García [3] is another recent contribution to this aspect of the theory from an altogether different perspective.

accepted that a significant loss of optic nerve fibers is needed to document the visual field loss (cf., [31]).

In optic neuropathy of Glaucoma a progressive loss of retinal ganglion cells occurs which brings about a decrease of RNFL thickness. Decrease of fibers can begin even five years before functional damage on the perimetry can be detected. Functional and structural damage in Glaucoma is present and the measurements of changes in the optic nerve could be correlated with damage observed in the visual field. The availability of devices that allow the analysis of fibers thickness of the layer is crucial [23,37].

Glaucomatous structural injury progresses and develops changes in the contour of the optic nerve. Different methods have been used to document the status of the optic nerve and RNFL [29,38].

At present commercial versions of optical imaging techniques that discriminate between healthy eyes and eyes with glaucomatous visual field loss are available: scanning laser polarimetry with variable corneal compensation (GDx VCC), confocal scanning laser ophthalmoscopy (HRT II, Heidelberg Retina Tomograph), and optical coherence tomography (Cirrus OCT). The sensitivities at high specificities were similar among the best parameters provided by each instrument.

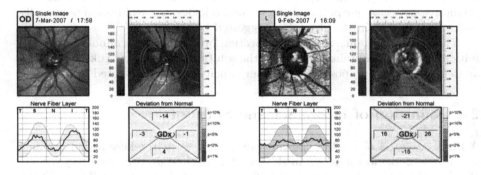

Fig. 1. Analysis with laser polarimetry for the measurement of the RNFL thickness using the NFA-II, GDX fibers analyzer (patients with normal and terminal Glaucoma).

In order to classify the eyes in glaucomatous and non-glaucomatous eyes, besides studying IOP (Goldmann tonometry) and the ophthalmoscopic study of the optic disc by biometry using Volk aspheric lens [27], Dicon TKS 4000 autoperimetry is used for the analysis of the visual field, and the laser polarimetry for the measurement of the RNFL thickness using the NFA-II, GDX fiber analyzer (Fig. 1).

A classification was separately performed for each eye of each patient. According to [7], these groups present different stages: 0 (normal eye), 1 (ocular hypertension), 2 (early Glaucoma), 3 (established Glaucoma), 4 (advanced Glaucoma), and 5 (terminal Glaucoma). Based on these stages, a non-glaucomatous eye corresponds to normal eye or ocular hypertension stages. A glaucomatous eye corresponds to an early Glaucoma stage or higher.

1.2 Contribution and Organization of the Paper

According to the discussion above we use source data from five characteristics of the patients: age, IOP, cup-to-disc ratio, the mean of all the values of the visual field in four quadrants (the superior nasal, superior temporal, inferior nasal and inferior temporal), and an experimental number extracted from all the values obtained by an image (employing NFA-II, GDX). Through recourse to suitable fuzzifications of the raw data, soft sets are suitably associated in a way that permits to devise soft rules. On these grounds we produce a prediction system according to which the risk of Glaucoma can be assessed.

Our approach is inspired by earlier applications of soft computing techniques in diagnosis. Yuksel *et al.* [41] apply soft set theory to diagnose prostate cancer risk. Slowiński [35] contributes to the application of rough sets to the analysis of an information system containing 122 patients (described by 12 attributes) with duodenal ulcer treated by highly selective vagotomy. Our approach differs from the method used by Yuksel *et al.* [41] in different respects. We introduce validation, which is missing in [41], and use our set of data in order to estimate the predictive power of our proposal. As to methodology, we avoid some technically controversial steps in the algorithm suggested by [41].

This paper is organized as follows. Section 2 recalls some terminology and definitions. Section 3 contains a review of the solution proposed by Yuksel *et al.* [41] as well as our own proposal. Finally, our conclusions are presented in Sect. 4.

2 Definition of Fuzzy Set and Soft Set

A fuzzy subset A of a set S is a function $\mu_A : S \to [0,1]$ where $\mu_A(x)$ is called the degree of membership of x in A. Henceforth FS(S) denotes the fuzzy subsets (FSs) of the set S. We can embed $\mathcal{P}(S)$, the set of all subsets of S, into FS(S) through the standard identification of $A \subseteq S$ with its characteristic function χ_A.

The usual description and terminology for soft sets refers to a universe of objects U and a universal set of parameters E. The fundamental reference for soft set based decision making draws on Maji, Biswas and Roy [20]. The main concept we use is the following:

Definition 1 (Molodtsov [22]). A pair (F, A) is a *soft set* over U when $A \subseteq E$ and $F : A \longrightarrow \mathcal{P}(U)$.

A soft set over U is regarded as a parameterized family of subsets of the universe U, the set A being the parameters. For each parameter $e \in A$, $F(e)$ is the subset of U approximated by e, that is, the set of e-approximate elements of the soft set. This concept has been investigated e.g., by Maji, Bismas and Roy [21] and by Feng and Li [12]. While [21] define concepts like soft subsets and supersets, soft equalities, intersections and unions of soft sets, *et cetera*, [12] give an extensive study of several types of soft subsets and soft equal relations.

In applications both U and A are usually finite, thus soft sets can be represented either by matrices or in tabular form (cf., Yao [40]). All cells are either 0 or 1. Rows are attached with objects in U, and columns are attached with parameters in A. It is also customary to give an abbreviated representation as shown in Example 1 below:

Example 1. Let $U = \{u_1, ..., u_5\}$ and $A = E = \{e_1, e_2, e_3, e_4\}$. A soft set (F, A) over U can be described as $F(e_1) = \{u_1, u_4\}$, $F(e_2) = \{u_3\}$, $F(e_3) = \varnothing$, and $F(e_4) = \{u_1, u_2, u_5\}$; or also in tabular or matrix form (see Table 1).

Table 1. Tabular and matrix representation of the soft set (F, A) in Example 1.

$$
\begin{array}{c|cccc}
 & e_1 & e_2 & e_3 & e_4 \\
\hline
u_1 & 1 & 0 & 0 & 1 \\
u_2 & 0 & 0 & 0 & 1 \\
u_3 & 0 & 1 & 0 & 0 \\
u_4 & 1 & 0 & 0 & 0 \\
u_5 & 0 & 0 & 0 & 1
\end{array}
\qquad
\begin{pmatrix}
1 & 0 & 0 & 1 \\
0 & 0 & 0 & 1 \\
0 & 1 & 0 & 0 \\
1 & 0 & 0 & 0 \\
0 & 0 & 0 & 1
\end{pmatrix}
$$

In order to design adequate soft rules for our expert system we make use of the following notion:

Definition 2 (Maji *et al.* [21]). Let (F, A) and (G, B) be two soft sets. Then (F, A) AND (G, B), henceforth denoted by $(F, A) \wedge (G, B)$, is defined as $(H, A \times B)$ where $H(a, b) = F(a) \cap G(b)$ for each $(a, b) \in A \times B$.

3 The Problem: Antecedents and a New Proposal

3.1 Antecedents

In this section we explore the problem of applying soft sets in decision making practice in medicine. Several AI techniques have been suggested as tools for the interpretation of automated visual field test results in patients with Glaucoma [18,33]. Using the optic disc topography parameters of the Heidelberg Retina Tomograph, neural network techniques can improve differentiation between glaucomatous and non-glaucomatous eyes [16,24,33]. Other types of machine learning classifiers, such as support vector machines, have also been reported to interpret visual fields adequately [4,6,14].

We can cite many antecedents of the use of soft computing techniques in medicine. Słowiński [35] applied rough sets in the analysis of duodenal ulcer to provide assessment in the treatment of new duodenal ulcer patients by HSV. This is in continuation of earlier applications of rough sets to this medical issue by Pawlak *et al.* [25]. Stefanowski and Słowiński [36] discuss problems connected with applications of rough set theory to identify the most important attributes and connected with induction of decision rules from the medical data set. [36] show that the causal relevancy of particular pre-therapy attributes can be determined by specifying the accuracy with which patients are assigned to particular recovery classes. Sanchez [32] pioneered the use of fuzzy techniques in medical diagnosis, an approach later extended by e.g., De *et al.* [11] to the setting of intuitionistic fuzzy sets; Saikia *et al.* [30] to the setting of intuitionistic fuzzy soft sets; and Chetia and Das [9] to the setting of interval-valued fuzzy soft sets, etc. Our main inspiration is Yuksel *et al.* [41], who use soft set theory to diagnose prostate cancer risk. Nevertheless, we can cite related uses of even fuzzy soft set theory in medical diagnosis (cf., Çelik and Yamak [8]).

3.2   Proposal of a New Soft Expert System for Glaucoma Diagnosis

We use a set of available data on five variables: (1) *age*; (2) *intraocular pressure* (IOP, expressed in millimeters of mercury); (3) *cup-to-disc ratio* (abbr. CDR, results were assigned as following: 0 for less than 0.4; 1 between 0.4–0.5; 2 between 0.5–0.6; 3 between 0.7–0.9); (4) *visual field mean* (abbr. VFM, mean of all the values of the visual field in superior nasal, superior temporal, inferior nasal, and inferior temporal quadrants); and (5) *polarimetry nerve fiber* (abbr. PNF, experimental number extracted from all the values on acquiring an image employing NFA-II, GDX).

Diagnosis of Glaucoma is known for all patients and corresponds to a total of 106 eyes. 53 eyes were randomly selected among the total set of available data in order to configure our expert system. The remaining eyes were used for validation purposes. In this section we proceed to explain the crucial part of the test, which is our algorithm for diagnosis.

Following the suggestion in [41], we first transform these data into fuzzy sets. Afterwards, by taking advantage of the standard inclusion of fuzzy sets into soft sets (cf., Molodtsov [22]), these fuzzy sets are transformed into suitable soft sets. Contrary to the spirit of [41] we do not invoke any parameter reduction of these soft sets, for which we find neither justification nor need. The crucial step is the construction of soft rules, which are subsequently analyzed in order to assess the Glaucoma risk. For this purpose each of the obtained rules yields a percentage.

Thus, for the diagnosis of Glaucoma we advance the following algorithm and give illustrative examples for each phase.

Algorithm - Setting up the Expert System

Step 1. Fuzzyfication of our data set with five variables (except for the CDR variable).

Step 2. The fuzzy sets corresponding to our data are transformed into soft sets via standard identification.

Step 3. The soft rules associated with our expert system are defined by the application of the AND operator (Definition 2) to the soft sets obtained

above. 15, 552 rules were obtained. We observe which patients satisfy each
rule.

Step 4. We calculate the Glaucoma risk percentage for each given particular
soft rule as follows: the set of patients for this rule is determined in Step
3. The number of patients with Glaucoma in this set is compared with the
total number of patients associated with this rule.

Algorithm - Application for Diagnosis. Based on the five parameters of a
newly arrived patient suspected of suffering from Glaucoma, the risk of actually
presenting Glaucoma is calculated as the maximum of the risks of all the rules
that the patient verifies (Step 4).

This is a detailed description of these steps illustrated with examples from
our data set.

Description of Step 1. In order to fuzzyficate our input data set we use several
membership functions for each variable described in medical literature (Fig. 2).

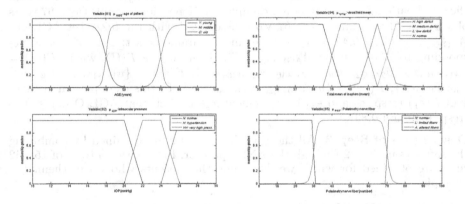

Fig. 2. Membership functions for our input variables.

The following linguistic variables are used: (1) for age: Y (young), M (medium),
and O (old); (2) for IOP: N (normal), H (high), and VH (very high hypertension); (3) for CDR: N (normal), S (slight), M (moderate), and H (high excavation);
(4) for VFM: H (high), M (medium), L (low), and N (normal deficit); and (5) for
PNF: N (normal), L (limit), and A (altered number of fibers).

Considering the width of the intervals associated to each linguistic variable
that the literature provides us, we define trapezoidal or triangular membership
functions. Although final results achieved were similar, sigmoid functions were
used in some cases.

In the case of the cup-to-disc ratio variable, the first two steps of fuzzifica-
tion/defuzzification are omitted since the possible values for this variable are 0,
1, 2 and 3. Thus, initial values of the CDR variable are maintained.

As an illustration we show the membership degrees of the following sample of input variables, where superindexes indicate the number of the variable:

$$\text{AGE(Y)}(x) = \begin{cases} \mu_Y^1(x) & \text{if } 0 < x < 40 \\ 0 & \text{if } x \geq 40 \end{cases} \qquad \text{IOP(VH)}(x) = \begin{cases} 0 & \text{if } 0 < x < 25 \\ \mu_{VH}^2(x) & \text{if } x \geq 25 \end{cases}$$

$$\text{VFM(L)}(x) = \begin{cases} 0 & \text{if } x < 41 \\ \mu_L^4(x) & \text{if } 41 \leq x \leq 42 \\ 0 & \text{if } x > 42. \end{cases}$$

Description of Step 2. In order to apply techniques from soft set theory, we resort to Molodtsov's procedure of transformation of fuzzy sets into soft sets.

We must be aware that Molodtsov's procedure considers soft sets on the universe $[0, 1]$. In order to conduct a practical study we need to select a subset of this infinite parameter set. The analysis of each membership function obtained in Step 1 suggests this selected set of parameters. Since the number of patients is limited, the parameter set must consist of a small number of elements (2 or 3).

In each of the newly defined soft sets, the universe of objects U coincides with the set of patients for whom data are employed. Hence, for example (u_1 is 97 years old, u_{35} is 72 y.o., and u_{24} is 67 y.o.): associated with the fuzzy set AGE(O), $A_{\text{AGE(O)}} = \{0.16, 0.49, 0.83\}$ is a pertinent parameter set; the soft set corresponding to AGE(O) and $A_{\text{AGE(O)}}$ is $F : A_{\text{AGE(O)}} \longrightarrow \mathcal{P}(U)$, where $F(e_1) = \{u_1, u_{10}, u_{21}, u_{24}, u_{28}, u_{30}, u_{35}, u_{40}, u_{41}, u_{45}, u_{47}\}$, $F(e_2) = \{u_1, u_{10}, u_{28}, u_{30}, u_{35}, u_{40}, u_{45}, u_{47}\}$, $F(e_3) = \{u_1, u_{10}, u_{28}, u_{30}, u_{40}, u_{47}\}$. In this example, an element x of $F(e_1)$ (resp. e_2 and e_3) is an element $x \in U$ such that $\text{AGE(O)}(x) \geq 0.16$ (resp. 0.49 and 0.83).

Description of Step 3. All the feasible soft rules are obtained by combining the soft sets in Step 2 through the AND operator. In this way, a total of $15,552$ rules are obtained for which we determine the patients who verify them. For example:

$$\text{AGE(Y)}(e_2) \wedge \text{IOP(H)}(e_2) \wedge \text{CDR(S)} \wedge \text{VFM(H)}(e_1) \wedge \text{PNF(N)}(e_3) = \{u_6, u_{20}, u_{23}\}. \tag{1}$$

Description of Step 4. The output of Step 3 allows us to associate each rule with a risk of Glaucoma as follows. For each of these rules, the ratio of patients with Glaucoma within the total of patients who verify each rule is computed. For example, the rule described by (1) presents a Glaucoma risk of 100 % because 3 out of the 3 patients listed suffer, in fact, from Glaucoma.

3.3   Testing the Performance of the Algorithm

The implementation of the model has been carried out by means of the scientific computation platform R2014a *Matlab*, using the toolbox of *Fuzzy Logic*.

The performance of classification of the designed model was validated with the remainder of the data of the other 50 % of the patients of the database. A correct classification of each eye in the diagnosis of Glaucoma (glaucomatous versus non-glaucomatous patient) has been achieved with an accuracy of 96.2 %. Specificity and sensitivity yield 1 and 0.95, respectively. Several statistical characteristics were calculated out of 53 total patients: true positive rate (39), false positive rate (0), true negative rate (12), false negative rate (2), precision (1), and F1-score (0.97).

4 Final Comments and Conclusion

Glaucoma constitutes a pathology of multifactorial etiology. Precocious diagnoses entail therapeutic actions which in a fundamental way affect the prognosis of the illness. Despite the increase of specificity and sensitivity of the diagnostic tests which are applied to detect Glaucoma, none stands alone a diagnostic criterion. Clinical judgment by an expert evaluator in Glaucoma remains the primary element for diagnosis.

In the present paper, an analysis of 106 eyes (including normal and glaucomatous patients in diverse stages) is used to develop an expert system. The expert system inputs 5 variables (age, intraocular pressure, cup-to-disc ratio, visual field mean, and polarimetry nerve fiber number) and outputs the diagnosis. The risk model is set up with half the data and contrasted with the diagnoses by a Glaucoma expert ophthalmologist. The performance of classification of the designed model is validated by the remaining data from our database. A correct classification of each eye has been achieved with an accuracy of 96.2 %. Specificity and sensitivity were 1 and 0.95, respectively. Hence, this method provides an efficient and accurate tool for the diagnosis of Glaucoma by means of soft computing techniques.

We contribute the inclusion of fuzzy soft sets in the diverse systems of clinical examination, standard perimetry, and analysis of the nerve fibers of the retina with scanning laser polarimetry (NFAII;GDx). Our proposal provides a new criterion for soft set based decision making that aims at facilitating the adequate diagnosis in a rapid and automated way.

Acknowledgments. Alcantud acknowledges financial support from the Spanish Ministerio de Economía y Competitividad (Project ECO2012–31933). The research of Santos-García was partially supported by the Spanish project Strongsoft TIN2012–39391–C04–04.

References

1. Aktaş, H., Çağman, N.: Soft sets and soft groups. Inf. Sci. **177**, 2726–2735 (2007)
2. Alcantud, J.C.R.: Some fundamental relationships among soft sets, fuzzy sets, and their extensions. Mimeo (2015)
3. Alcantud, J.C.R., Santos-García, G.: A new criterion for soft set based decision making problems under incomplete information. Mimeo (2015)

4. Bowd, C., Hao, J., Tavares, I.M., Medeiros, F.A., Zangwill, L.M., Lee, T.W., Sample, P.A., Weinreb, R.N., Goldbaum, M.H.: Bayesian machine learning classifiers for combining structural and functional measurements to classify healthy and glaucomatous eyes. Invest. Ophthalmol. Vis. Sci. **49**(3), 945–953 (2008)
5. Bowd, C., Zangwill, L.M., Berry, C.C., Blumenthal, E.Z., Vasile, C., Sánchez-Galeana, C., Bosworth, C.F., Sample, P.A., Weinreb, R.N.: Detecting early Glaucoma by assessment of retinal nerve fiber layer thickness and visual function. Invest. Ophthalmol. Vis. Sci. **42**(9), 1993–2003 (2001)
6. Burgansky-Eliash, Z., Wollstein, G., Chu, T., Ramsey, J.D., Glymour, C., Noecker, R.J., Ishikawa, H., Schuman, J.S.: Optical coherence tomography machine learning classifiers for Glaucoma detection: a preliminary study. Invest. Ophthalmol. Vis. Sci. **46**(11), 4147–4152 (2005)
7. Caprioli, J.: Discrimination between normal and glaucomatous eyes. Invest. Ophthalmol. Vis. Sci. **33**(1), 153–159 (1992)
8. Çelik, Y., Yamak, S.: Fuzzy soft set theory applied to medical diagnosis using fuzzy arithmetic operations. J. Inequal. Appl. **2013**(1), 82 (2013)
9. Chetia, B., Das, P.K.: An application of interval valued fuzzy soft sets in medical diagnosis. Int. J. Contemp. Math. Sci. **38**(5), 1887–1894 (2010)
10. Cook, C., Foster, P.: Epidemiology of Glaucoma: what's new? Can. J. Ophthalmol. **47**(3), 223–226 (2012)
11. De, S.K., Biswas, R., Roy, A.R.: An application of intuitionistic fuzzy sets in medical diagnosis. Fuzzy Sets Syst. **117**(2), 209–213 (2001)
12. Feng, F., Li, Y.: Soft subsets and soft product operations. Inf. Sci. **232**, 44–57 (2013)
13. Fingeret, M., Medeiros, F.A., Susanna, R.J., Weinreb, R.N.: Five rules to evaluate the optic disc and retinal nerve fiber layer for Glaucoma. Optometry **76**(11), 661–668 (2005)
14. Gordon, M.O., Beiser, J.A., Brandt, J.D., Heuer, D.K., Higginbotham, E.J., Johnson, C.A., Keltner, J.L., Miller, J.P., Parrish, R.K., Wilson, M.R., Kass, M.A.: The ocular hypertension treatment study: baseline factors that predict the onset of primary open-angle Glaucoma. Arch. Ophthalmol. **120**(6), 714–720 (2002). discussion 829–30
15. Han, B.H., Li, Y., Liu, J., Geng, S., Li, H.: Elicitation criterions for restricted intersection of two incomplete soft sets. Knowl. Based Syst. **59**, 121–131 (2014)
16. Henson, D.B., Spenceley, S.E., Bull, D.R.: Artificial neural network analysis of noisy visual field data in Glaucoma. Artif. Intell. Med. **10**(2), 99–113 (1997)
17. Hernández-Galilea, E., Santos-García, G., Suárez-Bárcena, I.: Identification of Glaucoma stages with artificial neural networks using retinal nerve fibre layer analysis and visual field parameters. In: Corchado, E., Corchado, J., Abraham, A. (eds.) Innovations in Hybrid Intelligent Systems. Advances in Soft Computing, vol. 44, pp. 418–424. Springer, Heidelberg (2007)
18. Lietman, T., Eng, J., Katz, J., Quigley, H.A.: Neural networks for visual field analysis: how do they compare with other algorithms? J. Glaucoma **8**(1), 77–80 (1999)
19. Maji, P., Biswas, R., Roy, A.: Fuzzy soft sets. J. Fuzzy Math. **9**, 589–602 (2001)
20. Maji, P., Biswas, R., Roy, A.: An application of soft sets in a decision making problem. Comput. Math. Appl. **44**, 1077–1083 (2002)
21. Maji, P., Biswas, R., Roy, A.: Soft set theory. Comput. Math. Appl. **45**, 555–562 (2003)
22. Molodtsov, D.: Soft set theory - first results. Comput. Math. Appl. **37**, 19–31 (1999)

23. Nukada, M., Hangai, M., Mori, S., Takayama, K., Nakano, N., Morooka, S., Ikeda, H.O., Akagi, T., Nonaka, A., Yoshimura, N.: Imaging of localized retinal nerve fiber layer defects in preperimetric Glaucoma using spectral-domain optical coherence tomography. J. Glaucoma **23**(3), 150–159 (2014)
24. Oddone, F., Centofanti, M., Iester, M., Rossetti, L., Fogagnolo, P., Michelessi, M., Capris, E., Manni, G.: Sector-based analysis with the heidelberg retinal tomograph 3 across disc sizes and Glaucoma stages. Ophthalmology **116**(6), 1106–11.e3 (2009)
25. Pawlak, Z., Slowiński, K., Slowiński, R.: Rough classification of patients after highly selective vagotomy for duodenal ulcer. Int. J. Man Mach. Stud. **24**(5), 413–433 (1986)
26. Qin, H., Ma, X., Herawan, T., Zain, J.M.: Data filling approach of soft sets under incomplete information. In: Nguyen, N.T., Kim, C.-G., Janiak, A. (eds.) ACIIDS 2011, Part II. LNCS, vol. 6592, pp. 302–311. Springer, Heidelberg (2011)
27. Quigley, H.A., Enger, C., Katz, J., Sommer, A., Scott, R., Gilbert, D.: Risk factors for the development of glaucomatous visual field loss in ocular hypertension. Arch. Ophthalmol. **112**(5), 644–649 (1994)
28. Quigley, H.A., Cone, F.E.: Development of diagnostic and treatment strategies for Glaucoma through understanding and modification of scleral and lamina cribrosa connective tissue. Cell Tissue Res. **353**(2), 231–244 (2013)
29. Rolle, T., Dallorto, L., Briamonte, C., Penna, R.R.: Retinal nerve fibre layer and macular thickness analysis with fourier domain optical coherence tomography in subjects with a positive family history for primary open angle Glaucoma. Br. J. Ophthalmol. **98**(9), 1240–1244 (2014)
30. Saikia, B.K., Das, P.K., Borkakati, A.K.: An application of intuitionistic fuzzy soft sets in medical diagnosis. Bio. Sci. Res. Bull. **19**(2), 121–127 (2003)
31. Sample, P.A., Taylor, J.D., Martinez, G.A., Lusky, M., Weinreb, R.N.: Short-wavelength color visual fields in Glaucoma suspects at risk. Am. J. Ophthalmol. **115**(2), 225–233 (1993)
32. Sanchez, E.: Inverses of fuzzy relations: application to possibility distributions and medical diagnosis. Fuzzy Sets Syst. **2**(1), 75–86 (1979)
33. Santos-García, G., Hernández-Galilea, E.: Using artificial neural networks to identify Glaucoma stages. In: Kubena, T. (ed.) The Mystery of Glaucoma, pp. 331–352. InTech, Rijeka (2011)
34. Shah, N.N., Bowd, C., Medeiros, F.A., Weinreb, R.N., Sample, P.A., Hoffmann, E.M., Zangwill, L.M.: Combining structural and functional testing for detection of Glaucoma. Ophthalmology **113**(9), 1593–1602 (2006)
35. Slowiński, K.: Rough classification of HSV patients. In: Slowiński, R. (ed.) Intelligent Decision Support. Theory and Decision Library, pp. 77–93. Springer, The Netherlands (1992)
36. Stefanowski, J., Slowiński, K.: Rough set theory and rule induction techniques for discovery of attribute dependencies in medical information systems. In: Komorowski, Jan, Żytkow, Jan M. (eds.) PKDD 1997. LNCS, vol. 1263. Springer, Heidelberg (1997)
37. Suh, M.H., Yoo, B.W., Kim, J.Y., Choi, Y.J., Park, K.H., Kim, H.C.: Quantitative assessment of retinal nerve fiber layer defect depth using spectral-domain optical coherence tomography. Ophthalmology **121**(7), 1333–1340 (2014)
38. Tatham, A.J., Weinreb, R.N., Zangwill, L.M., Liebmann, J.M., Girkin, C.A., Medeiros, F.A.: Estimated retinal ganglion cell counts in glaucomatous eyes with localized retinal nerve fiber layer defects. Am. J. Ophthalmol. **156**(3), 578–87.e1 (2013)

39. Tjon-Fo-Sang, M.J., de Vries, J., Lemij, H.G.: Measurement by nerve fiber analyzer of retinal nerve fiber layer thickness in normal subjects and patients with ocular hypertension. Am. J. Ophthalmol. **122**(2), 220–227 (1996)
40. Yao, Y.: Relational interpretations of neighbourhood operators and rough set approximation operators. Inf. Sci. **111**, 239–259 (1998)
41. Yuksel, S., Dizman, T., Yildizdan, G., Sert, U.: Application of soft sets to diagnose the prostate cancer risk. J. Inequal. Appl. **2013**(1), 229 (2013)
42. Zadeh, L.: Fuzzy sets. Inf. Control **8**, 338–353 (1965)
43. Zangwill, L.M., Bowd, C., Berry, C.C., Williams, J., Blumenthal, E.Z., Sánchez-Galeana, C.A., Vasile, C., Weinreb, R.N.: Discriminating between normal and glaucomatous eyes using the Heidelberg Retina Tomograph, gdx nerve fiber analyzer, and optical coherence tomograph. Arch. Ophthalmol. **119**(7), 985–993 (2001)
44. Zou, Y., Xiao, Z.: Data analysis approaches of soft sets under incomplete information. Knowl. Based Syst. **21**(8), 941–945 (2008)

Retinal Vessel Detection Based on Fuzzy Morphological Line Enhancement

Pedro Bibiloni$^{(\boxtimes)}$, Manuel González-Hidalgo, and Sebastià Massanet

Department of Mathematics and Computer Science,
Universitat de les Illes Balears, Palma, Spain
{p.bibiloni,manuel.gonzalez,s.massanet}@uib.es

Abstract. The paradigm of Fuzzy Morphology extends the concept of binary morphology to handle grayscale images. Fuzzy Morphology provides meaningful, local and simple operations that, when properly combined, form powerful transformations. We use this approach to segment out vessels in eye-fundus images, which can be used to diagnose medical conditions such as diabetic retinopathy. To automatically estimate the presence of such conditions, distinguishing vessels from other artifacts becomes a necessary initial step. To address the problem of segmenting curvilinear-like objects such as vessels, our methodology consists on applying the same structuring element rotated several times. We construct a vessel segmentation method and compare it with current state-of-the-art alternatives, showing the potential of our approach.

Keywords: Aggregation Function · Curvilinear Objects · Eye-fundus · Fuzzy Mathematical Morphology · Implication · t-norm · Vessel Segmentation

1 Introduction

Retinal eye-fundus images can be used by experts to detect medical conditions such as diabetic retinopathy or glaucoma. Along with technological improvements and the decreasing cost of eye-fundus cameras, an automated algorithm to estimate the influence of such conditions can help to widespread their use. Being this the final goal, we focus on an essential first step: the detection of vessels. The attributes of the tree-like vessel structure, such as their tortuosity or width, provide information towards correctly diagnosing illnesses. Besides, the ability to segment veins and arteries from other features and noise provides a shortcut to detect big and minor artifacts, which are also essential towards detecting diseases.

Vessel segmentation in retinal images has been a highly discussed topic during the last years. A number of techniques have been applied to vessel segmentation, including wavelets and Gabor filters, matched filtering, variational methods and mathematical morphology [4].

© Springer International Publishing Switzerland 2015
J.M. Puerta et al. (Eds.): CAEPIA 2015, LNAI 9422, pp. 61–70, 2015.
DOI: 10.1007/978-3-319-24598-0_6

Among all of them, we can highlight the method presented by Niemeijer *et al.* [10] and further improved by Staal *et al.* [12]. Besides publishing a public database, DRIVE, they introduced a method that computes a number of features per pixel and, to decide if a pixel represents a vessel or not, uses a k-Nearest Neighbors classifier. Soares *et al.* [11] introduced a similar method that leverages features based on multiscale Morlet wavelets, which are orientable, and a bayesian classifier called Gaussian mixture.

Regarding mathematical morphology techniques, Zana and Klein [13] presented a method in which the sum of top hat transformations is postprocessed by means of the Laplacian operator. Mendonça and Campilho [9] detect vessel centers with directional differential operators, followed by a region growing method. Lastly, the method that this document represents is an extension of the method presented in [2], in which a single top hat transformation is followed by a hysteresis step. In this document, the curvilinear shape of vessels is further leveraged in order to achieve a more accurate segmentation.

Structure of the Document. In Sect. 2, the automatic segmentation method is described, specifying the purpose of each step that it performs. Section 3 includes quantitative measures to compare our method with other segmentation algorithms, including a second segmentation expert and the method in which this one is based. In Sect. 4 we discuss the results obtained, the method itself and some possible improvements towards a better segmentation.

2 Automatic Segmentation

2.1 Nature of Images

Firstly, we present a description of a typical eye-fundus image, like the one shown in Fig. 1, focusing our attention on the features that characterize vessels. Our method is designed to leverage as much as possible the attributes here presented.

The images used in this paper are medium-size RGB eye-fundus retinal images. These images include the macula (darker circular region corresponding to the high-resolution vision), the optic disc (bright circle which is the termination of the optic nerve), the vessels, and might also contain artifacts (small

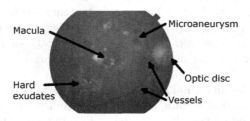

Fig. 1. Eye-Fundus sample image (14th image of the STARE database) (Color figure online).

white or yellow exudates, small or big hemorrhages and more specific pathologies). Besides pathologies, these images usually present other types of noise:
they usually have non-uniform illumination (both between different images and
within the same one), a non-flat background texture and central vessel reflex
(a lighter ridge along the center of some vessels, specially arteries).

The green channel is the one we will use due to its high contrast with regard
to the vessels, offering the red and blue ones very little information. A vessel
is a typically connected region of pixels with less green intensity values than
those located in their local background. Locally, they form a curvilinear object:
their width is *small* compared to their length, and their width does not change
abruptly. Besides, smooth bifurcations appear and some vessels have a central
lighter area, corresponding to the already mentioned central reflex. Globally, the
structure formed by all vessels is tree-shaped. It is originated at the optic disc
and grows towards the rest of the retina, surrounding the macula.

2.2   Description of the Algorithm

Our algorithm has several clearly differentiated stages, all of them with a specific
purpose. All these stages can be visualized in Fig. 2, where the 16th image of
the DRIVE database has been used as input sample. Each of them prepares the
image for the next step or leverages one specific characteristic inherent to the
vessel's nature. The rest of the section is dedicated to describing the method in
detail and linking it with the features that it leverages. Parameters or specific
details of our implementation can be found in the next section.

Preprocessing. (Stage 2 in Fig. 2). We preprocess the green channel of the
images by means of two steps: histogram equalization and Gaussian filtering.
This stage has three goals: firstly, it increases local contrast, enhancing the veins
and arteries; secondly, it faces non-uniform illumination and removes some noise;
lastly, it homogenizes the images taken in different conditions.

The first preprocessing step is a Contrast Limited Adaptive Histogram Equalization (CLAHE) [14]. The goal of *Histogram Equalization* is to modify the values
of pixels in order to change the shape of the histogram. *Adaptive* means that each
pixel is manipulated with the histogram of a local subregion around it. Finally,
in a *Contrast Limited* technique, values higher than a predefined threshold are
cut off to avoid noise amplification.

The second step consists on a 3×3 Gaussian shape with which the whole
image is filtered. The optimal size of this filter is a trade-off between preserving small vessels (only possible with small structuring elements) and removing
undesired noise (more effective with larger sizes).

Multidirectional Fuzzy Top-Hats. (Stage 3 in Fig. 2). Once the image has
been preprocessed, the detection of vessels should be carried out. In this step,
we leverage the fact that vessels are thin and dark objects to separate them from
regions that do not have these two qualities.

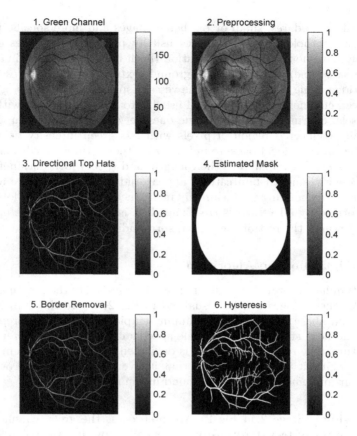

Fig. 2. Step by step execution of our method, using the 16th image of the DRIVE database.

For this purpose, we use a technique from fuzzy mathematical morphology which is based on the *black top-hat transform*. Let's consider that an image of size $n_1 \times n_2$ pixels is represented as a function $f : \{1, \ldots, n_1\} \times \{1, \ldots, n_2\} \to [0, 1]$. Let A and B be two images, where B will be referred to as the structuring element. Let $\overline{B}$ denote the reflection with respect to the center[1] of the structuring element B. Let $C : [0,1]^2 \to [0,1]$ be a fuzzy conjunction, and let $I : [0,1]^2 \to [0,1]$ be a fuzzy implication, which respectively extend the binary-logic conjunction and implication, as defined in [6]. The dilation ($\mathcal{D}$), erosion ($\mathcal{E}$), closing ($\mathcal{C}$) and black top-hat ($\mathcal{BTH}$) are defined as follows:

---

[1] We use the concept of *reflection with respect to the center* of an image B as its rotation 180° around the central point. According to our notation, and assuming that B has size $n_1 \times n_2$, it is formally defined as $\overline{B}(x_1, x_2) = B(n_1 + 1 - x_1, n_2 + 1 - x_2)$. Although the definition is general, we will only consider structuring elements with n_1, n_2 odd.

$$\mathcal{D}_C(A,B)(y) = \sup_x C\big(B(x-y), A(x)\big),$$
$$\mathcal{E}_I(A,B)(y) = \inf_x I\big(B(x-y), A(x)\big),$$
$$\mathcal{C}_{C,I}(A,B) = \mathcal{E}_I(\mathcal{D}_C(A,B), \overline{B}),$$
$$\mathcal{BTH}_{C,I}(A,B) = \mathcal{C}_{C,I}(A,B) - A,$$

where the supremum and infimum's ranges are such that both $B(x-y)$ and $A(x)$ are well defined.

In our case, we use a t-norm and its residual implicator as in [6], which fulfill the required properties [8, Prop. 45] so that the black top-hat transform detects darker regions in A that fit into the structuring element B.

To enhance vessels, which locally behave like curvilinear shapes, a linear-shaped structuring element is considered. To capture vessels with different orientations, we repeat this procedure rotating the structuring element several times, obtaining different black top-hat transformations, as shown in Fig. 3. Finally, we combine all these transformations with a pixel-wise aggregation function [1] due to their monotonic nature.

Border Removal. (Stages 4 and 5 in Fig. 2). After the fuzzy top hat step, we will suppress any false positives that our estimation generates outside the retina or near its limit.

To do so, (1) we create a mask to separate the retina from the almost black background that surrounds it, (2) this mask is slightly increased to include the boundary line, and (3) false positives can finally be removed.

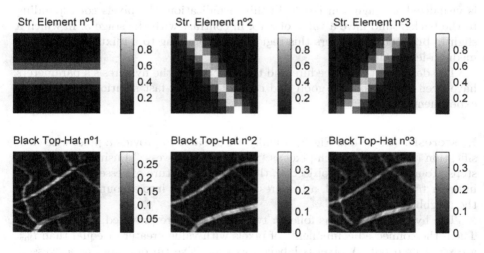

Fig. 3. Black Top-Hats with different curvilinear structuring elements, obtained with image 19th of DRIVE database for $(x,y) \in [300,400]^2$. For the sake of visualization we consider three rotations, but we remark that our algorithm uses six of them, as specified in Sect. 3.1.

Firstly, we will estimate the mask. Using the RGB original image, its pixel-wise luminance [5], $Y(x_1, x_2)$, is computed and is then filtered by means of a convolution with a normalized 3×3 flat element:

$$Y(x_1, x_2) = 0.299 \cdot R(x_1, x_2) + 0.587 \cdot G(x_1, x_2) + 0.114 \cdot B(x_1, x_2),$$

$$F(x_1, x_2) = Y(x_1, x_2) * \frac{1}{9} \begin{bmatrix} 1 & 1 & 1 \\ 1 & 1 & 1 \\ 1 & 1 & 1 \end{bmatrix}.$$

A hysteresis, explained at the end of this section, is performed over the filtered image $F(x_1, x_2)$. The thresholds are estimated from the filtered image itself:

$$t_{\text{low}} = \frac{\text{mean}\{F(x_1, x_2)\}}{2},$$

$$t_{\text{high}} = \frac{0.2 \cdot \text{mean}\{F(x_1, x_2)\} + 0.8 \cdot \text{max}\{F(x_1, x_2)\}}{2}.$$

Secondly, the mask will be enlarged to include the limits of this area, which can also contain false positives. The result of this step corresponds to stage 4 in Fig. 2. To achieve this goal, we apply a fuzzy erosion $\mathcal{E}$ to the bright area detected with the hysteresis (which corresponds to the retina), using a 10×10 pixel Gaussian function with standard deviation $\sigma = 2.5$ and the Goguen implication:

$$I_G(x, y) = \begin{cases} y/x, & x > y, \\ 1, & x \leqslant y. \end{cases}$$

Thirdly, we remove false positives by performing the pixel-wise product of this eroded mask with the estimated mask already generated. The result of this step is visualized as stage 5 in Fig. 2. In this visualization, the pixels corresponding to the background have a value of zero, in contrast with the stage 3, in which a slightly brighter tone covers this region, corresponding to a mixture of low and medium-level values.

The design of this procedure and the selection of the hysteresis's parameters have been shown to be a good and computationally fast solution by means of experimentation.

Hysteresis. (Stage 6 in Fig. 2). Finally, we are able to provide a pixel-wise classification (i.e. labelling each pixel as "vessel" or "non-vessel") using the previous steps. To accomplish this objective, the connected nature of vessels is leveraged: in order to classify a pixel, a hysteresis process takes into account the values of the neighbouring pixels.

The hysteresis works as follows: two thresholds are provided, t_{low} and t_{high}. Then, the connected components of pixels with value greater or equal than t_{low} are segmented out. A pixel is labelled as a positive (in our case, as a "vessel" pixel) if it belongs to a connected component in which at least one pixel has a value greater or equal than t_{high}.

The parameters t_{low} and t_{high} are specified in Sect. 3.1.

3 Experimental Results

3.1 Methodology

After obtaining an automatic segmentation, a quantitative measure of the correctness of method should be estimated. This measure should be coherent with the nature of the problem: we are trying to separate vessel pixels (positive instances) from non-vessel pixels (negative instances). These two classes are asymmetric: non-vessel pixels, which include a huge variety of objects, constitute the 80 % of the whole image. In order to handle different errors in a meaningful way, we use the F_1-score: the harmonic mean of precision (Pr) and recall (Re). This measure can also be expressed in terms of true positives (TP), true negatives (TN), false positives (FP) and false negatives (FN):

$$F_1 = \left(\frac{1/2}{\text{Pr}} + \frac{1/2}{\text{Re}} \right)^{-1} = \left(\frac{1/2}{\frac{\text{TP}}{\text{TP+FP}}} + \frac{1/2}{\frac{\text{TP}}{\text{TP+FN}}} \right)^{-1} = \frac{2\text{TP}}{2\text{TP} + \text{FN} + \text{FP}}.$$

In contrast, accuracy (Ac), which has been used in the context of vessel segmentation, is defined as:

$$\text{Ac} = \frac{\text{TP} + \text{TN}}{\text{Total Pixels}}.$$

Accuracy does not seem an appropriate indicator given the asymmetry of vessel pixels (around 15 %) and non-vessel pixels (the other 85 % of them). Accuracy measures the amount of pixels correctly classified, penalizing equally a false positive and a false negative. This property biases the methods towards *predicting less vessel pixels* than there actually are, because 85 % of pixels do not belong to a vessel. As a naive case, if no information is known about any pixel at all, an accuracy of 85 % can still be obtained by assigning all pixels the non-vessel label. This bias is not present when using the F_1-score.

To test our method we have segmented the vessels in a number of eye-fundus images contained in two databases whose pixel-wise ground truth is known. The DRIVE database [12] contains forty 565×584 images with at least one expert segmentation. They have low levels of noise and present none or small artifacts. The STARE database [7] has a number of 605×700 images, twenty of which have been manually segmented twice. They also have low levels of noise but present a wider range of pathologies.

Since both databases present different attributes, we have optimized our method independently in each of them. Surprisingly, the parameters selected are the same in both cases except for the hysteresis threshold, which is a good indicator of the robustness of our method. The number of rotated structuring elements was set to 6 through experimentation (that is, rotating the structuring element each $30°$). The curvilinear structuring element is a Gaussian shape along a base line with the corresponding inclination, in a 11×11 window and with approximately 3-pixel width. All black top hats were computed with the minimum t-norm and its corresponding residual implicator, the Gödel implication:

$$C(x, y) = \min(x, y), \qquad I(x, y) = \begin{cases} 1, & \text{if } x \leqslant y, \\ y, & \text{if } x > y. \end{cases}$$

To combine the top hat transforms, the pixel-wise maximum was selected due to its performance. Finally, the hysteresis values used were different: for the DRIVE database we used $t_{\text{low}} = 0.125$ and $t_{\text{high}} = 0.220$, whereas the STARE database provided better results with $t_{\text{low}} = 0.170$ and $t_{\text{high}} = 0.305$. Our method has been implemented in C and Matlab R2014a®.

3.2 Comparison with Other Methods

The results of our method have been compared against other method's automatic segmentations with the performance measure F_1−score. Among the methods used for comparison purposes, we include a second expert segmentation, the original method that we are improving with this work, and a variety of other proposed methods. Regarding the DRIVE database, we evaluated all methods in the 20 images of the test set, whereas the training set was only used by the algorithms that had a parameter training stage. On the other hand, all 20 images of the STARE database were evaluated, using the leave-one-out strategy[2] when training samples were needed. A summary of the results obtained can be found in Table 1.

A Wilcoxon Signed Rank test with a significance level of $\alpha = 0.05$ has been used to check the statistical superiority of our method with respect to the other ones. This test compares the hypothesis of whether the median of the difference of one distribution minus the other is greater than zero or not. Although this test compares the median instead of the mean, it is used due to its robustness against non normality, which is present in our distributions.

The methods by Chanwimaluang and Soares were executed with the implementations provided by their authors, the latter configured with the kNN classifier. The rest of segmentations were obtained from [7,10]. In this last case, the values included in the table are only the ones from which segmentations were available, since the implementation of the methods was not.

The results in Table 1 show the potential of our method. It not only improves the method in which it is based [2] with statistical significance, but is also better than a number of other techniques. Our method provides results close to the second expert segmentation, which can be considered a theoretical limit with respect to how good an algorithm could perform. However, some other methods are also very close to this limit, even obtaining better results in some situations.

---

[2] Leave-one-out consists on training a method with all samples but one, and evaluate the trained classifier to the last one. This procedure is repeated with each sample to obtain all segmentations. Leave-one-out is useful when we have very few samples because the estimation given is realistic: to evaluate one sample, its ground truth is never used.

Table 1. Statistical values obtained in the comparison of methods using the F_1-score as performance measure.

	DRIVE		STARE	
	Mean	(Std. Dev)	Mean	(Std. Dev)
2nd expert	0.788	(0.021)	0.740	(0.038)
Our method	0.757	(0.023)	0.709	(0.078)
Former method [2]	0.725	(0.046)	0.683[a]	(0.145)
Zana [13]	0.747[a]	(0.038)	–	–
Chanwimaluang [3]	0.670	(0.040)	0.638	(0.080)
Niemeijer [10]	0.749[a]	(0.034)	–	–
Staal [12]	0.764	(0.030)	–	–
Soares [11]	0.748[a]	(0.027)	0.698[a]	(0.079)
Hoover [7]	–	–	0.651	(0.062)

[a]Indicates that differences with our method are not statistically significative

Specifically, the algorithm published by Staal *et al.* [12] improves our method in the DRIVE database, although the comparison is not possible with the STARE database, which has a wider range of pathologies: segmentations are not available for these images.

4 Conclusions and Future Work

In this document we have presented a method to segment vessels in eye-fundus images. It is grounded in a model of the vessels within these retinal images, which is based on observation and experimental verification. The algorithm uses histogram equalization, black top hats based on fuzzy mathematical morphology and two-dimensional hysteresis, among other techniques.

The promising results obtained, specially in pathological images, motivate the further study of the algorithm. Other t-norms and residual implications can be used to perform the black top hat transformations, other aggregation functions can be used to merge them, and other parameters such as the thresholds of the hysteresis can be further adjusted or dynamically estimated. By doing so, the algorithm could be generalized to other databases with different characteristics, such as wider pathology diversity and increased noise level.

Regarding future work, two lines become predominant. Firstly, improvements beyond parameter optimization can still be achieved by using all three channels of the RGB images, instead of focusing on the green one, and studying a binarization method to enhance curvilinear objects, instead of the isotropic hysteresis procedure currently used. Secondly, the work may be extended in order to extract more information towards an automatic diagnosis: identification and classification of exudates, cotton wool spots or hemorrhages seems the appropriate next step, easier once a vessel segmentation procedure is provided.

Aknowledgments. This work was partially supported by the projects TIN2013-42795-P and TIN2014-56381-REDT (LODISCO network). P. Bibiloni also benefited from the fellowship FPI/1645/2014 of the *Conselleria d'Educació, Cultura i Universitats* of the *Govern de les Illes Balears* under an operational program co-financed by the European Social Fund.

References

1. Beliakov, G., Pradera, A., Calvo, T.: Aggregation Functions: A Guide for Practitioners, vol. 361. Springer, Heidelberg (2007)
2. Bibiloni, P., González-Hidalgo, M., Massanet, S.: Vessel segmentation of retinal images with fuzzy morphology. VipIMAGE 2015 (2015, forthcoming)
3. Chanwimaluang, T., Fan, G.: An efficient blood vessel detection algorithm for retinal images using local entropy thresholding. In: Proceedings of the 2003 International Symposium on Circuits and Systems 2003, ISCAS 2003, vol. 5, pp. 21–24. IEEE (2003)
4. Fraz, M.M., Remagnino, P., Hoppe, A., Uyyanonvara, B., Rudnicka, A.R., Owen, C.G., Barman, S.A.: Blood vessel segmentation methodologies in retinal images–a survey. Comput. Meth. Programs Biomed. **108**(1), 407–433 (2012)
5. Gonzalez, R.C., Woods, R.E., Eddins, S.L.: Digital Image Processing Using MATLAB, 2nd edn. Gatesmark Publishing, Knoxville (2004)
6. González-Hidalgo, M., Massanet, S., Mir, A., Ruiz-Aguilera, D.: On the choice of the pair conjunction-implication into the fuzzy morphological edge detector. IEEE Trans. Fuzzy Syst. **23**(4), 872–884 (2015)
7. Hoover, A., Kouznetsova, V., Goldbaum, M.: Locating blood vessels in retinal images by piecewise threshold probing of a matched filter response. IEEE Trans. Med. Imaging **19**(3), 203–210 (2000)
8. Kerre, E.E., Nachtegael, M.: Fuzzy Techniques in Image Processing, vol. 52. Springer Science and Business Media, Heidelberg (2000)
9. Mendonça, A.M., Campilho, A.: Segmentation of retinal blood vessels by combining the detection of centerlines and morphological reconstruction. IEEE Trans. Med. Imaging **25**(9), 1200–1213 (2006)
10. Niemeijer, M., Staal, J., van Ginneken, B., Loog, M., Abramoff, M.D.: Comparative study of retinal vessel segmentation methods on a new publicly available database. In: Fitzpatrick, J.M., Sonka, M. (eds.) Medical Imaging 2004, vol. 5370, pp. 648–656. International Society for Optics and Photonics, Bellingham (2004)
11. Soares, J.V., Leandro, J.J., Cesar, R.M., Jelinek, H.F., Cree, M.J.: Retinal vessel segmentation using the 2-D Gabor wavelet and supervised classification. IEEE Trans. Med. Imaging **25**(9), 1214–1222 (2006)
12. Staal, J., Abràmoff, M.D., Niemeijer, M., Viergever, M.A., van Ginneken, B.: Ridge-based vessel segmentation in color images of the retina. IEEE Trans. Med. Imaging **23**(4), 501–509 (2004)
13. Zana, F., Klein, J.C.: Segmentation of vessel-like patterns using mathematical morphology and curvature evaluation. IEEE Trans. Image Process. **10**(7), 1010–1019 (2001)
14. Zuiderveld, K.: Contrast limited adaptive histogram equalization. In: Paul, S.H. (ed.) Graphics Gems IV, pp. 474–485. Academic Press Professional Inc., San Diego (1994)

A Linguistic Approach for Self-Perceived Health State: A Real Study for Diabetes Disease

Rocio de Andrés Calle[1]([✉]), Teresa González-Arteaga[2],
José Carlos R. Alcantud[1], and Marta Peral[3]

[1] Faculty of Economics and Business, Institute of Enterprise (IME),
University of Salamanca, 37008 Salamanca, Spain
{rocioac,jcr}@usal.es
[2] Faculty of Science, University de Valladolid, 47011 Valladolid, Spain
teresag@eio.uva.es
[3] Centro de Atención Primaria de Laguna de Duero, 47140 Valladolid, Spain
mperalh@saludcastillayleon.es

Abstract. The concept of life quality is a subjective feeling that only
patient is able to define. The absence of disease is one of the determi-
nants of well-being and life quality. Generally, self-perceived health status
is measured by specific or generic questionnaires. The health information
collected in the questionnaires is usually expressed by numerical values
although the indicators evaluated are qualitative and subjective. This
contribution proposes a linguistic approach where health information
provided by patients is modelled by means of linguistic information in
order to manage the uncertainty and subjectivity of such assessments.
The contribution introduces a new model for measuring self-perceived
health that can manage linguistic information and computes a final
linguistic evaluation for each patient, applying an effective aggregation
operator. A real case study is also presented to show the usefulness and
effectiveness of the proposed model in the case of diabetes disease.

Keywords: Health perception · Linguistic modelling of health state ·
Linguistic health index

1 Introduction

Traditionally, the measure of the health state has been analyzed from an objective perspective by means of biochemical, physiological and anatomical indexes.
However, the health status has recently been considered as a multi-dimensional
concept which can be measured from different points of view: the degree of physical disability, the degree of psychological disability and the degree of disability
for interacting with the society (see [9]). Some of these aspects may be measured
by means of clinical test but others need to be measured taking into account the
perceptions that patients have on them. Keeping in mind such points, several
methodologies have been developed to measure self-perceived health status (see
[10,24], among others).

© Springer International Publishing Switzerland 2015
J.M. Puerta et al. (Eds.): CAEPIA 2015, LNAI 9422, pp. 71–81, 2015.
DOI: 10.1007/978-3-319-24598-0_7

In this paper we focus on measuring self-perceived health of patients with diabetic disease. We select this disorder because it is chronically debilitating and its high prevalence in the population. Some subjective factors that may impact in the quality of life of diabetic patients are: chronic feeling of being sick, changes in lifestyle, secondary physical disability, changes in the social relationships as a result of the disease, other complications such as visual impairment and problems related to sexual life and so forth. In the literature, there are diverse studies about how diabetes disease affects the quality of life (see [3]). As in the general case, a descriptive questionnaire is the tool used to study the impact of the diabetic disease on the quality of life (see *Diabetes Attitude Scale* (DAS) [1], *Diabetes Care Profile* (DCP) [11] and *Diabetes Quality of Life* (DQLF) [12], among others). The current methods provide only a quantitative precise values for representing self-perceived health information.

In this contribution we propose the use of the *Fuzzy Linguistic Approach* (see [26]) to model and assess the aforementioned subjective health factors. This approach provides a direct way to model qualitative information by means of linguistic variables and has been successfully used for this purpose in other evaluation fields (see [6,20,22], among others). Furthermore, we consider a flexible evaluation framework in the sense of allowing patients to express their own health perceptions in different linguistic scales according to the questionnaire issue. We must emphasize that the main and novel contribution of this work is to provide a suitable way of managing self-perceived health information but not to develop a general index to measure such an issue.

Finally, we also report on the results of a real application that illustrates our contribution. We build on real data from type 2 diabetes patients. The initial sample consisted of 72 patients of whom 18 completed all the test questions. Due to the fact that the paper's goal is focused on increasing the flexibility and versatility of the self-perceived health information, we do not take into account in this example some usual demographic aspects like age, gender, lifestyle, smoking habits, etc. We benefit from the novel modelization in order to produce a self-perceived health index for diabetes patients.

The paper is organized as follows. Section 2 is devoted to review in short the necessary linguistic concepts and methods for our proposal. In Sect. 3 we introduce our proposal to manage self-perceived health information from diabetes patient. Section 4 includes a real case of study. And the paper is concluded in Sect. 5.

2   Linguistic Background

Due to the fact that our proposal deals with multiple linguistic scales, we introduce some concepts and tools to manage multiple linguistic scales in a precise way.

2.1   Fuzzy Linguistic Approach

Self-perceived health information is usually expressed by means of numerical values although it is subjective, uncertain or vague. The fuzzy linguistic approach represents qualitative aspects as linguistic values by means of linguistic variables (see [27]). This approach is adequate when attempting to qualify phenomena related to human perceptions as in the problem we address here: self-perceived health. The use of the fuzzy linguistic approach implies to choose the appropriate linguistic descriptors for the term set and their semantics. An important parameter to be determined is the *granularity of uncertainty*, i.e., the cardinality of the linguistic term set used for showing the information that indicates the capacity of distinction that can be expressed; the more knowledge the more granularity (see [2]).

The use of linguistic variables implies processes of *computing with words* (CW) (see [18,19]) such as their fusion, aggregation, comparison, etc. To perform these computations there exist different models (see [7,8,14]). In this contribution we use a symbolic approach based on the *fuzzy linguistic 2-tuple* (see [14]) because it improves precision and interpretability of the results (see for more details [23]).

2.2 Managing Multi-granular Linguistic Information

Since our proposal considers the use of multi-granular linguistic frameworks for evaluating health state we need to accomplish processes of CW with this type of information. To solve these problems, different approaches have been proposed (see [4,5,15,17,21]).

Among the aforementioned methodologies we used the proposal by Herrera and Martínez [15] due to its flexibility, simplicity and its adjusting to our problem (see Fig. 1). This approach includes the following three stages:

1. First Stage: Choosing the basic linguistic term set. In order to unify information in a unique expression domain, first of all, a common expression domain so-called *Basic Linguistic Term Set* (BLTS) is determined. Henceforth it is noted as $\overline{S}$. This term set keeps the maximum granularity of all the linguistic term sets involved in the problem.
2. Second Stage: Transforming multi-granular linguistic information into fuzzy sets in the BLTS. The gathering information are unified by means of fuzzy sets on BLTS according to the following transformation function.

Definition 1. [13] Let $S = \{s_0, s_1, \ldots, s_h\}$ and $\overline{S} = \{\overline{s}_0, \overline{s}_1, \ldots, \overline{s}_g\}$ be two linguistic term sets, with $h \leq g$. The *linguistic transformation function* $T_{S\overline{S}} : S \longrightarrow \mathcal{F}(\overline{S})$ is defined by:

$$T_{S\overline{S}}(s_j) = \{(\overline{s}_0, \gamma_0), (\overline{s}_1, \gamma_1), \ldots, (\overline{s}_g, \gamma_g)\}$$

being,

$$\gamma_i = \max_y \min \{\mu_{s_j}(y), \mu_{\overline{s}_i}(y)\}, \ i = 0, 1, \ldots, g,$$

where $\mathcal{F}(\overline{S})$ is the set of fuzzy sets on $\overline{S}$, and μ_{s_j} and $\mu_{\overline{s}_i}$ are the membership functions of the linguistic labels $s_j \in S$ and $\overline{s}_i \in \overline{S}$, respectively.

3. Third Stage: Transformation into linguistic 2-tuples. The results obtained from the previous stage are difficult to understand by the health researcher. Moreover they introduce complexity in the computations. Because of these facts, we transform them into linguistic 2-tuples in the BLTS. This model represents the linguistic information through a 2-tuple (s, α), where s is a linguistic term and α is a numerical value which represents the symbolic translation. So, being $\beta \in [0, g]$ the value generated by a symbolic aggregation operation, we can assign a 2-tuple (s, α) that expresses the equivalent information of that given by β.

Definition 2. [14] Let $S = \{s_0, \ldots, s_g\}$ be a set of linguistic terms. The *2-tuple set associated with* S is defined as $\langle S \rangle = S \times [-0.5, 0.5)$. We define the function $\Delta_S : [0, g] \longrightarrow \langle S \rangle$ given by

$$\Delta_S(\beta) = (s_i, \alpha), \quad \text{with} \quad \begin{cases} i = \text{round}\,(\beta), \\ \alpha = \beta - i, \end{cases}$$

where *round* assigns to β the integer number $i \in \{0, 1, \ldots, g\}$ closest to β.

We note that Δ_S is bijective and $\Delta_S^{-1} : \langle S \rangle \longrightarrow [0, g]$ is defined by $\Delta_S^{-1}(s_i, \alpha) = i + \alpha$. In this way, the 2-tuples of $\langle S \rangle$ will be identified with the numerical values in the interval $[0, g]$.

The 2-tuple fuzzy linguistic representation model has associated a linguistic computational model (see [14]), that accomplishes processes of CW with symmetrical and triangular-shaped labels in a precise way. Keeping in mind that our objective here is to transform fuzzy sets in the BLTS into linguistic 2-tuples, we present the function χ that carries out this transformation.

Definition 3. [16] Given the linguistic term set $\overline{S} = \{\overline{s}_0, \overline{s}_1, \ldots, \overline{s}_g\}$, the function $\chi : \mathcal{F}(\overline{S}) \longrightarrow \langle \overline{S} \rangle$ is defined as:

$$\chi\left(\{(\overline{s}_0, \gamma_0), (\overline{s}_1, \gamma_1), \ldots, (\overline{s}_g, \gamma_g)\}\right) = \Delta_{\overline{S}}\left(\frac{\sum\limits_{j=0}^{g} j\,\gamma_j}{\sum\limits_{j=0}^{g} \gamma_j}\right).$$

3   A Linguistic Proposal to Model the Health Information Provided by Diabetes Patients

This section introduces a novel model for evaluating self-perceived health state. The aim of this problem is to evaluate the health of diabetes patients taking into account their own opinions of different aspect related to their disease. We now present the main features we consider for the arisen problem.

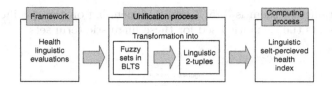

Fig. 1. Approach based on information fusion into BLTS

3.1   The Framework

It is supposed a set of patients $X = \{x_1, \ldots, x_n\}$ who have to evaluate their state of health by means of using a descriptive system composed of two parts. The first one consist of a 12-question survey based on $DQOL$ questionnaire (see Fig. 2). Due to medical research interests, the issues are classified in two different categories regarding *Physical* and *Psychological* effects (question numbers 3, 6, 7, 8, 9, 10 and 1, 2, 4, 5, 11, 12, respectively). And the second one includes a *General Linguistic Scale* (GLS). In this part patients have to answer the question: "How often would you say your health state is good?".

As shown in Fig. 2, patients use different linguistic term sets to assess each issue. Concretely, there are four different linguistic term sets. The granularity

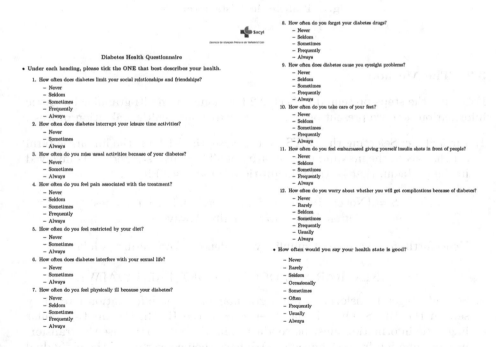

Fig. 2. Diabetes health questionnarie

of the uncertainty of them is 3, 5, 7 and 9, depending on the specific question. Figure 3 presents the semantic used for these linguistic term sets.

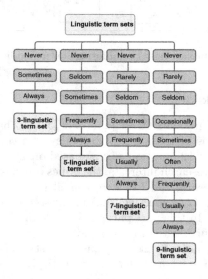

Fig. 3. Diabetes linguistic term sets

3.2 The Method

Following the steps presented in Sect. 2.2 for managing multi-granular linguistic information here we present our method to carry out health evaluation process.

1. First Stage: Selecting the BLTS. In this case, the BLTS is the linguistic term set that keeps the maximum granularity of all the linguistic term sets involved in the problem, that is, the 9-linguistic term set (see Fig. 4).

$$\overline{S} = \{\text{Never}, \text{Rarely}, \text{Seldom}, \text{Occasionally}, \text{Sometimes},$$
$$\text{Often}, \text{Frequently}, \text{Usually}, \text{Always}\}$$

Henceforth, for the sake of simplicity, we denote these terms as follows

$$\overline{S} = \{\text{NEV}, \text{RAR}, \text{SEL}, \text{OCC}, \text{SOM}, \text{OFT}, \text{FRE}, \text{US}, \text{ALW}\}.$$

2. Second Stage: Transforming multi-granular linguistic information into fuzzy sets in the BLTS. Once it has been chosen the BLTS, the multi-granular linguistic information must be conducted in it. To do so, we use the transformation function from Definition 1. We have then converted all the individual evaluations into fuzzy sets on $\overline{S}$ (see Fig. 1).

3. Third Stage: Transformation into linguistic 2-tuples. The results obtained
   previously are difficult to understand by the health researcher. Because of
   this, we transform them into linguistic 2-tuples in the BLTS by means of the
   function in Definition 3. Now, the evaluation is easy to carry out.

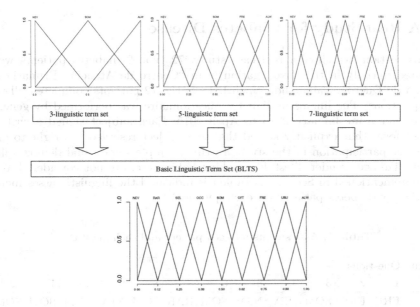

Fig. 4. Choosing the BLTS

3.3 Computing Process

The aim of the computing process is to evaluate and rank patients for different
purposes of pharmaceutical companies, hospital specialists, researchers into clinical practice, among others. For this objective, it is interesting to obtain a global
assessment for each patient that summarizes her health state. To do so, individual health perceptions are aggregated by using aggregation operators that allow
to operate in a symbolic way and have good properties. So, the use of 2-tuple
OWA operator seems suitable (see [14]).

The aggregation process to obtain a global health index for each diabetes
patient consists of the following steps:

1. Computing *Physical* and *Psychological* Index: For each patient, x_j, their
   assessments are aggregated for each group of questions.[1] As a result we get a
   Physical and Psychological index for each patient, I_{Phy} and I_{Psy}.

---

[1] The 2-tuple OWA operator needs a weighting vector that can be determined by
different methods based on weight generating functions. In this step equal weight
for each issue are considered for aggregating self-perceptions.

2. Computing *Global health* Index: the previous indexes and the assessment given for each patient in the GLS are aggregated. A global self-perceived health index is obtained after this process, I_H. In this step we propose the use of Yager's linguistic quantifiers [25] in order to generate OWA weights.

4   A Real Study for Diabetes Disease

In this section, we show a real case study. 72 type 2 diabetes patients were recruited initially in this investigation from "Centro de Atención Primaria de Laguna de Duero", Valladolid, (Spain). 18 of the 72 patients completed all the test questions. The linguistic diabetes questionnaire was performed by general practitioner from January 2015 to April 2015. Each subject signed a written consent form that explicitly stated that the subject reserved the right to end his or her participation in the study. In this example some usual demographic aspects like age, gender, lifestyle, smoking habits, etc. are not considered as it was aforementioned in Sect. 1. In Table 1 is indicated the linguistic assessments provided by diabetes patients for each question.

Table 1. Assessments for each patient and each question

Patient	Questions											
	1	2	3	4	5	6	7	8	9	19	11	12
1	FRE	FRE	SOM	NEV	NEV	SOM	RAR	SOM	NEV	SOM	SOM	SOM
3	FRE	SEL	FRE	NEV	ALW	NEV	RAR	SOM	SOM	ALW	SOM	SOM
5	NEV	SEL	SEL	SOM	ALW	NEV	NEV	NEV	SOM	ALW	SOM	NEV
7	FRE	FRE	FRE	NEV	ALW	NEV	SOM	SOM	NEV	ALW	SOM	RAR
8	FRE	FRE	FRE	NEV	ALW	SOM	SOM	SOM	SOM	ALW	SOM	RAR
18	SEL	SOM	SEL	SOM	SOM	NEV	SOM	NEV	SOM	ALW	SOM	NEV
21	NEV	SEL	FRE	NEV	NEV	SEL	SOM	SOM	SOM	ALW	SOM	NEV
27	FRE	FRE	FRE	ALW	ALW	SOM	SEL	SOM	SOM	ALW	NEV	NEV
28	FRE	FRE	NEV	NEV	ALW	NEV	SOM	SOM	SOM	NEV	SOM	SOM
33	FRE	SOM	SOM	SOM	ALW	SEL	RAR	SOM	NEV	ALW	SOM	RAR
34	SOM	FRE	FRE	SOM	ALW	NEV	RAR	SOM	SOM	ALW	SEL	NEV
36	FRE	FRE	FRE	SOM	ALW	SOM	SOM	SOM	NEV	ALW	SOM	SOM
45	SOM	FRE	FRE	NEV	ALW	NEV	SEL	SOM	SOM	SOM	SOM	NEV
48	FRE	FRE	FRE	NEV	ALW	NEV	RAR	SOM	SOM	ALW	SOM	SEL
55	FRE	FRE	FRE	NEV	ALW	SOM	SOM	SOM	NEV	ALW	SOM	NEV
59	SEL	FRE	FRE	SOM	SOM	SOM	SOM	SOM	NEV	SOM	SOM	USU
61	SEL	NEV	SEL	NEV	ALW	NEV	SOM	SOM	SOM	ALW	SOM	NEV
62	FRE	SEL	FRE	SOM	NEV	SOM	SOM	SOM	SOM	ALW	SOM	RAR

Table 2. Physical index, Psychological index and GLS assessments. Global self-perceived health index for different linguistic quantifiers

Patient	GLS	Partial index		Global index	
		Phy.	Psy.	Linguistic quantifier	
				Most of	As many as
1	SOM	OFT	(OFT, 0.46)	(OFT, 0.12)	(OFT, 0.31)
3	FRE	(FRE, −0.45)	(FRE, −0.20)	(FRE, −0.15)	(FRE, −0.07)
5	FRE	(SOM, 0.11)	(OFT, 0.01)	(OFT, 0.28)	(FRE, −0.33)
7	SOM	(FRE, 0.11)	(OFT, 0.46)	(FRE, −0.33)	(FRE, −0.11)
8	FRE	(FRE, 0.11)	(FRE, 0.46)	(FRE, 0.20)	(FRE, 0.34)
18	SOM	(SOM, 0.33)	(FRE, 0.32)	(OFT, 0.30)	(OFT, 0.23)
21	FRE	(SOM, 0.11)	(FRE, 0.44)	(FRE, −0.32)	(FRE, −0.15)
27	SOM	USU	(OFT, 0.45)	(FRE, −0.13)	(FRE, 0.48)
28	FRE	(OFT, 0.22)	(OFT, 0.37)	(FRE, −0.46)	(FRE, −0.21)
33	FRE	(FRE, 0.11)	(OFT, 0.33)	(FRE, 0.03)	(FRE, 0.07)
34	USU	(FRE, 0.33)	OFT	(USU, −0.49)	(USU, −0.22)
36	SOM	(USU, −0.45)	(FRE, 0.01)	(FRE, 0.16)	(FRE, 0.37)
45	FRE	(FRE, −0.11)	OFT	(FRE, −0.08)	(FRE, −0.04)
48	FRE	(FRE, 0.11)	(OFT, 0.21)	(FRE, 0.03)	(FRE, 0.07)
55	SOM	(FRE, 0.11)	(FRE, −0.22)	(FRE, −0.13)	FRE
59	USU	(FRE, −0.45)	(FRE, −0.08)	(FRE, 0.21)	(USU, −0.36)
61	SOM	(SOM, 0.11)	(FRE, −0.32)	(OFT, −0.47)	(OFT, 0.15)
62	FRE	(OFT, 0.11)	(FRE, 0.46)	(FRE, 0.12)	(FRE, 0.31)

According to the process proposed in Sect. 3, first the information is conducted into a unique linguistic term set, BLTS. In this case as we have aforementioned we consider that the BLTS is

$$\overline{S} = \{\text{NEV}, \text{RAR}, \text{SEL}, \text{OCC}, \text{SOM}, \text{OFT}, \text{FRE}, \text{US}, \text{ALW}\}.$$

To transform the input health information into FS; we apply the transformation function from Definition 1. When all information is expressed by means of fuzzy sets defined in the BLTS, we transform every fuzzy set in $\overline{S}$ into a linguistic 2-tuple by Definition 3. Once the information has been unified, the assessments provided by patients are aggregated following the steps given in Subsect. 3.3.

The results are shown in Table 2. This table shows partial results obtained: Physical and Psychological index. In addition, it includes the GLS assessments for each patient and the global self-perceived health index for each patient. Final global health indexes are computing by means of two different linguistic quantifiers ("most of" and "as many as").

5   Concluding Remarks

In this contribution we have presented a linguistic descriptive system to measure self-perceived health status of diabetes patients. Patients under study express by linguistic variables their subjective perceptions about their own health. In our proposal diabetes patients could express their evaluations in different linguistic scales according to the question answered, defining a multi-granular linguistic evaluation framework. The presented proposal not only obtain a global health index for each patient, but also it obtains partial indexes, Physical and Psychological. Moreover, the global health index includes the overall opinion of patients about their health by means of a general linguistic scale (GLS). All these results, partial and global, are expressed in a linguistic way in order to improve the understanding of such results by the practitioners. Consequently, this approach offers an increment of flexibility and an improvement in the treatment of self-perceived health information.

Acknowledgements. The authors thank Editors of Lecture Notes in Artificial Intelligence, three anonymous referees and Luis Martínez for their valuable comments and suggestions. The authors acknowledge financial support by the Spanish Ministerio de Ciencia e Innovación under Projects Project ECO2012–32178 (R. de Andrés Calle and T. González-Arteaga), CGL2008-06003-C03-03/CLI (R. de Andrés Calle) and ECO2012–31933 (J.C.R. Alcantud).

References

1. Anderson, R.M., Donnelly, M.B., Dedrick, R.F.: Measuring the attitudes of patients towards diabetes and its treatment. Patient Edu. Couns. **16**(3), 231–245 (1990)
2. Bonissone, P.P., Decker, K.S.: Uncertainty in Artificial Intelligence. North-Holland, Amsterdam (1986)
3. Bradley, C.: Importance of differentiating health status from quality of life. Lancet **357**(9249), 7–8 (2001)
4. Chang, S.L., Wang, R.C., Wang, S.Y.: Applying a direct multi-granularity linguistic and strategy-oriented aggregation approach on the assessment of supply performance. Eur. J. Oper. Res. **117**, 1013–1025 (2007)
5. Chen, Z., Ben-Arieh, D.: On the fusion of multi-granularity linguistic label sets in group decision making. Comput. Indus. Eng. **51**, 526–541 (2006)
6. de Andrés, R., García-Lapresta, J.L., Martínez, L.: A multi-granular linguistic model for management decision-making in performance appraisal. Soft Comput. **14**, 21–34 (2010)
7. Degani, R., Bortolan, G.: The problem of linguistic approximation in clinical decision making. Eur. J. Oper. Res. **2**, 143–162 (1988)
8. Delgado, M., Verdegay, J.L., Vila, M.A.: On aggregation operations of linguistic labels. Int. J. Intel. Syst. **8**, 351–370 (1993)
9. EuroQol: A new facility for the measurement of health-related quality of life. Health Policy **16**, 199–208 (1990)
10. EuroQol: Measuring Self Reported Population Health: An International Perspective Based on EQ-5D. SpringMed Publishing, Hungary (2004)

11. Fitzgerald, J.T., Davis, W.K., Connell, C.M., Hess, G.E., Funnell, M.M., Hiss, R.G.: Development and validation of the diabetes care profile. Eval. Health Prof. **19**, 208–230 (1996)

12. The DCCT Research Group: Reliability and validity of a diabetes quality-of-life measure for the diabetes control and complications trial (DCCT). Diab. Care **11**, 725–732 (1988)

13. Herrera, F., Herrera-Viedma, E., Martínez, L.: A fusion approach for managing multi-granularity linguistic terms sets in decision making. Fuzzy Sets Syst. **114**, 43–58 (2000)

14. Herrera, F., Martínez, L.: A 2-tuple fuzzy linguistic representation model for computing with words. IEEE Trans. Fuzzy Syst. **8**, 746–752 (2000)

15. Herrera, F., Martínez, L.: A model based on linguistic 2-tuples for dealing with multi-granularity hierarchical linguistic context in multiexpert decision-making. IEEE Trans. Fuzzy Syst. Man Cybern. **31**, 227–234 (2001)

16. Herrera, F., Martínez, L., Sánchez, P.J.: Managing non-homogeneous information in group decision making. Eur. J. Oper. Res. **166**, 115–132 (2005)

17. Huynh, V.N., Nakamori, Y.: A satisfactory-oriented approach to multiexpert decision-making with linguistic assessments. IEEE Trans. Fuzzy Syst. Man Cybern. Part B **35**, 184–196 (2005)

18. Kacprzyk, J., Zadrozny, S.: Computing with words in decision making: through individual and collective linguistic choice rules. Int. J. Uncertainty, Fuzziness Knowl.-Based Syst. **9**, 89–102 (2001)

19. Lawry, J.: A methodology for computing with words. Int. J. Approximate Reason. **28**, 51–89 (2001)

20. Martínez, L.: Sensory evaluation based on linguistic decision analysis. Int. J. Aproximated Reason. **44**, 148–164 (2007)

21. Martínez, L., Espinilla, M., Liu, J.: An extended hierarchical linguistic model for decision-making problems. Comput. Intel. **3**, 489–512 (2011)

22. Martínez, L., Espinilla, M., Pérez, L.G.: A linguistic multi-granular sensory evaluation model for olive oil. Int. J. Comput. Intel. Syst. **1**, 148–158 (2008)

23. Rodríguez, R.M., Martínez, L.: An analysis of symbolic linguistic computing models in decision making. Int. J. Gen. Syst. **42**, 121–136 (2013)

24. Ware, J.E.J., Sherbourne, C.D.: The MOS 36-Item short-form health survey (SF-36): I. Conceptual framework and item selection. Med. Care **30**(6), 473–483 (1992)

25. Yager, R.R.: An approach to ordinal decision making. Int. J. Approximate Reason. **12**, 237–261 (1995)

26. Zadeh, L.: The concept of a linguistic variable and its applications to approximate reasoning. Inf. Sci. Part I and Part II (8), Part III (9), 199–249, 301–357, 43–80 (1975)

27. Zadeh, L.: From computing with numbers to computing with words from manipulation of measurements to manipulation of perceptions. Int. J. Appl. Math. Comput. Sci. **12**(3), 307–324 (2002)

Applying Neuroevolution to Estimate the Difficulty of Learning Activities

Francisco J. Gallego-Durán[✉], Carlos J. Villagrá-Arnedo,
Rafael Molina-Carmona, and Faraón Llorens-Largo

Departamento de Ciencia de la Computación e Inteligencia Artificial,
Universidad de Alicante, Alicante, Spain
{fgallego,villagra,rmolina,faraon}@dccia.ua.es

Abstract. Learning practical abilities through exercises is a key aspect of any educational environment. To optimize learning, exercise difficulty should match abilities of the learner so that the exercises are neither so easy to bore learners nor so difficult to discourage them. The process of assigning a level of difficulty to an exercise is traditionally manual, so it is subject to teachers' bias. Our hypothesis is about the possibility of establishing a relation between human and machine learning. In other words, we wonder if exercises that are difficult to be solved by a person are also difficult to be solved by the computer, and vice versa.

To try to bring some light to this problem we have used a game for learning Computational Logic, to build neuroevolutionary algorithms to estimate exercise difficulty at the moment of exercise creation, without previous user data. The method is based on measuring the computational cost that neuroevolutionary algorithms take to find a solution and establishing similarities with previously gathered information from learners.

Results show that there is a high degree of similarity between learner difficulty to solve different exercises and neuroevolutionary algorithms performance, suggesting that the approach is valid.

Keywords: Difficulty estimation · Neuroevolution · Learning

1 Introduction

In training and education, difficulty plays a key role in learning practical abilities. In order to optimize learning, difficulty of any given exercise should match abilities of the learner. Matching the abilities means being so difficult as to be an interesting challenge and so easy to be reachable with a limited effort. Otherwise, learners have greater probability of dropping-out.

Correctly estimating the difficulty of a given activity/exercise is the first step to optimize the process of learning within this context. Some research work has been carried out calibrating difficulty by analyzing student historical data [10], or using linear regression to estimate difficulty based on user data [1] or even on generating exercises automatically with a given established difficult [12].

© Springer International Publishing Switzerland 2015
J.M. Puerta et al. (Eds.): CAEPIA 2015, LNAI 9422, pp. 82–91, 2015.
DOI: 10.1007/978-3-319-24598-0_8

However, there are few improvements on this field, and all of them concentrate in predicting based on previous data.

Some research has also been made on the interrelations between human and machine learning [5], but there are no previous experiences on relating learning costs from both worlds. In particular, there are no works about estimating the difficulty of activities/exercises using Neuroevolution (NE) algorithms.

Neuroevolution is the use of Evolutionary Algorithms (EA) to train Artificial Neural Networks (ANN), usually by means of a reinforcement scheme [14,16]. It involves the automatic generation of network topologies and the optimization of weights to produce trained ANNs. NE algorithms train ANNs in a reinforced, non-supervised way, which make them particularly suitable for tasks where there is no previous input-output data or data has to be collected while learning.

Since the first uses of EAs to evolve ANNs, lots of NE algorithms have been designed and tested with a diverse variety of problems [2,3,8,11], getting progressively greater results. NE has shown potential to deal with complex problems like learning how to play Atari games directly from visual input [6].

This work develops the idea of using Neuroevolution algorithms to estimate exercise difficulty at the moment of exercise creation, without previous user data. In particular, this idea is applied to an educative game called PLMan [15]. Although this work depends on PLMan, results are expected to be easily transferable to other areas of application.

In Sect. 2, the background of this work is presented. Section 3 presents the way to measure difficulty. The integration of this measurement in the NE algorithm is the aim of Sect. 4. In Sect. 4 the experiments and results are presented. Finally, conclusions and further work make up the final section.

2   Background

2.1   PLMan: An AI Programming Game

The basis of our research is a game called PLMan [15]. The game was built as an automated and fun way to aid students in learning functional programming with Prolog, as well as some useful abilities in Computational Logic.

In this game, students program the AI of a Pac-Man like character, creating a Prolog knowledge base. Each exercise comes in the form of a new maze, for which students have to program an AI able to get all the dots, dodging the perils. They start constructing bunches of simple rules in the form *"If you see an enemy to your left, move right"*[1], that lets them solve the first mazes. Mazes increase in complexity and programming requirements, encouraging students to learn more about Prolog and to be creative in the solution.

Lots of different mazes have been created for PLMan, with different layouts, objects to get and use, enemies and obstacles to avoid and even problems to solve. These mazes are organized into 4 stages and 5 levels of difficulty per stage. For each new exercise (i.e. maze), students pick up their desired difficulty

---

[1] in Prolog: `rule :- see(normal, left, 'E'), doAction(move(right))`.

level (from 1 to 5) and they are presented with a random maze. Students have to beat the 4 stages and a checkpoint to get the maximum grade. At each stage, students solve 1 to 5 different mazes (depending on the stage).

Every time a new maze is created for PLMan, it has to be assigned to a stage and a level of difficulty. This is manually done by the teachers, estimated on their experience. However useful, this estimation is far from optimal. The main aim of this work is to obtain the best possible maze-difficulty mapping in order to reduce student drop-out, as well as having a way to automatize the process.

2.2 Neuroevolution

This research is based on the HyperNEAT algorithm [3]. HyperNEAT is based on Neuroevolution of Augmenting Topologies (NEAT) [14], which is a direct-encoding NE algorithm featuring speciation that evolves populations of ANNs starting from the most simple possible topologies and increasingly complexifying them. Topologies grow as mutations add new neurons and/or links, creating more complex ANNs over time. This encourages finding simpler ANNs, as topologies with less neurons/links are explored first. NEAT was the first algorithm to include a registry to track genetic innovations (new neurons/links) over time. This tracking let NEAT create a new kind of crossover operator, matching genes through their entry in the registry of innovations. This new way of crossing over ANNs partially dealt with the Permutations Problem [9].

The main limitation of NEAT, its direct-encoding scheme, made it unsuitable for trying to find large-scale ANNs with patterns and regularities. Then, Compositional Pattern Producing Networks (CPPNs) [13] were created as an indirect encoding scheme to overcome this impossibility. CPPNs are a kind of networks similar to ANNs, but with an important difference: each node, instead of being a neuron, is a mathematical function. Therefore, a CPPN is a composition of functions that can produce outputs full of symmetries, patterns and regularities. By encoding a composition of functions as a network, CPPNs profited from the ideas behind NEAT. Then CPPN-NEAT was created as an algorithm to evolve increasingly complex CPPNs able to produce different spatial patterns with symmetries and regularities.

Spatial patterns produced by CPPNs are considered as neuron connectivity patterns by HyperNEAT [4]. Therefore, CPPNs become an indirect encoding scheme which can produce large-scale ANNs. As CPPNs are typically made of continuous functions, connectivity patterns can be used in different granularities, producing ANNs of varying number of nodes, but with same regularities and connectivity patterns. HyperNEAT takes a population of CPPNs as genotypes and evolves them with CPPN-NEAT.

For a CPPN to produce an ANN, a previously defined geometric *substrate* is required. A substrate is a collection of nodes placed in a N-dimensional space, thus having a vector of coordinates $\mathbf{x}^i = (\mathbf{x}_1^i, \mathbf{x}_2^i, ..., \mathbf{x}_n^i)$ for each node i. Typically, in a 2D-space neurons would be scattered in $[-1, 1] \times [-1, 1]$. Once a neuron substrate is defined, links and weights are added querying the CPPN with the coordinates of each possible pair of neurons $(\mathbf{x^i}, \mathbf{x^k}) \forall i, k$, where the output value from the CPPN represents the weight (w^{ik}) of the link from $\mathbf{x^i}$ to $\mathbf{x^k}$.

As links and weights are the output of a function of the relative location of neurons in space, the resulting topology for the ANN is related to the geometry of the substrate. This is an interesting characteristic of HyperNEAT, because it produces ANNs with the ability of "understanding" geometry relations between their inputs. This is important for us, as our automatic controllers need to understand geometric information contained in PLMan mazes to solve them.

3   Measuring Difficulty

The main goal of these research is to find an automatic way to make an optimal estimation of the difficulty of PLMan mazes. Let's define some terms:

- Executing a maze: simulating all the states of a maze (z), from its initial state, the actions taken by the main character (controlled by an AI α) and all the entities in the maze (enemies, objects...). Simulation, done using PLMan software, ends when the main character dies or eats all the dots.
- AI score:

$$s(z, \alpha) = \frac{\sum_{i=1}^{n} \delta^i(z, \alpha)}{n\delta(z, \phi)} \qquad (1)$$

where z: a given maze; n: number of test executions; α: an AI defined as a Prolog knowledge base; ϕ: a theoretical perfect AI function that achieves the best solution for any given maze; $\delta(z, \alpha)$: number of eaten dots at the end of an execution of the game, over the z maze, with α AI controlling the main character (i is used to distinguish between n different executions).
- Easiness:

$$e_t(z) = \frac{1}{m_z} \sum_{i=1}^{m_z} s(z, \alpha_t^i) \qquad (2)$$

where m_z: number of students trying to solve z; α_t^i: AI created by student i at time t;
- Difficulty:

$$D_t(z) = 1 - \frac{1}{t} \int_0^t e_t(z) dt \qquad (3)$$

In the end, the goal of a student ϵ should be getting the maximum $s_\epsilon(z, \alpha) | \forall z \in Z_\epsilon$, being $Z_\epsilon = \{z_\epsilon^i\}$ the set of mazes assigned to ϵ. So, this definition considers the expected goal of students and their average cost, mapping them over time, yielding much information than a simple static value.

These ideas are better understood with an example. Figure 1 shows $e_t(z_{22})$ and $D_t(z_{22})$ for maze z_{22}. $e_t(z_{22})$ reveals the average progression of students towards solving z_{22}. This graph gives general information about cost required to solve z_{22} (in average) as well as the advance in its mastery over time. As any student ϵ invests more time $t_k > t_j \Rightarrow s(z_{22}, \alpha_{t_k}^\epsilon) > s(z_{22}, \alpha_{t_j}^\epsilon)$. Therefore, $e_{t_k} > e_{t_j}$, yielding that z_{22} gets easier over time.

D_t is then defined to take into account the way e_t evolves over time. Although D_t is an instant value in time, its value depends on the entire range $[t_0, t]$. As can easily be deduced from Fig. 1, the evolution of the curve matters in terms of difficulty of a maze, as it represents kind of a "learning curve", so to speak. This evolution is captured in its area (greater area, greater difficulty), hence the definition of D_t in terms of the area of the curve. Therefore, values like $e_2(z_a) = e_2(z_b) = 0.75, D_2(z_a) = 0.13, D_2(z_b) = 0.35$ tell that mazes z_a and z_b are 75 % solved after 2 h of work, on average. However, the difficulty to get to that 75 % is greater on z_b because students, on average, expend more time on lower values of e_t. In other words, they find more difficulties to code better AIs, until they get one that solves 75 % of the maze.

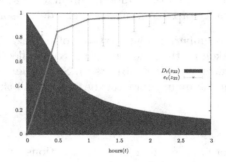

Fig. 1. $e_t(z_{22})$ and $D_t(z_{22})$ for maze z_{22}. Actual student data $(m_z = 42, n = 5)$

4   Proposed Method

Definitions at Sect. 3 let us compare maze difficulties and have a graphical understanding of them from student data. However, the goal of this research is to have optimal difficulty estimations at the time when a maze is created. This means that estimations are to be based only on the maze itself.

4.1   ANN Architectural Setup

Based mainly on results shown by [6] about the ability of NE to learn how to play Atari games, this research started posing this question: could $D_t(z)$ and NE algorithm learning cost for z have similarities? If there are enough similarities between the time/cost a NE algorithm takes to solve a maze z and the time students take, then it would be possible to use the NE algorithm as an estimation.

In order to test for similarities, the first step is to design a way to make NE learn how to play and solve PLMan mazes. Figure 2 shows the overall substrate design for HyperNEAT training. As PLMan is a console application that draws using terminal characters, objects are directly identified by their character. Therefore, the input layer can be structured as a series of substrates, each one receiving the information of the actual screen location of a given object. This input-layer design changes for each maze z, as it requires as many nodes as characters are used to draw z on screen. For instance, maze z_{22} requires 19×11 nodes for each input-layer substrate, having 4 input substrate, one for each object $O \in \{\text{'@'}, \text{'E'}, \text{'.'}, \text{'\#'}\}$. Also, as PLMan can have a single object in its inventory at a time, mazes with objects have also a special input substrate. This substrate is designed as a line of nodes, each one representing one possible object that PLMan can have in its inventory.

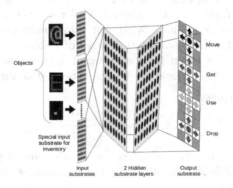

Fig. 2. ANN architecture. 2 fully-connected, recursive, hidden substrate layers are the core, along with maze-adapted substrate inputs and an output substrate with the 20 available actions for PLMan geometrically distributed as 4 virtual controllers.

The output layer has been designed with a geometrical disposition of the 20 possible actions the main character can do at a given turn. This leads to the layout with 12×3 nodes shown in Fig. 2, with 4 blocks of 5 actions, each one for one major action ($A \in \{\text{move, get, use, drop}\}$) and the direction towards the action is performed. This layout involves geometrical relationships amongst the actions and their directions, making easier for HyperNEAT to understand them. Output nodes without meaning (in grey) are not connected to the network.

Finally, the 2 hidden substrate layers have 16×10 nodes in layer 1 and 8×5 in layer 2. Layers are fully connected in forward sense (from input to output), without connections between nodes from the same layer. Also, there are recurrent links from output layer to hidden layer 2 and from hidden layer 2 to hidden layer 1. The decreasing distribution of nodes in hidden layers also aims to forcing the construction of high-level representations for decision-taking. This overall design has been drawn as an oversimplification of some known theories about the way the visual cortex works [7], in a similar way that [6] and others do.

It is important to notice that trained ANNs will not do the exact same work as students do. Students code AI controllers (α) in Prolog knowledge bases. These α controllers are then tested executing them along with PLMan software to get their scores $s(z, \alpha)$ for a given maze z. ANNs, on the contrary, play PLMan game directly selecting desired actions to perform. At each PLMan turn, ANNs are feeded with the status of the screen and inventory, and they output the action the main character is to perform. Despite the differences, the question remains valid: if there are similarities, one could be used as estimator for the other.

4.2 Similarity Measures

The next step is defining the way in which training cost is measured, as well as the training limits to be set. Then, there is also a need for a method to measure similarity between training cost values and D_t for any given maze z.

To measure the training cost of the ANNs for a given maze z, lets extend the definitions of $s(z, \alpha), e_t(z)$ and $D_t(z)$, but using training epochs (t'), instead of working hours and ANN agents (ω) instead of Prolog knowledge bases (α). Therefore, given an ANN agent from a group of agents that have been trained during t' epochs ($\omega_{t'} \in \Omega_{t'}$), these are be the extended definitions:

- ANN score and easiness:

$$s(z, \omega) = \frac{\sum_{i=1}^{n} \Delta^i(z, \omega)}{\delta(z, \phi)} \qquad (4)$$

where $\Delta(z, \omega)$ is the number of eaten dots at the end of the game, over the maze z with the ANN ω controlling the main character, similarly to $\delta(z, \alpha)$.
- ANN group easiness:

$$e_{t'}(z, \Omega_{t'}) = \frac{1}{|\Omega_{t'}|} \sum_{\forall \omega_{t'} \in \Omega_{t'}} s(z, \omega_{t'}) \qquad (5)$$

so, $|\Omega_{t'}| = 1, \omega_{t'} \in \Omega_{t'} \Rightarrow e_{t'}(z, \Omega_{t'}) = s(z, \omega_{t'})$, that is, the easiness coincides with the score when measured for individual ANNs, instead of groups.
- ANN Estimated maze difficulty:

$$D_{t'}(z, \Omega_{t'}) = 1 - \frac{1}{t'} \int_0^{t'} e_{t'}(z, \Omega_{t'}) dt' \qquad (6)$$

Then, a measure of similarity between $D_t(z)$ and $D_{t'}(z, \Omega_{t'})$ is the last step before proceeding with experiments. The problem here is that t and t' represent two different units that are not directly comparable, hence $D_1(z)$ and $D_1(z, \Omega_1)$ may represent very different points in time. To overcome this problem, a transformation from one timespace to the other is required. Lets call T and T' the timespaces for hours and epochs respectively, and define this transformation

$$\Theta(t) = t \frac{\max_{\forall t_i' \in T'} (t_i')}{\max_{\forall t_j \in T} (t_j)} = t' \qquad (7)$$

By using this transformation, timespaces T and T' are isomorphic, making the curves defined by $D_t(z)$ and $D_{t'}(z, \Omega_{t'})$ comparable. To extend the comparison to the whole range, a definition of similarity for difficulties is required:

$$\sigma_t(z, \Omega_{\Theta(t)}) = 1 - \frac{1}{t} \int_0^t |e_{\Theta(t)}(z, \Omega_{\Theta(t)}) - e_t(z)| dt \qquad (8)$$

This final notion of similarity defined in Eq. 8 is simple, yet effective: graphically it refers to the area between two difficulty curves escaled to $[0, 1]$ making an inverse proportion with t, and detracted from 0. This yields a final result in $[0, 1]$ that tends to 1 when difficulties are to be considered similar, and tends to 0 as they differ. It is also important to state that difficulties are always compared with respect to a point in time t. Moreover, $\lim_{t \to 0} \sigma_t(z, \Omega_{\Theta(t)}) = \lim_{t \to +\infty} \sigma_t(z, \Omega_{\Theta(t)}) = 1 \; \forall z, \Omega$. This happens because any maze is equally impossible to solve at $t = 0$ and has to be completely solved at $t = +\infty$. Therefore, difficulty curves at those extreme points in time are to be considered equal for any maze and estimator ANN. These are interesting properties of the definition as they match conceptually with expected results in reality.

5   Experimental Setup and Results

Experiments carried out use data about past-term student performance (336 first-year students using PLMan). PLMan software, along with a web-based system were setup to collect data about mazes and different solutions achieved by students during time. Relevant students' data are composed by their assigned mazes and the results from their programming sessions. From every session, data are sampled every 15 min, obtaining the best scores for each maze.

For these experiments, a subset $|Z| = 60$ of PLMan mazes has been considered, that accomplish the criteria of having been played by at least 10 % of the students (36 or more). This improves the signal/noise ratio of the sample.

For each maze $z \in Z$, a training session using HyperNEAT has been carried out. The relevant data got from the training sessions is the total number of generations carried out and the score of the best individual $s(z, \omega_{t'})$ at each training epoch (t'). Training sessions finish when $s(z, \omega_{t'}) = 1.0$ or when a fixed limit of 500 epochs is reached.

It is interesting to see that HyperNEAT is able to find a perfect solution for 90 % of the mazes considered, which validates the training setup. This result is not surprising as mazes considered range from easy to high medium difficulties, as the number of working hours clearly shows. Problems for HyperNEAT start with the most difficult mazes, where lots of objects need to be used, as well as some planification is required. However, as a fair point, is important to state that lots of students also fail to get the maximum score at these mazes.

The most interesting part are the sigma values $(\sigma_t(z, \Omega_{\Theta(t)}))$. They represent the notion of similarity between difficulty $(D_t(z))$ and estimation $(D_{t'}(z, \Omega_{t'}))$. Similarity values distributed in the range $[0.7142, 0.9807]$, $\mu = 0.8786$, $\sigma = 0.0651$. This results are way higher than expected, and clearly show that training cost can be used as a good predictor of difficulty.

More interesting than the raw numbers are the graphs that show the evolution of easiness and difficulty values in time. To illustrate this added value, graphs for mazes $z = 25, 59$ are shown in Fig. 3. Easiness is drawn in green and difficulty in red, using dashed lines for calculated values and normal lines for estimated values comming from ANNs; error bars are omitted for clarity. Figure 3(left) represents values for a relatively easy maze (all students solved it completely in less than 2.5 h). For this kind of maze, estimation is very accurate, showing very simmilar curves. Although this graph seems an important step forward, cases like Fig. 3(right) result more interesting. This figure shows that HyperNEAT finds different solutions and has a different timing than students on average. However, even with such differences, the definition of difficulty proves to be very stable, showing not too dissimilar lines. Difficulties here have clearly different measures, but their similarity make the estimation very useful as initial predictor.

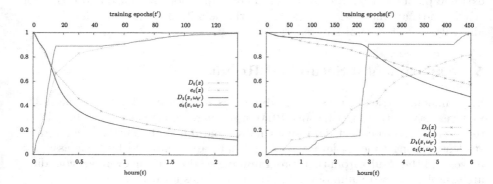

Fig. 3. Evolution of easiness and difficulty for maze $z = 25$ (left) and $z = 59$ (right), along with estimations coming from ANN $\omega_{t'}$

6   Conclusions and Further Work

This research has presented a novel application of Neuroevolution: an ability to estimate difficulty of newly created exercises, before having any kind of user data. This is an interesting application for educational or training environments, where badly estimating difficulty of exercises contributes to increasing learners drop-out. In particular, this paper has focused on doing this estimation for mazes of the PLMan game, which has also been presented.

This work started with questioning the possibility of using the training cost of NE algorithms as an estimator of the learning cost of student or, in other words, asking whether they could be similar or not. New definitions of difficulty and similarity are created for the particular problem being studied: solving PLMan mazes. The definitions presented have proven useful for the problem analyzed. In particular, the notion of difficulty has shown high stability; sharp differences in the way mazes are solved by NE with respect to students do not impede establishing great similarities with respect to their difficulty. This is a contribution of this research that deserves being further studied in the future, to better understand the advantages and drawbacks of this approach.

Experimental results give similarities far beyond expected, meaning that there is a clear relation in the way PLMan mazes are learnt by NE and students. This relation proves useful to predict maze difficulties with good accuracy.

Although definitions created in this research could prove limited to be extrapolated to other fields, the most important conclusion is that there is a exploitable learning relation, that future research could expand further beyond.

References

1. Cheng, I., Shen, R., Basu, A.: An algorithm for automatic difficulty level estimation of multimedia mathematical test items. In: Eighth IEEE International Conference on Advanced Learning Technologies, 2008, ICALT 2008 (2008)
2. Clune, J., Beckmann, B.E., Pennock, R.T., Ofria, C.: HybrID: a hybridization of indirect and direct encodings for evolutionary computation. In: Kampis, G., Karsai, I., Szathmáry, E. (eds.) ECAL 2009, Part II. LNCS, vol. 5778, pp. 134–141. Springer, Heidelberg (2011)
3. Gauci, J., Stanley, K.: Generating large-scale neural networks through discovering geometric regularities. In: Proceedings of the 9th Annual Conference on Genetic and Evolutionary Computation. ACM (2007)
4. Gauci, J., Stanley, K.O.: Autonomous evolution of topographic regularities in artificial neural networks. Neural Comput. **22**(7), 1860–1898 (2010)
5. Griffiths, T.L.: Connecting human and machine learning via probabilistic models of cognition. In: Technical Program, 10th Annual Conference of the International Speech Communication Association (2009)
6. Hausknecht, M., Khandelwal, P., Miikkulainen, R., Stone, P.: Hyperneat-ggp: a hyperneat-based atari general game player. In: Proceedings of the 14th Annual Conference on Genetic and Evolutionary Computation. ACM, New York (2012)
7. Olshausen, B.A.: Principles of image representation in visual cortex. In: Chalupa, L.M., Werner, J.S. (eds.) The Visual Neurosciences, pp. 1603–1615. MIT Press, Cambridge (2003)
8. Opitz, D.W., Shavlik, J.W.: Connectionist theory refinement: genetically searching the space of network topologies. J. Artif. Intell. Res. **6**, 177–209 (1997)
9. Radcliffe, N.J.: Genetic set recombination and its application to neural network topology optimisation. Neural Comput. Appl. **1**, 67–90 (1993)
10. Ravi, G., Sosnovsky, S.: Exercise difficulty calibration based on student log mining. In: Mdritscher, F., Luengo, V., Lai-Chong Law, E., Hoppe, U. (eds.) Proceedings DAILE 2013: Workshop on Data Analysis and Interpretation for Learning Environments (2013)
11. Risi, S., Lehman, J., Stanley, K.O.: Evolving the placement and density of neurons in the hyperneat substrate. In: Proceedings of the 12th Annual Conference on Genetic and Evolutionary Computation. ACM (2010)
12. Sadigh, D., Seshia, S.A., Gupta, M.: Automating exercise generation: a step towards meeting the MOOC challenge for embedded systems. In: Proceedings Workshop on Embedded Systems Education (WESE) (2012)
13. Stanley, K.O.: Compositional pattern producing networks: a novel abstraction of development. Genet. Program. Evolvable Mach. **8**(2), 131–162 (2007)
14. Stanley, K.O., Miikkulainen, R.: Evolving neural networks through augmenting topologies. Evol. Comput. **10**(2), 99–127 (2002)
15. Villagrá-Arnedo, C., Castel De Haro, M., Gallego-Durán, F.J., Pomares Puig, C., Suau Pérez, P., Cortés Vaíllo, S.: Real-time evaluation. In: EDULEARN09 Proceedings. IATED, Barcelona (2009)
16. Whitley, D., Starkweather, T., Bogart, C.: Genetic algorithms and neural networks: optimizing connections and connectivity. Parallel Comput. **14**(3), 347–361 (1990)

Evolutionary Product Unit Logistic Regression: The Case of Agrarian Efficiency

Carlos R. García-Alonso[1]($\boxtimes$), César Hervás-Martínez[2],
Salud MillánLara[1], and Mercedes Torres-Jiménez[1]

[1] Department of Mathematics and Engineering, Universidad Loyola Andalucía,
Escritor Castilla Aguayo 4, 14004 Córdoba, Spain
{cgarcia, smillan, mtorres}@etea.com
[2] Department of Computing and Numerical Analysis, University of Córdoba,
Córdoba, Spain
chervas@uco.es

Abstract. By using a high-variability sample of real agrarian enterprises previously classified into two classes (efficient and inefficient), a comparative study was carried out to demonstrate the classification accuracy of logistic regression algorithms based on evolutionary product-unit neural networks. Data envelopment analysis considering variable returns-to-scale (BBC-DEA) was chosen to classify selected farms (220 olive tree farms in dry farming) as efficient or inefficient by using surveyed socio-economic variables (agrarian year 2000). Once the sample was grouped by BCC-DEA, easy-to-collect descriptive variables (concerning the farm and farmer) were then used as independent variables in order to find a quick and reliable alternative for classifying agrarian enterprises as efficient or inefficient. Results showed that our proposal is very promising for the classification of complex structures (farms).

Keywords: Neural networks · Classification · Product-Unit · Evolutionary algorithms · Agrarian technical efficiency

1 Introduction

The logistic regression, is a special case of generalized linear model methodology where the assumptions of normality and the constant variance of the residuals are not satisfied.

In this paper LR is improved (to include the nonlinear effects of the covariates) taking into account the combination of linear and product-unit models [5, 7–9, 13, 16, 18]. Product-unit functions (PU) are nonlinear basis functions (mathematical transformations of the input variables) designed using the product of the covariates raised to arbitrary powers (real values). The nonlinear basis functions of the proposed model correspond to a special class of feed-forward neural networks, namely product-unit neural networks, PUNN, introduced by Durbin and Rumelhart [5] and developed recently where product-unit neural networks (PUNN) express strong covariate interactions. In this way, the LR model can be structured, on one hand, with all covariate product units: logistic regression by the product-unit model (LRPU) or, on the other,

J.M. Puerta et al. (Eds.): CAEPIA 2015, LNAI 9422, pp. 92–102, 2015.
DOI: 10.1007/978-3-319-24598-0_9

with both PU and initial covariates: logistic regression by the initial and the product-units covariates model (LRLPU).

The objective of this paper was to check the accuracy and interpretability of our hybrid classification algorithms as an alternative for classifying sets of observations in an uncertain environment where a great deal of interaction between our input variables was expected. According to this goal, LRPU and LRLPU algorithms were compared with LR and LDA, selecting a relevant problem in the agrarian economy framework: the productive efficiency of agrarian enterprises (olive tree farms).

The olive farm has been selected not only for its enormous importance in the Andalusian economy but also for the great environmental impact it can exert in reinforcing its role in the sustainable development of territories and in helping maintain the population in rural zones. Nowadays the European Union (EU) agrarian sector is more or less subsidised, and this circumstance requires it to be socially committed; that is, its financial support should be socially justified in terms of employment, environmental maintenance, food quality, efficiency, best practices and so on [6, 15]. So a subsidised farm should aspire to efficiency in a sustainable environment. According to the productive approach to technical efficiency, the farm is mainly devoted to producing output to be sold in the market to obtain a financial profit. A productively efficient farm implies using input that reasonably avoids over-utilization [17].

Data Envelopment Analysis (DEA) was applied to determine the technical efficiency of Decision Making Units (DMUs, farms) without previous assumptions like, for example, the knowledge of production functions [1–4]. In order to apply DEA it is necessary to know the exact values of all the inputs consumed (i.e. fertilizers, pesticides, etc.) for every DMU as well as the outputs produced (i.e. revenues, etc.). However, a key advantage of DEA over other approaches like the econometric Stochastic Production Frontier (SPF) is that DEA does not require any pre-described structural relationship between the inputs and resultant outputs, so allowing greater flexibility in the frontier estimation. It can also accommodate multiple outputs into the analysis. A disadvantage of the technique, however, is that it does not account for random variation in the output, and so attributes any apparent shortfall in output to technical inefficiency. However the main objective of this work is focused in forecasting with simple and only a few information the efficiency of a DMU and is not so important the methodology used to compute the technical efficiency.

In this paper, 220 olive-tree farms in dry farming were selected and grouped into efficient and inefficient groups (DEA) using the socio-economic variables surveyed. The division or classification obtained was then used to check our classification algorithms but now considering only easy-to-collect variables describing the structure of the farm and the farmer. Our hypothesis was that it was possible to classify farms as efficient or inefficient by using only these descriptive and easy-to collect variables as the independent ones (instead of difficult-to-obtain and expensive socio-economic ones). Obviously, all of them were different from those employed in DEA.

The classification results obtained using these variables could prove to be especially relevant for decision makers (politicians, rural development program managers, etc.) who could use this classification for rural planning purposes: for example, to identify those farms that should be the principle aid recipients due to their superior or inferior productive efficiency and compare them to the rest in order to improve the management and degree of competitiveness of the less efficient ones.

This paper is structured as follows: in Sect. 2 the classification methods to be used for determining farm efficiency were described; Sect. 3 briefly describes the DEA model used; in Sect. 4 the selection of the variable set is justified in a very relevant and strategic agrarian group in Andalusia (olive-tree farms in dry farming) and summarizes efficiency results in DEA models; classification results are statistically described in Sect. 5; the most relevant findings obtained using our hybrid classification models are described in Sect. 6.

2   Classification Methods

2.1   Logistic Regression with Product-Unit Covariates

Usually in real classification problems, it is not possible to assume that the generic function for determining the best classifier is always linear. According to that, several approaches for modelling non-linear systems have been proposed recently: the method of fractional polynomials and the method of fitting a generalized additive model.

In this study, based on the latest researched models, we propose a new alternative for a non-linear function $f(\mathbf{x}, \boldsymbol{\beta})$ by the inclusion of product-unit functions in the structure of the function $f(\mathbf{x}, \boldsymbol{\beta})$ establishing therein two parts: the first one is linear and the other, non-linear, made up of covariates formed as product-unit functions in the form:

$$B_j = B(\mathbf{x}, \mathbf{w_j}) = \prod_{l=1}^{p} x_l^{w_{jl}} \quad \text{for } j = 1, \ldots, m \text{ and } l = 1, \ldots, p \tag{1}$$

The non-linear part of the function can be represented as a product-unit neural network. The network has p inputs that represent the covariates of the model, m nodes in the hidden layer: the number of basis functions and one node in the output layer (in a two-class classification problem there is only one dependent variable Y -efficiency- that can only have values of 0 or 1). The activation function of the jth node in the hidden layer is given by (1), where Wjl is the weight of the connection between the input node l and the hidden node j. In this way, a LR by product-units and initial covariates model, LRLPU, is given by:

$$f(\mathbf{x}, \boldsymbol{\theta}) = \mathbf{x}^T \boldsymbol{\alpha} + \mathbf{B}^T(\mathbf{x}, \mathbf{W}) \boldsymbol{\beta} \tag{2}$$

where: $\mathbf{x}^T = (1, x_1, \ldots, x_p)$, $\mathbf{B}^T(\mathbf{x}, \mathbf{W}) = [B_1(\mathbf{x}, \mathbf{w_1}), \ldots, B_m(\mathbf{x}, \mathbf{w_m})]$ which $B_j(\mathbf{x}, \mathbf{w_j})$ as (4), and the parameters $\boldsymbol{\theta} = (\boldsymbol{\alpha}, \boldsymbol{\beta}, \mathbf{W})$, $\boldsymbol{\alpha} = (\alpha_0, \alpha_1, \ldots, \alpha_p)$, $\boldsymbol{\beta} = (\beta_1, \ldots, \beta_m)$ and $\mathbf{W} = (\mathbf{w_1}, \ldots, \mathbf{w_j})$ being $\mathbf{w_j} = (w_{j1}, \ldots, w_{jp})$ in which $w_{jl} \in R$. The LRPU model only includes BT(x, W)β (product-units). So the new conditional distribution is:

$$p(\mathbf{x}, \boldsymbol{\theta}) = \frac{\exp(\mathbf{x}^T \boldsymbol{\alpha} + \mathbf{B}^T(\mathbf{x}, \mathbf{W}) \boldsymbol{\beta})}{1 + \exp(\mathbf{x}^T \boldsymbol{\alpha} + \mathbf{B}^T(\mathbf{x}, \mathbf{W}) \boldsymbol{\beta})} \tag{3}$$

In this case, the decision boundaries are generalized surface response models. If we have a training data set $D\{(\mathbf{x_i},y_i)\}$ for $i = 1, \ldots, n$, we will use the method of maximum likelihood to estimate the parameters α and β -second step- because W was estimated previously by an evolutionary algorithm (EA) -first step- in the linear predictor $\mathbf{x}_i^T\alpha + \mathbf{B}^T(\mathbf{x}_i, \mathbf{W})\beta$. Each sample observation follows Bernouilli distribution, so since the observations are independent, the likelihood function is just:

$$L(y_1, y_2, \ldots, y_n) = \prod_{i=1}^{n} p_i^{y_i}(1 - p_i)^{1-y_i} \tag{4}$$

And the negative log-likelihood for those observations is:

$$\ln L(y_1, y_2, \ldots, y_n, \alpha, \beta) = \sum_{i=1}^{n} \left[y_i f(\mathbf{x}_i, \alpha, \beta) - \ln(1 + e^{f(\mathbf{x}_i, \alpha, \beta)}) \right] \tag{5}$$

Numerical search methods could be used to compute maximum likelihood estimates (MLE) $\hat{\alpha}$ and $\hat{\beta}$. However, it turns out that we can use iteratively reweighed least squares (IRLS) to actually find the MLE. We use the SPSS computer program that implements IRLS for the LR model. In order to define the LR using only product units as covariates, the LRPU model simplifies Eq. (2) establishing $\alpha = (\alpha_0, 0, \ldots, 0)$, in this form, we obtain logistic regression models where the linear and non-linear structure of the $f(\mathbf{x}, \beta)$ function has been modelled only with associated covariates to underlying interactions within the initial covariates.

2.2 The Estimation of Coefficients

The methodology proposed to estimate both LRPU and LRLPU parameters is a three step procedure based on the combination of an evolutionary algorithm, EA, (global explorer) and a local optimization procedure (local exploiters) carried out by a maximum-likelihood optimization method. In the first step, the EA is applied to design the structure and training of the weights of a PU neural network. It begins the search with an initial population, and at each iteration, the population is updated using a population-update algorithm. The evolutionary process determines the number m of potential basis functions of the model and the corresponding vectors $\mathbf{w}_j$ of exponents. The structure of our proposed EA is the following (more information can be seen in [10, 13, 14, 16]):

(1) Generate a random initial population of size N.
(2) Repeat the following steps until the stopping criterion is fulfilled:
   (a) Calculate the fitness of every individual in the population and rank the individuals regarding their fitness.
   (b) The best individual is copied into the new population (elitism).
   (c) The best 10 % percent of individuals of the population are replicated and substitute the worst 10 % individuals.

(d) Apply parametric mutation to the best 10 % of individuals.
(e) Apply structural mutation to the remaining 90 % of individuals.

For a dichotomous problem we consider the mean squared error (MSE) of an individual f of the population as:

$$MSE(f) = \frac{1}{n}\sum_{i=1}^{n}(y_i - f(\mathbf{x}_i))^2 \qquad (6)$$

where the y_i are the target values (0 or 1) and the $f(\mathbf{x}_i)$ are the estimated values. We define the fitness function by means of a strictly decreasing transformation of the MSE (7):

$$A(f) = \frac{1}{1 + MSE(f)}. \qquad (7)$$

In this paper we have used the following algorithm parameters: the exponents w_{ji} are initialized in the interval $(-5, 5)$ and the coefficients β_{kj} are initialized in $(-10, 10)$. In addition, the maximum number of nodes in the hidden layer is m = 4. The size of the population is N = 1000. The number of nodes that can be added or removed in a structural mutation is one or two. The number of connections that can be added or removed in a structural mutation is a number from one to six. The stopping criterion is reached whenever one of the following two conditions is fulfilled: (i) for 20 generations there is no improvement either in the average performance of the best 20 % of the population or in the fitness of the best individual; or (ii) the algorithm achieves 100 generations.

Once the basis functions have been determined by the EA, in a second step, we consider a transformation of the input space by adding the nonlinear transformations of the input variables given by the basis functions obtained by the EA. The model is linear in these new variables together with the initial covariates. The remaining coefficients α and β are calculated by the maximum-likelihood optimization method.

The third step is a backward-step procedure where the covariates of the model obtained in the second step are pruned sequentially (starting with the full model with all the covariates) until further pruning do not improve the fit. At each phase, the least significant covariate is deleted (the greatest critical p-value in the hypothesis test) to predict the response variable, where the associated coefficient equal to zero is the hypothesis to be contrasted. The procedure finishes when all tests provide p-values smaller than the fixed significance level, and the model obtained fits well.

3   Technical Efficiency: The DEA Model

In order to evaluate the relative performance of a set of decision making units (DMU) that produce multiple outputs consuming multiple inputs, DEA methods are well-known non-parametric data-oriented approaches that have developed greatly since the seminal paper of Charnes et al. [3]. DEA does not need the a priori assumptions associated with other approaches for performance appraisal such as, for example, statistical regression ones. Recent relative efficiency definitions assume that a DMU can be considered 100 % efficient in a set of selected DMU if, and only if, according to existing information (inputs and outputs), there is not any real evidence that some inputs or outputs could be improved without worsening any of their inputs or outputs. Based on this definition, many different DEA models have been developed, including the economic concept of returns to scale. Returns to scale can be considered variable when a proportional increase or decrease in all the inputs implies more (increasing returns to scale) or less (decreasing returns to scale) than proportional input increase or decrease. DEA models immediately assume this realistic approach [2, 4].

If we are analysing a set of DMU where each DMU j (j = 1, 2,..., n) produces identical outputs in different quantities, y_{rj} (r = 1, 2,..., s) and consumes also identical inputs in different amounts, x_{ij} (i = 1, 2,..., m), according to the standard variable returns to scale model (BCC-DEA), the technical efficiency of a selected DMU can be evaluated using the primal "envelopment form" using the following linear model:

$$\text{Min } \theta_0 - \varepsilon \left(\sum_{i=1}^{m} s_i^- + \sum_{r=1}^{s} s_r^+ \right) \tag{8}$$

Subject to

$$\theta_0 x_{i0} = \sum_{j=1}^{n} x_{ij}\lambda_j + s_i^- \; i = 1, 2, \ldots, m \quad \lambda_{r0} = \sum_{j=1}^{n} y_{rj}\lambda_j - s_r^+ \; r = 1, 2, \ldots, s$$

$$\sum_{j=1}^{n} \lambda_j = 1 \quad \lambda_j, s_i^-, s_r^+ \geq 0 \forall i, r, j$$

ε being a non-Archimedean element smaller than any positive real number, λ_j the model variables and s_i^- and s_i^- the corresponding slacks.

According to model [6], a DMU is efficient if and only if min $\theta_0 = 1$ ($\theta_0^* = 1$) and all slacks are zero. The input-oriented BCC model, that is the most realistic approach in the agrarian sector, analyses the possibility of reducing input consumption to produce the same amount of outputs in every DMU analysed [2, 4].

Once the DEA model is solved, it classifies the DMU set (agrarian enterprises) into two groups: inefficient (Y = 0) and efficient (Y = 1). In this paper, the relative technical efficiency of olive tree farms in dry farming was calculated using survey-based socio-economic variables (see Table 1).

4 Experimental Design: Selection and Justification of the Variable and Decisional Framework

The samples of real agrarian enterprises were randomly selected to be representative at a provincial level according to the Andalusian distribution of farm sizes and agrarian activities: crops and cattle [6, 11, 15]. The socio-economic structure of these agrarian

Table 1. Socio-economic variables of surveyed olive tree farms to calculate productive efficiency using BCC-DEA (source: CAC 3/2001 project)

		DEA	Variable description
1	SC1	Input	Energy structural costs (electricity and liquid and solid fuels, 10^2 €)
2	SC2	Input	Other structural costs except for structural hand labour (10^2 €)
3	SC3	Input	Taxes (10^2 €)
4	SHL	Input	Structural hand labour cost (10^2 €)
5	SR	Output	Structural revenues including non-agrarian revenues (10^2 €)
6	FHL	Input	Family hand labour over total hand labour on the farm (%)
7	ICO	Input	Input costs of the farm crops (10^2 €)
8	CCO	Input	Other costs of the farm crops (10^2 €)
9	HLC	Input	Total hand labour costs of farm crops (10^2 €)
10	CR	Output	Total crop revenues (10^2 €)
11	SUB	Input	Total crop subsidies (10^2 €)

enterprises, obtained from very detailed survey questionnaires, attempted to achieve the greatest possible precision in determining their productive structure, costs and revenues.

Our classification problem can be structured in three sequential phases: In the first, olive tree farms in the dry farming set from the original databases were selected in order to analyse the potential for reproducing efficiency results obtained from BCC-DEA of LR, LRPU and LRLPU models as compared to LDA. This strategic group is nowadays one of the most important ones in Andalusia[1] The sample analysed was made up of 220 complex farms spread all throughout Andalusia. In the second phase, BCC-DEA was chosen to calculate the productive efficiency, relative, of the sample considered. Only socio-economic variables (11 in total) were taken into account as stated in Table 1 (9 DEA inputs, agrarian resources, x_{ij} and 2 DEA outputs y_{rj}, economic results). The set of variables selected to calculate farm efficiency using BCC-DEA are very difficult to collect in the field and relatively difficult to calculate. In the third phase, the classification was carried out using DEA. From a productive point of view, 61 olive tree farms (27.73 %) were considered efficient (Y = 1). The resulting pre-classification produced a non-balanced structure, a circumstance that added an additional difficulty to the inner statistical variability of the training samples (Table 3) that is reproduced in the generalization ones.

Once the original set of farms was divided into two groups, efficient or inefficient, a selected easy-to-collect set of variables in the field that describe these farms and the corresponding farmers (Table 2) was considered the input group. The productive efficiency of each DMU (farm) was the dependent variable, for classification purposes.

---

[1] These farms represent 59 % of Spanish agricultural land and 27 % of that in the EU. Moreover. Andalusia is the main olive-producing region in Spain yielding more than 70 % of the total production. There are whole areas devoted to the olive oil sector, which represents 30 % of Andalusian agricultural employment. The sample analysed was made up of 220 complex farms spread all throughout Andalusia.

Table 2. Descriptive variables of surveyed olive-tree farms in dry farming

		Variable description
1	RE[1]	Region. Sample design
2	CA[1]	Total cultivated area of the farm (hectares)
3	PO[1]	Percentage of olive tree area over CA (%)
4	NC[1]	Number of farm crops
5	YL[1]	Olive tree yield (ton of olives/hectare)
6	HL[1]	Percentage of non-family hand labour cost over total production costs of the farm (%)
7	NRE[1]	Does the manager or the family have non-agrarian revenues? (Yes or No)
8	TR[1]	Number of farm tractors
9	ST[1]	Training level of the farm manager. (1: None, 2: Basic, 3: High school level, 4: Professional training, 5: First university degree, 6: University master o higher degree)
10	AS[1]	Does the manager have agrarian studies? (Yes or No)
11	AG[1]	Farmer age (< 40 years old, between 40 and 55, between 55 and 65 and > 65 years old)
12	SX[1]	Manager sex (1: Male, 2: Female)
13	CON[1]	Does the farm manager sell directly to consumers? (Yes or No)
14	WH[1]	Does the farm manager sell directly to wholesalers? (Yes or No)
15	RT[1]	Does the farm manager sell directly to retailers? (Yes or No)
16	IN[1]	Does the farm manager sell directly to industry? (Yes or No)
17	COO[1]	Is the farmer a cooperative member? (Yes or No)
18	HE[2]	Average altitude of the farm municipality (meters over sea level)
19	SL[2]	Average slope of the farm municipality (%)
20	ER[2]	Percentage of agrarian soils in the farm municipality where erosion can be considered moderate (%)

SIMA: Andalusian Municipality Information System (2005).

In the classification process, ten different training/generalization samples were designed using approximately 60 % of the farms for training and the remaining 40 % for generalization (see Table 3).

In order to evaluate and compare the accuracy of the classification models proposed, the Correct Classification Rate (CCR), Producer's Accuracy (PA) and User's Accuracy (UA) variables were selected. The first one (CCR) can be defined as the percentage of total correct classified observations with respect to the total number of observations. The PA is the number of farms correctly classified as a given class with respect to the total number of farms that belongs to that class (also called true positive). UA is calculated as the number of farms correctly classified in a class with respect to the total number of farms that was classified as that class by the algorithm (also called precision rate). The best classification method, is that where both PA and UA parameters are equal to one.

Table 3. Basic statistics of descriptive variables in total sample

Variable	Mean	Standard Deviation	VariationCoefficient
CA	17,68	27,61	156 %
PO	87,76	25,61	29 %
NC	1,40	0,91	65 %
YL	3,29	2,27	69 %
HL	45,02	30,51	68 %
TR	0,75	0,92	123 %
ST	2,48	1,35	55 %
AG	2,15	0,89	42 %
HE	539,90	202,44	37 %
SL	76,03	25,77	34 %
ER	37,25	29,81	80 %

5   Results

We explain our classification into efficient and non-efficient farms through three logistic models: standard LR, LR only with product-unit covariates (LRPU) and LR with product-unit and initial covariates (LRLPU).

The best mean results obtained (Table 4) in terminus of CCR were reached with LRLPU models, in training (81.2 %) and in the generalization set (74.1 %). In all the samples selected, the CCR was greater than or equal to 70 %, which is an excellent classification ratio considering the complexity of the olive-tree farm database.

If we compare the percentage of farms correctly classified in each class (PA), inefficient farms were more easily recognized in general than efficient ones. In the first case (inefficient), the best results were obtained with LRPU (96.1 and 93.2 % respectively in training and generalization set) while in the second (efficient), these rates fell to 46.3 % and 31.6 % in each one of the sets with the LRLPU application, (the

Table 4. Mean % of cases (in ten partitions) correctly classified using, LR, LRPU and LRLPU model.

CLASS	Training set PA			Generalization set PA		
	LR	LRPU	LRLPU	LR	LRPU	LRLPU
Y = 0 Inefficient	95,4	96,1	95,4	89,3	93,2	90,9
Y = 1 Efficient	39,4	33,3	40,4	23,2	21,9	31,6
CLASS	Training set UA			Generalization set UA		
	LR	LRPU	LRLPU	LR	LRPU	LRLPU
Y = 0 Inefficient	80,23	78,74	80,45	75,9	75,9	77,8
Y = 1 Efficient	76,8	76,4	77,4	54,9	63,4	63,8
Total Farms	Training set CCR			Generalization set CCR		
	79,7	78,4	81,2	71,1	73,4	74,1

best in this class). If we observe the UA coefficient obtained from the models, we can see that LRLPU reached the best results in all groups and classes (Table 4). So we can affirm that LRLPU model was the best in the classification of both total and efficient farms, and LRPU was the best in the classification of inefficient farms.

LRLPU stands out especially in comparison with LDA (Table 5). The non-parametric Krushkal-Wallis test was carried out and it detected significant differences between the mean results of the CCR obtained with the methodologies applied (sig. = 0.04; α = 0.05). We can affirm that LR with PU (LRPU and LRLPU) were among the best positions with respect to the mean results.

Table 5. Fitness statistics of selected classification methods in the generalization sets

Method	CCR Mean	VariationCoeff.	PA Inefficient	PA Efficient	UA Inefficient	UA Efficient
LDA	58,5	1,7 %	66,8	43,4	79,5	28,2
LR	71,1	6,4 %	89,6	23,2	75,9	54,9
LRLPU	74,1	3,7 %	90,9	31,6	77,8	63,8
LRPU	73,4	1,6 %	93,2	21,9	75,9	63,4

6 Conclusions

In realistic and non-balanced classification situations, when considering the productive efficiency of olive-tree farms in dry farming, LRPU and LRLPU models have demonstrated their accuracy in terms of CCR, PA and UA parameters. Our best models, LRPU and LRLPU, are really very precise in classifying productively inefficient farms. They have problems adjusting their predictions to reality when efficient farms are taken into consideration (other classification algorithms showed worse results). This problem probably has two justifications, one structural: the global data set had many more inefficient farms; the second, related to the super-efficiency problem (BCC-DEA cannot easily distinguish efficiency levels within the efficient set). But in our specific case, the study of inefficient farms is more useful than one for efficient farms because inefficient farms do not manage input consumption appropriately and can contribute to processes of erosion, pollution, etc. LRPU and LRLPU algorithms may also be an alternative to analyse efficiency levels within the efficient set of farms originally classified using BCC-DEA.

Acknowledgements. This work has been subsidized by the project TIN2014-54583-C2-1-R of the Spanish Ministerial (MINECO), FEDER funds and the P11-TIC-7508 project of the Junta de Andalucía (Spain).

References

1. de Andrés, J., Landajo, M., Lorca, P.: Forecasting business profitability by using classification techniques: A comparative analysis based on Spanish case. Eur. J. Oper. Res. **167**, 518–542 (2005)

2. Banker, R.D., Cooper, W.W., Seiford, L.M., Thrall, R.M., Zhu, J.: to scale in different DEA models. Eur. J. Oper. Res. **154**(2), 345–362 (2004). [40]
3. Charnes, A., Cooper, W.W., Rhodes, E.: Measuring the efficiency of decision making units. Eur. J. Oper. Res. **2**(6), 429–444 (1978)
4. Cooper, W.W., Seiford, L.M., Zhu, J.: Data envelopment analysis: history, models and interpretations. In: Cooper, W.W., Seiford, L.M., Zhu, J. (eds.) Handbook on Data Envelopment Analysis, pp. 1–40. Kluwer Academic Publishers, Boston (2004)
5. Durbin, R., Rumelhart, D.: Product units: a computationally powerful and biologically plausible extensión to backpropagation networks. Neural Comput. **1**, 133–142 (1989)
6. García-Alonso, C.R., Marín, H.: An integrated model to study the structural and financial sustainability of agricultural enterprises. Acta Hortic. **674**, 313–320 (2005)
7. García-Pedrajas, N., Hervás-Martínez, C., Muñoz-Pérez, J.: Covnet: a cooperative coevolutionary model for evolving artificial neural networks. IEEE Trans. Neural Netw. **14**(3), 575–596 (2003)
8. Gutiérrez, P.A., Hervás-Martínez, C., Martínez-Estudillo, F.J.: Logistic regression by means of evolutionary radial basis function neural networks. IEEE Trans. Neural Netw. **22**, 246–263 (2011)
9. Gutiérrez, P.A., Segovia-Vargas, M.J., Salcedo-Sanz, S., Hervás-Martínez, C., Sanchís, A., Portilla-Figueras, J.A., Fernández-Navarro, F.: Hybridizing logistic regression with product unit and RBF networks for accurate detection and prediction of banking crises. OMEGA Int. J. Manage. Sci. **38**, 333–344 (2010)
10. Ismail, A., Engelbrecht, A.P.: Global optimization algorithms for training product unit neural networks. In: IJCNN-2000, vol. 1, pp. 132–137. IEEE Computer Society (2000)
11. MacFarlane, R.: Modelling the interaction of economic and socio-behavioural factors in the prediction of farm adjustment. J. Rural Stud. **12**(4), 365–374 (1996)
12. MAPA (Ministerio de Aricultura, Pesca y Alimentación) Anuario de Estadística Agroalimentaria, Ministerio de Agricultura, Pesca y Alimentación. Madrid (2005)
13. Martínez-Estudillo, A.C., Martínez-Estudillo, F., Hervás-Martínez, C., García-Pedrajas, N.: Evolutionary produc-tunit based neural networks for regression. Neural Netw. **19**, 477–486 (2006)
14. Martínez-Estudillo, F., Hervás-Martínez, C., Martínez-Estudillo, A.C., García-Pedrajas, N.: Hybridation of evolutionary algorithms and local search by means of a clustering method. IEEE Trans. Syst. Man and Cybern. Part. B. Cybern. **36**(3), 534–546 (2006)
15. Sadras, V., Roget, D., Krause, M.: Dynamic cropping strategies for risk management in dry-land farming systems. Agric. Syst. **76**(3), 929–948 (2003)
16. Torres, M., Hervás, C., García, C.: Multinomial logistic regression and product unit neural network models: Application of a new hybrid methodology for solving a problem in the livestock sector. Expert Syst. Appl. **36**, 12225–12235 (2009)
17. Webster, J.P.G.: Assessing the economic consequences of sustainability in agriculture. Agric. Ecosyst. Environ. **64**(2), 95–102 (1997)
18. Yao, X., Liu, Y.: A new evolutionary system for evolving artificial neural networks. IEEE Trans. Neural Netw. **8**(3), 694–713 (1997)

Knowledge Representation, Reasoning and Logic

On Coarser Interval Temporal Logics and their Satisfiability Problem

Emilio Muñoz-Velasco[1]([✉]), Mercedes Pelegrín-García[2], Pietro Sala[3], and Guido Sciavicco[2]

[1] Department of Applied Mathematics, University of Malaga, Málaga, Spain
emilio@ctima.uma.es
[2] Department of Information, Engineering and Communications,
University of Murcia, Murcia, Spain
{mariamercedes.pelegrin,guido}@um.es
[3] Department of Computer Science, University of Verona, Verona, Italy
pietro.sala@univr.it

Abstract. The primary characteristic of interval temporal logic is that intervals, rather than points, are taken as the primitive ontological entities. Their computational behaviour is generally bad, and several restrictions have been considered in order to define decidable and computationally affordable temporal logics based on intervals. In this paper we take inspiration from Golumbic and Shamir's coarser interval algebras, which generalize the classical Allen's Interval Algebra, in order to define two previously unknown variants of Halpern and Shoham's logic (HS). We prove that one of them (denoted here by HS_7) is still generally undecidable, while the other one (HS_3) becomes, perhaps surprisingly, PSpace-complete, at least in the finite case.

1 Introduction

Time intervals, rather than time points, are regarded in interval temporal logics as the primitive ontological entities, and the truth of formulae is defined accordingly. These logics can be applied in many fields, such as hardware and real-time system verification, language processing, constraint satisfaction and planning, among others [1,12,20,21]. Moreover, interval temporal logics have been considered as the basis for temporal extensions of Description Logic [2–4,22]. The most influential interval temporal logic is probably Halpern and Shoham's Modal Logic of Allen's Relations (HS) [15], and it is well-known that the satisfiability problem for HS, interpreted over most interesting classes of linearly ordered sets is (highly) undecidable.

The different strategies that have been used to obtain fragments of HS that perform better can be summarized as follows: (i) limiting the set of modalities that are included in the language; (ii) interpreting the language over semantically incomplete linear structures; (iii) limiting the nesting of temporal modalities; (iv) restricting the applicability of boolean operators and/or relaxing the semantics of the modal operators. The few fragments or variants of HS that have

© Springer International Publishing Switzerland 2015
J.M. Puerta et al. (Eds.): CAEPIA 2015, LNAI 9422, pp. 105–115, 2015.
DOI: 10.1007/978-3-319-24598-0_10

been proven to be decidable show complexities that range from NP-complete to NExpTime-complete, ExpSpace-complete, and even non-primitive recursive; undecidability is still the rule even when sub-propositional fragments are considered [7–11,18].

Allen's Interval Algebra (IA) [1] can be seen as the backbone of HS: modal operators in the HS repository can be mapped one-by-one over Allen's interval relations. In [14] Golumbic and Shamir propose to reduce the set of binary relations between intervals by defining *coarser* relations that correspond to logical disjunctions of Allen's relations. In this way, two natural coarser algebras emerge, namely IA_7 and IA_3. The former encompasses seven relations, by preserving the original relations *before,after*, and *equal to*, by joining *meets* and *overlaps* into a single relation (and similarly for their inverse ones), and by joining *during, starts*, and *finishes* into a single relation (and, again, similarly for their inverse ones). The latter encompasses only three relations: the original *before* and *after*, plus a relation (*intersects*) that can be viewed as the disjunction of all the remaining ones (and therefore is the inverse of itself and includes equality). In this work we propose two fragments of HS based on the same idea: HS_7 retains from HS the modal operators that correspond to *before* and *after*, and includes new ones corresponding each to one of the relations of IA_7, except equality; similarly, HS_3 features three modal operators, one for each of IA_3's binary relation. These logics can be naturally applied to the same fields as full HS; moreover they reflect the idea underlying the standard SQL:2011 [16], where interval relations are not necessarily Allen's ones (for example, *later* is interpreted as the disjunction of Allen's *meets* and *later*). We prove here that while (not surprisingly) HS_7 is still undecidable when interpreted over every interesting class of linearly ordered sets, HS_3 becomes PSPACE-complete at least in the finite case. Given the generally bad computational behaviour of interval logics (e.g., in the universe of the syntactical fragments of HS, the decidable ones account for around 10 % of the expressively different ones - see, for example, [7]) this result strikes out as an interesting exception. While the PSPACE-hardness of HS_3 holds in all considered cases, its decidability in the infinite cases is an open problem, although our exploratory analysis suggests that PSPACE-membership of HS_3 in the finite case should be transferrable to the infinite cases as well.

2 Preliminaries

Let $\mathbb{D} = \langle D, < \rangle$ be a strict (i.e., irreflexive) linearly ordered set. A *strict interval* (resp., *non-strict interval*) over $\mathbb{D}$ is an ordered pair $[x, y]$, where $x, y \in D$ and $x < y$ (resp., $x \leq y$). In the recent literature, the *strict semantics*, where only strict intervals are considered, is usually adopted. This conforms to the definition of interval adopted by Allen in [1], but differs from the one given by Halpern and Shoham in [15]. If we exclude the identity relation, there are 12 different relations between two intervals in a linear order, often called *Allen's relations* [1]: the six relations R_A (adjacent to), R_L (later than), R_B (begins), R_E (ends), R_D (during), and R_O (overlaps), depicted in Fig. 1, and their inverses, that is,

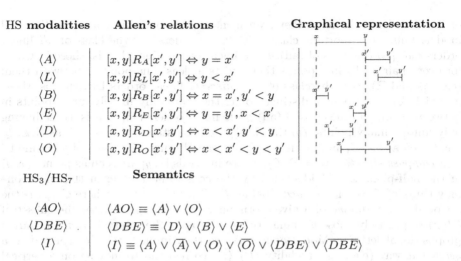

HS modalities	Allen's relations	Graphical representation
$\langle A \rangle$	$[x,y]R_A[x',y'] \Leftrightarrow y = x'$	
$\langle L \rangle$	$[x,y]R_L[x',y'] \Leftrightarrow y < x'$	
$\langle B \rangle$	$[x,y]R_B[x',y'] \Leftrightarrow x = x', y' < y$	
$\langle E \rangle$	$[x,y]R_E[x',y'] \Leftrightarrow y = y', x < x'$	
$\langle D \rangle$	$[x,y]R_D[x',y'] \Leftrightarrow x < x', y' < y$	
$\langle O \rangle$	$[x,y]R_O[x',y'] \Leftrightarrow x < x' < y < y'$	

HS$_3$/HS$_7$	Semantics
$\langle AO \rangle$	$\langle AO \rangle \equiv \langle A \rangle \vee \langle O \rangle$
$\langle DBE \rangle$	$\langle DBE \rangle \equiv \langle D \rangle \vee \langle B \rangle \vee \langle E \rangle$
$\langle I \rangle$	$\langle I \rangle \equiv \langle A \rangle \vee \langle \overline{A} \rangle \vee \langle O \rangle \vee \langle \overline{O} \rangle \vee \langle DBE \rangle \vee \langle \overline{DBE} \rangle$

Fig. 1. Allen's interval relations, the corresponding HS modalities, and the semantic definitions HS$_3$/HS$_7$ modalities.

$R_{\overline{X}} = (R_X)^{-1}$, for each $X \in \{A, L, B, E, D, O\}$. We interpret interval structures as Kripke structures, with Allen's relations playing the role of the accessibility relations. Thus, we associate a universal modality $[X]$ and an existential modality $\langle X \rangle$ with each Allen relation R_X. For each $X \in \{A, L, B, E, D, O\}$, the *transposes* of the modalities $[X]$ and $\langle X \rangle$ are the modalities $[\overline{X}]$ and $\langle \overline{X} \rangle$, corresponding to the inverse relation $R_{\overline{X}}$ of R_X. Halpern and Shoham's logic HS [15] is a multi-modal logic with formulae built from a finite, non-empty set $\mathcal{AP}$ of atomic propositions (also referred to as proposition letters), the classical propositional connectives, and a pair of modalities for each Allen relation:

$$\varphi ::= \bot \mid p \mid \neg\varphi \mid \varphi \vee \varphi \mid \varphi \wedge \varphi \mid \langle X \rangle\varphi \mid \langle \overline{X} \rangle\varphi,$$

where $p \in \mathcal{AP}$ and $X \in \{A, L, B, E, D, O\}$. The other propositional connectives and constants (e.g., $\rightarrow$, and $\top$), as well as the dual modalities (e.g., $[A]\varphi \equiv \neg\langle A \rangle\neg\varphi$), can be derived in the standard way. Well-formed HS$_3$-formulae can be obtained by the above grammar when $X \in \{L, I\}$, while HS$_7$-formulae are defined under the restriction that $X \in \{L, AO, DBE\}$.

The semantics of (HS and) both HS$_3$ and HS$_7$ is given in terms of *interval models* $M = \langle \mathbb{I}(\mathbb{D}), V \rangle$, where $\mathbb{D}$ is a linear order, $\mathbb{I}(\mathbb{D})$ is the set of all (strict) intervals over $\mathbb{D}$, and V is a *valuation function* $V : \mathcal{AP} \mapsto 2^{\mathbb{I}(\mathbb{D})}$, which assigns to each atomic proposition $p \in \mathcal{AP}$ the set of intervals $V(p)$ on which p holds. The *truth* of a formula on a given interval $[x, y]$ in an interval model M is defined by structural induction on formulae; propositional letters and Boolean connectives are treated in the standard way, while the semantic rules for the modal operators can be immediately deduced from Fig. 1. Formulae of HS, and therefore of HS$_3$ and HS$_7$, can be interpreted over a class of interval models (built on a given class of linear orders). Among others, we mention the following classes of (interval models built on important classes of) linear orders: *(i)* the class of *all* linear orders Lin; *(ii)* the class of (all) *dense* linear orders Den, that is, those in which for every pair of distinct points there exists at least one point in between them (e.g., $\mathbb{Q}$ and $\mathbb{R}$); *(iii)* the class of (all) *discrete* linear orders Dis, that is, those in which for every pair of distinct points there are only finitely many points in between them; *(iv)* the class of (all) *finite* linear orders Fin, that is, those having only finitely many points; *(v)* the classes built on standard sets such as $\mathbb{N}, \mathbb{Z}, \mathbb{Q}$, etc. Given a class $\mathcal{C}$, and given $\mathbb{D} \in \mathcal{C}$, one can alternatively think of a HS-model as a *compass structure* $\mathcal{G} = (\mathbb{D}, \mathcal{L})$, where intervals $[x, y]$ are seen as points (x, y) in the half-plane $\mathbb{D} \times \mathbb{D}$ identified by the constraint $x < y$; in this view, one may think of $\mathcal{L}$ as an *extended* labeling $\mathcal{L} : \mathbb{D} \times \mathbb{D} \to 2^{Cl(\varphi)}$, where $Cl(\varphi)$ is the set of all sub-formulae of a given formula φ, and $\mathcal{L}(x, y)$ denotes the subset of $Cl(\varphi)$ of precisely those formulae that are true at the interval $[x, y]$ (including propositional letters). Modal operators are then immediately interpreted in a *geometric* way (e.g., the modality $\langle B \rangle, \langle \overline{B} \rangle$ correspond to moving on a vertical line in the plane, while $\langle E \rangle, \langle \overline{E} \rangle$ correspond to moving on a horizontal line). Such an interpretation (see, e.g. [19]) works nicely also for fragments of HS such as HS$_3$ and HS$_7$; we will alternately use compass structures and interval models in the rest of the paper.

In this paper we focus on the decidability of the satisfiability problem for both HS$_3$ and HS$_7$. The relative expressive power of HS, HS$_3$, and HS$_7$ is unknown, but partial results seem to indicate that it holds HS$_3 \prec$ HS$_7 \prec$ HS ($\prec$ is read as *is strictly less expressive than*). As a matter of fact, we can easily prove that HS$_3 \prec$ HS in the finite case: a simple counterexample based on bisimulation (cfr. [13]) proves that, for example, $\langle B \rangle$ cannot be expressed in HS$_3$. Recent results [9, 18] for the AB$\overline{B}$A fragment of HS gives us a partial result concerning the satisfiability problem for HS$_3$: it turns out that HS$_3 \prec$ AB$\overline{B}$A (the modal operators $\langle L \rangle$ and $\langle \overline{L} \rangle$ are immediately expressed in terms of $\langle A \rangle$ and $\langle \overline{A} \rangle$, while the operator $\langle I \rangle$ can be obtained by means of a combination of the modalities in AB$\overline{B}$A). Since AB$\overline{B}$A is decidable, but not primitive recursive, in the finite case [18] as well as in the cases of Den, $\mathbb{Q}$ [9], so is HS$_3$. Here we prove that its satisfiability problem is in fact PSPACE-complete (a much stronger result) in the finite case and PSPACE-hard in all other classes. Similarly, we know that the HS$_7$-modality $\langle DBE \rangle$ is enough to obtain undecidability in the finite/discrete case, as well as the cases of $\mathbb{N}$ and $\mathbb{Z}$ [17]; based on existing results, though, the status of HS$_7$ interpreted in Lin, $\mathbb{Q}$ or Den is unknown. We prove here that, not surprisingly, it is undecidable when interpreted on each of the mentioned classes of linearly ordered sets; our proof also applies to all cases already covered from [17].

3 Decidability and Hardness Results for HS$_3$

In this section, we first prove that the satisfiability problem for HS$_3$ is PSPACE-hard, regardless of the class of linearly ordered sets on which it is interpreted. PSPACE-hardness is proven via a (logspace) reduction from the classical

Quantified Boolean Formula (QBF) satisfiability problem, shown to be PSPACE-hard in [23]. A Quantified Boolean formula is an expression of the form $\theta \equiv Q_1 p_1 \ldots Q_n p_n f$, where f is a formula of propositional logic and, for all $1 \leq i \leq n$, Q_i is either $\forall$ or $\exists$. We can assume without loss of generality that the formula θ is closed (i.e., every variable in f is quantified).

Theorem 1. *The satisfiability problem for* HS_3 *over* Fin, Dis, Den, $\mathbb{N}$, $\mathbb{Z}$, $\mathbb{Q}$, *and* Lin *is* PSPACE-*hard.*

Proof (Sketch). Let $\theta = Q_1 p_1 \ldots Q_n\ p_n f$ be a given closed Quantified Boolean formula. We build a HS_3-formula Φ_θ such that Φ_θ is satisfiable over a linear order if and only if θ is true. Given θ, we define $P_\forall = \{i : 1 \leq i \leq n, Q_i = \forall\}$; the formula Φ_θ, that uses an *universal* operator defined as $[G]\phi \equiv [I][I]\phi$, is the conjunction of the following formulae:

$$\phi_1 \equiv [G](\bigwedge_{1 \leq i \leq n+1}(h_i \to \bigwedge_{1 \leq i \leq n+1}[I]\neg h_i)) \wedge [G](\bigwedge_{1 \leq i \leq n}(h_i \to \langle I \rangle \langle I \rangle h_{i+1}))$$

$$\phi_2 \equiv \langle I \rangle h_1 \wedge [\overline{G}]f \wedge [G]\bigwedge_{i \in P_\forall}(\overline{h_i} \to (\langle I \rangle \langle I \rangle (h_{i+1} \wedge p_i) \wedge \langle I \rangle \langle I \rangle (h_{i+1} \wedge \neg p_i)))$$

$$\phi_3 \equiv [G]\bigwedge_{2 \leq i \leq n}((h_i \wedge p_{i-1}) \to$$
$$[I]\bigwedge_{1 \leq j \leq i-1}([I]\neg h_j \to [I](\bigvee_{i+1 \leq j \leq n+1} h_j \to p_{i-1})))$$

$$\phi_4 \equiv [G]\bigwedge_{2 \leq i \leq n}((h_i \wedge \neg p_{i-1}) \to$$
$$[I]\bigwedge_{1 \leq j \leq i-1}([I]\neg h_j \to [I](\bigvee_{i+1 \leq j \leq n+1} h_j \to \neg p_{i-1})))$$

Each h_i $(1 \leq i \leq n)$ represents the node in the $(\theta\text{-})$tree in which we choose the value of the variable p_i (see Fig. 2). Assuming that θ has at least one proposition, $\langle I \rangle h_1$ (in ϕ_2) forces that h_1 holds somewhere, and, then, we force the existence of a choice for each proposition (ϕ_1); intervals representing choices are not pairwise intersecting (ϕ_1), giving rise to a tree-like structure. For each universally quantified variable, we have intervals, in the correct sub-tree, that witness both the false and the true value for it (ϕ_2). Values are propagated in the correct sub-trees (ϕ_3, ϕ_4) in such a way that the interval labeled with h_{n+1} is also labeled with the chosen truth values for each proposition, so to serve as a witness for the satisfiability of θ: in particular, if some of the h_{n+1}-labeled intervals do not satisfy f, then $[G]f$ is not satisfied either. Notice that this particular result holds also for the fragment of HS_3 with the sole operator $\langle I \rangle$.   □

Now, we prove that the satisfiability problem for HS_3 is decidable in PSPACE in the particular case of finite linear orders, giving us a completeness result in this case. While transferring such a result to other discrete classes is a purely technical problem, for the non-discrete ones it might require a deeper analysis.

Theorem 2. *The satisfiability problem for* HS_3 *over* Fin *is* PSPACE-*complete.*

Proof (Sketch). Let φ be an HS_3 formula, and $\mathcal{G} = (\mathbb{D}, \mathcal{L})$ be a compass structure for it. We prove that if $|\mathbb{D}|$ is greater than a certain limit (that will be obtained below) then there exists a compass structure $\mathcal{G}' = (\mathbb{D}', \mathcal{L}')$ for φ with $|\mathbb{D}'| < |\mathbb{D}|$. The *contraction* method obtained in this way can be iterated in order to obtain a model whose cardinality is less than or equal to the given limit. Since one can

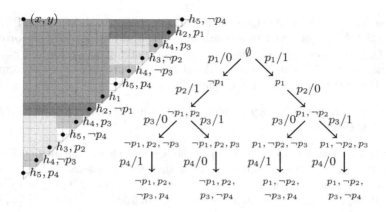

Fig. 2. A tree-model for $\theta = \forall p_1 \exists p_2 \forall p_3 \exists p_4 (p_1 \vee p_2) \wedge (\neg p_1 \vee \neg p_2) \wedge (p_3 \vee p_4) \wedge (\neg p_3 \vee \neg p_4)$ (right-hand side) and its embedding into a compass structure (left-hand side).

design an algorithm that only keeps trace of a *constant number of horizontal lines* (later referred to as *rows*) of a structure at the same time, finite satisfiability can be checked in PSPACE. The intuitive idea of the contraction procedure is as follows: *(i)* we describe a *row* of the compass structure in such a way that the number of different descriptions is bounded; *(ii)* whenever the cardinality of the model is grater that the limit, then there must be two different rows $y_1 < y_2$ with the same description; *(iii)* a smaller (contracted) model can be obtained by keeping the part of the original model below row y_1, and suitably reconstructing the rest of the model using the part of the original model above row y_2, thus eliminating the portion of the model y_1 and y_2.

Given $\mathcal{G} = (\mathbb{D}, \mathcal{L})$ that satisfies φ, for a point (x, y) we can define $\mathcal{R}eq_{I\overline{L}}(x, y) = \{\langle I \rangle \psi, [I] \psi, \langle \overline{L} \rangle \psi, [\overline{L}] \psi \mid \langle I \rangle \psi, [I] \psi, \langle \overline{L} \rangle \psi, [\overline{L}] \psi \in \mathcal{L}(x, y)\}$; clearly, we have that $|\mathcal{R}eq_{I\overline{L}}(x, y)| \leq |\varphi|$. Now, given an element $y \in \mathbb{D}$, let $\mathcal{R}eq_{I\overline{L}}(y) = \{\mathcal{R}eq_{I\overline{L}}(x, y) : 0 \leq x \leq y\}$. Since $\langle I \rangle$ and $\langle \overline{L} \rangle$ are transitive, $|\mathcal{R}eq_{I\overline{L}}(y)| \leq |\varphi|$ and its elements may be arranged in a sequence $R_1 \subset \ldots \subset R_{|\mathcal{R}eq_{I\overline{L}}(y)|}$. The number of possible different chains $\mathcal{R}eq_{I\overline{L}}(y)$ is bounded by $|\varphi|^{|\varphi|} = 2^{|\varphi| \log(|\varphi|)}$. Let $count_y : \mathcal{R}eq_{I\overline{L}}(y) \to \{1, \ldots, |\varphi|\}$ be a function such that for each $R \in \mathcal{R}eq_{I\overline{L}}(y)$ we have $count_y(R) = \min(2 \cdot |\varphi| + 1, |\{x : \mathcal{R}eq_{I\overline{L}}(x, y) = R\}|)$. Observe that for any given $\mathcal{R}eq_{I\overline{L}}(y)$ we may have $(2 \cdot |\varphi| + 1)^{|\varphi|} = 2^{|\varphi| \log(2 \cdot |\varphi| + 1)}$ possible $count_y$ functions. To each y we associate a minimal set $\mathcal{W}_y \subseteq \{0, \ldots, y\}$ that satisfies: *(i)* for all $\psi \in Cl(\varphi)$ such that there exists $0 \leq x \leq y$ and $y' > y$ with $\psi \in \mathcal{L}(x, y')$ there exists $x' \in \mathcal{W}_y$ and $y' > y$ such that $\psi \in \mathcal{L}(x', y')$, and *(ii)* for every $0 \leq x'' \leq y$ and $y'' > y$ with $\psi \in \mathcal{L}(x'', y'')$, we have $y'' \leq y'$ or *(iii)* for every $0 \leq x'' \leq y$ and $y'' > y$ with $\psi \in \mathcal{L}(x'', y'')$, we have $x'' \geq x'$. Now, if $R_{\mathcal{W}_y} = \{\psi : \exists x \exists y (0 \leq x \leq y \wedge y' > y \wedge \psi \in \mathcal{L}(x, y'))\}$, we have that $|R_{\mathcal{W}_y}| \leq |\varphi|$, and, thus, the number of possible $R_{\mathcal{W}_y}$ is bounded by $2^{2 \cdot |\varphi|}$. Let $f_y : \mathcal{R}eq_{I\overline{L}}(y) \to \{0, \ldots, y\}$ such that, for every $R \in \mathcal{R}eq_{I\overline{L}}(y)$, $\mathcal{R}eq_{I\overline{L}}(f_y(R), y) = R$ and $\mathcal{R}eq_{I\overline{L}}(f_y(R) + 1, y) \neq R$. Similarly to $\mathcal{R}eq_{I\overline{L}}(x, y)$, for every point (x, y) we can also define $\mathcal{R}eq_L(x,y) = \{\langle L\rangle\psi, [L]\psi \mid \langle L\rangle\psi, [L]\psi \in \mathcal{L}(x,y)\}$. Let us observe that for every $0 \leq x, x' \leq y$, we have $\mathcal{R}eq_L(x,y) = \mathcal{R}eq_L(x',y)$ and thus we can simply identify with $\mathcal{R}eq_L(y) = \mathcal{R}eq_L(x,y)$ for some $0 \leq x \leq y$. It is easy to see that $|\mathcal{R}eq_L(y)| \leq |\varphi|$. Notice that $\mathcal{R}eq_L(y)$ is a set of sub-formulae of φ, while $\mathcal{R}eq_{I\overline{L}}(y)$ is a set of sets of sub-formulae of φ whose cardinality cannot exceed $|\varphi|$. At this point, for each y we let $row(y) = (\mathcal{R}eq_L(y), \mathcal{R}eq_{I\overline{L}}(y), count_y, R_{\mathcal{W}_y})$. Taking into account the number of different component of each $row(y)$, we have that the possible values for $row(y)$ is roughly bounded by

$$|\varphi| \cdot 2^{|\varphi|\log(|\varphi|)} \cdot 2^{|\varphi|\log(2|\varphi|+1)} \cdot 2^{|\varphi|} = |\varphi| \cdot 2^{|\varphi|(\log(2|\varphi|+1)+\log(|\varphi|)+1)}.$$

If $|\mathbb{D}|$ exceeds such a limit, then there must exist two rows $y_1 < y_2$ with $row(y_1) = row(y_2)$. Thus, we can define a non-decreasing function $g : \{0, \ldots, y_1\} \to \{0, \ldots, y_2\}$ such that: (i) for every $x \in \{0, \ldots, y_1\}$ we have $\mathcal{R}eq_{I\overline{L}}(x,y) = \mathcal{R}eq_{I\overline{L}}(x, g(x))$, and (ii) $\mathcal{W}_{y_2} \subseteq Img(g)$. Let $\Delta = y_2 - y_1$; we can finally build the compass structure $\mathcal{G}' = (\mathbb{D}', \mathcal{L}')$ with $|\mathbb{D}'| = |\mathbb{D}| - \Delta$, where $\mathcal{L}'$ is defined as follows: (i) $\mathcal{L}'(x,y) = \mathcal{L}(x,y)$ for every $0 \leq x \leq y \leq y_1$, (ii) $\mathcal{L}'(x,y) = \mathcal{L}(x + \Delta, y + \Delta)$ for every $y_1 < x \leq y \leq |\mathbb{D}'|$, and (iii) $\mathcal{L}'(x,y) = \mathcal{L}(g(x), y + \Delta)$ for every $y_1 < x \leq y_1 < y \leq |\mathbb{D}'|$.

The above proof, usually called *small model theorem*, provides the necessary insights for developing a PSPACE decision procedure for HS$_3$ over Fin. First observe that each formula φ may be rewritten into an equi-satisfiable formula $\varphi' = \varphi \vee \langle I\rangle\varphi \vee \langle L\rangle\varphi$: it is easy to see there exists a compass structure $\mathcal{G} = (\mathbb{D}, \mathcal{L})$ for φ if and only if there exists a compass structure $\mathcal{G}' = (\mathbb{D}, \mathcal{L}')$ for φ' with $\varphi' \in \mathcal{L}(0,1)$. Then, we may assume w.l.o.g. that $\varphi = \varphi' \vee \langle I\rangle\varphi' \vee \langle L\rangle\varphi'$ for some formula φ'. A non-deterministic procedure can be designed that works as follows (where φ is the formula to be checked for satisfiability):

1. A counter y is initialized to the value 0. Let F be an atom with $F \cap \{\langle I\rangle\psi \in Cl(\varphi)\} = \emptyset$ and $\varphi \in F$ - if such an atom does not exist we answer NO (unsatisfiable) - and let $row(y) = (\{\langle L\rangle\psi, [L]\psi \in F\}, \{\{\langle I\rangle\psi, [I]\psi, \langle\overline{L}\rangle\psi, [\overline{L}]\psi \in F\}\}, count_y, \{\psi : \langle I\rangle\psi \in F\})$ where $count_y(\{\langle I\rangle\psi, [I]\psi, \langle\overline{L}\rangle\psi, [\overline{L}]\psi \in F\}) = 1$;
2. We generate a row $row(y+1) = (\mathcal{R}eq_L(y+1), \mathcal{R}eq_{I\overline{L}}(y+1), count_{y+1}, R_{\mathcal{W}_{y+1}})$ which is *compatible* with $row(y) = (\mathcal{R}eq_L(y), \mathcal{R}eq_{I\overline{L}}(y), count_y, R_{\mathcal{W}_y})$ - if such a row does not exist we answer NO, and if $\mathcal{R}eq_L(y + 1) \cap \{\langle L\rangle\psi \in Cl(\varphi)\} = R_{\mathcal{W}_{y+1}} = \emptyset$ we answer YES;
3. If $y + 1 = |\varphi| \cdot 2^{|\varphi|(\log(2|\varphi|+1)+\log(|\varphi|)+1)} + 1$ we answer NO, and, otherwise, we update y to $y + 1$ and we go back to step 2.

It is easy to see that such a procedure may be implemented in polynomial space. As a matter of fact, the procedure requires to store only the counter for y and at most two *rows* at the same time; therefore, it suffices to prove that they can be represented in polynomial space w.r.t. $|\varphi|$. Since y cannot exceed $2^{|\varphi|(\log(2|\varphi|+1)+\log(|\varphi|)+1)}$, we have that $|\varphi|(\log(2|\varphi|+1) + \log(|\varphi|) + 1)$ bits are enough to represent it. Since $|\mathcal{R}eq_{I\overline{L}}(y)| = |Dom(count_y)| \leq |\varphi|$, we have that $count_y$ takes $|\varphi|^2(\log(2|\varphi|+1) + \log(|\varphi|) + 1)$ bits to be represented. Finally, we have that $|\mathcal{R}eq_L(F)| \leq |\varphi|$, that $|\mathcal{R}eq_{I\overline{L}}(y)| \leq |\varphi|$, that each element in $\mathcal{R}eq_{I\overline{L}}(y)$

requires $|\varphi|$ bits to be represented, and that $R_{\mathcal{W}_y}$ requires $2 \cdot |\varphi|$ bits to be represented. Summing up, we need $(\log(2|\varphi|+1)+\log(|\varphi|)+1)(2|\varphi|+1)+2|\varphi|^2+4|\varphi|$ bits to handle the whole computation correctly, and thus the satisfiability of HS_3 over Fin is in PSPACE, as we claimed.   □

4 Undecidability Results for HS₇

In this section we show that the satisfiability problem for HS_7 interpreted in any of the classes Dis, Den, $\mathbb{N}, \mathbb{Z}, \mathbb{Q}$, and Lin is undecidable (recall that Dis, $\mathbb{N}$ and $\mathbb{Z}$ were already covered by the results in [17]). Undecidability is proven via a reduction [6] from the so-called Octant Tiling Problem (OTP). This is the problem of establishing whether a given finite set of tile types $\mathcal{T} = \{t_1, \ldots, t_N\}$ can tile the second octant of the integer plane $\mathcal{O} = \{0 \le i \le j\}$. For every tile type $t_i \in \mathcal{T}$, let $right(t_i)$, $left(t_i)$, $up(t_i)$, and $down(t_i)$ be the colors of the corresponding sides of t_i. To solve the problem, one must find a function $f : \mathcal{O} \to \mathcal{T}$ such that $right(f(n,m)) = left(f(n+1,m))$ and $up(f(n,m)) = down(f(n,m+1))$. By exploiting an argument similar to the one used in [5] to prove the undecidability of the Quadrant Tiling Problem, it can be shown that the Octant Tiling Problem is undecidable too. Notice that the OTP, as well as our reduction, is unrelated to interpreting models as compass structures (as we did in the previous section).

Theorem 3. *The satisfiability problem for* HS_7 *over* Dis, Den, $\mathbb{N}, \mathbb{Z}, \mathbb{Q}$, *and* Lin *is undecidable.*

Proof (Sketch). Given an instance $\mathcal{T}$ of the OTP, where $\mathcal{T}$ is a finite set of tiles types, we build an HS_7-formula $\Phi_{\mathcal{T}}$ in such a way that $\Phi_{\mathcal{T}}$ is satisfiable if and only if $\mathcal{T}$ tiles $\mathcal{O}$, assuming, here, that the underlying linear order presents at least one infinite ascending chain. We set the tiling framework by forcing the existence of an infinite chain of *unit* intervals (or, simply, *units*, denoted by the propositional letter u). Let us define an *universal* modality as $[G]\phi \equiv \phi \wedge \bigwedge_{X \in \{L, AO, DBE\}}([X]\phi \wedge [\overline{X}]\phi)$, a language $\mathbf{L} = \{*\} \cup \mathcal{T}$, and let us identify each tile $t_1, \ldots, t_N$ with a propositional letter whose symbol is used in the reduction. First, we have:

$$\phi_1 \equiv u_0 \wedge \neg * \wedge \bigwedge_{l=0,1}[G](u_l \to \langle AO \rangle u_{(l+1) \bmod 2}) \wedge [G](u \leftrightarrow (u_0 \vee u_1))$$
$$\phi_2 \equiv [G](u \to (\langle DBE \rangle \top \wedge [DBE]\neg u)) \wedge [G]((u_0' \wedge u_1') \to \bot)$$
$$\phi_3 \equiv \bigwedge_{l=0,1}[G](u_l \to [DBE]u_l')$$
$$\phi_4 \equiv [G](u \to [DBE]u') \wedge [G]((u' \wedge [AO]\neg u) \to u_b) \wedge [G]((u' \wedge [\overline{AO}]\neg u) \to u_e)$$
$$\phi_5 \equiv [G](u_b \to [AO]\neg u) \wedge [G](u_e \to [\overline{AO}]\neg u)$$

Assuming that $M, [x, y] \Vdash \phi_1 \wedge \ldots \wedge \phi_5$ we can prove that there exists an infinite sequence $x < y = y_0 < y_1 < \ldots$ such that: *(i)* for each $i \ge 0$, $M, [y_i, y_{i+1}] \Vdash u$; *(ii)* if $[z, t] \ne [y_i, y_{i+1}]$, for each $i \ge 0$, then $M, [z, t] \Vdash \neg u$, unless $t < x$ or $z > y_i$ for each $i \in \mathbb{N}$; *(iii)* for each $i \ge 0$, every interval of the type $[y_i, z]$, $z < y_{i+1}$, satisfies u_b(and at least there exists one interval of this type), and every interval of the type $[z, y_{i+1}]$, $z > y_i$, satisfies u_e (and at least there exists one interval of this type). Now, consider the following formulae:

$$\phi_6 \equiv C_1 \wedge \bigwedge_{l=0,1} [G](C_l \rightarrow \langle AO \rangle C_{(l+1) \bmod 2}) \wedge [G](C \leftrightarrow (C_0 \vee C_1))$$

$$\phi_7 \equiv \bigwedge_{l=0,1} [G](C_l \rightarrow [DBE]C_l') \wedge [G]((C_0' \wedge C_1') \rightarrow \bot)$$

$$\phi_8 \equiv [G](C \rightarrow ([AO]\neg u_e \wedge [\overline{AO}]\neg u_b)) \wedge [G](C \rightarrow ([DBE]\neg C \wedge \langle DBE \rangle \top))$$

$$\phi_9 \equiv [G](u \leftrightarrow \bigvee_{s \in \mathbf{L}} s) \wedge [G] \bigwedge_{s, s' \in \mathbf{L}, s \neq s'} (s \wedge s' \rightarrow \bot)$$

$$\phi_{10} \equiv \langle AO \rangle (\langle AO \rangle (\bigvee_{i=1,\dots,N} t_i \wedge \langle AO \rangle *)) \wedge [G]((u \wedge \langle AO \rangle C) \rightarrow \langle AO \rangle *)$$

$$\phi_{11} \equiv [G]((u \wedge \langle \overline{AO} \rangle C) \rightarrow \langle \overline{AO} \rangle *) \wedge [G](* \rightarrow (\langle AO \rangle C \vee \langle \overline{AO} \rangle C))$$

$$\phi_{12} \equiv [G]((u \wedge \neg *) \rightarrow \langle AO \rangle Corr) \wedge [G]((u \wedge \neg * \wedge [AO]\neg *) \rightarrow \langle \overline{AO} \rangle Corr)$$

$$\phi_{13} \equiv [G]((u \wedge \neg * \wedge \langle AO \rangle *) \rightarrow [AO](Corr \rightarrow \langle AO \rangle (u \wedge [AO](u \rightarrow \neg *))))$$

$$\phi_{14} \equiv [G](Corr \rightarrow [AO]\neg u_e) \wedge [G](Corr \rightarrow [\overline{AO}]\neg u_b) \wedge [G](* \rightarrow [AO]\neg Corr)$$

$$\phi_{15} \equiv [G](Corr \rightarrow ([DBE]\neg Corr \wedge [DBE]\neg C \wedge [\overline{DBE}]\neg C \wedge \neg C))$$

Formulae from ϕ_6 to ϕ_{15}, in conjunction with the above observations, imply the existence of an infinite sequence of indexes $k_0 < k_1 < \dots$ such that $y_0 = y_{k_0}$ and: (i) for each $j \geq 0$, $M, [y_{k_j}, y_{k_{j+1}}] \Vdash C$; if $[z, t] \neq [y_{k_j}, y_{k_{j+1}}]$, for each $j \geq 0$, then $M, [z, t] \Vdash \neg C$, unless $t < x$ or $z > y_i$ for each $i \in \mathbb{N}$. Moreover, these formulae guarantee that: (i) each u-interval of the type $[y_i, y_{i+1}]$ satisfies precisely one letter from $\mathbf{L}$; (ii) the C-interval $[y_{k_0}, y_{k_1}]$ is composed by exactly three units; (iii) each C-interval of the type $[y_{k_j}, y_{k_{j+1}}]$ is such that both its first unit $[y_{k_j}, y_{k_j+1}]$ and its last unit $[y_{k_{j+1}-1}, y_{k_{j+1}}]$ satisfies $*$; (iv) no other interval $[z, t]$ satisfies $*$ unless $t < x$ or $z > y_i$ for each $i \in \mathbb{N}$. In the context of the structure above described, every level of the octant (C-interval) is composed by an integer number of units, the first one and the last one of which are the only $*$-intervals. We can therefore refer to the m-th $\neg *$-interval of a level as the m-th tile of that level, and we are therefore interested in connecting the m-th tile of a given level with the m-th tile of the next one. This is taken care of by means of requirements from ϕ_{12} to ϕ_{14}, which allow us to prove that: (i) for each $i, j \geq 0$, if the interval $[y_{k_j+i}, y_{k_j+i+1}]$ is a $\neg *$-interval, then the point y_{k_j+i+1} starts a $Corr$-interval; (ii) for each $i, j > 0$, if the interval $[y_{k_j+i+1}, y_{k_j+i+2}]$ is a $\neg *$-interval, then the point y_{k_j+i} ends a $Corr$-interval; (iii) for each $j > 0$ the points y_{k_j}, y_{k_j-1}, and y_{k_j-2} do not finish any $Corr$-interval; (iv) by a simple combinatorial argument, every tile of a level is connected (via $Corr$) to its corresponding tile of the next one, and, if the level is not the first one and the tile is not the last one of the level, the tile is also connected to the corresponding one of the preceding level; (v) finally, as a consequence of the above points, every level features precisely as many tiles as the preceding level plus one. To conclude, the following constraints:

$$\phi_{16} \equiv \bigwedge_{i=1,\dots,N} [G](t_i \rightarrow [AO](Corr \rightarrow \langle AO \rangle (\bigvee_{j=1,\dots,N \mid up(t_i)=down(t_j)} t_j)))$$

$$\phi_{17} \equiv \bigwedge_{i=1,\dots,N} [G]((t_i \wedge [AO]\neg *) \rightarrow [AO](\bigvee_{j=1,\dots,N \mid right(t_i)=left(t_j)} t_j))$$

allow us to prove that: (i) for each pair $[y_i, y_{i+1}]$, $[y_{i+1}, y_{i+2}]$ of $\neg *$-intervals, if $[y_i, y_{i+1}]$ satisfies $t_r \in \mathcal{T}$ and $[y_{i+1}, y_{i+2}]$ satisfies $t_s \in \mathcal{T}$ then $right(t_r) = left(t_s)$; (ii) for each interval $[y_i, y_j]$ satisfying $Corr$, if $[y_{i-1}, y_i]$ satisfies $t_r \in \mathcal{T}$ and $[y_j, y_{j+1}]$ satisfies $t_s \in \mathcal{T}$ then $up(t_r) = down(t_s)$. □

Table 1. A summary of the results of this paper (denoted by [t.p.]).

	Fin	Dis	Den	N	Z	Q	Lin
HS	Und [15]	Und [15]	Und [15]	Und [15]	Und [15]	Und [15]	Und [15]
HS$_7$	Und [17]	Und [17]	Und [t.p.]	Und [17]	Und [17]	Und [t.p.]	Und [t.p.]
HS$_3$	PSPACE-c [t.p.]	PSPACE-h [t.p.]	PSPACE-h [t.p.] NPR [9]	PSPACE-c [t.p.]	PSPACE-c [t.p.]	PSPACE-h [t.p.] NPR [9]	PSPACE-h [t.p.]

5   Conclusions

In this paper we studied two previously unknown variants of Halpern and Shoham's logic (HS), inspired by Golumbic and Shamir's interval algebras, which generalize the classical Allen's Interval Algebra with coarser interval relations. While HS$_7$ (the finest of them) is still generally undecidable, HS$_3$ (the coarsest of them) becomes PSPACE-complete in the finite case and, at least, PSPACE-hard in the other cases (Table 1). Decidability in the infinite cases is still an open problem (via embedding we only know that it is decidable, but not primitive recursive - NPR, over Den and $\mathbb{Q}$), although our exploratory analysis of these cases suggests that HS$_3$ should be PSPACE-complete regardless of the class in which it is interpreted.

Acknowledgments. The authors acknowledge the support from the Spanish fellowship program *'Ramon y Cajal' RYC-2011-07821* (G. Sciavicco), and the Spanish Project *TIN12-39353-C04-01* (G. Sciavicco and E. Muñoz-Velasco).

References

1. Allen, J.F.: Maintaining knowledge about temporal intervals. Commun. ACM **26**(11), 832–843 (1983)
2. Artale, A., Bresolin, D., Montanari, A., Ryzhikov, V., Sciavicco, G.: DL-lite and interval temporal logics: a marriage proposal. In: Proceedings of the 21st European Conference of Artificial Intelligence (ECAI), pp. 957–958 (2014)
3. Artale, A., Franconi, E.: A temporal description logic for reasoning about actions and plans. J. Artif. Intell. Reasoning **9**, 463–506 (1998)
4. Bettini, C.: Time-dependent concepts: representation and reasoning using temporal description logics. Data Knowedge Engeneering **22**(1), 1–38 (1997)
5. Börger, E., Grädel, E., Gurevich, Y.: The Classical Decision Problem. Perspectives of Mathematical Logic. Springer, Berlin (1997)
6. Bresolin, D., Della Monica, D., Goranko, V., Montanari, A., Sciavicco, G.: The dark side of interval temporal logic: marking the undecidability border. Ann. Math. Artif. Intell. **71**(1–3), 41–83 (2014)
7. Bresolin, D., Della Monica, D., Montanari, A., Sala, P., Sciavicco, G.: Interval temporal logics over finite linear orders: the complete picture. In: Proceedings of the 20th European Conference on Artificial Intelligence (ECAI), pp. 199–204 (2012)
8. Bresolin, D., Della Monica, D., Montanari, A., Sala, P., Sciavicco, G.: Interval temporal logics over strongly discrete linear orders: the complete picture. In: Proceedings of the 4th International Symposium on Games, Automata, Logics, and Formal Verification (GANDALF). EPTCS, vol. 96, pp. 155–169 (2012)

9. Bresolin, D., Della Monica, D., Montanari, A., Sala, P., Sciavicco, G.: On the complexity of fragments of the modal logic of Allen's relations over dense structures. In: Dediu, A.-H., Formenti, E., Martín-Vide, C., Truthe, B. (eds.) LATA 2015. LNCS, vol. 8977, pp. 511–523. Springer, Heidelberg (2015)

10. Bresolin, D., Della Monica, D., Montanari, A., Sciavicco, G.: The light side of interval temporal logic: the Bernays-Schönfinkel fragment of CDT. Ann. Math. Artif. Intell. **71**(1–3), 11–39 (2014)

11. Bresolin, D., Muñoz-Velasco, E., Sciavicco, G.: Sub-propositional fragments of the interval temporal logic of Allen's relations. In: Fermé, E., Leite, J. (eds.) JELIA 2014. LNCS, vol. 8761, pp. 122–136. Springer, Heidelberg (2014)

12. Chaochen, Z., Hansen, M.R.: Duration Calculus: A Formal Approach to Real-Time Systems. EATCS: Monographs in Theoretical Computer Science, Springer (2004)

13. Della Monica, D., Goranko, V., Montanari, A., Sciavicco, G.: Expressiveness of the interval logics of Allen's relations on the class of all linear orders: complete classification. In: Proceedings of the 22nd International Joint Conference on Artificial Intelligence (IJCAI), pp. 845–850. AAAI Press (2011)

14. Golumbic, M., Shamir, R.: Complexity and algorithms for reasoning about time: a graph-theoretic approach. J. ACM **40**(5), 1108–1133 (1993)

15. Halpern, J., Shoham, Y.: A propositional modal logic of time intervals. J. ACM **38**(4), 935–962 (1991)

16. Klarman, S.: Practical querying of temporal data via OWL 2 QL and SQL:2011. In: Proceedings of the 19th International Conference on Logic for Programming, Artificial Intelligence, and Reasoning (LPAR). EPiC Series, vol. 26, pp. 52–61. Center for Artificial Inteligence Research (2014)

17. Marcinkowski, J., Michaliszyn, J.: The undecidability of the logic of subintervals. Fundam. Inf. **131**(2), 217–240 (2014)

18. Montanari, A., Puppis, G., Sala, P.: Maximal decidable fragments of halpern and Shoham's modal logic of intervals. In: Abramsky, S., Gavoille, C., Kirchner, C., Meyer auf der Heide, F., Spirakis, P.G. (eds.) ICALP 2010. LNCS, vol. 6199, pp. 345–356. Springer, Heidelberg (2010)

19. Montanari, A., Puppis, G., Sala, P., Sciavicco, G.: Decidability of the interval temporal logic $A\bar{B}\bar{B}$ on natural numbers. In: Proceedings of the 27th Symposium on Theoretical Aspects of Computer Science (STACS), pp. 597–608. Inria Nancy Grand Est & Loria (2010)

20. Moszkowski, B.: Reasoning about digital circuits. Ph.D. thesis, Department of Computer Science, Stanford University, Stanford, CA (1983)

21. Pratt-Hartmann, I.: Temporal prepositions and their logic. Artif. Intell. **166**(1–2), 1–36 (2005)

22. Schmiedel, A.: Temporal terminological logic. In: Proceedings of the 8th National Conference on Artificial Intelligence (AAAI), pp. 640–645. AAAI Press (1990)

23. Stockmeyer, L., Meyer, A.: Word problems requiring exponential time (Preliminary Report). In: Proceedings of the 5th Annual ACM Symposium on Theory of Computing (STOC), pp. 1–9. ACM (1973)

Characterizing and Computing HBG-PCs for Hybrid Systems Fault Diagnosis

Belarmino Pulido[✉], Carlos Alonso-González, Anibal Bregon, and Alberto Hernández

Departamento de Informática, Universidad de Valladolid, Valladolid, Spain
{belar,calonso,anibal}@infor.uva.es
pascu216@gmail.com

Abstract. Possible Conflicts (PCs) are those minimally redundant subsystems, computed offline, that can be used for consistency-based diagnosis of physical systems. In this work we characterize Possible Conflicts for hybrid systems diagnosis in the Hybrid Bond Graph modelling framework, introducing the notion of HBG-PCs. We provide a method to compute the complete set of HBG-PCs before causality is assigned in the model, removing a previous assumption that the system model should have a valid causal assumption when every switching junction was set to ON. We call this new concept Structural HBG-PC. We illustrate these issues with an prototypical example and discuss our contributions against other proposals in the literature.

1 Introduction

Hybrid systems are physical systems that exhibit a continuous behaviour which can be modified due to changes in its configuration. Examples of hybrid systems are the ABS brake system commonly found in the automotive industry or air-conditioning systems that can provide heat and/or cold air. The kind of hybrid systems we focus on have a continuous behaviour controlled by discrete events. The behavioural model of this kind of systems is made up of the continuous behavioural model for each working mode and the discrete events which trigger the changes between them.

Hybrid systems fault diagnosis has to be accurate and efficient, because it is vital that they work in a nominal and safe state, and the diagnosis process must accommodate to the changes in the system state. There are many proposals in the model-based fault diagnosis community[1]: based on hybrid modeling [1,2], hybrid state estimation [3,4], or a combination of online state tracking and residual evaluation [5,6]. All these proposals have at least one of the following difficulties: either it is necessary to pre-enumerate all possible configurations or working modes in the system (and to provide models for all of them), or they

---

[1] The Artificial Intelligence approach to model-based diagnosis it is usually knwon as DX, while the Control Theory approach to the same problem is usually known as FDI.

© Springer International Publishing Switzerland 2015
J.M. Puerta et al. (Eds.): CAEPIA 2015, LNAI 9422, pp. 116–127, 2015.
DOI: 10.1007/978-3-319-24598-0_11

need to determine somehow the actual working mode, including the actuators' configuration and the continuous behaviour.

Some authors have proposed Hybrid Bond Graphs (HBGs) [7] as a modelling technique for hybrid systems. HBG modeling is an extension for hybrid systems of the well known Bond-Graph (BG) modelling approach [8]. Its main advantage is that they do not need a pre-enumeration of all possible modes to track the system behaviour. Hybrid behaviour is introduced by means of idealized switching junctions that connect or disconnect parts of the system. BG and HBG models provide a graphical description of the system model and its main advantage is that different kinds of numerical equations can be automatically derived from them, and these equations can be used to simulate system behaviour.

Possible Conflicts (PCs) were defined to work with a set of algebraic or differential equations [9], but the concept was later extended to work with BG models [10]. Initially PCs were computed from the Temporal Causal Graph (TCG) associated with the BG once causality was assigned using the Sequential Causal Assignment Process (SCAP) algorithm. Later on, we proposed to derive PCs for hybrid systems using HBGs [11]. We called Hybrid PCs (HPCs) to such extension. Main assumption in that approach was that there exists a valid causal assignment for any bond in the model in integral causality when every switching junction was set to ON. The causality within the HPC models could be changed using HSCAP, which is the extended version of SCAP for hybrid systems, whenever a mode change was detected [12]. In this work we remove that requirement and we propose a formal characterization of the HPCs in the HBG framework, together with a method to compute HBGs from a non-causal HBG.

The organization of this work is as follows. First, we introduce the concepts about BG modelling, and the PC approach for consistency-based diagnosis in the BG framework, that will be illustrated using a running example. Afterwards we extend PCs to HBG terminology, and provide the algorithms to compute HBG-PCs. We finish by discussing about related work and drawing some conclusions.

2   Characterizing PCs in the BG Modelling Framework

2.1   Running Example

To illustrate our approach we will use a simple electric circuit that exhibits the major feature of hybrid systems: a pair of physical switches that provide the system with four potentially different working modes (even though one of the combinations is not a feasible mode). This system is shown in Fig. 1(a).

2.2   Hybrid Bond-Graphs for Hybrid Systems Modelling

Bond Graph modeling approach is a domain-independent energy-based topological modeling language for physical systems [2,8]. Several types of primitive elements are used to build BGs: storage elements (capacitors, C, and inductances, I), dissipative elements (resistors, R) and elements for energy transformation

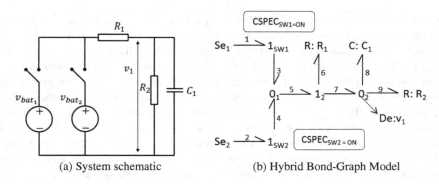

(a) System schematic   (b) Hybrid Bond-Graph Model

Fig. 1. An electric system fed with two power sources. Each power source can be selected using a switch.

(transformers, TF, and gyrators, GY). There are also effort and flow sources (Se and Sf), which are used to define interactions between the system and the environment. Elements in a BG are connected by 0 or 1 junctions (representing ideal parallel or series connections between components, respectively). Each bond has associated two variables (effort and flow).

Hybrid Bond Graphs extend Bond-Graphs by including idealized switching junctions, SW for short, to allow mode changes in the system. If a SW is set to *ON*, it behaves as a regular junction. When it changes to *OFF*, all bonds incident on the junction are deactivated forcing 0 flow (or effort) for 1 (or 0) junctions. Those junctions are implemented as a finite state machine *control specification (CSPEC)*. Transitions between the CSPEC states can be triggered by endogenous or exogenous variables, called guards. CSPECs capture controlled and autonomous changes as described in [12].

Figure 1(b) shows the HBG model for our electric system. In that model there are two switching junctions: 1_{sw_1} and 1_{sw_2}, in this case both of them set to ON. That HBG model has no causal assignment to the bonds in the graph. Figure 2 shows different configurations of the system when we set to OFF any of these SWs. For the sake of readability we turn grey in the HBG those SW and its related bonds when they are switched to OFF.

2.3   Possible Conflicts from BG Models

The PC approach is a dependency-compilation technique from the DX community [9] for consistency-based diagnosis in continuous systems. PCs compile offline those minimal structurally overdetermined subsets of equations from the system model capable of generating fault hypotheses from observed measurement deviations, i.e. they are the basis to check the consistency between observed and estimated variables in the system.

The structural and causal information required to compute the set of PCs can be derived automatically from a set of equations, which can be a set of Algebraic Differential Equations or a Bond-Graph model [10].

To extend the PCs approach for hybrid systems diagnosis, we chose the HBG models, because it is not necessary to enumerate every working mode beforehand [2]. Moreover, efficient proposals exist to automatically change the causality in the model whenever a change in the system mode occurs [12].

We initially relied upon two main assumptions to compute the set of PCs: it was possible to use integral causality to solve the underlying equations, and there was a complete valid causal assignment for the system model when every SW was set to ON. These subsystems were called Hybrid PCs [11]. Now we propose to remove both assumptions and still compute the set of Hybrid PCs. Main reason is that some systems do not have a VCA under integral causality when every SW is ON, because such configuration will never be set. That is the case of our running example, because it is not a valid configuration and we will never have both SWs in Fig. 1 set to ON.

To avoid such requirement we propose to compute the set of Hybrid PCs without initially considering causality. We will call these subsystems Structural Hybrid Bond-Graph Possible Conflicts (SHBG-PCs). In order to define SHBG-PCs we proceed first by defining PCs for BG modelling, then extending them to HBG models.

Definition 1. *(BG) A BG is a connected graph made up of elements and bonds:* $\{E, B\}$, *where* $E = St \cup M$. *M represents sensors (De, Df) and St, the set of structural elements, is made up of* $St = S \cup PSV \cup J_t$. *S represents effort or flow Source elements (Se, Sf). PSV contains passive elements (resistors, R, capacitors, C, or inductance elements, I). J_t is the total set of junctions:* $J_t = J \cup T$, *where T are transformers, TF, or gyrators, GY, and J is the set of 0- or 1-junctions.*

Each element is connected by means of bonds, $B \subset E \times E$.

Not every relation between elements e_i, e_j is allowed for each bond $b_k \in B$: for each $(e_i, e_j) \in B$, $e_i \in J_t$ *or* $e_j \in J_t$ *or* $(e_i, e_j) \in Jt$.

Exceptionally there could be combinations of one source and one passive element that would not respect that generic rule, but we do not consider those systems as significant for fault diagnosis. Moreover, BGs are usually extended by adding a number to each bond, in order to facilitate the enumeration of each effort and flow variable.

Each bond $b_k \in B$ represents a relation or equation among system (effort and flow) variables. The elements in $S \cup PSV$ provide the behavioural model by means of the set of its constituent equations. The elements of J_t provide the structural model of the system. The set M determines which variable in the system can be observed (the observational model).

Causality expresses computational dependencies between effort and flow variables in a BG [12]. Once causality is assigned to the bonds in a BG model, we know how to use the equations for behaviour simulation. The SCAP algorithm [8] has been used to assign causality automatically to the BG. A BG with a valid global causal assignment and without sensors defines a just-determined set of equations, where S elements are the exogenous variables or inputs [13]. Causality is graphically depicted as strokes in the edges, either at the tail or at the head.

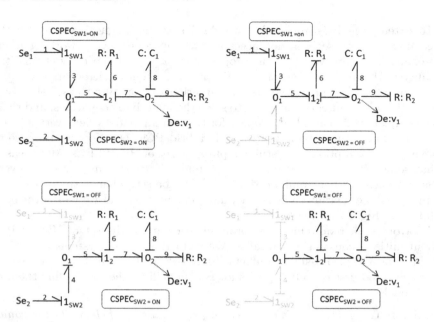

Fig. 2. HBG-PCs for the running example under the four possible working modes.

A BG with a valid causal assignment (VCA) is known as a Causally Enhanced BG [2] or Causal BG [13]:

Definition 2. *(Causal BG) It is a BG = $\{E, B\}$, where each bond, $b_i \in B \subset E \times E$ is extended with a label causality = { "effort", "flow"}, that signals which variable (effort or flow) fix the causality in the bond: $b_i = (e_i, e_j, causality)$.*

Figure 2 shows four different configurations for the HBG in Fig. 1(b). Each one of them is a BG if we think that a SW set to ON is a regular junction. Three of the configurations have a VCA. Only the one in the upper left corner have no VCA, which corresponds to the two SWs set to ON.

Adding sensors in a BG introduces analytical redundancy in the system model, because we can at least estimate and observe each variable related to the sensor. As it is the usual procedure in model-based fault diagnosis, sensors are the potential source of discrepancies. This is the main idea behind building Analytical Redundancy Relations (ARRs) or Diagnostic Bond-Graphs (DBGs) for FDI using BGs [13]. PCs also rely on these concepts although they were not originally defined on the BG framework. Extending the concept of PCs to BGs requires finding the set of subsystems in a BG with minimal analytical redundancy, which in turn requires introducing the three following definitions.

Definition 3. *(Degenerated junction (J_d)) A degenerated 1-j (equivalently 0-j) is a one-port element that must be obtained from a valid 1-j (equiv. 0-j) in a BG that is connected to a flow sensor Df (equiv. effort, De) or a flow source, Sf* *(equiv. effort, Se). Given a bond, b, and a measurement Df_1, the 1- degenerated junction (equiv. 0-j) changes the junction behavioural model:*

- *$f_b := Df_1$ (instead of the set of equalities $f_a = f_c = f_b$ for a 3-port 1-junction with determining bond b). If b is linked to a source, the equation would be $f_b := Sf_1$.*
- *there is no restriction for the conjugated variable, e_b (instead of $e_b = e_a + e_c$).*

Degenerated junctions provide the value for exactly one variable, of exactly the same type (effort/flow) of the adjacent measurement or source. In our running example in Fig. 1(b) there is no degenerated junctions. We could create one by removing bonds 8 and 9, and elements C_1 and R_2 in junction 0_2.

Definition 4. *(sBG) A sub Bond Graph, sBG, derived from a $BG = \{E, B\}$, is a partially connected subgraph: $sBG = \{E', B'\} \subseteq \{E, B\} \mid E' = St' \cup M'$ and $St' = S' \cup PSV' \cup J'$ with $S' \subseteq S, PSV' \subseteq PSV, M' \subseteq M$ and $B' \subseteq E' \times E' \subset B$. $J' = J'_o \cup J'_d, J'_o \subseteq J_t$, and J'_d is a set of zero or more degenerated junctions. Additionally if $j_d \in J'_d$ was derived from $j_o \in J_t$ then $j_o \notin J'$.*

A *sBG* is a partial subgraph from a BG that is made of some of the constituent elements of BG, and also a set of junctions J_o from the original BG. But there is also a potentially empty set of degenerated 1- and 0-junctions, J_d, that will be used to split the BG in terms of sources or measurements and they are used to determine the value of flow/effort variables. If j_d is a degenerated junction derived from an original junction $j_o \in J$, then by definition $j_o \notin J'$. In particular, we are interested in those *sBGs* with analytical redundancy:

Definition 5. *(RBG) A Redundant Bond Graph, RBG, is defined as a sBG whose underlying model has analytical redundancy.*

Now we have the necessary concepts to define a PC in the BG framework:

Definition 6. *(Bond-Graph Possible Conflict (BG-PC)) Given a valid BG with a VCA, a BG-PC is a RBG, $\{E_{pc}, B_{pc}\}, E_{pc} = St_{pc} \cup M_{pc}$, such that BG-PC $\subset BG$, and BG-PC is minimal in the sense that $\nexists RBG' \subset BG$ with $RBG' \subset$ BG-PC.*

The existence of a BG-PC $\subset$ BG requires that BG had analytical redundancy: there must exist $d' \in M_{pc}$ such that the VCA of BG-PC allows estimation of d' from dualized sensors and/or sources: d' is the discrepancy node of the BG-PC and it is unique (otherwise the analytical redundancy in BG-PC would not be minimal).

Figure 2 shows two RBGs due to the presence of sensor $De : v_1$: the upper right and the lower left corners. The HBG in the upper left corner has redundancy, but no VCA. The HBG in the lower right corner has VCA but no redundancy, hence it is not a RBG.

3   Characterizing HBG-PCs

HBG models have no genuine new elements w.r.t. a BG model. Only a SW changing its state can modify the underlying set of equations. Consequently, using HBG models instead of BG models makes little difference in the way PCs are defined. Hence, extending the concept for hybrid systems is rather straightforward if every SW is ON:

Definition 7. *(HBG-PC:) It is a BG-PC, where some elements $J_{sw} \subseteq J'$ are switching junctions, and has a VCA when all the switching junctions of J_{sw} are set to ON.*

In Bregon et al. [11,14] we demonstrated that the set of PCs in an HBG when every SW is set to ON provides the smaller set of PCs, and any analytically redundant subsystem will be part of one of these PCs[2]. The reason is that a change in one SW going from ON to OFF will neither introduce new measurements in the system nor increase the number of state variables. Hence, it can not be the source of new redundancy. Switching from ON to OFF and viceversa, will only connect or disconnect parts of the system.

We now propose to remove the assumption that there is a VCA when every SW is set to ON: such configuration might have no valid causal model. This is not surprising. Some systems have multiple structural configurations and several are not compatible among them. These configurations are usually known beforehand because they represent the *limited* set of valid operation modes in the system. But a well designed system must have at least one VCA for some configuration of SWs set to ON and/or OFF[3]. If we assume that a SW set to OFF disconnect a part of the system, each one of these valid configurations represent a subsystem where our assumption for BG-PCs holds: it must have a VCA when every SWs in that subsystem is set to ON. If we are able to find the maximal subsets of SWs where our assumption holds, we can guarantee that there will be no new genuine and smaller BG-PCs.

Definition 8. *(maxJ$_{sw}$) Given a RBG and its set of SW, J_{sw}, a maximal subset $maxJ_{sw} \subseteq J_{sw}$, satisfies the following properties:*

– *RBG has a VCA when all the SW in $maxJ_{sw}$ are set to ON*
– *$\forall sw' \in \{J_{sw} \setminus maxJ_{sw}\}$, RBG has no VCA with all the SW in $maxJ_{sw} \cup \{sw'\}$ set to ON.*

Since each BG-PC in a BG model is related to a sensor, and changing a SW to from ON to OFF does not introduce new redundancy, we can search for HBG-PCs in two steps: first, we search for structural redundancy, assuming every SW is ON, without considering causality. We call these new subsystems containing

---

[2] Exceptionally some degenerated subsystems can appear, but they had no interest for diagnosis purposes.

[3] Otherwise there would be parts of the system that will be never used, or there is no need for such SW in the model.

analytical redundancy *Structural HBG-PCs*, or *SHBG-PC* for short. Second, we check for those maximal SW configurations in each *SHBG-PC* for VCAs. Each one of these valid configurations is a HBG-PC.

Definition 9. *(Structural HBG-PC:) It is a RBG such that* $\forall\, maxJ_{sw} \subseteq J_{sw}$, *each* $RBG' \subseteq RBG$, *obtained by means of the following operations, is a HBG-PC:*

- *setting all the* SW *in* $\{J_{sw} \setminus maxJ_{sw}\}$ *to* OFF
- *keeping in RBG' all the* SW *in* $maxJ_{sw}$ *to* ON
- $J_{sw} = \bigcup maxJ_{sw}$.

Each SHBG-PC defines the maximal set of elements in the HBG that can be a part of a HBG-PC related to the discrepancy node in the SHBG-PC (which is the sensor introducing the redundancy).

Searching for the sets $maxJ_{sw}$ is a worst case exponential problem. However, the way we compute SHBG-PCs help us with this problem. Next we introduce the required algorithms to compute SHBG-PCs.

3.1   Computing HBG-PCs

Computing structural HBG-PCs from HBGs is straightforward: structural HBG-PCs are searched traversing the HBG from the sensors to sources and/or other sensors, collecting all its components, except those of the degenerated junctions linked to dualized sensors. There is, however, one exception to this rule, due to the presence of non-parametric paths: paths of the HBG that allow propagating flow or effort form a source or sensor independently of passive elements. Given that we are looking for minimal redundancy, the passive elements of non-parametric paths should not be included in the structural HBG-PC.

Algorithm 1 assumes the original HBG model is correct and that effort/flow sensors will be only connected to 0/1 junctions, respectively. It also assumes that non-parametric paths do not traverse switching junctions. The HBG is modelled as a set of nodes (elements) connected through bonds. The algorithm first identifies nodes in Non-Parametric paths in the HBG[4]. Then it performs depth-first search for minimal paths from every *sensor* available to source or sensor elements. Such paths describe Redundant Bond Graphs, *SHPC*. Each node in the *TentativePath* is required to compute the effort/flow variable in the *sensor*.

The algorithm is able to find HBG-PCs that contains only sources and/or sensors to estimate the value of *sensor*, together with junction elements. These are called non-parametric BG-PCs, and can be regarded as degenerated BG-PCs because they can only detect faults in sensor, but they can not be used to diagnose parametric faults. For that reason, they are not included in this framework.

---

[4] It is straightforward propagating from sensor/sources an traversing non-parametric junctions.

Algorithm 1. HPC ALGORITHM

Input: Set of nodes in Bond Graph: nodeSet
Output: Set of SHBG-PCs
1 Mark nodes belonging to Non-Parametric-Paths to sources/sensors;
2 **for** *each sensor* {*De or Df*} *in nodeSet* **do**
3 $\quad$ $SHPC := \{\}; TentativePath := \{\}$; Remove *sensor* from *nodeSet*;
4 $\quad$ Add *sensor* to SHPC; Mark *sensor* as discrepancy-node for $SHPC$;
5 $\quad$ Add any node adjacent to *sensor* $\in nodeSet$ to *TentativePath*;
6 $\quad$ $[SHPC, ok] := buildRBG(nodeSet, SHPC, TentativePath)$
7 $\quad$ **if** $ok == 1$ *AND SHPC is a non parametric BG-PC* **then**
8 $\quad\quad$ Insert SHPC in SHBG-PCs;

Algorithm 2. BUILD RBG

Input: Set of nodes, *nodeSet*, current RBG, $SHPC$, and current path, *TentativePath*
Output: Updated $SHPC$ and *TentativePath*, and error code, *ok*
1 **while** *TentativePath is not empty AND ok != -1* **do**
2 $\quad$ Extract *node* from *TentativePath*;
$\quad$ $[SHPC, TentativePath, ok] := analyzeEl(node, SHPC, TentativePath)$

Algorithm 3. ANALYZEEL

Input: Current *node*, current $SHPC$, and current search path *TentativePath*
Output: Updated $SHPC$ and *TentativePath*, and error code *ok*
1 $ok := 0$
2 **if** *node is not in SHPC* **then**
3 $\quad$ Add *node* to $SHPC$;
4 $\quad$ **if** *node is a junction linked to sensor/source s AND s* $\notin TentativePath$ **then**
5 $\quad\quad$ $ok := 1$; Add s to $SHPC$;
6 $\quad$ **else if** *node is a junction in a Non-Parametric Path to s' AND*
7 $\quad$ $s' != SHPC.DiscrepancyNode$ **then**
8 $\quad\quad$ $ok := 1$; Add nodes in Non-Parametric Path to s' to $SHPC$;
9 $\quad$ **else if** *there is a non-empty subset of nodes adjacent to node* **then**
10 $\quad\quad$ Add every 1-Port element, E in *subset* to $SHPC$
11 $\quad\quad$ Add every junction in *subset* to *TentativePath*
12 $\quad$ **else**
13 $\quad\quad$ $ok := -1$

Algorithm 2 extracts in each step a *node* from the *TentativePath*. The *node* is analysed by Algorithm 3. The search stops successfully if the *TentativePath* is empty.

Each element in *TentativePath* is analysed by means of Algorithm 3. Depending on the type of *node*, different actions are performed. If *node* is a junction, and there is a source or sensor adjacent to *node*, the search will stop. Same happens if the junction belongs to a Non-Parametric Path linked to a sensor or source different from the original discrepancy sensor. Otherwise, we collect any element, not previously visited, adjacent to the junction, and store them in the current $SHPC$. If there are other junctions adjacent to *node* they are stored in *TentativePath*, and the search continues.

Once we have found a SHBG-PC it is necessary to find the sets $maxJ_{sw}$ to determine if it defines a HBG-PC. As mentioned in the previous section this problem has a worst case exponential complexity. However, finding first the SHBG-PCs using structural information we reduce the complexity of the search, turning a global search into a local search (within the SHBG-PC). Moreover, in order to determine the presence of a HBG-PC we only need to find one maximal set with at least one VCA. It can be useful to have the complete set of $maxJ_{sw}$ for each SHBG-PC, that can be computed offline, but it is not mandatory.

4   Case Study

We will illustrate the performance of the algorithms in our running example. The HBG model is correct and has redundancy (given by sensor $De{:}v1$), but if we run HSCAP when "every SW ON" there is no Valid Causal Assignment.

Algorithm 1, for only sensor $De : v_1$, search backwards from the adjacent 0-j, and includes every single element in the HBG in the SHBG-PC structure. In this case, there are two non-parametric paths: $\{Se_1, 1_{sw_1}, O_1\}$, and $\{Se_2, 1_{sw_2}, O_1\}$. Since the whole structural model has no VCA, we start the search for maximal configurations of SW set to ON: we alternatively switch SWs to OFF: 1_{sw_1} and 1_{sw_2}. Both of them have a VCA, hence it is not necessary to search further.

Figure 2 shows the four configurations for the non-causal model in Fig. 1(b). The upper right side and the lower left side contain the only two configurations with a VCA. The two remaining configurations do not comply with the HBG-PC definition: one has no VCA and the other one it is not a RBG. Finally, the SHBG-PCs is exactly the union of elements in both RBG'. Results are summarized in the Table 1:

Table 1. RBGs found in the electric circuit. Only two out of four configurations of SWs have VCA, providing two Redundant Bond-Graphs for the SHBG-PC containing the whole system model.

RBG'	Sensor	$maxJ_{sw}$	Elements
1	v_1	$\{1sw_1\}$	$\{Se_1, 0_1, 1_1, R_1, 0_2, C_1, R_2\}$
2	v_1	$\{1sw_2\}$	$\{Se_2, 0_1, 1_1, R_1, 0_2, C_1, R_2\}$

We have tested the algorithms in larger systems with more complex HBG models (a four tank hybrid systems, and a Reverse Osmosis System), finding the complete set of HBG-PCs that can be found using previous approaches. Due to lack of space we can not include neither the description of the systems, their HBG models or the results[5]. The reader can find a complete description of these results in [15].

---

[5] http://www.infor.uva.es/~belar/HBGPCS_results/results.pdf   has   a   complete description of the systems and the results.

5   Conclusions

The main contribution is the introduction of the Structural HBG-PC, because it allows to find HBG-PCs for hybrid systems without imposing any condition on the global causality of the system model [12]. In previous works [11], we imposed the assumption that the systems had a VCA when every SW was set to ON. Now SHBG-PCs can be computed independently of any causal assignment, which is a main difference with other approaches relying upon HBG models [2,13].

This work provides an alternative characterization for HBG-PCs, based on maximal sets of SWs set to ON with a VCA. This definition generalizes the former one [14] when the maximal set is the whole set of SWs. However, if the system does not fulfill this requirement, the concept of SHBG-PC still helps us to deal locally with non valid SW configurations, while containing the whole set of HBG-PCs for every feasible configuration.

A SHBG-PC covers a set of maximal switching junctions. The actual HBG-PCs must be obtained searching within the SHBG-PC, without further search in the global model. Finding maximal sets of SWs has a worst case exponential cost. However, it is not strictly needed to compute these sets, unless we want to characterize offline the families of HBG-PCs for each valid configuration. It is enough to check out that there is one VCA for anyone of the valid configurations.

As in previous works, Structural HBG-PCs allows to track hybrid system behaviour with only local changes in the model, because a change in a SW is local to the structural model. When a change in the system mode requires a change in a SW from ON to OFF or viceversa, we only need to run a HSCAP-like algorithm within the SHBG-PC to determine a new diagnosis model.

Further research is needed to integrate *HBG-PCs* that are completely non-parametric with all theirs SWs set to ON. In this proposal we only cover for a special case when there are non-parametric paths close to a sensors or sources.

Acknowledgments. This work has been supported by Spanish MINECO under DPI2013-45414-R grant.

References

1. Mosterman, P., Biswas, G.: Diagnosis of continuous valued systems in transient operating regions. IEEE Trans. Syst. Man Cyber. Part B **29**(6), 554–565 (1999)
2. Narasimhan, S., Biswas, G.: Model-based diagnosis of hybrid systems. IEEE Trans. Syst. Man Cyber. Part A **37**(3), 348–361 (2007)
3. Hofbaur, M.W., Williams, B.C.: Hybrid estimation of complex systems. IEEE Trans. Syst. Man Cybern. Part B Cybern. **34**(5), 2178–2191 (2004)
4. Rienmüller, Th., Bayoudh, M., Hofbaur, M.W., Travé-Massuyès, L.: Hybrid estimation through synergic mode-set focusing. In: Proceedings of IFAC Safeprocess 2009, pp. 1480–1485. Barcelona, Spain (2009)
5. Benazera, E., Travé-Massuyès, L.: Set-theoretic estimation of hybrid system configurations. IEEE Trans. Syst. Man Cyber. Part B **39**, 1277–1291 (2009)

6. Bayoudh, M., Travé-Massuyès, L., Olive, X.: Coupling continuous and discrete event system techniques for hybrid system diagnosability analysis. In: Proceeding of ECAI 2008, pp. 219–223. IOS Press, Amsterdam, The Netherlands (2008)
7. Mosterman, P.J., Biswas, G.; Behavior generation using model switching - a hybrid bond graph modeling technique. In: Society for Computer Simulation, pp. 177–182. SCS publishing (1994)
8. Broenink, J.F.: Introduction to physical systems modelling with bond graphs. In: SiE Whitebook on Simulation methodologies (1999)
9. Pulido, B., Alonso-González, C.: Possible Conflicts: a compilation technique for consistency-based diagnosis. IEEE Trans. Syst. Man Cyber. Part B **34**(5), 2192–2206 (2004)
10. Bregon, A., Pulido, B., Biswas, G., Koutsoukos, X.: Generating Possible Conflicts from Bond Graphs using Temporal Causal Graphs. In: Proceeding of the 23rd European Conference on Modelling and Simulation, ECMS 2009, Madrid, Spain (2009)
11. Bregon, A., Alonso, C., Biswas, G., Pulido, B., Moya, N.: Fault diagnosis in hybrid systems using Possible Conficts. In: Proceedings of the IFAC SAFEPROCESS 2012. Mexico D.F., Mexico (2012)
12. Roychoudhury, I., Daigle, M.J., Biswas, G., Koutsoukos, X.: Efficient simulation of hybrid systems: a Hybrid Bond Graph approach. In: SIMULATION: Transactions of the Society for Modeling and Simulation International, April 2010
13. Samantaray, A.K., Bouamama, B.O.: Model-based Process Supervision: A Bond Graph Approach. Springer, London (2008)
14. Moya, N.: Fault Diagnosis of Hybrid Systems with Dynamic Bayesian Networks and Hybrid Possible Conficts. Ph.D. thesis, ETSI. Informatica. Universidad de Valladolid (2013)
15. Hernández-Cerezo, A.: Diagnosis de sistemas hibridos mediante Posibles Conflictos Hibridos (in Spanish). Master thesis, ETSI Informatica, University of Valladolid, Valladolid, Spain, July 2015

Clinical Decision Support System for the Diagnosis and Treatment of Fuzzy Diseases

Rubén Romero-Córdoba, Jose Ángel Olivas, Francisco Pascual Romero[✉],
and Francisco Alonso-Gómez

SMILe Research Group, High School of Computing of Castilla-La Mancha,
Paseo de la Universidad, 4, 13071 Ciudad Real, Spain
{ruben.romcor,pacoalonso40}@gmail.com
{joseangel.olivas,FranciscoP.Romero}@uclm.es

Abstract. The application of smart programs and services in the medical field is nowadays a reality that guarantees patients a quality healthcare. In the present article, it is proposed the development of a Clinical Decision Support System (CDSS) in order to diagnose a set of "fuzzy diseases".This concept refers to the diseases that are not diagnosable through a concrete clinical test or symptom. Then, the diagnosis of a "fuzzy diseases" set is based in the exclusion of symptoms and tests results, due to the similarity between them. For dealing with these inconveniences, in this paper it has been designed a reasoning method which uses mainly a theory about the conceptual categorization from the Psychology field [1,2] and the prototypes concept of Zadeh [3]. Through the use of this model, it was obtained a satisfactory result in the evaluation of patients.

Keywords: Prototype set theory · Fuzzy sets · CDSS · Fibromyalgia · Diferential diagnosis

1   Introduction

The growth of the computing systems in the health field has been reflected in reports such as "2013 Annual Report of the U.S. Hospital IT Market" [4]. The report was carried out in the year 2014 and it revealed a large growth of these systems in the US hospitals. Standing out the application of AI techniques, especially in the knowledge engineering [5] area.

One line of work in that field is the development of CDSS. In this paper, it is proposed to create one of these systems, that may be used in a real medical environment. The main goal is the creation of a method for representing and performing a diagnostic with a group of diseases whose diagnostic process has not been clearly defined. For that, it will be used several techniques related with the Prototype concept and the categorization of types. With the aim of

J.M. Puerta et al. (Eds.): CAEPIA 2015, LNAI 9422, pp. 128–138, 2015.
DOI: 10.1007/978-3-319-24598-0_12

applying these techniques, it has been chosen a set of diseases that have many similarities between them and simultaneously they have a strong similarity with Fibromyalgia. This allows to perform a diagnostic with a set of "fuzzy diseases".

Fibromyalgia prevalence in overall levels is between 2 % and 5 % of the world population and it predominates in people about 20 and 50 years old [6], with a higher proportion of women (10 times more than men) [7]. The total amount of affected people in different countries are not negligible [7,8]: 3.2 % in Germany, 2.4 % in Spain, 2 % in EEUU, 1.4 % in France, 3.7 % in Italy, 3.6 % in Portugal and 2.5 % in Sweden. In Spain, 15 % of the rheumatology consults and between 5 % and 10 % of the primary healthcare are dedicated to these patients, which means a total expense in public health of about 11 million euros per year. Therefore, it can be determined that the development of a CDSS may reduce costs and improve the healthcare quality.

The work will be organized as follows: In section two, a short introduction for evaluating the currents reasoning techniques used in CDSS that treat diseases of this type, and for describing the diseases chosen. In the next section, it is displayed the developed design of the system and finally a description of the performed evaluations and their results. To finish, the conclusions are described as well as several improvements to perfect the system.

2   Background

The CDSS is destined to perform a diagnostic and/or treatment of diseases through an exclusion process, it has been designed with multitude of methods and techniques. The main ones being those whose reasoning is based in probabilistic models [9], those based on fuzzy reasoning [10,11], those based on neural networks [12–15], other are based on the theory of frames and finally, there is a group that uses hybrid methods [16].

However, the application of these techniques has been destined for a disease diagnostic process in which there is clearly a distinguishing feature. In the case of the study proposed in this article, the designed system will not have diseases with a distinguishing feature due to the similarity and disparity of symptoms. The illnesses chosen are: Polymyositis, Rheumatoid Arthritis, Systemic Lupus Erythematosus, Polymyalgia Rheumatic and Hypothyroidism, being the common nexus, and the most difficult to diagnose, Fibromyalgia.

Fibromyalgia is characterized as a chronic disease that affects to the soft parts of the Locomotor System and that presents a high sensibility in multiple points of the body in which there is a generalized presence of chronic muscuoloskeletal pain. The pain symptoms usually coexist with others such as: fatigue, sleep disturbances, memory problems, concentration, joint stiffness, headaches, feeling of swelling in the hands, anxiety, depression, and so on.

Many times, Fibromyalgia is confounded with other illnesses, because its symptoms are very similar. It does not have any known cause and it does not produce any type of changes in tissues or cells. The diagnostic is mainly clinic and the results of the tests are not enough to detect it. To diagnose it, the doctor must perform different tests in order to rule out diseases like: Polymyositis, Rheumatoid Arthritis, Systemic Lupus Erythematosus, Polymyalgia Rheumatic, Hypothyroidism and so on. Once they are discarded, the medical history of the patient, as well as his symptomatology, are studied. After that, a process of physical exploration begins where the trigger points are detected and those affected are accounted. These points are called *objective indicators* (Fig. 1).

In the absence of a cura-
tive treatment, the aim is to
relieve the symptoms through
a personalized one, depending on multiple factors as the
trigger points affected or the
symptoms. The pharmacologic
treatments are usually combined with others alternatives
like acupuncture. In a nutshell,
Fibromyalgia is present, with a
high incidence, in many countries and affects patients with a
large amount of different symptoms. However, there is very little information about its causes,
which has a negative impact,
both physically and psycholog-

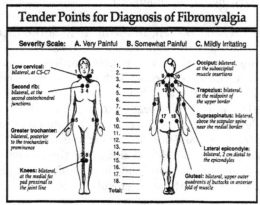

Anatomic location of tender points according to the American College
of Rheumatology 1990 classification criteria for fibromyalgia.

Fig. 1. Distribution of tender points.

ically on patients who have to be constantly monitored. Moreover, for health institutions it is a relevant problem, owing to the high presence of patients with a disease not clearly defined, not correctly treated, or wrongly diagnosed.

3   Design of a CDSS for Fuzzy Diseases

The approach given to the detection and treatment of diseases that are highly similar comes as a result of the developed theories whose primary concept is the prototype. The prototype concept turns around the notion of membership of an element in relation to a class. The prototypes theory of Psychology, enunciated by some scientists such as Eleanor Rosch [1, 2] or Bremermann [17] suggest that an item belongs to a class or prototype, if it resembles, in a high level, the maximum representative of the class. Later and carrying on this idea, Zadeh introduced the concept of "fuzzy prototype" [3] to reformulate the basic ideas exposed by the psychology scientists. The main improvements exposed are based on the fact that an element belonging to a group is not always a good representative of the class to which it belongs [18]. Moreover, a prototype is not an element with a defined limit and simples features, but rather, a fuzzy object and then, it may possess certain "degree" of membership to one or more classes. Therefore, he determined that not only the most characteristic element defines a prototype, but that it establishes a system of membership to determine the similarity of an object with a prototype.

Then, based on these theories, the fact that an element has a higher proximity with some classes or others has allowed to devise a method for detecting and treating diseases with a high similarity index. The diseases would be then the prototypes and the symptoms their features. The prototypes may have an internal classification of its features: "resolutive facts", "indicative facts" and "others".

In a medical context, if a prototype represents a disease, the resolutive facts would constitute the evidences or symptoms that confirm or refute the disease. Moreover, the indicative facts would suspect that it may have some similarities due to the symptoms and the results of the patients' tests. Finally the "others" group may contain special conditions imposed by experts in the field, and from their experiences, comments about the disease, etc. Another important detail of the prototype design would be the classification of symptoms or evidences that would be part of it, giving them a category of importance (this being a linguistic or numerical label), which will determine the degree of compliance with the prototype. That degree of compliance is evaluated by a function of affinity.

As shown in Fig. 2, by inputing a set of symptoms and tests results associated with a patient, the affinity function mission is to find the greatest similarity among the multiple prototypes defined. These contain input values: "known", "unknown" or "non-existent" of the different prototypes that represent the disease. The "known" one will create an assessment based on their affinity with each of the prototypes. The fact of lack of certain symptoms will also be treated in a favorable or unfavorable way in terms of affinity, and the "non-existent facts" would have a different treatment. With all this, affinity function maintains a

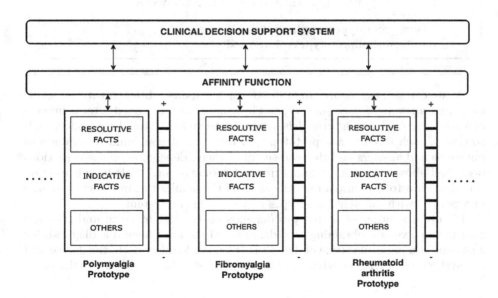

Fig. 2. Affinity function structure.

vector of the prototypes ordered by affinity. The basic structure of the algorithm used for quantification performed is shown below:

Algorithm 1. rate prototypes algorithm

```
def rate_ patterns (PatientAnswers) :
    similprototypesVector = getprototypeVector();
    for ( answer in PatientAnswers)do
        for ( prototype in similprototypesVector)do
            iterationValue = 0
            prototypeAnswerValue =
            prototype.getAnswer(userAnswer)
            if
            (prototypeAnswerValue.hasAnswer(userAnswer))then
                if
                (prototypeAnswerValue.isKnowed(userAnswer))then
                    iterationValue +=
                    prototypeAnswerValue.equals(answer)?
                        prototype.getPositiveValueOf(answer) :
                        prototype.getNegativeValueOf(answer)
                else
                    iterationValue +=
                    prototypeAnswerValue.isAsked(userAnswer) ?
                        getValueOfNotAskedAnswer() :
                        getValueOfNotValueKnowed()
            prototype.valoration += iterationValue
    sort_prototypes(similprototypesVector)
    return similprototypeVectorSorted
```

As we can see, the algorithm evaluates each response obtained with the questions and answers of each prototype. These have been obtained after a process of knowledge engineering in which, doctors intervened to build the conceptualization of each disease in a prototype. In this way, it was build a database of questions and answers and the assessment of them, depending on the conditions described above: "known", "unknown" and "nonexistent." This base is used by the algorithm to generate a quantification of the similarities in the clinical case of a patient with different prototypes registered in the system.

Finally, the order of prototypes depends on the weight given and they are returned in a vector, obtaining an ordered list of the most favorable diagnosis for a patient at a particular time of diagnosis. This would allow both, the doctor and the system, to determine what may be the next step in the patient evaluation.

4   System Evaluation

In this section, it is described first the basic workflow of a patient evaluation, then it is presented a complex clinic case for study, with details, about how the system behaves in a reasoning process. Later, it is shown a resume of all the evaluations carried out and their results.

4.1   Evaluation Workflow

The procedure followed by the CDSS in the process of reasoning correspond to the following flowchart (Fig. 3):

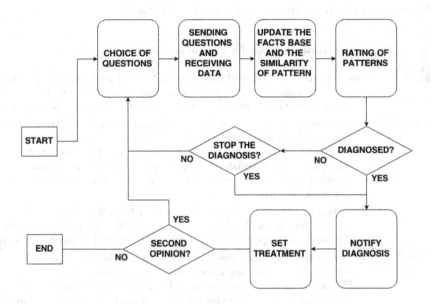

Fig. 3. CDSS Workflow.

As shown in the picture, the first step is the choice of questions to ask. On it, the system evaluates what questions choose to ask, for extract the key responses at each point of diagnosis. For example, if diagnosis is in a starting point, it shows the initial questions chosen to know to where guide the process. In later iterations the disease set is ordered by similarity for each patient and it is used to choose the questions to ask belonging to the prototype which has more similarity. This process also enable that the evaluation of the questions will be at the same time in all prototypes.

The structure of the questions in each prototype will follow the scheme explained above, being the most urgent symptoms assessed before the others. This is what the system uses at each iteration to choose the most appropriate questions in each case. Then the answers to the questions asked will be received and using these, a quantification of the similarity of input data with respect to the prototypes is performed. And finally prototypes are ordered by similarity.

If the patient has been diagnosed, the diagnosis is notified, and a treatment, depending on the symptoms reported, is established, giving the possibility to the doctor to make a second diagnosis. In the case that the patient has been sufficiently evaluated or the data are contradictory, this question is not performed and the system itself gives information about the most likely diagnosis.

4.2   A Complex Clinical Case

To illustrate in more detail the process undertaken by the core reasoning system, it will be exposed a real clinic case of a patient (Table 1):

Table 1. Complex clinical case overview

Patient	The patient is a 52 year-old resident in Ciudad Real (Spain) who has attended high frequency of primary care consultations, describing a symptom that could be framed within the scope of the system.
Clinical case	It is proposed an evaluation for the Clinical decision support system designed for a case with a number of symptoms such as skin affectations nonspecific, unspecific blood disorders (including leucopenia and lymphopenia), presence of debility proximal muscle (typical of patients with polymyalgia) and poor response to corticosteroids.
	With this symptomatic frame, it is wanted to perform a check for a positive diagnosis of Fibromyalgia, given the high proximity with Polymialgia, Hyporthyroidism, Polymyositis and Dermatomyositis
Results	The expected result is a positive diagnosis for Fibromyalgia and several alternative diagnosis: Polymyalgia Rheumatica, Hypothyroidism, Polymyositis or Dermatomyositis. As for the results obtained by the clinical decision support system, the main diagnostic is the same that the expert formulated. Among the alternatives, the system has determined, by order of similarity: Hypothyroidism, Dermatomyositis Polymyalgia Rheumatica

After the evaluation of the algorithm described (Algorithm 1), the system determines that the more viable prototype is Lupus. Not having detected a fact that ratifies or disproves the hypothesis, it asks a serie of data with which it continues working on this hypothesis. Then, it determines that Lupus can not be, because the symptoms fit more into a typical case of Rheumatoid Arthritis. Therefore, the similarity function has changed the order of prototype's vector because now there is a higher affinity with other prototype.

In a subsequent iteration, it detects that it could be a case of Hypothyroidism and it continues asking questions in order to carry on refining the order of the vector until suspecting the patient has Fibromyalgia. At that time, it evaluates the main facts, and as it is later the prototype with more similarity, it studies its indicative facts and later, its tangential facts. Finally, it determines that the prototype with more similarity with respect to the patient's clinical case corresponds with the Fibromyalgia prototype. That is when a new process begins to establish a treatment.

To finish, it recommends to closely monitor three diseases highly related, by the similarity of his symptoms in this clinic case: Hypothyroidism, Dermatomyositis Polymyalgia Rheumatica, in this order (Fig. 4).

Fig. 4. Diagnosis obtained by the system

4.3 Summary of Cases Evaluated

The verification of the results of the system was carried out by evaluating ten patients at the health center of Daimiel (Spain), through the supervision of Dr. Francisco Alonso Gomez. The patients have been diagnosed earlier and it has been proven that the medication chosen by the expert for the disease is the correct dose level that allow them to lead a relatively normal life. The summary of the assessment for patients was as follows (Table 2):

As it can be seen, it has reached a high degree of similarity between the medical diagnosis, verified by the expert, and the provided by the CDSS (about

Table 2. Cases evaluated

Case	Clinic case verified	CDSS diagnosis
1	**Rheumatoid Arthritis**	**Rheumatoid Arthritis**
2	**Dermatomyositis**	**Dermatomyositis**
3	**Polymyositis**	**Polymyositis**
4	**Hypothyroidism**	**Hypothyroidism**
5	**Lupus**	**Lupus**
6	**Polymyalgia Rheumatica**	**Polymyalgia Rheumatica**
7	C.C. between **Lupus** y Rheumatoid Arthritis (alt.)	**Rheumatoid Arthritis**, Alt: Dermatomyositis, Polymyalgia Rheumatica
8	C.C. of a patient who is expected to have Polymyalgia Rheumatica and their symptoms might be confused with Polymyositis and Dermatomiositis	**Polymyalgia Rheumatica**, Alt: Polymyositis, Dermatomyositis or A.Rheumatoid Arthritis
9	C.C. of **Hypothyroidism**. Due to the symptoms of this case, the diagnosis may be confused with Polymyositis or even with Fibromyalgia	**Hypothyroidism**, Polymyositis, Polymyalgia Rheumatica or Fibromyalgia
10	C.C. whose diagnosis could be Polymyalgia Rheumatica, Hypothyroidism, Polymyositis or Dermatomyositis	**Fibromyalgia**, Alt: Hypothyroidism, Polymyalgia Rheumatica, Dermatomyositis

98 %). The case of the patient 7 has been partially verified by the CDSS, as it has detected one of the two pathologies with greater similarity between the symptoms: Rheumatoid Arthritis.

However, it has not detected the possible presence of Lupus in the patient. Nevertheless, the reasoning followed was verified and accepted by the expert. Considering the recorded data in the time of diagnosis and tests conducted by the expert without help system, it can be determined that the CDSS has been a tool, in combination with the doctor, that has reduced the time of diagnosis, the number of consultations and the cost of testing for the healthcare institution.

5 Conclusions and Future Work

The main goal of this paper is to propose a CDSS as a powerful and essential tool for a doctor as a stethoscope and that it may be useful in the diagnostic and treatment of the fuzzy diseases. In this sense, it has been worked using several techniques of AI that have allowed to model each disease as a prototype for giving to diagnostic and treatment process a higher flexibility.

In this case, the system described aims to improve the healthcare assistance of the patients with difficult identifiable diseases, enhancing the standard of living of each one. Moreover, for healthcare institutions it supposes a save considerable cost, taking into account the figures provided in the introduction of this document.

Finally, with regard to future works, it is proposed several improvements related to perfect the system. Among others, it includes the extraction of conclusions of medical reports, written through a linguistic processing of unstructured text, in order to increase the independence of the system, in terms of patient data extraction. Moreover, it is proposed a generalization of the model defined, to built several interconnected CDSS allowing the diagnostic and treatment of diseases in multiples groups. This lets also an easy way for a disease definition, using the prototype concept.

References

1. Rosch, E.H.: Natural categories. Cogn. Psychol. **4**, 328–350 (1973)
2. Rosch, E.: Cognitive representation of semantic categories. J. Exp. Psychol. Gen. **104**(3), 192–233 (1975)
3. Zadeh, L.A.: A note on prototype set theory and fuzzy sets. Cognition **12**, 291–297 (1982)
4. HIMSS. 2013 annual report of the u.s. hospital it market. Technical report (2014)
5. Gómez, A., Juristo, N., Montes, C., Pazos, J.: Ingeniería del Conocimiento. Ed. Centro de Estudios Ramón Areces S.A., Madrid, España (1997)
6. Torres, L., Elorza, J.: Medicina del Dolor, 6th edn. Elsevier, España (1997)
7. Buse, J.W., Garcia-Gomez, M., Ebrahim, S., Connell, G., Coomes, E.A., Bruno, P., Malik, K., Torrance, D., Ngo, T., Kirmayr, K., Avrahami, D., Riva, J.J., Struijs, P., Brunarski, D., Burnie, S.J., LeBlanc, F., Steenstra, I.A., Mahood, Q., Thorlund, K., Montori, V.M., Sivarajah, V., Alexander, P., Jankowski, M., Lesniak, W., Faulhaber, M., Bała, M.M., Schandelmaier, S., Guyatt, G.H.: Systematic review and network meta-analysis of interventions for fibromyalgia: a protocol. Syst. Rev. J. **2** (2013)
8. de Miquel, C.A., Cmpayo, G.J., Flórez, M.T., Gómez Arguelles, J.M., Blanco Tarrio, E., Gobbo Montoya, M., Pérez Martin, Á., Martínez Salio, A., Vidal Fuentes, J., Altarriba Alberch, J., de la Cámara, A.G.: Interdisciplinary consensus document for the treatment of fibromyalgia. Actas Esp. Psiquiatr. **2**(38), 108–120 (2010)
9. Ameri, A., Moshtaghi, H.: Design and development of an expert system in differential diagnosis of maxillofacial radio-lucent lesions. In: IRCSE 2008: IDT Workshop on Interesting Results in Computer Science and Engineering. Mälardalen University. Västerås, Sweden, October 2008
10. Douali, N., Roo, J.D., Papageorgiou, E.I., Jaulent, M.-C.: Case based fuzzy cognitive maps (cbfcm): new method for medical reasoning. In: IEEE International Conference on Fuzzy Systems (2011)
11. Maseleno, A., Hasan, M.M.: Skin infection detection using dempster-shafer theory. In: 2012 International Conference on Informatics, Electronics Vision (ICIEV), pp. 1147–1151, May 2012
12. Cunninghamb, I., Fishera, A., Lakea, S., Chandnab, A.: Web-strabnet: a web-based expert system for the differential diagnosis of vertical strabismus (squint). Comput. Math. Methods Med. **11**(1), 89–97 (2010)

13. Pancerz, K., Gomula, J., Szkola, J.: Copernicus - an expert system supporting differential diagnosis of patients examined using the mmpi test - an index-rule approach. In: HEALTHINF, pp. 323–328 (2011)
14. Gomula, J., Pancerz, K., Szkola, J.: Computer-aided diagnosis of patients with mental disorders using the copernicus system. In: 2011 4th International Conference on Human System Interactions (HSI), pp. 274–280, May 2011
15. Vicente, J., Garcia-Gomez, J.M., Vidal, C., Marti-Bonmati, L., del Arco, A., Robles, M.: SOC: a distributed decision support architecture for clinical diagnosis. In: Barreiro, J.M., Martín-Sánchez, F., Maojo, V., Sanz, F. (eds.) ISBMDA 2004. LNCS, vol. 3337, pp. 96–104. Springer, Heidelberg (2004)
16. Cucu, R., Avram, C., Astilean, A., Farcas, I.-G., Machado, J.: E-health decision support system for differential diagnosis. In: 2014 IEEE International Conference on Automation, Quality and Testing, Robotics, pp. 1–6 (2014)
17. Bremermann, H.J.: Pattern recognition. In: Systems Theory in the Social Sciences, pp. 116–159 (1976)
18. Armstrong, S.L., Gleitman, L.R., Gleitman, H.: What some concepts might not be. Cognition 13, 363–308 (1983)

Public and Secret Forgetting of Propositional Formulas

Ángel Nepomuceno-Fernández, Enrique Sarrión-Morrillo,
Fernando Soler-Toscano[✉], and Fernando R. Velázquez-Quesada

Group of Logic, Language and Information, University of Seville, Seville, Spain
{nepomuce,esarrion,fsoler,FRVelazquezQuesada}@us.es

Abstract. This paper presents two operations over Kripke models for representing the act of an agent forgetting the truth-value of a given propositional formula. The first is a form of 'public' forgetting (built over previous monoagent proposals) after which all agents know that the forgetful one has indeed forgotten the given formula; the second is a form of 'secret' forgetting after which the forgetful agent knows what has happened but the rest of them remain oblivious of the action.

Keywords: Public forgetting · Secret forgetting · Epistemic logic · Dynamic epistemic logic · Knowledge representation · Multi-agent system

1 Introduction

Epistemic notions, such as knowledge and belief, are subject to the effect of different epistemic actions, many of which have been studied in the literature [1–3]. However, the epistemic action of *knowledge forgetting* has not received much attention.[1] A possible reason is its similarities with *belief contraction*, an action that, semantically, relies on a plausibility ordering that defines beliefs as the most plausible situations, and thus provides an ordering among what is not believed but has not been discarded. However, such ordering is not natural when dealing with knowledge: there does not seem to be an ordering among the epistemic possibilities that are known *not* to be the case.

This paper presents a logical treatment under possible worlds semantics of the action of *forgetting whether*, understood here as forgetting the formula's truth-value.[2] This work extends the forgetting of (sets of) atomic propositions of [8] to propositional formulas, and the forgetting of propositional formulas in single agent settings of [9] to multi-agent scenarios (i.e., public and secret versions of the action). Additionally, the present approach produces smaller epistemic models and adheres tighter to the original epistemic state of the involved agents.

---

[1] Still, some approaches in the *knowledge representation* area deal with the forgetting of sets of atomic propositions in single-agent scenarios (e.g., [4,5]).

[2] Thus, this action is unrelated to others that involve, e.g., changes in awareness [6,7].

© Springer International Publishing Switzerland 2015
J.M. Puerta et al. (Eds.): CAEPIA 2015, LNAI 9422, pp. 139–149, 2015.
DOI: 10.1007/978-3-319-24598-0_13

2 Basic Definitions

Throughout this text, *At* denotes a designated countable non-empty set of atoms (propositional variables) and *Ag* a countable non-empty set of agents.

Definition 1 (Language $\mathcal{L}_\Box^{Ag}$). *The grammar of $\mathcal{L}_\Box^{Ag}$ is given by*

$$\varphi ::= \top \mid p \mid \neg\varphi \mid \varphi \wedge \varphi \mid \Box_i\varphi$$

with $p \in At$ and $i \in Ag$. Formulas of the form $\Box_i\varphi$ are read as "agent i knows that φ is the case". The symbols $\bot$, $\vee$, $\rightarrow$, $\leftrightarrow$ and $\Diamond_i$ are defined as usual.

Formulas of $\mathcal{L}_\Box^{Ag}$, the basic multi-agent epistemic language, are interpreted in *Kripke (possible worlds)* models, as described below.

Definition 2 (Multi-agent Model). *A multi-agent Kripke frame (or, simply, a frame) is a tuple $\langle W, R \rangle$ where W is a non-empty set of possible worlds and $R : Ag \rightarrow \wp(W \times W)$ a function that assigns a binary relation over W to each agent $i \in Ag$ (R_i is agent i's accessibility relation). A multi-agent Kripke model (or, simply, a model) is a frame equipped with an atomic valuation $V : At \rightarrow \wp(W)$. A pointed multi-agent model is a pair $(\mathcal{M}, w)$ with $\mathcal{M}$ a model and w a world in it (the evaluation point).*

Definition 3 (Satisfaction for $\mathcal{L}_\Box^{Ag}$). *Let $\mathcal{M} = \langle W, R, V \rangle$ be a model. The relation $\models$ between pointed models and formulas in $\mathcal{L}_\Box^{Ag}$ is defined as follows.*

$$
\begin{aligned}
\mathcal{M}, w &\models p & &\text{iff} & &w \in V(p) \\
\mathcal{M}, w &\models \neg\varphi & &\text{iff} & &\mathcal{M}, w \not\models \varphi \\
\mathcal{M}, w &\models \varphi \wedge \psi & &\text{iff} & &\mathcal{M}, w \models \varphi \text{ and } \mathcal{M}, w \models \psi \\
\mathcal{M}, w &\models \Box_i\varphi & &\text{iff} & &\text{for all } u \in W, R_i wu \text{ implies } \mathcal{M}, u \models \varphi
\end{aligned}
$$

As usual, $\mathcal{M} \models \varphi$ states that $\mathcal{M}, w \models \varphi$ for all worlds w in $\mathcal{M}$. If X is a class of models, $\mathsf{X} \models \varphi$ states that $\mathcal{M} \models \varphi$ for all $\mathcal{M} \in \mathsf{X}$. The formula φ is valid when $\mathcal{M} \models \varphi$ for every model $\mathcal{M}$, a case denoted by $\models \varphi$.

As the definition of the model shows, no assumption is made about the accessibility relations; thus, the structures might be understood as representing not the agents' knowledge but rather their beliefs. This work uses the first interpretation because, as the semantic interpretation states, $\Box_i\varphi$ holds when φ is the case in all the agent's epistemic possibilities, a definition that follows the spirit of "knowledge" (*"I know φ when it holds in all the situations I consider possible"*) instead of that of beliefs (*"I believe φ when it holds in the most plausible situations among those I consider possible"*).

Recall the following known result for the language $\mathcal{L}_\Box^{Ag}$.

Proposition 1. *Let $\mathcal{M}, \mathcal{M}'$ be two models with $\mathcal{M} = \langle W, R, V \rangle$ and $\mathcal{M}' = \langle W', R', V' \rangle$. If $(\mathcal{M}, w)$ and $(\mathcal{M}', w')$ are At^*-bisimilar (see Sect. 2.2 of [10]) then, for every formula $\varphi \in \mathcal{L}_\Box^{Ag}$ whose atoms appear all in At^*, $(\mathcal{M}, w) \models \varphi$ if and only if $(\mathcal{M}', w') \models \varphi$.*

The following definition will be useful.

Definition 4 (Clausal Form). *If π is a propositional formula, then π's clausal form $\mathcal{C}(\pi)$ (i.e., its minimal conjunctive normal form) is defined as the set of all clauses (set of literals interpreted disjunctively) that are minimal non-tautological consequences of π.*

Note how $\mathcal{C}(\pi)$ is the set of π's prime implicates [11]. Such set, which can be generated by several algorithms (e.g., [11–14]; see [15] for more), has been already used for epistemic concerns, mainly on proposals following the *AGM* approach for belief revision [1] in which the agent's beliefs are represented syntactically (e.g., [16,17]).

3 Public Forgetting

Definition 5 (Language $\mathcal{L}_{\Box\ddagger^P}^{Ag}$). *The language $\mathcal{L}_{\Box\ddagger^P}^{Ag}$ extends $\mathcal{L}_{\Box}^{Ag}$ with expressions of the form $[\ddagger_a^P \pi]\varphi$ with π a propositional formula and $a \in Ag$ an agent, read as "after agent a publicly forgets whether π, φ is the case". Expressions of the form $\langle\ddagger_a^P \pi\rangle\varphi$ are defined in the standard way (as $\neg[\ddagger_a^P \pi]\neg\varphi$).*

For the semantic interpretation of the new formulas, note how $\Box_a\varphi$ is the case when φ holds in all agent a's epistemic alternatives. Then, in order for her to forget the truth-value of a given *contingent* propositional formula π (so she does not know that it holds but also she does not know that it fails), she needs to consider as possible not only (at least) one situation where π fails, but also (at least) one situation in which $\neg\pi$ fails (and thus π holds). First, note how, given a possible world, there are several ways to falsify a given formula π. If its clausal form $\mathcal{C}(\pi) = \{D_1, \ldots, D_n\}$ is used, then it is clear than in order to make π false at some world, at least one clause in $\mathcal{C}(\pi)$ should be false in it; thus, there are $2^n - 1$ different forms of falsifying π. However, falsifying an arbitrary non-empty collection of clauses is problematic, both because of the combinatorial explosion and because the negations of different clauses might be mutually inconsistent. In fact, the *minimal* change approach suggest that, in order to falsify π, it is enough to falsify only one of its clauses.

The 'forgetting' operation defined in this section creates one copy of the original model: if the original world makes π true, then the copy falsifies a fixed clause of $\mathcal{C}(\pi)$, but if the original world makes π false, then the copy falsifies a fixed clause of $\mathcal{C}(\neg\pi)$.

Definition 6 (Public Forgetting). *Let $\mathcal{M} = \langle W, R, V\rangle$ be a model, $a \in Ag$ be an agent, π a propositional formula, and D_1, D_2 two finite non-tautological clauses.*

The model $\mathcal{M}_{a,\pi}^P\binom{D_1}{D_2} = \langle W', R', V'\rangle$ is such that (1) $W' := W \times \{0,1\}$; (2) $R_a' := \{((w,i),(u,j)) \in W' \mid R_a wu \text{ and } i,j \in \{0,1\}\}$ and, for every agent $b \in Ag$ with $b \neq a$, $R_b' := \{((w,i),(u,i)) \in W' \mid R_b wu \text{ and } i \in \{0,1\}\}$; (3) for every $p \in At$ and $w \in W$, (3.1) $(w,0) \in V'(p)$ if and only if $w \in V(p)$, and (3.2) $(w,1) \in V'(p)$ if and only if at least one of the following holds: (3.2.1) $w \in V(p)$ and $\mathcal{M},w \models \pi$ and $p \notin D_1$, or (3.2.2) $w \in V(p)$ and

$\mathcal{M}, w \models \neg\pi$ and $p \notin D_2$, or **(3.2.3)** $\mathcal{M}, w \models \pi$ and $\neg p \in D_1$, or **(3.2.4)** $\mathcal{M}, w \models \neg\pi$ and $\neg p \in D_2$.

The operation produces a model $\mathcal{M}^P_{a,\pi}\binom{D_1}{D_2}$ whose domain has two types of worlds. Worlds of the form $(w, 0)$ (the 'area 0') preserve the original valuation: an atom p is true on $(w, 0)$ if and only if p was already true on w. On the other hand, in those of the form $(w, 1)$ (the 'area 1') all literals in either D_1 or else D_2 have been falsified, according to whether π holds or not in w. For the accessibility relations, that of the forgetful agent a is extended in an uniform way, making a world (u, j) accessible from a world (w, i) when u is accessible from w in the original model. For the rest of the agents, their respective relation is as the original within each copy, but no arrow goes from one area to the other.

Definition 7 (Satisfaction for $\mathcal{L}^{Ag}_{\Box \ddagger P}$). *Let $\mathcal{M} = \langle W, R, V \rangle$ be a model and w a world of W. Definition 3 is extended to formulas in $\mathcal{L}^{Ag}_{\Box \ddagger P}$ with*

$$\mathcal{M}, w \models [\ddagger^P_a \pi]\varphi \quad iff \quad \mathcal{M}^P_{a,\pi}\binom{D_1}{D_2}, (w, 0) \models \varphi \text{ for all } D_1 \in \mathcal{C}(\pi), D_2 \in \mathcal{C}(\neg\pi)$$

Thus, φ is the case after agent a publicly forgets the truth-value of π, $[\ddagger^P_a \pi]\varphi$, when φ holds independently of the clauses D_1 and D_2 that are chosen to falsify π and $\neg\pi$ (respectively) in the added worlds.

4   The Effect of Publicly Forgetting Whether π

The model $\mathcal{M}^P_{a,\pi}\binom{D_1}{D_2}$ is the result of agent a publicly considering new possibilities. If π was true at a given w, then π is false at $(w, 1)$, but if π was false at w, it is now true at $(w, 1)$. This is done by falsifying in $(w, 1)$ all literals in either D_1 (if π was true at w) or else in D_2 (otherwise). In each case, atoms not occurring in the clause keep their original truth-value. Thus,

Lemma 1. *Let $\mathcal{M} = \langle W, R, V \rangle$ be a model and π a propositional formula that is neither a tautology nor a contradiction (so both $\mathcal{C}(\pi)$ and $\mathcal{C}(\neg\pi)$ are non-empty sets of contingent clauses), with $D_1 \in \mathcal{C}(\pi)$ and $D_2 \in \mathcal{C}(\neg\pi)$, and a forgetful agent a. Then, for any $w \in W$,*

$$\mathcal{M}^P_{a,\pi}\binom{D_1}{D_2}, (w, 0) \models \pi \quad iff \quad \mathcal{M}, w \models \pi \tag{1}$$

$$\mathcal{M}^P_{a,\pi}\binom{D_1}{D_2}, (w, 1) \not\models \pi \quad iff \quad \mathcal{M}, w \models \pi. \tag{2}$$

Proof. By Definition 6, $(w, 0)$ and w satisfy exactly the same atoms, so (1) is immediate. For (2), suppose $\mathcal{M}, w \models \pi$; then the truth-value of every literal in D_1 has been falsified in $(w, 1)$. Hence, $\mathcal{M}^P_{a,\pi}\binom{D_1}{D_2}, (w, 1) \not\models \bigvee D_1$ and therefore $\mathcal{M}^P_{a,\pi}\binom{D_1}{D_2}, (w, 1) \not\models \pi$. On the other hand, when $\mathcal{M}, w \not\models \pi$, all literals in D_2 are falsified, so $\mathcal{M}^P_{a,\pi}\binom{D_1}{D_2}, (w, 1) \not\models \bigvee D_2$ and then $\mathcal{M}^P_{a,\pi}\binom{D_1}{D_2}, (w, 1) \not\models \neg\pi$ so $\mathcal{M}^P_{a,\pi}\binom{D_1}{D_2}, (w, 1) \models \pi$.

Example 1. Consider the following pointed model $(\mathcal{M}, w_0)$ in which both agents a and b know p (i.e., $\mathcal{M}, w_0 \models \Box_a p \wedge \Box_b p$):

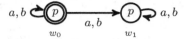

Consider the action of agent a forgetting whether p. Given that $\mathcal{C}(p) = \{\{p\}\}$, there is only one clause to be chosen: $\{p\}$. Similarly, $\mathcal{C}(\neg p) = \{\{\neg p\}\}$, so the only clauses that can be considered for a to forget whether p are $D_1 = \{p\}$ and $D_2 = \{\neg p\}$. The pointed model $(\mathcal{M}_{a,\pi}^P\binom{\{p\}}{\{\neg p\}}), (w_0, 0))$ appears below, with the bottom row being the copy in which each world switches π's truth-value:

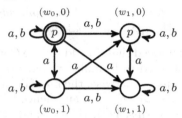

As a result of the action, from $(w_0, 1)$ agent a considers possible worlds where p holds as well as worlds where p fails. Thus, $\mathcal{M}_{a,\pi}^P\binom{D_1}{D_2}, (w_0, 0) \models \neg\Box_a p \wedge \neg\Box_a \neg p$ and hence $\mathcal{M}, w_0 \models \Box_a p \wedge [\ddagger_a^P p](\neg\Box_a p \wedge \neg\Box_a \neg p)$. With respect to agent b, from $(w_0, 1)$ she considers possible only worlds where p holds; thus, $\mathcal{M}_{a,\pi}^P\binom{D_1}{D_2}, (w_0, 0) \models \Box_b p$ and hence $\mathcal{M}, w_0 \models \Box_b p \wedge [\ddagger_a^P p]\Box_b p$. However, while at $(\mathcal{M}, w)$ agent b knew a knew p, $\mathcal{M}, w_0 \models \Box_b \Box_a p$, at $(\mathcal{M}_{a,\pi}^P\binom{D_1}{D_2}), (w_0, 0))$ agent b knows that a does not know whether p, $\mathcal{M}_{a,\pi}^P\binom{D_1}{D_2}, (w_0, 0) \models \Box_b(\neg\Box_a p \wedge \neg\Box_a \neg p)$.

In the previous example, note how, if w_1 did not have reflexive arrows and it were the evaluation point in $\mathcal{M}$ (and hence $(w_1, 0)$ the evaluation point at the model after the operation), then the agent would know p before the action (by vacuity), but she would still know p afterwards (by vacuity too). The following proposition shows that this counterintuitive outcome of the 'forgetting whether' action can only occur when the knowledge of the agent is inconsistent.

Proposition 2. *Let π be a propositional formula that is neither a tautology nor a contradiction. Then, $\models [\ddagger_a^P \pi](\Box_a \neg \pi \vee \Box_a \pi) \leftrightarrow \Box_a \bot$.*

Proof. Let $\mathcal{M} = \langle W, R, V \rangle$ be a model. From right to left, if $\mathcal{M}, w \models \Box_a \bot$ then there is no u such that $R_a w u$ so, by Definition 6, there is no (u, i) such that $R'_a(w, 0)(u, i)$ (regardless of the clauses used); hence, $\mathcal{M}_{a,\pi}^P\binom{D_1}{D_2}, (w, 0) \models \Box_a \neg \pi \vee \Box_a \pi$ and therefore $\mathcal{M}, w \models [\ddagger_a^P \pi](\Box_a \neg \pi \vee \Box_a \pi) \leftrightarrow \Box_a \bot$.

From left to right, suppose $\mathcal{M}, w \models \neg\Box_a \bot$; then there is $u \in W$ such that $R_a w u$ and therefore, independently of the chosen clauses D_1 and D_2, there are $(u, 0)$ and $(u, 1)$ in W' such that $R'_a(w, 0)(u, 0)$ and $R'_a(w, 0)(u, 1)$. By Lemma 1, $(u, 0)$ and $(u, 1)$ assign opposite truth-values to π, so $\mathcal{M}_{a,\pi}^P\binom{D_1}{D_2}, (w, 0) \models \Diamond_a \neg\pi \wedge$

$\Diamond_a \pi$, that is, $\mathcal{M}^P_{a,\pi}\binom{D_1}{D_2}, (w, 0) \models \neg(\Box_a \pi \vee \Box_a \neg \pi)$. But π is neither a tautology nor a contradiction, so both $\mathcal{C}(\pi)$ and $\mathcal{C}(\neg \pi)$ are non-empty sets of contingent clauses and therefore $\mathcal{M}, w \models \langle \ddagger^P_a \pi \rangle \neg(\Box_a \pi \vee \Box_a \neg \pi)$, that is, $\mathcal{M}, w \not\models [\ddagger^P_a \pi](\Box_a \pi \vee \Box_a \neg \pi)$.

As a particular case, if π is an atom p, then $\mathcal{C}(p) = \{\{p\}\}$ is non-empty and contains only contingent clauses, so $[\ddagger^P_a p](\Box_a p \vee \Box_a \neg p) \leftrightarrow \Box_a \bot$ is valid. More interestingly, recall that an agent's knowledge is consistent at w if and only if w has at least one accessible world. Thus, in the class of models where this consistency property holds, called *serial* and denoted by Ser, the forgetting action achieves its intended result.

Corollary 1. *For any non-tautological and non-contradictory propositional formula* π, Ser $\models \langle \ddagger^P_a \pi \rangle \top \wedge [\ddagger^P_a \pi](\neg \Box_a \pi \wedge \neg \Box_a \neg \pi)$.

The reader might have noticed that, in addition to Corollary 1, both Lemma 1 and Proposition 2 are restricted to formulas π that are neither tautologies nor contradictions. This is because, otherwise, the proof does not go through: in such cases, either $\mathcal{C}(\pi) = \varnothing$ or else $\mathcal{C}(\neg \pi) = \varnothing$, and hence there are no clauses to be applied. As a consequence of this, both $[\ddagger^P_a \top]\varphi$ and $[\ddagger^P_a \bot]\varphi$ are valid for any formula φ. Nevertheless, neither $\langle \ddagger^P_a \top \rangle \top$ nor $\langle \ddagger^P_a \bot \rangle \top$ are satisfiable.

On Minimality. The following proposition shows how the forgetting operation is indeed minimal with respect to the changes in the agents' knowledge, as it does not affect the truth-value of formulas not sharing atoms with the forgotten one.

Proposition 3. *Let* π *be a propositional formula that is neither a tautology nor a contradiction (so* $\mathcal{C}(\pi)$ *and* $\mathcal{C}(\neg \pi)$ *are non-empty sets of contingent clauses). Then, for every agent* a *and every formula* $\varphi \in \mathcal{L}^{Ag}_\Box$ *whose atoms do not appear in literals of* $\bigcup \mathcal{C}(\pi)^3$, $\models \varphi \leftrightarrow [\ddagger^P_a \pi]\varphi$.

Proof. The proof uses a bisimulation argument. First, take any model $\mathcal{M} = \langle W, R, V \rangle$. Take any $D_1 \in \mathcal{C}(\pi)$ and any $D_2 \in \mathcal{C}(\neg \pi)$ with π be a contingent propositional formula, and let At_π be the set of atoms in literals of $\bigcup \mathcal{C}(\pi)$. Given Definition 6, the relation Z between the domains of $\mathcal{M}$ and $\mathcal{M}^P_{a,\pi}\binom{D_1}{D_2}$ defined as

$$Z := \{(u, (u, k)) \in (W \times W') \mid u \in W \text{ and } k \in \{0, 1\}\}$$

is a $(At \setminus At_\pi)$-bisimulation. Hence, for every formula $\varphi \in \mathcal{L}^{Ag}_\Box$ whose atoms do not appear in At_π and every $u \in W$, $\mathcal{M}, u \models \varphi$ iff $\mathcal{M}^P_{a,\pi}\binom{D_1}{D_2}, (u, k) \models \varphi$. The actual proof is straightforward, as for any pointed model $(\mathcal{M}, w)$ the pair $(w, (w, 0))$ is in the $(At \setminus At_\pi)$-bisimulation.

In particular, the change in the knowledge of the forgetful agent is minimal, as if φ does not contain atoms in $\bigcup \mathcal{C}(\pi)$, then $\models \Box_a \varphi \leftrightarrow [\ddagger^P_a \pi]\Box_a \varphi$.

---

[3] Trivially, the atoms in literals of $\bigcup \mathcal{C}(\pi)$ are the same as in $\bigcup \mathcal{C}(\neg \pi)$, hence the same as in $\bigcup \mathcal{C}(\pi) \cup \bigcup \mathcal{C}(\neg \pi)$ too.

Example 2. Consider the following pointed single-agent model.

Observe how the agent knows neither $p \wedge q$ (she considers w_1 possible) nor $\neg(p \wedge q)$ (she considers w_0 possible). Again, there are two possible outcomes for an action of forgetting whether the already 'unknown' $p \wedge q$ is the case:

$\mathcal{M}'$ (choosing $\{p\}$ and $\{\neg p, \neg q\}$) $\mathcal{M}''$ (choosing $\{q\}$ and $\{\neg p, \neg q\}$)

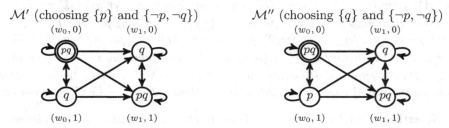

In both pointed models, $\mathcal{M}'$ and $\mathcal{M}''$ respectively, the agent still knows neither $p \wedge q$ nor $\neg(p \wedge q)$. However, in both cases the action has affected her information. In the leftmost pointed model $(\mathcal{M}', (w_0, 0))$ she considers possible a $\neg p \wedge q$-world, $(w_1, 0)$, from which there is an accessible $p \wedge q$-world, $(w_1, 1)$ (that is, $\mathcal{M}', (w_0, 0) \models \Diamond(\neg p \wedge q \wedge \Diamond(p \wedge q)))$, something that did not happen at $(\mathcal{M}, w_0)$ (that is, $\mathcal{M}, w_0 \not\models \Diamond(\neg p \wedge q \wedge \Diamond(p \wedge q)))$. In the rightmost pointed model $(\mathcal{M}'', (w, 0))$ she considers possible a $p \wedge \neg q$-world, $(w_0, 1)$ (that is, $\mathcal{M}'', (w_0, 0) \models \Diamond(p \wedge \neg q))$, something that did not happen at $(\mathcal{M}, w_0)$ (that is, $\mathcal{M}, w_0 \not\models \Diamond(p \wedge \neg q))$. Thus, forgetting whether is the case a formula whose truth-value is not known to begin with can affect the agent's information by giving her 'new reasons' to not know the formula's truth-value. Also, observe that in $\mathcal{M}'$ the agent still knows q but not in $\mathcal{M}''$, so difference choices of clauses produce different effects.

Proposition 3 shows that the forgetting operation does not affect the truth-value of formulas not involving atoms in the clausal form of the one forgotten one. The following result goes one step beyond, showing how the *propositional* knowledge of agents other than the forgetful remains unaffected too.

Proposition 4. *If π is a propositional formula that is neither a tautology nor a contradiction and b an agent different from a then, for every propositional formula π' (including π), $\models \Box_b \pi' \leftrightarrow [\ddagger_a^P \pi] \Box_b \pi'$.*

Proof. The core of the proof are two facts of the new model: the atomic valuation of the area 0 is as in the original model, and the accessibility relation of agents other than a does not go from one area to the other. Formally, let $(\mathcal{M}, w)$ be a pointed model with $\mathcal{M} = \langle W, R, V \rangle$. Let π be a propositional formula; let b an agent different from a.

Observe first how, from the definition of the valuation V' in $\mathcal{M}_{a,\pi}^P \binom{D_1}{D_2}$ for any $D_1 \in \mathcal{C}(\pi)$ and $D_2 \in \mathcal{C}(\neg\pi)$, worlds $v \in W$ and $(v, 0) \in W'$ have the same atomic valuation; hence, for every propositional formula π',

$$\mathcal{M}, v \models \pi' \quad \text{iff} \quad \mathcal{M}_{a,\pi}^P \binom{D_1}{D_2}, (v, 0) \models \pi'$$

For the proof, from left to right, suppose $\mathcal{M}, w \models \Box_b \pi'$; *then, for every* $u \in W$, $R_b w u$ *implies* $(\mathcal{M}, u) \models \pi'$. *Consider now the set of all* R_b'-*successors of* $(w, 0)$ *in a model* $\mathcal{M}_{a,\pi}^P \binom{D_1}{D_2}$ *for arbitrary* $D_1 \in \mathcal{C}(\pi)$ *and* $D_2 \in \mathcal{C}(\neg \pi)$; *from the definition of* R_b', *the set is given by* $\{(u, 0) \in W' \mid R_b w u\}$. *Thus, if* $(u, 0)$ *is in such set, then* $R_b w u$ *and hence* $\mathcal{M}, u \models \pi'$ *so, by the initial observation,* $\mathcal{M}_{a,\pi}^P \binom{D_1}{D_2}, (u, 0) \models \pi'$. *Since* $(u, 0)$ *is an arbitrary* R_b'-*successor of* $(w, 0)$, $\mathcal{M}_{a,\pi}^P \binom{D_1}{D_2}, (w, 0) \models \Box_b \pi'$; *since* D_1 *and* D_2 *are arbitrary,* $\mathcal{M}, w \models [\ddagger_a^P \pi] \Box_b \pi'$.

From right to left, suppose $\mathcal{M}, w \models [\ddagger_a^P \pi] \Box_b \pi'$. *Then, for any* $D_1 \in \mathcal{C}(\pi)$ *and* $D_2 \in \mathcal{C}(\neg \pi)$, $\mathcal{M}_{a,\pi}^P \binom{D_1}{D_2}, (w, 0) \models \Box_b \pi'$ *and therefore, for every* $(u, k) \in W'$, *if* $R_b'(w, 0)(u, k)$ *then* $\mathcal{M}_{a,\pi}^P \binom{D_1}{D_2}, (u, k) \models \pi'$. *Now take any* $u \in W$ *such that* $R_b w u$. *By its definition,* $R_b'(w, 0)(u, 0)$ *and therefore* $\mathcal{M}_{a,\pi}^P \binom{D_1}{D_2}, (u, 0) \models \pi'$. *But then, by the initial observation,* $\mathcal{M}, u \models \pi'$. *Hence,* $\mathcal{M}, w \models \Box_b \pi'$, *as required.*

Nevertheless, under the reasonable assumption of consistency, the epistemic knowledge of all the agents (including the forgetful one) change.

Proposition 5. *If* π *is a propositional formula that is neither a tautology nor a contradiction, and* $i \in Ag$, *then* $\mathsf{Ser} \models [\ddagger_a^P \pi] \Box_i (\neg \Box_a \pi \wedge \neg \Box_a \neg \pi)$.

Proof. The key observation is that, while the worlds in the original model and those of in the area 0 are propositionally equivalent (initial observation in proof of Proposition 4), they are not modally equivalent, as in the new model such worlds have accessibility arrows for the forgetful agent a. Formally, let $\mathcal{M}, w$ be a pointed model with $\mathcal{M} = \langle W, R, V \rangle$; let π be a propositional formula and take arbitrary $D_1 \in \mathcal{C}(\pi)$ and $D_2 \in \mathcal{C}(\neg \pi)$.

For agents b other than a, consider the set of all R_b'-successors of $(w, 0)$ in $\mathcal{M}_{a,\pi}^P \binom{D_1}{D_2}$; from the definition of R_b', this set is given by $\{(u, 0) \in W' \mid R_b w u\}$. Now take any element $(u, 0)$ in such set and focus on its first component u. Since $\mathcal{M}$ is serial, there is $v \in W$ such that $R_a u v$; from this and the definition of R_a' it follows that both $(v, 0)$ and $(v, 1)$ are R_a'-successors of $(u, 0)$. If $\mathcal{M}, v \models \pi$ then $\mathcal{M}_{a,\pi}^P \binom{D_1}{D_2}, (v, 0) \models \pi$ and $\mathcal{M}_{a,\pi}^P \binom{D_1}{D_2}, (v, 1) \models \neg \pi$ *(Lemma 1)*; otherwise, $\mathcal{M}, v \models \neg \pi$ so $\mathcal{M}_{a,\pi}^P \binom{D_1}{D_2}, (v, 0) \models \neg \pi$ and $\mathcal{M}_{a,\pi}^P \binom{D_1}{D_2}, (v, 1) \models \pi$ *(Lemma 1 again)*. In both cases $\mathcal{M}_{a,\pi}^P \binom{D_1}{D_2}, (u, 0) \models \Diamond_a \pi \wedge \Diamond_a \neg \pi$, and thus $\mathcal{M}_{a,\pi}^P \binom{D_1}{D_2}, (u, 0) \models \neg \Box_a \pi \wedge \neg \Box_a \neg \pi$. Since $(u, 0)$ is an arbitrary R_b'-successor of $(w, 0)$, then $\mathcal{M}_{a,\pi}^P \binom{D_1}{D_2}, (w, 0) \models \Box_b (\neg \Box_a \pi \wedge \neg \Box_a \neg \pi)$; since D_1 and D_2 are arbitrary, $\mathcal{M}, w \models [\ddagger_a^P \pi] \Box_b (\neg \Box_a \pi \wedge \neg \Box_a \neg \pi)$.

For agent a, the set of R_a'-successors of $(w, 0)$ in $\mathcal{M}_{a,\pi}^P \binom{D_1}{D_2}$ has more elements, as it is given by $\{(u, k) \in W' \mid R_b w u \wedge k \in \{0, 1\}\}$. Nevertheless, the extra elements also satisfy the property as, again by the seriality of M, every $(u, 1)$ in such set can reach, via R_a', both a world satisfying π and another satisfying $\neg \pi$. Thus, $\mathcal{M}_{a,\pi}^P \binom{D_1}{D_2}, (u, 1) \models \neg \Box_a \pi \wedge \neg \Box_a \neg \pi$, and therefore $\mathcal{M}, w \models [\ddagger_a^P \pi] \Box_a (\neg \Box_a \pi \wedge \neg \Box_a \neg \pi)$.

5   Secret Forgetting

Definition 8 (Language $\mathcal{L}^{Ag}_{\Box\ddagger s}$). *The language $\mathcal{L}^{Ag}_{\Box\ddagger s}$ extends $\mathcal{L}^{Ag}_{\Box}$ with expressions of the form $[\ddagger^S_a \pi]\varphi$ with π a propositional formula and $a \in Ag$ an agent, read as "after agent a secretly forgets whether π, φ is the case". Expressions of the form $\langle\ddagger^S_a \pi\rangle\varphi$ are defined in the standard way (as $\neg[\ddagger^S_a \pi]\neg\varphi$).*

Definition 9 (Secret Forgetting). *Let $\mathcal{M} = \langle W, R, V\rangle$ be a model, $a \in Ag$ be an agent, π a propositional formula, and D_1, D_2 finite non-tautological clauses.*
    The model $\mathcal{M}^S_{a,\pi}\binom{D_1}{D_2} = \langle W', R', V'\rangle$ is such that (1) $W' := W \times \{0,1,2\}$; (2) the relation R'_a is the union of $\{((w,i),(u,j)) \in W' \mid R_a wu,\ i,j \in \{0,1\}\}$ and $\{((w,2),(u,2)) \in W' \mid R_a wu\}$ and, for every agent $b \in Ag$ with $b \neq a$, the relation R'_b is $\{((w,i),(u,2)) \in W' \mid R_b wu$ and $i \in \{0,1,2\}\}$; (3) for every $p \in At$ and $w \in W$, (3.1) $(w,k) \in V'(p)$, with $k \in \{0,2\}$, if and only if $w \in V(p)$, and (3.2) $(w,1) \in V'(p)$ if and only if at least one of the following holds: (3.2.1) $w \in V(p)$ and $\mathcal{M}, w \models \pi$ and $p \notin D_1$, or $w \in V(p)$ and $\mathcal{M}, w \models \neg\pi$ and $p \notin D_2$, or (3.2.2) $\mathcal{M}, w \models \pi$ and $\neg p \in D_1$, or (3.2.3) $\mathcal{M}, w \models \neg\pi$ and $\neg p \in D_2$.

The domain in $\mathcal{M}^S_{a,\pi}\binom{D_1}{D_2}$ has three types of worlds. Those of the form $(w,0)$ and $(w,2)$ preserve the original valuation; in those of the form $(w,1)$ all literals in either D_1 or else D_2 have been falsified, according to whether π holds or not in w (just as in $\mathcal{M}^P_{a,\pi}\binom{D_1}{D_2}$). With respect to accessibility, areas 0 and 1 are only visible for agent a; the rest of the agents can only conceive worlds in area 2.

Definition 10 (Satisfaction for $\mathcal{L}^{Ag}_{\Box\ddagger s}$). *Let $\mathcal{M} = \langle W, R, V\rangle$ be a model and w a world of W. Definition 3 is extended to formulas in $\mathcal{L}^{Ag}_{\Box\ddagger s}$ with a new clause.*

$$\mathcal{M}, w \models [\ddagger^S_a \pi]\varphi \quad \text{iff} \quad \mathcal{M}^S_{a,\pi}\binom{D_1}{D_2}, (w,0) \models \varphi \text{ for all } D_1 \in \mathcal{C}(\pi), D_2 \in \mathcal{C}(\neg\pi).$$

Example 3. Consider the pointed model $(\mathcal{M}, w)$ in which a and b know p.

$$a,b \circlearrowleft \boxed{p}\ \ w$$

Given that $\mathcal{C}(p) = \{\{p\}\}$ and $\mathcal{C}(\neg p) = \{\{\neg p\}\}$, the only clauses that can be considered when agent a forgets secretly whether p are $D_1 = \{p\}$ and $D_2 = \{\neg p\}$. The resulting pointed model is

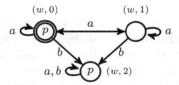

Observe how, while worlds $(w,0)$ and $(w,2)$ have the same atomic valuation, world $(w,1)$ falsifies p. With respect to the accessibility relations, from the valuation point agent a considers a possibility satisfying p, $(w,0)$, as well as another

falsifying it, $(w, 1)$. On the other hand, from the evaluation point agent b considers just one possibility, $(w, 2)$, in which everything is as before. Thus,

$$\mathcal{M}, w \models (\Box_a p \wedge \Box_b \Box_a p) \wedge [\ddagger_a^S p](\neg \Box_a p \wedge \Box_b \Box_a p)$$

A proof similar to that of Proposition 2 shows that, under the reasonable assumption of consistency, after the operation the forgetful agent has indeed forgotten the relevant formula. Nevertheless, now the whole knowledge of the rest of the agents remains intact.

Proposition 6. *If π is a propositional formula that is neither a tautology nor a contradiction; let a and b be different agents. For every formula $\varphi \in \mathcal{L}_\Box^{Ag}$,*

$$\models \Box_b \varphi \leftrightarrow [\ddagger_a^S \pi] \Box_b \varphi.$$

Proof. By bisimulation. Take any model $\mathcal{M} = \langle W, R, V \rangle$ and any $D_1 \in \mathcal{C}(\pi)$ and $D_2 \in \mathcal{C}(\neg\pi)$ with π a contingent propositional formula. Given Definition 9, the following relation between the domains of $\mathcal{M}$ and $\mathcal{M}_{a,\pi}^S \binom{D_1}{D_2}$:

$$Z := \{(u, (u, 2)) \in (W \times W') \mid u \in W\}$$

is an At^*-bisimulation. Hence, for every $\varphi \in \mathcal{L}_\Box^{Ag}$ and every $u \in W$, $\mathcal{M}, u \models \varphi$ iff $\mathcal{M}_{a,\pi}^S \binom{D_1}{D_2}, (u, 2) \models \varphi$.

For the actual proof, let a and b be different agents, π a contingent propositional formula, and take any pointed model $(\mathcal{M}, w)$ with $\mathcal{M} = \langle W, R, V \rangle$. From left to right, if $\mathcal{M}, w \models \Box_b \varphi$ then, for every $u \in W$, $R_b w u$ implies $\mathcal{M}, u \models \varphi$. Now, take any $D_1 \in \mathcal{C}(\pi)$ and any $D_2 \in \mathcal{C}(\neg\pi)$, and consider the set of R_b'-successors of $(w, 0)$: from the definition of R_b', such set is $\{(u, 2) \in W' \mid R_b w u\}$. Then, for any $(u, 2)$ in it, $R_b w u$ so $\mathcal{M}, u \models \varphi$ and therefore $\mathcal{M}_{a,\pi}^S \binom{D_1}{D_2}, (u, 2) \models \varphi$. Hence, $\mathcal{M}_{a,\pi}^S \binom{D_1}{D_2}, (w, 0) \models \Box_b \varphi$ and thus $\mathcal{M}, w \models [\ddagger_a^S \pi] \Box_b \varphi$.

From right to left, take any $D_1 \in \mathcal{C}(\pi)$ and any $D_2 \in \mathcal{C}(\neg\pi)$, and suppose $\mathcal{M}_{a,\pi}^S \binom{D_1}{D_2}, (w, 0) \models \Box_b \varphi$. Then for every $(u, k) \in W'$, $R_b'(w, 0)(u, k)$ implies $\mathcal{M}_{a,\pi}^S \binom{D_1}{D_2}, (u, k) \models \varphi$. Now consider the set of R_b-successors of w: for any u in such set, $R_b w u$ and then, from the definition of R_b', $R_b'(w, 0)(u, 2)$; thus, $\mathcal{M}_{a,\pi}^S \binom{D_1}{D_2}, (u, 2) \models \varphi$ and therefore $\mathcal{M}, u \models \varphi$. Hence, $\mathcal{M}, w \models \Box_b \varphi$.

6 Conclusions and Future Work

The present paper uses the possible world semantics to represent the changes that occur in an multi-agent epistemic model when an agent, publicly o secretly, *forgets whether* (i.e., forgets the truth-value) a propositional formula is the case as represented by its 'minimal' conjunctive normal form. The presented forgetting operations can be modelled using action models, which providing a method for obtaining its axiom system. Also, other forms of forgetting can be studied. For example, we can define a simpler forgetting action where the agent simply forgets that a given formula is true. For this action, not only public and secret versions can be defined, but also a private one (in the latter, an agent forgets that a formula π is true and the other agents know that the forgetful agent has forgotten that π is true or $\neg\pi$ is true, but not which one).

Acknowledgements. We acknowledge support from projects FFI2014-56219-P (Minist. Economía y Competitividad) and P10-HUM-5844 (Junta de Andalucía).

References

1. Alchourrón, C.E., Gärdenfors, P., Makinson, D.: On the logic of theory change: partial meet contraction and revision functions. J. Symbolic logic **50**(2), 510–530 (1985)
2. van Ditmarsch, H., van der Hoek, W., Kooi, B.: Dynamic Epistemic Logic. Synthese Library Series, vol. 337. Springer, Netherlands (2008)
3. van Benthem, J.: Logical Dynamics of Information and Interaction. Cambridge University Press, Cambridge (2011)
4. Zhang, Y., Zhou, Y.: Properties of knowledge forgetting. In: Proceedings of the 10th International Workshop on Non-Monotonic Reasoning (NMR-2008), pp. 68–75 (2008)
5. Zhang, Y., Zhou, Y.: Knowledge forgetting: properties and applications. Artif. Intell. **173**(16–17), 1525–1537 (2009)
6. van Benthem, J., Velázquez-Quesada, F.R.: The dynamics of awareness. Synthese **177**(Suppl.–1), 5–27 (2010)
7. van Ditmarsch, H., French, T., Velázquez-Quesada, F.R., Wang, Y.: Knowledge, awareness, and bisimulation. In Schipper, B.C. (ed.) TARK, pp. 61–70 (2013)
8. van Ditmarsch, H., Herzig, A., Lang, J., Marquis, P.: Introspective forgetting. Synth. (Knowl. Ration. Action) **169**(2), 405–423 (2009)
9. Fernández-Duque, D., Nepomuceno-Fernández, Á., Sarrión-Morrillo, E., Soler-Toscano, F., Velázquez-Quesada, F.R.: Forgetting complex propositions. Logic J. IGPL. Draft: arXiv:1507.01111 [cs.LO] (2015, Submitted)
10. Blackburn, P., de Rijke, M., Venema, Y.: Modal Logic. Cambridge Tracts in Theoretical Computer Science, vol. 53. Cambridge University Press, Cambridge (2001)
11. Quine, W.V.O.: The problem of simplifying truth functions. Am. Math. Mon. **59**(8), 521–531 (1952)
12. de Kleer, J.: An improved incremental algorithm for generating prime implicates. In Swartout, W.R. (ed.) Proceedings of the 10th National Conference on A.I, pp. 780–785. AAAI Press/The MIT Press, San Jose, CA, 12–16 July 1992
13. Kean, A., Tsiknis, G.K.: An incremental method for generating prime implicants/implicates. J. Symb. Comput. **9**(2), 185–206 (1990)
14. Rymon, R.: An SE-tree-based prime implicant generation algorithm. Ann. Math. Artif. Intell. **11**(1–4), 351–366 (1994)
15. Bittencourt, G.: Combining syntax and semantics through prime form representation. J. Log. Comput. **18**(1), 13–33 (2008)
16. Pagnucco, M.: Knowledge compilation for belief change. In: Sattar, A., Kang, B.-H. (eds.) AI 2006. LNCS (LNAI), vol. 4304, pp. 90–99. Springer, Heidelberg (2006)
17. Zhuang, Z.Q., Pagnucco, M., Meyer, T.: Implementing iterated belief change via prime implicates. In: Orgun, M.A., Thornton, J. (eds.) AI 2007. LNCS (LNAI), vol. 4830, pp. 507–518. Springer, Heidelberg (2007)

Intelligent Systems and Environment

Intelligent Systems and Environment

Estimation of Species Richness Using Bayesian Networks

A.D. Maldonado[1]([✉]), R.F. Ropero[2], P.A. Aguilera[2], R. Rumí[1], and A. Salmerón[1]

[1] Department of Mathematics, University of Almería, Almería, Spain
{amg457,rrumi,antonio.salmeron}@ual.es
[2] Informatics and Environment Laboratory, Department of Biology and Geology, University of Almería, Almería, Spain
{rosa.ropero,aguilera}@ual.es

Abstract. We propose a new methodology based on continuous Bayesian networks for assessing species richness. Specifically, we applied a restricted structure Bayesian network, known as tree augmented naive Bayes, regarding a set of environmental continuous predictors. Firstly, we analyzed the relationships between the response variable (called the *terrestrial vertebrate species richness*) and a set of environmental predictors. Secondly, the learnt model was used to estimate the species richness in Andalusia (Spain) and the results were depicted on a map. The model managed to deal with the *species richness - environment* relationship, which is complex from the ecological point of view. The results highlight that landscape heterogeneity, topographical and social variables had a direct relationship with species richness while climatic variables showed more complicated relationships with the response.

Keywords: Terrestrial vertebrate species richness · Continuous Bayesian networks · Probabilistic reasoning · Regression

1 Introduction

Species richness is the target of many hypotheses. Two of the main approaches for explaining the distribution of biodiversity are (1) the "habitat heterogeneity hypothesis" [21], which assumes that species richness increases as the habitat becomes structurally more complex; and (2) the "species energy hypothesis" [14], which establishes that regional richness is limited by the energy available to the system (i.e. solar radiation, measured as temperature, evapotranspiration, precipitation or net primary productivity, among others) [31]. Therefore, landscape structure, climate, topography and also social processes may condition species richness [26]. Bayesian networks (BNs), which belong to the so-called *probabilistic graphical models*, have great potential for dealing with complex systems. BN applications to the Environmental Sciences area have undergone a considerable increase in recent years [1].

© Springer International Publishing Switzerland 2015
J.M. Puerta et al. (Eds.): CAEPIA 2015, LNAI 9422, pp. 153–163, 2015.
DOI: 10.1007/978-3-319-24598-0_14

BNs can deal with continuous, discrete and hybrid (both simultaneously) data without imposing restrictions on the interactions among the variables thanks to the development of models, such as *Mixture of Truncated Exponentials* (MTE) [22]. For more information, read [18,28]. In the case of regression and classification issues, some fixed or restricted structures have been developed to emphasize the importance of one variable of interest. The simplest case is the Naive Bayes structure, which assumes complete conditional independence between the explanatory variables given the response. A step forward was taken with the allowance of dependencies between the explanatory variables, introduced by the tree augmented naive Bayes (TAN) structure [11]. In spite of the fact that TAN provides better accuracy than the NB model, the former has been applied just once to solve a classification problem in the Environmental Sciences and Ecology area [2].

Applications of BNs to species richness are scarcely found in the literature [15, 24]. The aim of this paper is to demonstrate that BNs are useful for evaluating the response of terrestrial vertebrate species richness to a number of environmental variables. In particular, we developed a TAN regression model from a set of explanatory variables (landscape heterogeneity, climatic, topographic and social variables) and a response variable (the terrestrial vertebrate species richness variable), and established the type of relationship between them. Afterwards, the learnt TAN regression model was used to estimate the terrestrial vertebrate species richness in Andalusia, which was depicted on a map.

2 Methodology

2.1 Study Area and Data Description

The study area is Andalusia, a region in southern Spain which occupies an area of 87 000 km^2 between 36°N - 38°44'N and 3°50'W - 0°34'E. Data from different thematic maps[1] were incorporated into a geographic information system- the so-called ArcGis (ESRI®ArcMap^{TM}10.0). A number of variables, considered to be representative of the landscape heterogeneity, climate, topography, and population in the study area, were selected by experts. A 10×10 km grid was used to calculate the value of each selected variable within each cell [27]. The coordinate system for all these datasets is based on the European Terrestrial Reference System 1989 (ETRS89).

These data yielded a matrix composed of 11 continuous variables taking values over 887 observations (each observation represents a 10×10 km cell), where the response variable is *terrestrial vertebrate species richness* (from now on referred to as richness) and the 10 explanatory variables are: *land-use heterogeneity* (Het)[2], *Shannon evenness index* (E_H) (see footnote 2), *patch density*

---

[1] Data sources: Andalusian Environmental Network, Spanish Inventory of Terrestrial Species, Spanish National Geographic Institute and Multiterritorial Information System of Andalusia.

[2] Variables representing landscape structure [3], calculated from the Andalusian Land Use and Land Cover Map.

(Patch) (see footnote 2), *average annual rainfall* (Rainfall), *average annual mean temperature* (T), *average annual mean potential evapotranspiration* (PET), *elevation range* (Z), *mean slope* (Slope), *mean aspect* (Aspect), and *human population density* (Pop). In order to prevent numerical instability problems, the data were rescaled to interval [0,1] by using the transformation

$$x' = \frac{x - x_{min}}{x_{max} - x_{min}}. \tag{1}$$

2.2 Probabilistic Graphical Models: Bayesian Networks

A Bayesian network (BN) is a statistical multivariate model for a set of variables $\mathbf{X} = \{X_1, \ldots, X_n\}$, which is defined in terms of two components:

1. Qualitative Component. A directed acyclic graph with a set of random variables (vertices, $\mathbf{X}$) and links between them representing dependence relationships.
2. Quantitative Component. A set of conditional probability functions quantifying the dependence relationships between the variables. The probability distribution of each variable, given its parents, is defined by

$$p(x_1, \ldots, x_n) = \prod_{i=1}^{n} p(x_i | pa(x_i)) \qquad \forall x_1, \ldots, x_n \in \Omega_{x_1, \ldots, x_n} \tag{2}$$

where Ω_{x_i} represents the set of all possible values of variable x_i and $pa(x_i)$ denotes an instantiation of the parents of X_i.

A Bayesian network can be used as a regression model if it contains a continuous response variable Y and a set of continuous or discrete explanatory variables $X_1, \ldots, X_n$. In this case of study, the response variable Y is species richness, which is considered continuous, and the set of explanatory variables $X_1, \ldots, X_n$ are the 10 other continuous variables mentioned in Sect. 2.1. Then, the value for Y given the observations $x_1, \ldots, x_n$ (i.e. the numerical prediction for Y, denoted as $\hat{y}$) is predicted by computing the conditional density $f(y|x_1, \ldots, x_n)$. To be more specific, the conditional expectation of the response variable (given the observed explanatory variables) is obtained as [10]

$$\hat{y} = g(x_1, \ldots, x_n) = E[Y|x_1, \ldots, x_n] = \int_{\Omega_Y} y f(y|x_1, \ldots, x_n) dy. \tag{3}$$

Considering that $f(y|x_1, \ldots, x_n)$ is proportional to $f(y) \times f(x_1, \ldots, x_n|y)$, the specification of an n dimensional density for $X_1, \ldots, X_n$ given Y is required in order to solve the regression problem, which increases the computational cost. However, this problem is simplified if the factorization encoded by the BN is used. Since building a network without restrictions is not always possible, networks with fixed or restricted and simple structures are utilized. The extreme case is the NB structure, where all the explanatory variables are considered independent given Y (see Fig. 1(a)). The strong assumption of independence behind NB models is somehow compensated by the reduction on the number of parameters to be estimated from data, since in this case, it holds that

$$f(y|x_1,\ldots,x_n) \propto f(y) \prod_{i=1}^{n} f(x_i|y),\tag{4}$$

which means that, instead of one n-dimensional conditional density, n one-dimensional conditional densities have to be estimated.

The impact of relaxing the independence assumption has been studied for regression oriented Bayesian networks [9], employing the so-called *tree augmented naive Bayes* (TAN) [11]. In TAN models, more dependencies are allowed, expanding the naive Bayes structure by permitting each feature to have one more parent besides Y (see Fig. 1(b)). The increase in complexity, in both the structure and the probability learning, results in richer and more accurate models. Therefore, the TAN structure was chosen as the qualitative component for our BN. In the next paragraph, the quantitative component, defined by MTE functions, is explained.

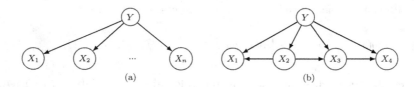

(a)   (b)

Fig. 1. Structure of a naive Bayes model (a) and a TAN model (b).

The MTE model is characterized by a function defined as follows. Let $\mathbf{W} = (W_1,\ldots,W_d)$ and $\mathbf{Z} = (Z_1,\ldots,Z_c)$ be sets of discrete and continuous parts respectively. A *Mixture of Truncated Exponentials* is a function defined for each fixed value of the discrete variables as

$$f(z_1,\ldots,z_c) = a_0 + \sum_{i=1}^{m} a_i \exp\left\{ \sum_{j=1}^{c} b_i^{(j)} z_j \right\}\tag{5}$$

where a_i, $i = 0,\ldots,m$ and $b_i^{(j)}$, $i = 1,\ldots,m$, $j = 1,\ldots,c$ are real numbers.

An MTE function is an *MTE density* if it integrates to 1. A *conditional MTE density* can be specified by dividing the domain of the conditioning variables and giving an MTE density of the conditioned variable for each configuration of splits of the other variables. The more the intervals used to divide the domain of the continuous variables, the better the MTE model accuracy (nevertheless, it increases the complexity of the model). To estimate the parameters of MTE densities, we followed the approach recently introduced in [19], which is based on least squares optimization.

Since the TAN structure (see Fig. 1(b)) is not unique for a given set of variables, the dependence structure among the explanatory variables is obtained as

$$I(X_i, X_j | Y) = \iiint f(x_i, x_j, y) \log \frac{f(x_i, x_j | y)}{f(x_i | y) f(x_j | y)} dx_i dx_j dy, \qquad (6)$$

where a maximum spanning tree whose arcs are labelled with the mutual information between the linked variables, conditional on the response variable, is constructed [9,11]. The integral above cannot be obtained in closed form for MTE densities, and therefore it has to be approximated. We adopt here the solution proposed in [9], consisting of estimating it from a sample of size m, $\{(X_i^{(k)}, X_j^{(k)}, Y^{(k)})\}_{k=1}^{m}$ drawn from the joint distribution $f(x_i, x_j, y)$, as

$$\hat{I}(X_i, X_j | Y) = \frac{1}{m} \sum_{k=1}^{m} \left(\log f(X_i^{(k)} | X_j^{(k)}, Y^{(k)}) - \log f(X_i^{(k)} | Y^{(k)}) \right). \qquad (7)$$

Once the model was obtained, the species richness estimation for each cell in the grid was calculated and depicted on a map. Note that each observation in the matrix has a code corresponding to each cell in the grid. Therefore, transferring the output of the model to the grid was possible by using the common code.

2.3 Probabilistic Reasoning

Probabilistic reasoning consists in computing the posterior probability of our variable of interest Y given some evidence of the observed variables $\mathbf{E}$ [17]. In this regard, we can observe the changes in the posterior probabilities of our response variable (richness) when new information is introduced in any of the explanatory variables. Therefore, if $\mathbf{e}$ influences Y positively, $P(Y \geq y | \mathbf{e}) \geq P(Y \geq y)$; if, on the contrary, the influence is negative, $P(Y \geq y | \mathbf{e}) \leq P(Y \geq y)$. In this way, the relationships between richness and the 10 environmental variables were tested by using 9 equidistant values from the domain of the explanatory variables as evidence. Therefore, 90 propagations were carried out in the model, obtaining as many posterior distributions of the response variable. The posterior distributions were summarized into their means and plotted on 10 graphs (1 per explanatory variable), which provided information about the type of relationship: direct, if the influence is positive; indirect, if the influence is negative; and curvilinear, if the influence changes its sign.

2.4 Validation of the Model

A k-fold cross validation [29] was carried out in order to test the TAN regression model. This technique randomly splits the dataset into k subsets and the method is repeated k times. In each step, one subset is used to test the model built from the remaining k-1 subsets (training subset). Then, the root mean squared error (RMSE), is computed in each step. Finally, the mean of the RMSE is computed to measure the accuracy of the model. In this paper, a k-value of 10 was applied.

3   Results and Discussion

Figure 2 shows the qualitative component of the TAN model, where each explanatory variable is conditioned on the response (richness) and by another explanatory variable. Each link between the response and the remaining variables shows a label symbolizing the type of relationship between them. The average RMSE of the TAN model, calculated as described in Sect. 2.4, is 21.57 while the standard deviation for the response variable (richness) is 24.00.

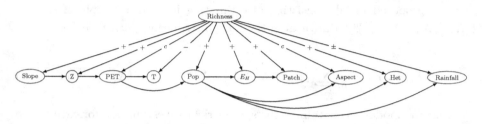

Fig. 2. TAN model obtained from the set of variables. Direct, inverse and curvilinear relationships between Richness and each explanatory variable are labelled as "+", "−" and "c" respectively. Rainfall is labelled as ± because its relationship with Richness changes from downtrend to uptrend. Z, range of elevation; PET, potential evapotranspiration; T, temperature; Pop, population density; E_H, Shannon evenness index; $Patch$, patch density; Het, land use heterogeneity.

Figure 3 depicts the relationships between richness and each explanatory variable. Richness presents a direct relationship with Heterogeneity, the Shannon evenness index (E_H), Patch density, range of elevation (Z), Slope and Population density, an inverse relationship with T and a curvilinear relationship with potential evapotranspiration (PET) and Aspect. On the other hand, Rainfall has a particular behavior, with its low values having an inverse relationship and its medium and high values having a direct relationship with richness.

Graphs in Fig. 3 indicate that landscape heterogeneity (estimated as land-use heterogeneity, Shannon evenness index and Patch density [3]) benefits species richness. Since habitats change at a high rate along an elevational gradient [16], the more the range of elevation (Z) varies, the more heterogeneous the landscape is. In addition, the greater the Z, the steeper the slope. Hence, Z and Slope have also a positive influence on richness, which corresponds with other studies [16,23]. These results meet the habitat heterogeneity hypothesis, which states that habitat heterogeneity provides more niches, facilitating specialization and therefore leading to the coexistence of a larger number of species [21].

Richness and Population density also have a direct relationship, which may seem arguable. Nevertheless, other studies that have found this relationship to be direct claim that this is because both variables have a hump-shaped relationship with primary productivity [4,6]. As productivity increases, more species can coexist, up to a point where the number of species begins to decrease. This point could be the result of species competition [12] and/or an increase in intensive agriculture, resulting in an increase in homogeneity.

Regarding PET, which may be interpreted as a measure of ambient energy [7,30], richness shows a unimodal response. The species energy hypothesis claims that higher energy availability increases net primary productivity, permitting more species to coexist. However, according to our results and other studies [7,13,16,20], energy may be relevant for explaining species richness only in high latitudes while other factors, such as landscape structure, become more important under warm climates [16,25]. In addition, richness can be indirectly correlated with energy availability in arid regions [20]. In our study area, the highest PET values occur in the Baetic depression, a vast flat and low-lying agricultural area located between the 2 main mountain ranges in Andalusia: the Sierra Morena and the Baetic Systems; and in the southeast, an arid region with high temperatures and scarce precipitation.

On the other hand, the relationship between richness and T is inverse. Different studies [5,7,8] have shown dissimilar results related to climate variables, which suggests that the pattern may vary geographically. In our study area, annual mean temperature varies widely from the coast to the inland but it especially depends on an altitudinal gradient, with mountain enclaves in the Baetic System having the lowest temperatures and the Baetic depression and some points on the Mediterranean Coast (southeast) having the highest. Concerning aspect, the unimodal relationship presented by richness - Aspect indicates that richness is greater at the south face, which receives the largest number of hours of sunshine in the study area.

Finally, rainfall shows an unusual relationship with richness. The v-shape on the *Rainfall* graph in Fig. 3 indicates that richness decreases when rainfall increases up to a medium-low value; from that point on their relationship is direct. This behavior could be related to agricultural practices and elevation. In our study area, the Baetic depression is a low-lying flat area, mainly covered by monocultures, with annual precipitation ranging between 500 and 750 mm, which corresponds to the minimum on the graph. On the other hand, in the Baetic System and the Sierra Morena mountain range, the highest mountains surpass 750 mm a year while the tablelands present less than 500 mm a year, corresponding to greater richness on the *Rainfall* graph. Thus, the lack of landscape heterogeneity in the Baetic depression reduces species richness.

The estimated value of richness for each cell in the study area was obtained from the TAN regression model and afterwards depicted on a map (Fig. 4). The study area is orographically and climatically diverse. It is no wonder that mountain ranges, i.e., the Sierra Morena and the Baetic Systems, show greater richness than cells lying on the Baetic depression since the former regions present higher elevation variations, hence higher slope and higher heterogeneity than the latter. These areas are also cooler and receive less insolation because of the cloudiness produced by the orographic effect, and therefore they present lower PET.

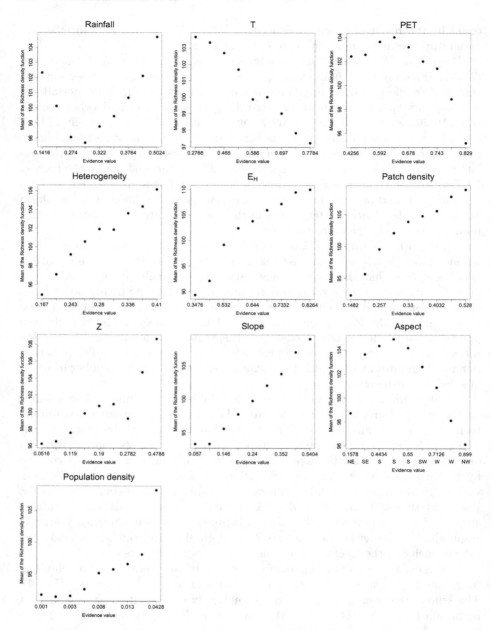

Fig. 3. Relationships between richness and the explanatory variables. Circles represent the mean of the density function of the richness variable.

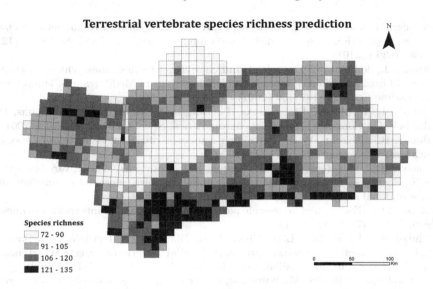

Fig. 4. Estimated values of terrestrial vertebrate species richness (number of species).

4 Conclusions

With this paper we sought to demonstrate some of the capabilities of BNs when dealing with species richness data, which is often limited and coarse-grained. Even though we did not include some potentially relevant variables, such as net primary productivity, temperature and rainfall range or specific land-use categories, the model managed to estimate the species richness given the selected explanatory variables. The inclusion of more variables may be considered for future work. The TAN regression model was able to deal with continuous data, avoiding the discretization process. In addition, by introducing new evidence in each explanatory variable separately, we obtained useful information about the relationship between the species richness and each explanatory variable. Following this idea, BNs can be used to create scenarios of change, which may be meaningful for future work.

Acknowledgements. This work has been supported by the Spanish Ministry of Economy and Competitiveness through project TIN2013-46638-C3-1-P, by Junta de Andalucía through projects P12-TIC-2541 and P11-TIC-7821 and by ERDF (FEDER) funds. A.D. Maldonado and R. F. Ropero are being supported by the Spanish Ministry of Education, Culture and Sport through an FPU research grant, FPU2013/00547 and AP2012-2117 respectively.

References

1. Aguilera, P.A., Fernández, A., Fernández, R., Rumí, R., Salmerón, A.: Bayesian networks in environmental modelling. Environ. Model. Softw. **26**, 1376–1388 (2011)

2. Aguilera, P.A., Fernández, A., Reche, F., Rumí, R.: Hybrid Bayesian network classifiers: application to species distribution models. Environ. Model. Softw. **25**(12), 1630–1639 (2010)
3. Atauri, J., de Lucio, J.: The role of landscape structure in species richness distribution of birds, amphibians, reptiles and lepidopterans in Mediterranean landscapes. Landscape Ecol. **16**, 147–159 (2001)
4. Balmford, A., Moore, J.L., Brooks, T., Burges, N., Hansen, L.A., Williams, P., Rahbek, C.: Conservation conflicts across Africa. Science **291**, 2616–2619 (2001)
5. Boone, R.B., Krohn, W.B.: Partioning sources of variation in vertebrate species richness. J. Biogeogr. **27**, 457–470 (2000)
6. Chown, S.L., van Rensburg, B.J., Gaston, K.J., Rodrigues, A.S.L., van Jaarsveld, A.S.: Energy, species richness and human population size: conservation implications at a national scale. Ecol. Appl. **15**(5), 1233–1241 (2003)
7. Currie, D.J.: Energy and large-scale patterns of animal- and plant- species richness. Am. Nat. **137**, 27–49 (1991)
8. Diniz-Filho, J.A.F., Bini, L.M., Vieira, C.M., Blamires, D., Terribile, L.C., Bastos, R.P., de Oliveira, G., de Souza Barreto, B.: Spatial patterns of terrestrial vertebrate species richness in the brazilian Cerrado. Zool. Stud. **42**(2), 146–157 (2008)
9. Fernández, A., Morales, M., Salmerón, A.: Tree augmented naive bayes for regression using mixtures of truncated exponentials: application to higher education management. In: Berthold, M., Shawe-Taylor, J., Lavrač, N. (eds.) IDA 2007. LNCS, vol. 4723, pp. 59–69. Springer, Heidelberg (2007)
10. Fernández, A., Salmerón, A.: Extension of Bayesian network classifiers to regression problems. In: Geffner, H., Prada, R., Machado Alexandre, I., David, N. (eds.) IBERAMIA 2008. LNCS (LNAI), vol. 5290, pp. 83–92. Springer, Heidelberg (2008)
11. Friedman, N., Geiger, D., Goldszmidt, M.: Bayesian network classifiers. Mach. Learn. **29**, 131–163 (1997)
12. Graham, J.H., Duda, J.J.: The humpbacked species richness-curves: a contingent rule for community ecology. Int. J. Ecol. **2011**, 1–15 (2011)
13. Hawkins, B.A., Porter, E.E., Diniz-Filho, J.A.F.: Productivity and history as predictors of the latitudinal diversity gradient of terrestrial birds. Ecology **84**(6), 1608–1623 (2003)
14. Hutchinson, G.E.: Homage to Santa Rosalia or Why are there so many kinds of animals? Am. Nat. **93**, 145–159 (1959)
15. Jellinek, S., Rumpff, L., Driscoll, D.A., Parris, K.M., Wintle, B.A.: Modelling the benefits of habitat restoration in socio-ecological systems. Biol. Conserv. **169**, 60–67 (2014)
16. Kerr, J.T., Packer, L.: Habitat heterogeneity as a determinant of mammal species richness in high-energy regions. Nature **385**, 252–254 (1997)
17. Lacave, C., Luque, M., Díez, F.J.: Explanation of Bayesian networks and influence diagrams in Elvira. IEEE Trans. Syst. Man Cybern. Part B Cybern. **37**, 952–965 (2007)
18. Langseth, H., Nielsen, T.D., Rumí, R., Salmerón, A.: Mixtures of Truncated Basis Functions. Int. J. Approximate Reasoning **53**(2), 212–227 (2012)
19. Langseth, H., Nielsen, T., Pérez-Bernabé, I., Salmerón, A.: Learning mixtures of truncated basis functions from data. Int. J. Approximate Reasoning **55**, 940–956 (2014)
20. Li, L., Wang, Z., Zerbe, S., Abdusalih, N., Tang, Z., Ma, M., Yin, L., Mohammat, A., Han, W., Fang, J.: Species richness patterns and water-energy dynamics in the drylands of northwest China. PLoS ONE **8**, e66450 (2013)

21. MacArthur, R.H., Wilson, E.O.: The Theory of Island Biogeography. Princeton University Press, Princeton (1967)
22. Moral, S., Rumí, R., Salmerón, A.: Mixtures of truncated exponentials in hybrid Bayesian networks. In: Benferhat, S., Besnard, P. (eds.) ECSQARU 2001. LNCS (LNAI), vol. 2143, pp. 156–167. Springer, Heidelberg (2001)
23. Moreno-Rueda, G., Pizarron, M.: The relative influence of climate, environmental heterogeneity, and human population on the distribution of vertebrate species richness in south-eastern Spain. Acta Oecologica 32, 50–58 (2007)
24. Mori, T., Saitoh, T.: Flood disturbance and predator-prey effects on regional gradients in species diversity. Ecology 95(1), 132–141 (2014)
25. van Rensburg, B.J., Chown, S.L., Gaston, K.J.: Species richness, environmental correlates and spatial scale: a test usign south african birds. Am. Nat. 159, 566–577 (2002)
26. Ruiz-Labourdette, D., Nogués-Bravo, D., Ollero, H.S., Schmitz, M.F., Pineda, F.D.: Forest composition in Mediterranean mountains is projected to shift along the entire elevational gradient under climate change. J. Biogeogr. 39, 162–176 (2012)
27. Schmitz, M., Pineda, F., Castro, H., Aranzabal, I.D., Aguilera, P.: Cultural landscape and socioeconomic structure. Environmental value and demand for tourism in a Mediterranean territory. Consejería de Medio Ambiente. Junta de Andalucía. Sevilla (2005)
28. Shenoy, P.P., West, J.C.: Inference in hybrid Bayesian networks using mixtures of polynomials. Int. J. Approximate Reasoning 52(5), 641–657 (2011)
29. Stone, M.: Cross-validatory choice and assessment of statistical predictions. J. R. Stat. Soci. Ser. B (Methodological) 36(2), 111–147 (1974)
30. Thornthwaite, C., Mather, J.: The Water Balance. Drexel Institute of Technology (Philadelphia) Laboratory of Climatology, vol. 8(1). Publications in climatology, Centerton (1955)
31. Wright, D.H.: Species-energy theory: an extension of species-area theory. Oikos 141, 496–506 (1983)

Automatic Generation of Air Quality Index Textual Forecasts Using a Data-To-Text Approach

A. Ramos-Soto[1]([⊠]), A. Bugarín[1], S. Barro[1], N. Gallego[2], C. Rodríguez[2], I. Fraga[2], and A. Saunders[2]

[1] Research Center on Information Technologies (CiTIUS),
University of Santiago de Compostela, Santiago de Compostela, Spain
{alejandro.ramos,alberto.bugarin.diz,senen.barro}@usc.es
[2] MeteoGalicia, Xunta de Galicia, Santiago de Compostela, Spain
calidadedoaire.cma@xunta.es

Abstract. In this paper we present a data-to-text service which automatically produces textual forecasts about the air quality state for every municipality in Galicia (NW Spain) for the Galician Meteorology Agency (MeteoGalicia). We discuss the context and the details about the conception of the service, as well as a technical and formal description of the solution adopted. This approach complements and is integrated into GALiWeather, a public service which currently issues in Meteogalicia's web page daily textual short-term weather forecasts including information about the sky state, precipitation, wind and temperatures.

Keywords: Linguistic descriptions of data · Natural language generation · Data-to-text · Air quality state

1 Introduction

As new ways to synthesize comprehensible information for human users from huge quantities of data are currently being explored, natural language generation (NLG) and, more specifically, data-to-text (D2T) approaches have gained increased attention in recent times. These systems help eliminate the gap between raw data and human users through the automatic generation of high quality texts that include relevant information extracted from the source data.

Data-to-text solutions have been successfully used in many real applied domains (see [1] for a thorough review of NLG and D2T systems). In this sense, we deployed GALiWeather [2], an application that uses techniques from the fuzzy sets field (linguistic descriptions of data) with some basic NLG processing in order to provide daily textual short-term weather forecasts for 315 municipalities in Galicia (NW Spain). GALiWeather was co-jointly conceived and developed with Meteogalicia (Galician Meteorology Agency) and has recently (May 2015) been released as a public service. Its forecasts were intended at first to provide information exclusively about weather conditions. However, due to the

© Springer International Publishing Switzerland 2015
J.M. Puerta et al. (Eds.): CAEPIA 2015, LNAI 9422, pp. 164–174, 2015.
DOI: 10.1007/978-3-319-24598-0_15

growing interest in the application showed by MeteoGalicia, GALiWeather was extended with an additional service which generates descriptions about the air quality state forecast.

Several systems have been described in the literature for creating automatic textual weather forecasts [3–5]. However, we are aware of only two systems which build air quality natural language texts, TEMSIS [6] and MARQUIS [7]. TEMSIS produces reports using environmental data about several pollutants taken from several measurement stations in the Saar-Moselle Region (France and Germany). This system is used as a tool which allows air quality experts to query for information, and thus it does not issue texts for the general public. It originally supported French and German languages, but several more were added, including English, Portuguese, Japanese and Chinese. MARQUIS is a more recent and ambitious approach, which generates air quality report bulletins for five different European regions.

Since TEMSIS, MARQUIS and our approach have originated in different contexts and have different motivations and objectives, it is unfeasible to formally compare them. In fact, in NLG literature comparisons are only made between different approaches that solve exactly the same problem (e.g. [8] is the only cited paper in [1] which compares different NLG solutions, all of which address the generation of textual weather forecasts using the same input data). However, it is interesting to provide a review on the similarities and differences among the three systems.

For instance, regarding input data, both TEMSIS and MARQUIS use raw input numeric data for individual pollutants, whereas our approach uses general air quality state information provided as graphical color labels.

With respect to end-users, TEMSIS reports are aimed at air quality experts, our approach generates descriptions for a general public and MARQUIS considers different end-user profiles depending on several variables. In this sense, another interesting fact is that both our approach and MARQUIS include relevant meteorological information related to the air quality descriptions.

Also related to the previous matter, the problem each service tries to address is also different. In the case of TEMSIS, it was meant as a support tool for experts. MARQUIS is a more flexible approach, although its focus is the generation of air quality bulletins for different kinds of users. In the case of our solution, its aim is to complement the main weather forecast generation service with air quality descriptions for non-expert users.

In this paper we discuss the details involving the creation of the air quality state forecast description service for GALiWeather, which include the approach and techniques used to model and implement the system and the evaluation methodology to validate the service.

2   Service Description

The air quality state description generation approach follows the same two-staged model used in GALiWeather's weather forecast generation [2]. Figure 1

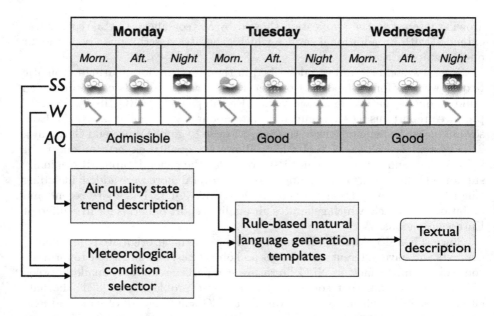

Fig. 1. Schema of the air quality state text generation.

shows a global schema of the whole process. Starting from a three day length short-term forecast which includes weather symbols and air quality indices as color labels, this process is composed of a content determination stage, which extracts the relevant information contained in the source data as an interme-diate linguistic description, and a linguistic realization stage, which converts the extracted information into a natural language text through the use of tem-plates. The resulting textual descriptions provide information about the air qual-ity index trend and relevant related weather conditions.

2.1 Input Air Quality State Forecast Data Characterization

MeteoGalicia's air quality database covers all the 315 Galician municipalities and includes air quality and meteorological forecast data in a three-day temporal window. Formally, following the terminology used in [2], each municipality M has an associated air quality forecast dataset, $AFD_M = \{AQ_M, SS_M, W_M\}$, which includes data series for air quality state (AQ_M), sky state (SS_M) and wind (W_M). For clarity reasons, without loss of generality, we will consider a single municipality data series in the explanations that follow ($AFD_M = AFD$).

This data includes labels and weather symbols represented by codes. For instance, the experts have characterized the air quality state values as labels which can be represented in colors associated to these labels (a "good" air qual-ity value for a given day is shown as a green color in the municipality forecast, as Fig. 2 shows). Likewise, sky state phenomena are characterized as 21 numerical codes (values in the interval [101,121]) and the wind phenomena as 34 numerical codes (values associated to a given intensity and direction in the interval [299,332]). These numerical codes are used to display graphical symbols in the forecast website (Fig. 2).

	Monday			Tuesday			Wednesday		
	Morn.	Aft.	Night	Morn.	Aft.	Night	Morn.	Aft.	Night
SS									
W									
AQ	Admissible			Good			Good		

With respect to the air quality state, it is expected to improve to good, favored by the rain during the coming days.

Fig. 2. Air quality state linguistic description example.

Each data series element in AFD is characterized in what follows:

– **Air Quality State** (AQ). It provides one label per day about the air quality state. $AQ = \{aq_1, aq_2, aq_3\}$, where $aq_i \in \{good, admissible, bad, hazardous\}$ $\forall aq_i \in AQ$.
– **Sky State** (SS). It provides three numerical codes per day (morning, afternoon, night) about two meteorological variables of interest, namely cloud coverage and precipitation. From a formal point of view, $SS = \{ss_1, \ldots, ss_i, \ldots, ss_9\}$, where $ss_i \in [101, 121], \forall ss_i \in SS$. Each code in the interval $[101, 121]$ has a specific sky state meaning (for example, 111 means "covered with rain").
– **Wind** (W). It provides three numerical codes per day about the wind intensity and direction. $W = \{w_1, \ldots, w_i, \ldots, w_9\}$, where $w_i \in [299, 332], \forall w_i \in W$. Each code in the interval $[299, 332]$ has an associated wind direction and intensity (for instance, 317 means "strong wind from the North").

For each forecast data series AFD, our application obtains a single textual description about the air quality state, which includes information about the general air quality trend and, when appropriate, relevant meteorological facts which complement the general description, including cloud coverage, precipitation and wind.

2.2 Content Determination Stage

The air quality state linguistic description obtained by our approach provides information about two items, the trend of the air quality state and optional additional comments about relevant meteorological states (Fig. 2). These two components are obtained independently.

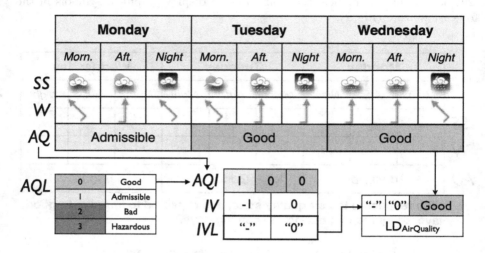

Fig. 3. Air quality state linguistic description creation.

Air Quality State Trend Description. Since the input dataset size is very reduced (three values) and consequently the number of possible cases, we have adopted a direct approach which converts the input data into a description that corresponds to one of several possible identified cases. This description is obtained as it follows:

– **Input:**
  • A set of ordered valid air quality state labels $AQL = aql_1, \ldots, aql_i, \ldots, aql_n$. In our case, $AQL = \{good, admissible, bad, hazardous\}$.
  • An air quality data series $AQ = \{aq_1, aq_2, aq_3\}$, where each element is a label defined in AQL.
– **Procedure.** From AQ, AQI is created by replacing the labels in AQ by their index order in AQL (for instance, if $AQ = \{admissible, good, good\}$, $AQI = \{1, 0, 0\}$). Then, the index variation among values is calculated $IV = \{iv_1 = aqi_2 - aqi_1, iv_2 = aqi_3 - aqi_2\}$. Finally, IVL is defined from IV by encoding the sign of the values iv_1 and iv_2 into labels as it follows:

$$ivl_j = \begin{cases} '+' & \text{if } iv_j > 0 \\ '-' & \text{if } iv_j < 0. \\ '0' & \text{if } iv_j = 0. \end{cases}$$

– **Output.** An air quality trend description composed of the results obtained in IVL and the air quality label for the last day:

$$LD_{AirQuality} \rightarrow (ivl_1, ivl_2, aq_3)$$

Figure 3 shows an example of this linguistic description creation process.

Meteorological Condition Description. In this case, as opposed to the rest of operators used in GALiWeather, the extraction of relevant meteorological conditions does not solely consist in generating descriptions by transforming data into linguistic labels. Instead, for the reasons mentioned above, we have adopted a direct rule-based approach, which first calculates the percentages of expected precipitation, cloud coverage types and relevant wind episodes along the whole three day term, for two days (starting on the second day) and for the last forecast day. This allows us to provide relevant meteorological conditions for every possible change in the air quality state (for instance, if the air quality state changes in the second day, two-day length percentages are used to determine if there are relevant weather conditions regarding this change).

In order to obtain the ratio of cloud coverage types, the sky state data series SS and a definition set of the different cloud coverage categories are needed. Following the nomenclature in [2], we define the cloud coverage linguistic variable $CCL = \{ccl_1, \ldots, ccl_k, \ldots, ccl_m\}$. Each linguistic term $ccl_k \in CCL$ has an associated crisp membership function $\mu_{ccl_k} : \mathbb{N} \to \{0, 1\}$, defined as:

$$\mu_{ccl_k}(ss_i) = \begin{cases} 1 & \text{if } ss_i \in ccl_k \\ 0 & \text{otherwise} \end{cases}$$

This allows us to obtain the apparition percentages for each ccl_k, for every period length. Figure 4 shows an example on how this percentages are obtained, with $CCL = \{clear, partiallycloudy, verycloudy\}$. In the case of precipitation, we follow a similar approach, but there is no distinction among precipitation types, as Fig. 4 shows.

Wind percentages are calculated in the same way, but the relevant wind episodes are given by a code interval.

Using the percentages for each meteorological variable, rules are applied to determine the most appropriate weather condition for each term length among the ones defined by the experts. These condition list is used as input of the natural language generation process, along with the air quality trend description.

2.3   Linguistic Realization Stage

The textual descriptions about the air quality state have a simple fixed structure which holds information about the air quality trend and an optional meteorological comment. Thus, the use of templates to produce natural language texts is appropriate for this case.

In fact, we have adapted the XML templates described in [2], which were extended to add support for the air quality state descriptions. Expressions and vocabulary are included in the template for every possible case. Then, according to the case the linguistic description represents, a corresponding specific expression is selected and completed with the values in the description.

The different air quality trend cases are defined as a grammar, which is used to parse the air quality linguistic description, where "Worsen" is "+", "Improve is "–" and "Maintain is "0":

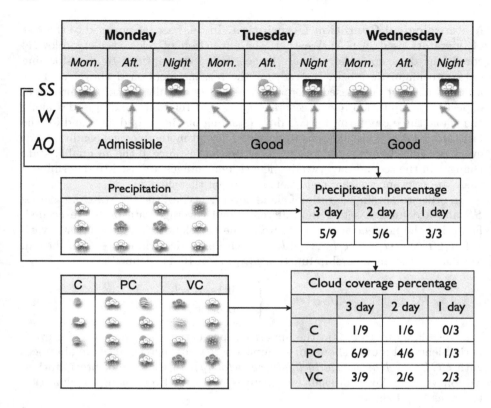

Fig. 4. Conditions operator.

$\langle$AQ$\rangle$→$\langle$ChangeType$\rangle$$\langle$ChangeLabel$\rangle$
$\langle$ChangeType$\rangle$→$\langle$Stable$\rangle$|$\langle$MediumChange$\rangle$|
$\langle$StartChange$\rangle$|$\langle$EndChange$\rangle$|$\langle$ProgressiveChange$\rangle$
$\langle$Stable$\rangle$→**MaintainMaintain** $\langle$MediumChange$\rangle$→**WorsenImprove**|
ImproveWorsen
$\langle$StartChange$\rangle$→**WorsenMaintain**|
ImproveMaintain
$\langle$EndChange$\rangle$→**MaintainWorsen**|**MaintainImprove**
$\langle$ProgressiveChange$\rangle$→**WorsenWorsen**|**ImproveImprove**
$\langle$ChangeLabel$\rangle$→**Good**|**Admissible**|**Bad**|**Hazardous**

When a specific *ChangeType* is detected, its associated template is selected and expert rules (which were provided by the air quality experts) check if the obtained weather conditions are relevant enough to be included as an additional comment in the description. For instance, if most of the short-term period forecast is rainy and the air quality is good, a comment explaining the how rain favors good air quality state is included in the final description.

3   Results and Evaluation

3.1   Examples

Although the number of possible cases contemplated in the descriptions is reduced, the combination of air quality state trends with relevant meteorological phenomena produces a high number of different potential scenarios. For instance, Fig. 5 shows a case where the air quality changes through the three day period, but remains good. It also includes a comment about wind, which is one of the weather conditions favoring a good air quality state.

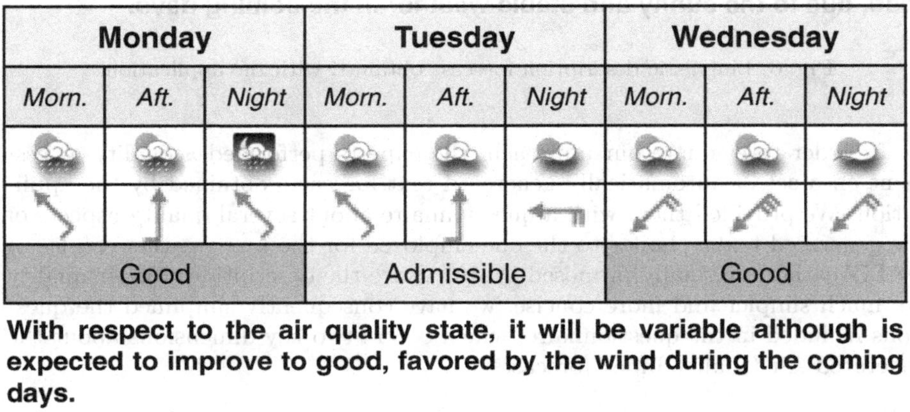

Monday			Tuesday			Wednesday		
Morn.	*Aft.*	*Night*	*Morn.*	*Aft.*	*Night*	*Morn.*	*Aft.*	*Night*
Good			Admissible			Good		

With respect to the air quality state, it will be variable although is expected to improve to good, favored by the wind during the coming days.

Fig. 5. Linguistic description forecast obtained with the application.

Figure 6 provides a case where the air quality progressively gets worse, changing from good to bad. In addition, a sunny weather condition, which is related to this kind of change, is also commented in the textual description.

3.2   Quality Assessment Evaluation

Evaluation processes are an essential duty in applied NLG systems [9], since they ensure that the automatically generated texts fulfill the required quality for end-users. In this sense, one of the most reliable and demanding evaluation methodologies in this area involves the participation of domain experts, although this is not always feasible due to the lack of specialized staff or simply availability issues. In our case, four experts participated in the knowledge engineering stages of the system (language requirements of the data-to-text system). Since our aim is to produce natural language information that is indistinguishable from the one the human experts produce and is backed by them, the validation process was made by the two experts that were able to take part in the evaluation process.

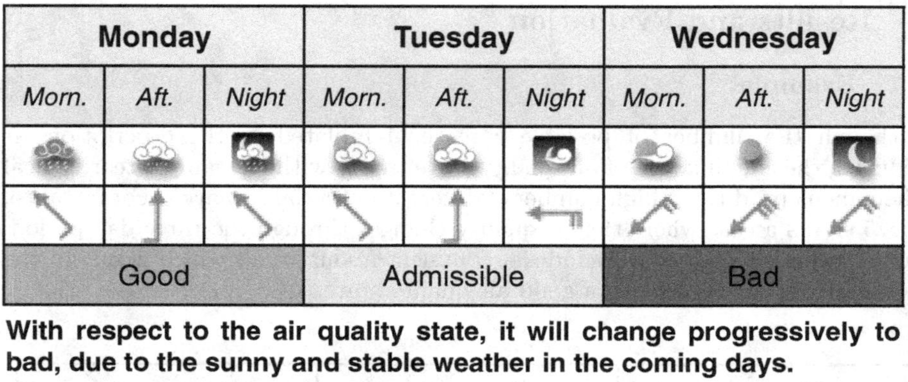

Monday			Tuesday			Wednesday		
Morn.	*Aft.*	*Night*	*Morn.*	*Aft.*	*Night*	*Morn.*	*Aft.*	*Night*
Good			Admissible			Bad		

With respect to the air quality state, it will change progressively to bad, due to the sunny and stable weather in the coming days.

Fig. 6. Linguistic description forecast obtained with the application.

In order to evaluate our approach, the experts performed a quality assessment on a set of automatically generated text forecasts obtained by the application. We provided them with a questionnaire about several quality aspects of the generated texts, similar to the one employed for the text weather service of GALiWeather, originally proposed in [10]. Since the descriptions for air quality are much simpler and more concise, we have consequently simplified the questions included in the questionnaire, which covers two key dimensions about the generated Air Quality Index forecasts:

- Relevance: Does the forecast include all the kind of information the expert would include?
- Truthfulness: Does the included information in the forecast reflect the numeric-symbolic forecast correctly?

The remaining dimension, "Manner", which deals with the format and presentation of the text, has been discarded due to the restricted vocabulary and expressions, which were directly defined by the experts. Consequently, this questionnaire is focused exclusively on the quality of the content of the descriptions. More specifically, the questionnaire we propose consists of two questions which deal in more depth with the previous two dimensions. Each of these questions were answered by the experts as a number in a 1–5 scale (from 1 "very negative" to 5 "very positive") :

- **Question 1:** "Indicate in which degree you identify the type of results expressed as the type of results expressed by yourself".
  This question determines the grade in which an expert identifies the generated forecast with the ones he creates.
- **Question 2:** "Do you agree with the provided descriptions? (a) For the air quality state trend (b) For the meteorological causes". This question considers the degree of truthfulness of the generated description, this is, the degree in which the content of the forecast reflects faithfully the information within the

numeric-symbolic forecast data. Question 2 is divided into two sub-questions, where the first one refers to the air quality state description and the second one addresses the meteorological conditions related to that Air Quality Index state.

Following this quality measure approach, the global quality Q of an automatically generated natural language weather forecast S_i is defined as the arithmetic mean of the two questions:

$$Q_{S_i} = \frac{p_1 + \overline{p_2}}{2} \tag{1}$$

The term p_1 is the score for Question 1 and $\overline{p_2}$ corresponds to the average score of the sub-questions a and b for Question 2. Thus, the global quality score GQ for the collection of automatically generated natural language forecasts is obtained as the average of the validation cases quality score: $GQ = \sum_{i=1}^{n} \frac{Q_{S_i}}{n}$, where $n = 15$ in each expert quality assessment.

Table 1. Validation questionnaire score

Expert	GQ	Standard deviation
Exp. 1	4.86	0.35
Exp. 2	4.73	0.45

For this evaluation process a set of 20 test cases was generated, which includes air quality data and meteorological data covering every possible case identified by the experts and their corresponding textual description. Two experts were provided with a sub-collection of this set, composed of 15 cases, where 10 of them are common and 5 are exclusive for each subject. The results of the questionnaire (Table 1), show a high satisfaction degree from the experts.

4   Conclusions

We have discussed the creation of a solution which extends the functionality of GALiWeather, allowing the generation of air quality state forecast descriptions as natural language texts. The quality of automatically generated prediction texts was assessed by two different experts, producing high satisfaction results which verified the validity of our approach. The automatic generation of forecast texts for Air Quality Index state has been incorporated into MeteoGalicia's municipality meteorological forecast service, along with the already present forecast texts. The automatically generated texts are publicly available in [11].

Acknowledgements. This work was supported by the Spanish Ministry for Economy and Competitiveness (grants TIN2011-29827-C02-02 and TIN2014-56633-C3-1-R) and by the European Regional Development Fund (ERDF/FEDER) and the Galician Ministry of Education (grants EM2014/012 and CN2012/151). A. Ramos-Soto is supported by the Spanish Ministry for Economy and Competitiveness (FPI Fellowship Program) under grant BES-2012-051878.

References

1. Ramos-Soto, A., Bugarín, A., Barro, S.: On the role of linguistic descriptions of data in the building of natural language generation systems. Fuzzy Sets Syst. (2015). http://dx.doi.org/10.1016/j.fss.2015.06.019
2. Ramos-Soto, A., Bugarín, A., Barro, S., Taboada, J.: Linguistic descriptions for automatic generation of textual short-term weather forecasts on real prediction data. IEEE Trans. Fuzzy Syst. **23**(1), 44–57 (2015)
3. Coch, J.: Interactive generation and knowledge administration in MultiMeteo. In: Proceedings of the Ninth International Workshop on Natural Language Generation, Niagara-on-the-lake, Ontario, Canada, pp. 300–303 (1998). Software demonstration
4. Goldberg, E., Driedger, N., Kittredge, R.: Using natural-language processing to produce weather forecasts. IEEE Exp. **9**(2), 45–53 (1994)
5. Sripada, S., Reiter, E., Davy, I.: SUMTIME-MOUSAM: configurable marine weather forecast generator. Exp. Update **6**(3), 4–10 (2003)
6. Busemann, S., Horacek, H.: Generating air-quality reports from environmental data. In: Busemann, S., Becker, T., Finkler, W. (eds.) DFKI Workshop on Natural Language Generation, DFKI Document D-97-06 (1997)
7. Wanner, L., Bohnet, B., Bouayad-Agha, N., Lareau, F., Nickla, D.: MARQUIS: generation of user-tailored multilingual air quality bulletins. Appl. Artif. Intel. **24**(10), 914–952 (2010)
8. Belz, A.: Automatic generation of weather forecast texts using comprehensive probabilistic generation-space models. Nat. Lang. Eng. **14**(4), 431–455 (2008)
9. Reiter, E.: Task-based evaluation of NLG systems: control vs real-world context. In: Proceedings of the UCNLG+Eval: Language Generation and Evaluation Workshop, UCNLG+EVAL 2011, Stroudsburg, PA, USA, pp. 28–32. Association for Computational Linguistics (2011)
10. Eciolaza, L., Pereira-Fariña, M., Trivino, G.: Automatic linguistic reporting in driving simulation environments. Appl. Soft Comput. **13**(9), 3956–3967 (2013)
11. MeteoGalicia: Meteogalicia's website. http://www.meteogalicia.es/web/prediccion/localidades/localidadesindex.action

Using a New Tool to Visualize Environmental Data for Bayesian Network Modelling

R.F. Ropero[1]([✉]), Ann E. Nicholson[2], and Kevin Korb[2]

[1] Informatics and Environment Laboratory, Department of Biology and Geology,
University of Almería, Almería, Spain
rosa.ropero@ual.es
[2] Faculty of Information Technology, Monash University,
Melbourne, VIC 3800, Australia

Abstract. This paper presents the software Omnigram Explorer, a visualization tool developed for interactive exploration of relations between variables in a complex system. Its objective is to help users gain an initial knowledge of their data and the relationships between variables. As an example, we apply it to the water reservoir data for Andalusia, Spain. Two Bayesian networks are learned using causal discovery, both with and without the information gleaned from this exploration process, and compared in terms of the Logarithmic loss and causal structure. Even though they show the same predictive accuracy, the initial exploration with Omnigram Explorer supported the use of prior information to achieve a more informative causal structure.

Keywords: Omnigram explorer · Natural complex systems · Bayesian networks · Data visualization · Water management

1 Introduction

Bayesian networks (BNs) are finding rapidly increasing application in Ecology and Environmental Science, modeling complex natural systems [3]. The development process is correspondingly complex, frequently involving extensive expert elicitation processes combined with the collection and automated mining of data from multiple sources (see [1,4,7,8]).

As a part of the process, visualizing the data available to build the models, or again visualizing artificial data generated by the models developed, has an important role. Data visualization can assist in understanding the key relationships between variables in a system, assisting in both model construction and validation. Data visualization done well can also greatly simplify communications with non-expert stakeholders. Some common data visualization approaches include the scatter plots and parallel coordinates [2].

© Springer International Publishing Switzerland 2015
J.M. Puerta et al. (Eds.): CAEPIA 2015, LNAI 9422, pp. 175–184, 2015.
DOI: 10.1007/978-3-319-24598-0_16

Here we use the new visualization tool, Omnigram Explorer[1] (OE) [10], to investigate a BN model of water reservoirs in Andalusia, Spain. OE provides new ways to interact with data sets, allowing for a visual sensitivity analysis of, for example, the effect of causal variables on downstream effect variables under a variety of conditions. The original intention behind OE was that it be an *interactive* tool, coordinating through an API with a BN to explore different initial conditions and their consequences. That is still the intention for the future, but it is currently restricted to working with static data sets, produced by a BN or otherwise, although it will use a BN defined by a Netica (www.norsys.com) dne file in its display, if one is provided. Here we simply illustrate OE's value with static data sets.

2   Omnigram Explorer

OE was designed as a tool for interactive exploration of relations between variables in an agent-based simulation [10]. It draws upon ideas for visualization in the *Attribute Explorer* [9], where data is presented in a set of histograms, one per variable. For more detail information about the data requirements see the link: http://www.tim-taylor.com/omnigram/.

To begin, a data file and model definition are necessary. The data file containing a joint data sample are loaded and presented by OE in a graphical form (Fig. 1(a)). Each variable is represented by a histogram, showing its sample distribution, with a maximum of 20 bins. If a bin is empty (e.g., bin 0 in *Rainfall* node in Fig. 1(a)), a thin horizontal line is drawn at the base. A small circle represents the mean (or, if the user chooses, the median). The range of values is indicated by the horizontal bar under the histogram. The initial histogram represents all the values read from the data file in a plain form, but a subset of them can be highlighted in a *linking and brushing* process (in dark red color).

2.1   OE Interaction Modes

OE allows you to designate some variables as input or outputs and to use Bayesian network links to represent causal structure or other dependencies, as you wish. At present these features are for display only.

The power of this tool lies in its interaction modes, where a variable or subset of variables can be selected and their relation with the remaining variables explored. The selected variables are the "focus" of attention, which is indicated visually by a red square indicator in the corner of the node. Having selected a focus, OE has four different modes of interaction.

---

[1] Omnigram Explorer is an open-source tool developed in Processing (http://processing.org). The source code, executables (for Windows, Mac and Linux), documentation and related material are available at http://www.tim-taylor.com/omnigram/.

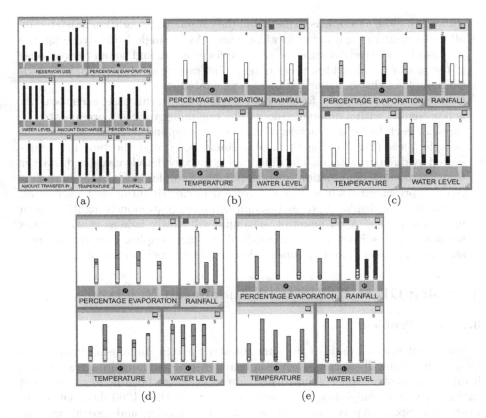

Fig. 1. Initial histograms for the reservoir example with the focus in *Rainfall* variable (a) and modes of interaction in OE for a subset of variables: Single node (b), Multi node (c), Omnibrushing (d) and Sample view (e) (Color figure online).

- Single Node Brushing (Fig. 1(b)), in which only one variable can be in the focus. When a range of values for that node is selected, all of the other variables are updated to show the corresponding sample values in their distributions (represented in dark blue). When changing the focal range, you can simultaneously watch the changes across the other variables, allowing you to intuitively discover the strength of dependencies between the variables. In the example of Fig. 1(b) the focus is on high levels of rainfall (red), and the distributions across other variables conditioned on that high level are displayed in blue.
- Multi Node Brushing (Fig. 1(c)) extends the previous interaction mode, with more than one variable in focus. When two or more variables are selected, OE indicates the ranges selected in red and shows the conditional distributions over other variables in dark blue. Samples which fail match one of the selected ranges are shown in light green; those which match all but two of the ranges are displayed in light red; white displays all other samples. The color, therefore,

shows how close a sample is to matching the conjunctive condition indicated by all the specified ranges in the focal variables. As in Single Node Brushing, the user can interactively change the range of focus nodes and watch the response of the rest of the variables, performing an interactive sensitivity analysis with the sample of the model or data which generated it.

- Omnibrushing (Fig. 1(d)) focuses on a single node. In this case, each focal bin is represented with a different colour. The remaining variables are updated to show for each bin what fraction of the data correspond to the focal bins.
- Sample View (Fig. 1(e)) again uses a single node, and the bins are represented by different colours. The difference is the way data is visualized. Rather than represent a conjunction of corresponding samples, each individual sample is represented itself as a small colored circle, simultaneously across all variables. The display iterates through samples, continuously lighting them up in a sequence. After being lit, a sample will slowly fade as other samples are selected, resulting in a rotating display of subsamples. How quickly new samples are selected and old ones fade is under the user's control.

3   Using OE to Understand Andalusian Reservoirs

3.1   The Problem

A prominent characteristic of the annual water cycle in Andalusia, Spain, is its irregularity. Rainfall alternates between heavy storms and long droughts. Historically, dam construction has been the main solution for both flood control and extending water availability, and there are now more than 1200 dams currently working in Spain. Apart from human water consumption and agriculture, the dams provide a minimum water flow during droughts, allowing biodiversity to be maintained in river beds.

International Panel of Climate Change (IPCC) predicts in Andalusia an increase in the annual average temperature and evaporation, along with a decrease in the rainfall, but with more frequent extreme weather events [5]. These changes will cause severe difficulties in Andalusian water management. New tools and techniques for understanding and managing the reservoirs are urgently needed [11].

3.2   Data Description

For our study we used the Water Quality Dataset from Andalusia (Environmental Information Network of Andalusia) and the National Environmental Statistics (National Government of Spain), from 1999 to 2008. From the reservoirs located in this region of Spain, we selected those that belong to the *Guadaliquivir* and *Guadalete-Barbate* river basin areas, which have no missing values, giving us complete data about 61 dams over the period.

The dataset consists of 6588 samples over the following eight variables (and their states, with continuous variables discretized using expert knowledge and taking into account the distributions of the variables). *Reservoir use* is a discrete variable with 10 states representing the main use/s of each reservoir classified by the regional Government of Andalusia (1 Hydroelectric; 2 General regulation; 3 Irrigation; 4 Human consumption; 5 Industry; 6 No information; 7 Ecological; 8 Irrigation and other; 9 Irrigation and consumption; 10 Consumption and others). *Temperature* (less than 10; 10–15; 15–20; 20–25 and 25–30°) and *Rainfall* (less than 0.03; 0.03–0.06 and more than 0.06 m³/m²) represent the climatic conditions near the dam. *Percentage Evaporation* is the percentage of the reservoir capacity that evaporates (less than 0.029; 0.029–0.035; 0.035–0.93 and more than 0.93 %). *Water level* indicates the height of the water column (less than 92; 92–257; 257–497 and 497–1039 m.a.s.l.) whilst *Percentage Full* expresses the percentage of the reservoir capacity that is currently used (0–25; 25–50; 50–75; 75–100; more than 100 %, during an event of a storm the reservoir can exceed the dam capacity). Finally, dam management is represented by *Amount Discharge* and *Amount Transfer in*. *Amount Discharge* refers to the amount of water that is released when floodgates are opened for ecological, water consumption or regulation purposes (less than 0.13; 0.13–1.36; 1.36–7.08 and more than 7.08 m³). By contrast, *Amount Transfer in* (less than 0.27; 0.27–1.42; 1.42–6.95 and more than 6.05 m³) is the amount of water deliberately added to the reservoir, e.g., pumped in from another reservoir.

3.3 OE Data Exploration Prior to Modeling

Here we illustrate the value of OE in initial data exploration, prior to any use of machine learning or BN modeling. Some other tools such as Weka or R software are also available and useful. The aim of this paper is not to compare OE with them, but to present it as an alternative of traditional statistical packages. Figure 1(a) shows the OE view of the data before choosing an interaction mode. *Water Level*, *Amount Transfer in* and *Amount Discharge* present homogeneous distributions, with similar number of samples in each bin.

The goal is to better understand the variables *Percentage Full* and *Water Level* in Andalusia and to predict their behavior under several future scenarios of management decision and those being predicted by the IPCC. So, first we explored the behavior of the system when *Rainfall* is altered. Using Omnibrushing (Fig. 2(a)) we could easily see that lower values of *Rainfall* are associated with higher *Temperature* values and are also associated with lower values of *Percentage Full*. However, the highest values of *Rainfall* are not particularly correlated with higher values of *Percentage Full*.

After we explored the distribution of the *Rainfall* variable in relation to the others, we used Single Node Brushing to explore the changes when we selected the lowest *Rainfall* value and moved through to the highest value (Fig. 3), attempting to identify correlations between the variables. There is a clear negative relation between *Rainfall* and *Temperature* and a clear positive relation with *Percentage Full*, *Water Level* and *Amount Transfer in*. However, the relationships with *Percentage Evaporation* are more ambiguous. When *Rainfall* values are higher, *Percentage Evaporation* tend to be more prevalent in the second bin.

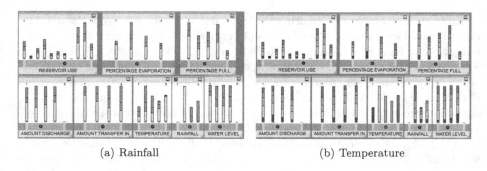

(a) Rainfall   (b) Temperature

Fig. 2. Omnibrushing for *Rainfall* and *Temperature*

Another variable of prime interest is *Temperature*. As with *Rainfall*, we use Omnibrushing (Fig. 2(b)) and Single Node Brushing (Fig. 3) to explore its relation with the rest of the variables. First, we can see that medium values are more prevalent in the rest of the variables than both extremes (bins 1 and 5). When we focus on a subset, bins 1 and 2 (corresponding to temperatures lower than 15°), we find that samples are fairly flat except for lower *Percentage Evaporation* and slightly higher values of *Rainfall*. If we move now to the highest bin (temperatures above 25°), more changes are evident. The sample size is markedly smaller, so inferences must be less certain, but this smaller sample shows low rainfall and higher water discharge, presumably to combat drought conditions.

Next we followed the same procedure with *Percentage Full*. One thing we observed was that both *Amount Transfer in* and *Amount Discharge* behave in the same way with respect to *Percentage Full* (Fig. 3(e) and (f)) and that the relation between all three is positive. We computed the Pearson correlation between *Amount Transfer in* and *Amount Discharge* conditioned on *Water Reservoir*, which was a very high 0.95. This suggests some redundancy between the two variables *Amount Transfer in* and *Amount Discharge*; however, we have already observed that they behave in *opposite* ways in high temperature conditions (Fig. 3).

Finally, we took advantage of the Multi Node Brushing and explored the system when both *Rainfall* and *Temperature* nodes were in focus. One of the possible scenarios for the future of Andalusia combines an increase in the annual temperature with a decrease in average rainfall. Using OE, we checked the sensitivity of the system to this change. With the *Rainfall* node focused on the lowest bin, we ran the focus on *Temperature* from the medium values (bin 3) to the highest value (Fig. 4). The remaining variables showed changes as the focus moved, allowing us to do interactive sensitivity analysis.

With this exploration process we gained some initial understanding of how the variables are related, but also some idea the system's causal structure. *Rainfall* and *Temperature* are clearly inversely related, whilst *Rainfall*, *Percentage Full* and *Water Level* are positively related. *Percentage Evaporation* is also related with both *Rainfall* and *Temperature*, but the relations seem to be more

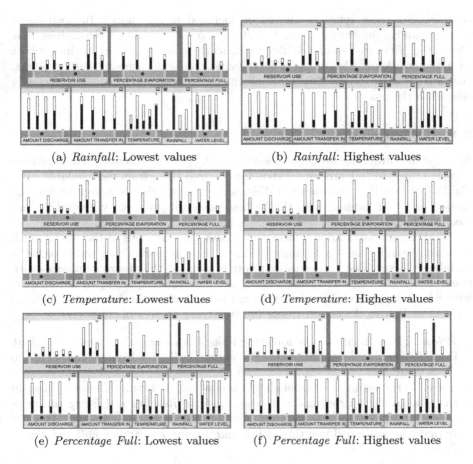

(a) *Rainfall*: Lowest values

(b) *Rainfall*: Highest values

(c) *Temperature*: Lowest values

(d) *Temperature*: Highest values

(e) *Percentage Full*: Lowest values

(f) *Percentage Full*: Highest values

Fig. 3. Single Node Brushing for *Rainfall*, *Temperature* and *Percentage Full* variables, focus on the lowest and highest values.

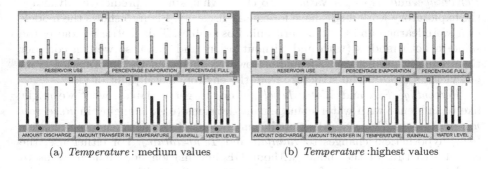

(a) *Temperature* : medium values

(b) *Temperature* :highest values

Fig. 4. Multi Node Brushing given the lowest value of *Rainfall*, for medium (a) to the highest (b) values of *Temperature*

complex. So, these relations should be included in the model. In both cases, *Rainfall* and *Temperature* seem to act as a possible cause of *Percentage Full*, *Percentage Evaporation* and *Water Level*, so they should appear in the network as parent of them. Also, given a fixed *Percentage Full*, *Amount Discharge* and *Amount Transfer in* provide similar information and should be considered closely related in the model.

3.4   BN Learning

We used the causal discovery program CaMML[2] (Causal discovery via Minimum Message Length) to learn causal structure (causal BNs) from the available data. CaMML uses a Bayesian metric (MML score) and stochastic search to find the model, or set of models, with the highest posterior probability given the data (see [4] Chap. 9, or [6]).

CaMML supports prior information about the structure of the model, such as what variables should be linked (Priors), or the partial (or total) order of variables (Tiers). The idea of using priors is to assist the discovery process with common sense background knowledge or genuine expert opinion, or, in this case, with what we think we have learned from data exploration. Inspired by OE, we tried the following Tiers and Priors (with varying degrees of confidence):

- *Priors:* There should be the following links: from *Rainfall* to *Percentage Full*, from *Percentage Evaporation* to *Percentage Full*, and from *Water Level* to *Percentage Full*.
- *Tiers:* Variables in the model should follow this structure: *Reservoir Use* in the first level, as a root node; in a second level *Rainfall* and *Temperature* as parent of *Percentage Evaporation*, *Amount Discharge* and *Amount Transfer ir* that are positioned in a third level; and, finally, *Percentage Full* and *Water Level*.

We ran CaMML on the data both with and without these priors and tiers. A *10-fold Cross Validation* was carried out to calculate the Logarithmic Loss using *Percentage Full* as target variable, to check what kind of predictive advantage the exploratory work might have for causal discovery. Figure 5 shows the models that were learned and their Logarithmic Loss values. This metric is exactly the same in both models (with and without priors and tiers), so we can consider them equally predictively adequate. However, including the information from OE yields a more useful structure from the environmental point of view.

Percentage Full and *Water Level* are our target variables, what we might like to influence with water management decisions (e.g., changing in *Reservoir use* or *Amount Transfer in*) or predict in response to climatic change scenarios (e.g., hypothetical changes to *Rainfall* and *Temperature*). For either use, the causal structure of the model without OE information does not allow us to model appropriately the effects on *Percentage Full* not *Water Level*, since, for

---

[2] https://github.com/rodneyodonnell/CaMML.

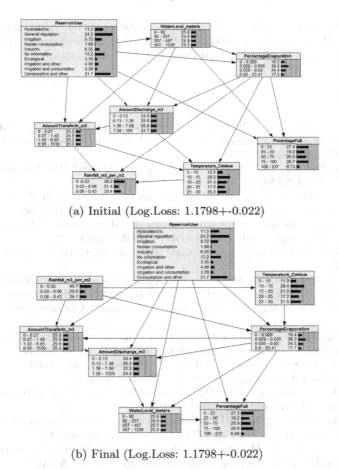

(a) Initial (Log.Loss: 1.1798+-0.022)

(b) Final (Log.Loss: 1.1798+-0.022)

Fig. 5. Netica displays and the Logarithmic Loss (Log.Loss) for the BNs learned both with (Final) and without (Initial) information from OE.

example, the climate change variables are child variables with respect to the rest of the model, while *Water Level* is spuriously shown as a causal factor for other variables. Reordering these variables in causally meaningful tiers was suggested by both common sense and the OE visualization process.

4   Conclusion

This paper describes the software Omnigram Explorer (OE) and its application to analysing and modeling water reservoirs in Andalusia. The initial exploration of the data with OE allowed the users to achieve a better understanding of the data, with the resultant causal structure better fitting the aims of modeling. The interactive graphical interface provides users with an easy and intuitive way to explore the data, as well as assisting the communication of results to non-specialists.

Acknowledgements. This work has been supported by ARC grant number DP110101758R. F. Ropero is supported by the FPU research grant, AP2012-2117, funded by the Spanish Ministry of Education, Culture and Sport.

References

1. Coreau, A., Treyer, S., Cheptou, P., Thompson, J.D., Mermet, L.: Exploring the difficulties of studying futures in ecology: what to do ecological scientists think? Oikos **119**, 1364–1376 (2010)
2. Heer, J., Bostock, M., Ogievetsky, V.: A tour through the visualization zoo. Commun. ACM **53**(6), 59–67 (2010)
3. Kelly, R., Jakeman, A.J., Barreteau, O., Borsuk, M., ElSawah, S., Hamilton, S., Henriksen, H.J., Kuikka, S., Maier, H., Rizzoli, E., Delden, H., Voinov, A.: Selecting among five common approaches for integrated environmental assessment and management. Environ. Model. Softw. **47**, 159–181 (2013)
4. Korb, K.B., Nicholson, A.E.: Bayesian Artificial Intelligence. CRC Press, Boca Raton (2011)
5. Méndez-Jiménez, M.: Estudio Básico de Adaptación al Cambio Climático (2012)
6. O' Donnell, R.: Flexible Causal Discovery with MML. Ph.D. thesis, Faculty of Information Technology (Clayton). Monash University, Australia, 3800, September 2000
7. Parrott, L.: Hybrid modelling of complex ecological systems for decision support: recent successes and future perspectives. Ecol. Inf. **6**, 44–49 (2011)
8. Ricci, P.F., Rice, D., Ziagos, J., LA Jr., C.: Precaution, uncertainty and causation in environmental decisions. Environ. Int. **29**, 1–19 (2003)
9. Spence, R., Tweedie, L.: The attribute explorer: information synthesis via exploration. Interact. Comput. **11**, 137–146 (1998)
10. Taylor, T., Dorin, A., Korb, K.: Omnigram explorer: a simple tool for the initial exploration of complex systems ECAL 2015 (2015, Submitted)
11. Teegavarapu, R.S.V.: Modeling climate change uncertainties in water resources management models. Environ. Model. Softw. **25**, 1261–1265 (2010)

Intelligent Web and Recommender Systems

Learning Parliamentary Profiles
for Recommendation Tasks

Luis M. de Campos[1]($\boxtimes$), Juan M. Fernández-Luna[1], Juan F. Huete[1],
Pável Calado[2], and Bruno Martins[2]

[1] Departamento de Ciencias de la Computación e Inteligencia Artificial,
ETSI Informática y de Telecomunicación, CITIC-UGR, Universidad de Granada,
18071 Granada, Spain
{lci,jmfluna,jhg}@decsai.ugr.es
[2] Instituto Superior Técnico e INESC-ID, Universidade de Lisboa, Lisboa, Portugal
{pavel.calado,bruno.g.martins}@ist.utl.pt

Abstract. We consider the problem of building a content-based recommender system in a parliamentary context, which may be used for two
different but related tasks. First, we consider a filtering task where, given
a new document to be recommended, the system can decide those Members of the Parliament who should receive it. Second, we also consider
a recommendation task where, given a request from a citizen, the system should present information on those deputies that are more involved
in the topics of the request. To build the system we collected, for each
Member of the Parliament, the text of corresponding speeches within
the parliament debates and generated, with different techniques, a profile that was used to match against the input (document or request).
We tested our methods using the documents of the regional Andalusian
Parliament at Spain, obtaining promising results.

Keywords: User profiles · Content-based recommender systems · Information filtering · Information retrieval · Parliamentary documents

1 Introduction

The application of Information and Communication Technologies (ICT) in public administration, called e-government, aims to improve public services and
democratic processes, as well as to strengthen support to the public [8]. Within
this general context, we focus on the specific case of national or regional parlia-
ments which, as other political institutions, produce a plethora of information
but may fail to reach the people who are interested in it. This communication
gap is related to citizens but also to the Members of the Parliament (MP) them-
selves [2]. As stated in [10] in the context of the European Parliament, "MPs
need to be selective in their information input". The same authors also stress
the need to "increase dissemination of information and to provide opportunities
for greater interaction between represented and representative". Our proposals
in this paper go in the direction of these two goals.

© Springer International Publishing Switzerland 2015
J.M. Puerta et al. (Eds.): CAEPIA 2015, LNAI 9422, pp. 187–197, 2015.
DOI: 10.1007/978-3-319-24598-0_17

Let us assume that a new document must be distributed among the MPs. This document may be external to the parliament (e.g., a news release) or internal, such as a parliamentary initiative[1]. The proposed system should be able to evaluate and decide those MPs who should receive it (a filtering task), according to their specific interests and the content of the document itself. On the other hand, consider an entity (e.g. a citizen or an institution) that wants to find the most appropriate MPs that can deal with a given request. In this case, the system should recommend who are these MPs, again taking into account their interests and the topical content of the request. In both cases, given an input to the system (either a new document that must be filtered or a request of a citizen), an automated procedure should determine those MPs who should receive this input.

Thus, our research may be framed within the field of content-based recommender/filtering systems [1, 9], which are systems that recommend an item to a user, based on a description of the item and a profile of the user's interests. We are not aware of any previous description of one such system in a parliamentary context.

The source of information to learn about the interests of the MPs, in order to build the corresponding MP profiles, will be the transcriptions of all their speeches within parliament debates (either in plenary sessions or in more specific committee sessions). These transcriptions are collected in the form of records of proceedings.

The rest of the paper is organized in the following way: in Sect. 2 we describe the different ways we are going to use to build the MP profiles, as well as how these profiles will be used by an Information Retrieval System (IRS) to match them against the inputs, providing as a result a ranked list of MPs. The profiles will act as documents in a document collection and the inputs (documents or requests) will play the role of queries. In Sect. 3 we give details of the experimental framework designed to test our proposals, using a collection of records of proceedings of the regional Parliament of Andalusia at Spain. Section 4 ends the paper with the conclusions and some proposals for future work.

2   Building and Using Profiles

Considering the revision of the state-of-the-art about profiles and personalized IR given in [4], we are going to contextualize the type of profiles that we are working with in this research. The profiles that we present are built implicitly, mining relevant documents for the users, in our case, MPs who participate in parliamentary debates (in opposition to those constructed by explicit information given by users). With respect to the temporal perspective, our proposed profiles are static in the sense that they are not updated with the time (the alternative is the dynamic profile, which is changed when the preferences of the users change). In order to incorporate new information, our profiles have to be

---

[1] An initiative is the literal transcription of the discussion in the parliament of a petition presented by specific MPs or groups.

re-built from the scratch and we could say that they represent a long-term snap-shot. The profiles at hand are only composed of a flat group of terms. We do not consider other type of information such as semantic networks or hierarchies, weighted concepts or association rules, for example.

Also in [4], the authors propose the following stages in the process of building profiles: (1) Collecting the user information; (2) Representing the profiles, and (3) Profile construction. Therefore, considering these phases, we are going to describe the decisions made to build the profiles, although previously we are going to explain how these profiles will be used after they are built.

2.1 Exploitation of the Profiles

It is important to remark that this paper, as stated in Sect. 1, is focused on the use of profiles for filtering tasks (and not for search personalization through query expansion [5]). In this case, we could consider that a citizen is looking for an MP who is involved in certain matters in which the citizen is interested in, expressed by means of a query to a retrieval system; or the case where given a new initiative that arrives to the system, we would like to know the names of those MPs who could be interested in it. In both cases, we have to use a more pure IR perspective, as the profiles would be considered documents from a classic IR view. The query could be the citizen's information need expressed as a set of keywords or the complete text included in an initiative. Then, an IRS indexing the document collection composed of the profiles would process the query, obtaining a ranked list of the MPs who are more involved with the content of the query as the result.

2.2 Collecting User Information

In this first stage, with the aim of extracting the information to build the profile, different mechanisms can be applied, as discussed in [4]. Taking into account that the context of this research are the parliamentary debates, and more specifically, their transcriptions of the MPs' interventions in the form of records of proceedings, as previously described in Sect. 1, we assume that we may build the MPs' profiles analyzing all their participations (speeches) in different initiatives discussed in committee or plenary sessions in the whole set of records of proceedings. For example, if an MP usually participates in debates related to agriculture, all their interventions will be around this topic and we could learn a profile composed of agriculture-related terms. That would be the case where the profile contains only one facet, but it is very easy to find the case where a politician is included in several commissions dealing with different topics, let us say education, environment and economics, for example. In these cases, the profiles originating from speeches could be considered multi-faceted and reflecting multiple preferences, as the MP is closer to several specific political areas.

Our approach considers, as the base for building the MPs' profiles, a collection of *documents*, each containing the whole text of all the speeches of a specific MP in the discussion of a particular initiative. We can represent as D the set of documents, each compiling all the interventions of the i-th MP, i.e. $D = \{d_1, \ldots, d_m\}$ (m being the number of MPs).

2.3 Representation

The second step is to determine the content of the profile and its internal organization. In our case, a specific MP's profile will be composed of a set terms extracted from the MPs' collection of interventions and finally weighted in order to reflect their importance or relevance in the complete profile. We assume term independence, so no type of relationships between terms is represented in the profile. Then, the profile of the i-th MP, P_i, is conceptually represented by a set of pairs term, weight, i.e. $P_i = \{(t_{i1}, w_{i1}), \ldots, (t_{in}, w_{in})\}$, where n is the number of terms included in the profile. An important question that we shall partially try to answer in the experimentation phase is what is the most appropriate size of the profile with the aim of best representing the MP's ideas expressed in their speeches.

Noticing that not only the size is important, another research question that we tackle in this article is whether the composition of the profile in terms of parts of speech could be relevant for its quality. We shall take into account profiles composed of (1) only nouns (proper and common), which tries to simulate, in a certain way, concepts included in the interventions; (2) Nouns plus verbs, complementing the concepts with actions related to them; and finally, (3) all parts of speech (APoS). In this last case, we assume that stop words are not good language elements to be considered in a profile. As such, they are removed given a list of the most common words in the corresponding language (prepositions, articles, conjunctions, etc.), adding also a set of very frequent words in the regional parliamentary domain (for example, "deputy" or "Andalusia"). At this point, APoS profiles could contain nouns, verbs, some adjectives and adverbs, and also dates and numbers.

2.4 Construction

Broadly speaking, the process of constructing a profile P_i is basically founded on computing a weight for each term in the set of documents D, and selecting those n terms with the highest value. Then, profile P_i is built filtering terms from d_i. This would be a term selection task. Next, we have to focus our attention on the weighting schemes used to measure the importance of the terms in the profile, and to rank them accordingly. Two of the more well-known approaches are tf and $tfidf$. The former simply reflects the raw occurrence of the term in the collection of speeches, d_i, i.e. it means that the most frequent terms appearing in the transcriptions of each MP are selected. Profiles weighted with this scheme will just contain the most common words of each MP. The latter, the $tfidf$, takes into account, not only term frequencies in documents but also their rarity within the whole collection. The idf component of a term t is the inverse document frequency computed as $log\left(\frac{|D|}{df_t}\right)$, where df_t is the number of documents where term t occurs. Profiles, which terms are selected based on this scheme, will contain a vocabulary more particular of the MP, weakening terms which appears very frequently in the speeches of other MPs.

In addition to these approaches, we add a new one, called *Difference* $(Diff)$, presented in [11] in the context of profiles used to personalize search results via query expansion. The foundation of this new weighting scheme is basically that if a term t is more frequent inside a document d_i than outside (the rest of documents), the term is representative of that $i - th$ MP. Otherwise, if the term occurs more times in the speeches of other MPs than in the ith MP, then it is not useful for her as a representative of her speeches. More formally, we define $f^+(t, d_i)$ as the frequency of t in d_i; $f^+(d_i)$ is the total number of terms in d_i; $f^-(t, d_i)$ and $f^-(d_i)$ are respectively the frequency of t and the number of terms in documents outside d_i. We then define the difference measure of t with respect to d_i, $Diff(t, d_i)$, as:

$$Diff(t, d_i) = \frac{f^+(t, d_i)}{f^+(d_i)} - \frac{f^-(t, d_i)}{f^-(d_i)} \tag{1}$$

The previous equation corresponds to the normalized frequency of t within d_i minus the normalized frequency of t outside d_i. If the final value is $Diff(t, d_i) \leq 0$, it means that t is more frequent outside than within d_i, so it is not representative of d_i. However, if the final value is $Diff(t, d_i) > 0$, this means that t represents d_i at a certain degree.

Using any of these three approaches we obtain as the output, for each MP, a set of n selected terms together with their corresponding weights.

Finally, and in order to facilitate the use of the profiles for any given search engine, we have decided not to use directly the sets of selected weighted terms as the profiles. Instead, we build each profile as a bag of words, replicating the selected terms several times, simulating the way a document contains term occurrences. This facilitates the profiles to be indexed by existing search engines, and therefore we can use their internal weighting schemes.

We propose two different alternatives for this purpose: The first one, noted as *R-tf*, is to replicate any selected term as many times as its tf (number of occurrences in d_i), reflecting its real occurrence pattern, independently on its weight. The second one, *R-Prop*, is designed according to the fact that if a term has got a higher weight, then it should be replicated more times than those with lower weights. To carry out this idea we apply a linear transformation to the original weight, considering the maximum and minimum weight values as well as the number n of terms to be included in the profile. This transformation is: $replications = (int) \left((n - 1) \frac{weight - min\_weight}{max\_weight - min\_weight} + 1 \right)$. Therefore, the term having maximum weight will have a replication value of n, while the one with minimum weight will have a replication value of 1. This way is intended to give occurrences of a term proportional to its weight.

3 Evaluation

In this section we describe the components of the evaluation framework, as well as the obtained results and conclusions. In order to evaluate the quality of the different profiles we shall try to measure their capability at predicting whether an MP might have some interest in a new initiative (considering only the content of the speeches). So, given one such initiative, the system will give as output a ranking of those MPs having the profiles that best match the target initiative (particularly, we shall focus on the top-10 MPs).

3.1 Evaluation Framework

The evaluation framework is composed by the following components:

Data Set: We use all the initiatives (5258) from the 8th term of office of the Andalusian Parliament at Spain[2], marked up in XML [3]. These initiatives contain a set of 12633 different interventions. From this set we shall build the profiles only for those deputies (or technical guests) who participate in more than 10 different initiatives, giving a total of 132 profiles.

Parameter Configuration: The different parameters that will be considered in these experiments are[3]: the number of terms in the profile, which takes values 50, 250, 500, 750 and 1000; The Part of Speech (the type of terms in the profile), which might be Noun (N), Noun+Verb (NV) and all PoS (A); The metrics for selecting the best terms in the profile are *tf* (t), *tfidf* (i) and *Diff* (d), and finally, the importance of the term in the profile that will be either *R-tf* (F) or *R-prop* (P). In total, a set of 90 different types of profile were built (plus one that consists of using all the terms in the MPs' speeches). We use the profiles in conjunction with the search engine library Lucene[4], considering three different similarity measures, namely BM25, Language Model and Cosine, giving a total number of 273 different evaluations.

Evaluation Methodology: In order to evaluate the performance of our proposals, we have used the repeated holdout method [7]: the set of initiatives is randomly partitioned into training (80 %) and test (20 %), and we repeat this process five times (the results presented in the study are the averages over the different rounds). The training set is used to learn the MP profiles. With respect to the initiatives in the test set, we remove the information related to the MPs who participate in their discussion, being totally anonymous. In these experiments we have considered, as ground truth, that a test initiative, j, will be relevant only to those n_j MPs who participate in it[5].

---

[2] http://www.parlamentodeandalucia.es.

[3] In parentheses we present the short acronym used in the figures and tables in this section.

[4] https://lucene.apache.org.

[5] We consider that this is a rather conservative assumption, because it is quite reasonable to think that an initiative can also be relevant to other MPs.

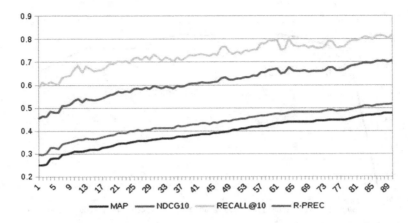

Fig. 1. Performance for the different evaluation metrics using BM25.

Evaluation Metrics: In order to evaluate the accuracy of our approach, we use the recall values considering the top-10 MPs, rec@10, that measures how many MPs, among the relevant MPs, appear in the top positions of the ranking and the Normalized Discounted Cumulative Gain [6], NDCG@10, which measures the ranking quality. Also, considering that the number of relevant MPs varies with the initiative (on the average there are 2.4 interventions per initiative) we shall also measure the accuracy on the top n_j positions using MAP@n_j (Mean Average Precision) and the R-precision (that represents the precision over the top n_j MPs).

3.2   Results

Although the selected metrics measure different features in the output ranking, it deserves to be mentioned that they all are highly correlated, with correlation values greater than 0.97 among all of them, independently of the used similarity function. In order to illustrate this fact, Fig. 1 presents the values obtained by each metric for each one of the 90 possible parameter configurations (in the x-axis) using BM25. We believe that this fact strengthens the conclusions obtained in this study because the results are consistent among the different metrics. Also, this helps us to reduce the number of results to be shown, focusing on the results obtained with one of them; particularly we have selected the NDCG@10 as the main metric through the main part of this section. We shall organize this section through 3 different research questions, the first two related to the parameter configuration and the last one devoted to analyzing the differences between the similarity measures.

Q1: Which is the right number of terms of the profile? In order to answer this question, we have run an intensive test considering different profile sizes, fixing the rest of the parameters to the configuration which gives the best results

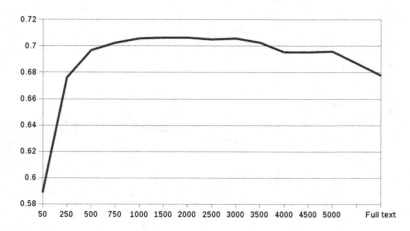

Fig. 2. NDCG@10 values, using BM25, when varying the size of the profile.

(discussed below). The results for the NDCG@10 metric and BM25 are presented in Fig. 2. From this figure we can see that using a few number of terms the results are not good enough, increasing to the best values using a profile size in the range 1000 to 5000 terms (which is better than considering all the terms), then the results decrease when the profile size increases.

From this result we can conclude that the best alternative is to consider a profile with around 1000 terms, being a good balance between size and quality of the results. Also, our experiment shows that for our proposal it is necessary to consider a huge number of terms in the profile (the results obtained using only 50 terms are quite poor). Note that this fact is against the profile's size necessary for helping the users to improve the search experience, i.e. to find those documents relevant to a given query. In this case, the use of large profiles is not convenient because of the query drift problem[6]. This also suggests that the search of the best profile in a filtering task is a different problem than, for instance, successfully personalize search results.

Q2: Which is the best configuration of profile parameters? In order to answer this question, we shall use the net chart presented in Fig. 3. This chart shows the NDGC@10 values for each candidate configuration when using BM25 as similarity measure. In the grid all the different accuracy values obtained with the same profile size, i.e., 50, 250, 500, 750 and 1000 have been connected by lines, so we can see easily how the performance varies with the configuration.

From this chart we can say that the best configuration is:

size = 1000; type = APoS, selection = *tfidf*, weight = *R-prop*.

---

[6] The change in the underlying *intent* between the original query and its expanded form.

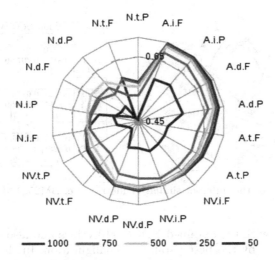

Fig. 3. NDCG@10 values for the profile sizes equals to 50, 250, 500, 750 and 1000 using BM25 as similarity metric.

Although this is important, other conclusions can also be obtained: Firstly, with respect to the part of the speech considered for selecting the terms in the profile, it seems that it is better not to consider any restriction about the selected terms, i.e. all the parts of the speech matter. Nevertheless, the tendencies in the results are different when using only nouns[7] versus the use of nouns and verbs or all PoS. Secondly, the best alternative for selecting terms for being included in the profile is to take into account *tfidf* weights, although there are not significant differences with respect to the use of Diff. In this sense, the results get worse when only the frequencies are taken into account. In other words, how helpful is a term to describe the user preferences does not depend only on the raw frequency of the term in the speech, but it also depends on how common is this term in the rest of the speeches, fact that has been taken into account by the other two metrics. It is worth to remark that this holds for all types of terms. Thirdly, there is not a clear winner with respect to the use of a frequency or proportional-based approaches to determine the weight of the terms in the profile (there is not statistical significance between the results, using a two-tail t-test we obtain a p-value equals to 0.00193). In this case, the best results have been obtained using a proportional criterion, although this criterion only wins in the 37.7 % of the configurations.

Q3: Is there any difference between the different similarity models? In order to tackle this question we shall discuss the results obtained using BM25, Language Model (LM) and Cosine (VECT), fixing the profile size to 1000. Figure 4

---

[7] We are not going to discuss their impact in this work, since the accuracy values obtained are worse in all the cases.

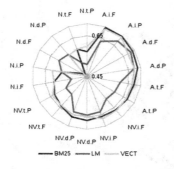

Param.	rec@10	NDCG	MAP	R-prec
BM25				
Full	0.7770	0.6778	0.4568	0.4959
A.i.P	0.8177	0.7074	0.4773	0.4876
%	5.23	4.37	4.48	-1.63
LM				
Full	0.7421	0.6176	0.3867	0.4329
A.d.F	0.8095	0.6903	0.4542	0.4953
%	9.08	11.77	17.45	14.41
VECT				
Full	0.7971	0.6876	0.4584	0.5030
A.i.P	0.8231	0.7036	0.4658	0.5087
%	4.39	2.32	1.61	1.13

Fig. 4. Results for the different similarity metrics, i.e. BM25, LM and VECT.

shows a net chart with the obtained NDCG@10 values and also a table with all the values obtained by the best parameter configuration. In this table we also present the results when we do not learn a profile, i.e. all the terms in the speech are considered (denoted as Full) that can be considered the baseline, and the improvements (in terms of percentage of gain, %) for each metric.

In this case, we can see that both BM25 and VECT exhibit a similar performance (particularly, when considering APoS or N+V) whereas LM behaves differently in tendencies and results. Thus, in the case of LM it seems that it is better to consider *Diff* as criterion guiding the term selection process (this is in some way congruent with the criterion used by LM to compute the terms weights). Also, it is interesting to note that although LM gives the worst results, greater improvements (with respect to the baseline) are obtained.

4   Conclusions

We have designed a new alternative to build user profiles in a Parliamentary context, which is based on considering parliamentary interventions as bags of words. In this sense, the profiles can be considered as new documents that can be indexed by a search engine. In this paper we have explored the effects of three features on the profile quality: the number of terms, their grammatical type and their associated weights (encoded as the frequency of a term in the profile). Our experimental results show that it is better to consider a large number of terms for describing the users' preferences, which suggests that a profile for filtering has different features than the ones used in search tasks. We have also explored the effect of the parts of the speech used in the profile, showing a strong evidence in favor of the use of all parts of the speech. Also, our results show that, in order to select the best terms, it is necessary to consider how common is a term in the other MPs speeches.

Although our current focus is on a parliamentary context, the ideas developed here could be used in other situations, for instance in recommending new technical papers to scientists, or in discovering those scientists who are more prominent for a given topic. For future work, we plan to tackle the fact that the profiles can be heterogeneous and also the impact of the time in the profile, i.e. analyzing short-term vs long-term users' interests.

Acknowledgements. Paper supported by the Spanish "Ministerio de Economía y Competitividad" under the project TIN2013-42741-P.

References

1. Belkin, N.J., Croft, W.B.: Information filtering and information retrieval: two sides of the same coin? Commun. ACM **35**, 29–38 (1992)
2. Busby, A., Belkacem, K.: 'Coping with the Information Overload': An Exploration of Assistants' Backstage Role in the Everyday Practice of European Parliament Politics. European Integration online Papers, vol. 17 (2013)
3. de Campos, L.M., Fernández-Luna, J.M., Huete, J.F., Martin-Dancausa, C.J., Tur-Vigil, C., Tagua, A.: An integrated system for managing the andalusian parliament's digital library. Program Electron. Libr. Inf. Syst. **43**, 121–139 (2009)
4. Gauch, S., Speretta, M., Chandramouli, A., Micarelli, A.: User profiles for personalized information access. In: Brusilovsky, P., Kobsa, A., Nejdl, W. (eds.) Adaptive Web 2007. LNCS, vol. 4321, pp. 54–89. Springer, Heidelberg (2007)
5. Pasi, G.: Issues in personalizing information retrieval. IEEE Intell. Inf. Bull. **10**, 3–7 (2010)
6. Jarvelin, K., Kekalainen, J.: Cumulative gain-based evaluation of IR techniques. ACM Trans. Inf. Syst. **20**, 422–446 (2002)
7. Lantz, B.: Machine Learning with R. Packt Publishing Ltd., UK (2013)
8. Palvia, S.C.J., Sharma, S.S.: E-government and e-governance: definitions/domain framework and status around the world wide web. Foundations of e-government. In: 5th International Conference on E-Governance, pp. 1–12 (2007)
9. Pazzani, M.J., Billsus, D.: Content-based recommendation systems. In: Brusilovsky, P., Kobsa, A., Nejdl, W. (eds.) Adaptive Web 2007. LNCS, vol. 4321, pp. 325–341. Springer, Heidelberg (2007)
10. Shamin, J., Neuhold, C.: 'Connecting Europe': the use of 'new' information and communication technologies within european parliament standing committees. J. Legislative Stud. **13**, 388–402 (2007)
11. Vicente-López, E., de Campos, L.M., Fernández-Luna, J.M., Huete, J.F.: Personalization of parliamentary document retrieval using different user profiles. In: Proceedings of the 2nd International Workshop on Personalization in eGovernment Services and Applications (PEGOV2014), pp. 28–37 (2014)

An Analysis of the Quality Issues of the Properties Available in the Spanish DBpedia

Nandana Mihindukulasooriya[✉], Mariano Rico, Raúl García-Castro, and Asunción Gómez-Pérez

Ontology Engineering Group, Departamento de Inteligencia Artificial,
Universidad Politécnica de Madrid, Madrid, Spain
{nmihindu,mariano.rico,rgarcia,asun}@fi.upm.es
http://www.oeg-upm.net

Abstract. DBpedia exposes data from Wikipedia as machine-readable Linked Data. The DBpedia data extraction process generates RDF data in two ways; (a) using the mappings that map the data from Wikipedia infoboxes to the DBpedia ontology and other vocabularies, and (b) using infobox-properties, i.e., properties that are not defined in the DBpedia ontology but are auto-generated using the infobox attribute-value pairs. The work presented in this paper inspects the quality issues of the properties used in the Spanish DBpedia dataset according to conciseness, consistency, syntactic validity, and semantic accuracy quality dimensions. The main contribution of the paper is the identification of quality issues in the Spanish DBpedia and the possible causes of their existence. The findings presented in this paper can be used as feedback to improve the DBpedia extraction process in order to eliminate such quality issues from DBpedia.

Keywords: DBpedia · Spanish DBpedia · Data quality · Conciseness · Consistency · Syntactic validity · Semantic accuracy

1 Introduction

Following the success of the web of documents (World Wide Web), there has been a big enthusiasm in creating a Web of Data by publishing data in a manner that can be easily understood by software programs. In 2014, there were more than 1,000 publicly available datasets containing more than 900,000 documents[1] which describe more than 8 million resources. Among these datasets, DBpedia [2] stands out as the central hub of Linked Open Data (LOD) because it provides a vast amount of information and most other datasets in the LOD cloud link to DBpedia.

DBpedia data come from Wikipedia, the vast online encyclopedia that grows daily with the selfless contributions of its editors. Until 2011 only data from

---

[1] http://linkeddatacatalog.dws.informatik.uni-mannheim.de/state/.

© Springer International Publishing Switzerland 2015
J.M. Puerta et al. (Eds.): CAEPIA 2015, LNAI 9422, pp. 198–209, 2015.
DOI: 10.1007/978-3-319-24598-0_18

the English language Wikipedia was extracted but, since then, several "local" DBpedia chapters were created for other Wikipedia languages. For the Spanish language, the Spanish DBpedia[2] (esDBpedia) was created in 2012 and currently there are 15 other "local" DBpedia chapters. Notice that 40 % of the pages in the Spanish Wikipedia do not have links to the English Wikipedia (canonicalized datasets[3] in the DBpedia); therefore, a significant percentage of the information stored in the Spanish DBpedia is not available in the English DBpedia. This fact places the Spanish DBpedia as a valuable and exclusive source of local information. Also we have to remark that the English DBpedia does not contain all the information stored in the local DBpedias, but only a minimum subset[4] (labels and abstracts, specifically).

These DBpedias need the collaboration of people to provide semantics to the data. We call this process "mapping" because it relates data from Wikipedia articles to elements of the DBpedia ontology[5]. This is done by using wiki-based tools available in the DBpedia website[6].

As shown in Fig. 1, the extraction process reads a Wikipedia page (in this example, from the Spanish DBpedia) which contains an infobox (highlighted in red in the figure) and extracts its attribute-value pairs. Infoboxes are templates for concepts (in this example, for the "Actor" concept) and are comprised of fields (attribute-value pairs). The extraction process generates one or several RDF triples from each attribute-value pair by using the information specified in the mappings.

The automatic generation of RDF data using the entities of the DBpedia ontology relies on the manual creation of mappings. In the case of the Spanish chapter of DBpedia, there have been three community events intended to show attendants the mapping process and to provide mappings for most used infobox templates[7]. Currently there are around 100 mappings which cover more than 80 % of the total data stored in the infoboxes of the Spanish Wikipedia.

However, many of these mappings have infobox fields that are neither related to DBpedia entities (properties or classes) nor to other ontology entities. In such cases, rather than ignoring these valuable data, the extraction process generates a triple relating the Wikipedia resource (as the subject), a property generated using the infobox field (as the predicate) and its value (as the object). On the one hand, the properties that are generated by the extractors using infobox fields can be distinguished because they have distinct namespace prefixes (*i.e.*, either http://es.dbpedia.org/property/ or http://dbpedia.org/property/). On the other hand, the DBpedia ontology properties have a different namespace (http://dbpedia.org/ontology/).

---

[2] http://es.dbpedia.org.

[3] See statistics for Spanish at http://wiki.dbpedia.org/services-resources/datasets/dataset-statistics.

[4] See the datasets loaded at http://wiki.dbpedia.org/services-resources/datasets/data-set-loaded-2014.

[5] http://mappings.dbpedia.org/server/ontology/.

[6] http://mappings.dbpedia.org.

[7] http://mappings.dbpedia.org/server/statistics/es/.

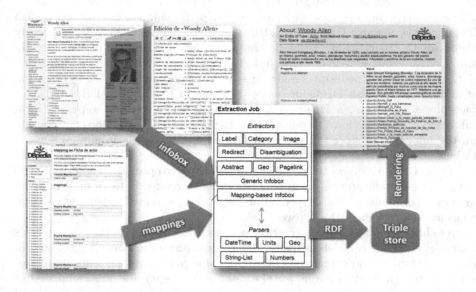

Fig. 1. DBpedia RDF data generation from Wikipedia infoboxes (Color figure online).

Table 1. Properties in the Spanish DBpedia dataset.

Property prefix	Properties		Triples	
	Num.	%	Num.	%
http://es.dbpedia.org/property/	19,885	52.53	18,021,389	10.66
http://dbpedia.org/property/	17,188	45.40	9,742,710	5.76
http://dbpedia.org/ontology/	576	1.52	86,602,281	51.21
http://xmlns.com/foaf/0.1/	12	0.03	8,132,328	4.81
http://www.w3.org/1999/02/22-rdf-syntax-ns#	8	0.02	12,298,451	7.27
http://www.w3.org/2000/01/rdf-schema#	7	0.02	5,366,982	3.17
http://www.w3.org/2002/07/owl#	6	0.02	16,523,751	9.77
http://purl.org/dc/terms/#	4	0.01	4,148,399	2.45
http://www.w3.org/2004/02/skos/core#	4	0.01	1,153,685	0.68
http://purl.org/dc/elements/1.1/	3	0.01	3,346,874	1.98
http://www.w3.org/ns/prov#	1	0.00	2,853,681	1.69
Other prefixes	163	0.43	911,131	0.54
Total	37,857	100	169,101,662	100

Table 1 illustrates the number of properties in the Spanish DBpedia categorized by the namespace prefix. In addition, the table also shows the number of triples that contain such properties. It can be seen that 37,073 $(19,885+17,188)$ out of 37,857 properties (i.e., 97.93 %) are auto-generated using the infobox fields. The triples that contain such properties constitute 16.42 % of all data available in the Spanish DBpedia.

Despite these "infobox-properties" are not defined in the DBpedia ontology, they are perfectly usable; for instance, in SPARQL queries. Moreover, infobox-properties provide valuable data specific for a given language because infobox templates are not shared among languages, that is, each Wikipedia language has its own infobox templates. However, properties in the DBpedia ontology are common to all languages and its language specificity is in the multilingual label assigned to each class and property.

The goal of this work is to analyze the 37,857 distinct properties used in the Spanish DBpedia 2014 dataset[8] in order to identify quality problems with respect to the conciseness, consistency, syntactic validity, and semantic accuracy quality dimensions. More concretely, the analysis aimed at identifying the common patterns of quality problems in the dataset, the root-causes of those patterns, and potential means for minimizing or eliminating those identified quality problems. Furthermore, the statistical data for each ontology element (class or property) extracted from the Spanish DBpedia dataset are made available online[9].

This paper is structured as follows: Sect. 2 describes how the statistical data that were used to identify quality issues were extracted; Sect. 3 presents the different quality dimensions that were analyzed in this paper and the results of such analysis; Sect. 4 discusses related work; and finally Sect. 5 provides some conclusions and lines future work.

2   Extraction of Property Statistics

This section describes the process that was used to extract statistical information about the property characteristics in the Spanish DBpedia dataset.

First, a list of all the properties used in the dataset was extracted using a SPARQL query. Based on the URI of the property, the local name and the namespace were identified and stored for further analysis. This categorization by namespace provides an overview about the composition of the dataset (See Table 1) and also enables performing an analysis on a subset of the properties, for example, the infobox-properties in the Spanish DBpedia.

Once the property list was extracted, for each property in the list, a set of statistics was extracted using a series of parametrized SPARQL query templates[10]; those statistics were analyzed in detail to identify quality issues under different dimensions. For each property, all the triples that contain that property as a predicate were considered. The subject and object instances/values of all

---

[8] The Spanish DBpedia 2014 dataset is the last publicly available version in July 2015.
[9] http://loupe.linkeddata.es/loupe/.
[10] http://loupe.linkeddata.es/loupe/methods.html#property.

Table 2. Overview of the property statistics.

Property statistics template		Example data
General information	URI	http://es.dbpedia.org/property/edad
	Local name	edad
	Namespace	http://es.dbpedia.org/property/
	Number of triples	4623
Subjects analysis	URI subject count	4623 (100 %)
	Blank node count	0 (0 %)
	Extracted Domain classes (i.e., ?subject a ?class)	dbpedia-owl:Agent 2611 (56.48 %)
		schema:Person 1515 (32.77 %)
		.... (rest omitted for brevity)
Objects analysis	URI object count	186 (4.02 %)
	Blank node object count	0 (0 %)
	Extracted range classes (i.e., ?object a ?class)	skos:Concept 17 (9.14 %)
		schema:Place 2 (1.08 %)
		.... (rest omitted for brevity)
	Literal object count	4437 (95.98 %)
	Numerical object count	2491 (53.88 %)
	Integer object count	2382 (51.52 %)
	Average of numerics	3.53
	Max numeric sample	8.79E11, 1.5E8, 1.5E7, 8.2E6, 8121540
	Min numeric sample	0.0, 0.5, 1.0, 1.08, 1.2

such triples were used to generate the statistics about the property as shown in Table 2. For the purpose of statistics generation and analysis, a closed world assumption was followed, *i.e.*, only the data that are present in the dataset were taken into consideration.

The objective of generating these statistics was to use them as input for the quality assessment process. The set of all the subjects of triples containing a given property were used to calculate IRIs and blank nodes counts, the type of each subject (if a class definition was found in the dataset), and the percentage of each type of subjects (see the extracted domain classes in Table 2). Similarly, the objects of the triples were analyzed to generate the counts of IRIs, blank nodes, and literals. For IRIs and blank nodes, their types and type percentages were extracted. For literals, a special attention was paid to numeric data types and those were categorized into decimals, doubles, floats, and integers.

The extracted statistics are not exhaustive, *i.e.*, the list of statistics can be extended by systematically analyzing other numeric types as well as non-numeric types such as date types, duration, and boolean. The set of SPARQL templates used in this study can be easily extended to cover such types.

Finally, the extracted property statistics were analyzed semi-automatically, both using manual inspection and a set of quality assessment services, to identify the quality problems that are described in the next section.

3 Analysis of Quality Dimensions

Four quality dimensions were used to analyze the quality issues of the Spanish DBpedia properties; each dimension is detailed next.

- **Conciseness.** A dataset is defined to be concise if it does not contain redundant concepts with different identifiers [7]. Conciseness refers to the minimization of redundant entities at both the schema level and data level [9]. In this study, we limit our scope to the analysis of properties used in the Spanish DBpedia including both the properties that are defined in the DBpedia ontology and other known ontologies and the properties that are generated by the DBpedia extractors using the infobox labels in Wikipedia. We identify the redundant properties in the Spanish DBpedia dataset (*i.e.*, the properties that are intended to mean the same relationship but have different identifiers – IRIs) and the possible causes for the existence of such redundant properties.
- **Consistency.** A dataset is defined to be consistent if it does not contain conflicting or contradictory data [5]. When an ontology is available, a reasoner can be used to verify whether the dataset is consistent with respect to the axioms defined in the ontology. However, as it was shown in Table 1, the majority of properties in the Spanish DBpedia are auto-generated infobox properties without any ontological axioms. Thus, we look at characteristics that can be checked without having an ontology. For this purpose, we assume OWL DL semantics (not RDFS Semantics) because the DBpedia ontology follows such semantics. We identify the properties that are both object and datatype properties simultaneously because according to OWL DL, the object domain (the set of all individuals) and the data domain (the data values) are strictly disjoint[11].
  Further, we analyze the extracted domain and range classes of properties using the method described in Sect. 2. The objective of this analysis is to identify subjects or objects that do not match the semantics of the property. We used manual inspection of domain and range classes with smaller percentages to identify such cases.
- **Syntactic Validity.** A given value is defined as syntactically valid or accurate when that value belongs to the legal value set (or value range) for the represented domain and when it does not violate the syntactic rules for the domain such as predefined formats [4]. Malformed datatype literals or literals

---

[11] http://www.w3.org/TR/owl2-direct-semantics/#Interpretations.

incompatible with the datatype range are examples of violations of syntactic validity [5]. Clustering and outlier detection techniques for datatypes and ranges are used to detect invalid values [8].

In this analysis, we looked for properties with values that have datatype definitions that do not match with their data values. For instance, the values declared as an integer containing a floating point value (e.g., `7.5^^xsd:integer`) or datatype definitions erroneously included inside a string value by mistake (e.g., `"2^^xsd:integer"`).

– **Semantic Accuracy.** Semantic accuracy of a dataset is defined as the degree to which data values correctly represent real world facts [9]. One metric that can be used to determine semantic accuracy is the detection of outliers based on different approaches such as statistical distribution-based methods, distance-based methods, and deviation-based methods. In this analysis, we used a simple outlier detection mechanism of 0.1 % negative numbers for numerical values. Usage of other outlier detection methods such as the ones mentioned in [8] is planned as future work.

3.1 Conciseness

We used an iterative process to identify duplicate property URIs that are intended to have the same meaning. As the first step, we alphabetically ordered the property list extracted as discussed in Sect. 2 using a Collator[12] for Spanish locale with the strength set to primary (*i.e.*, the differences such as capitalization or accents are not considered significant). Then, we selected several samples of 100 adjacent properties from different places of the list and analyzed them manually to find common patterns of duplicate properties. Based on that analysis, the following list of causes for duplicate property URIs were identified.

– Capitalization irregularities: e.g., `partidosEnPrimera`, `partidosenprimera`, `partidosenPrimera`.
– Synonyms: e.g., `causaDeMuerte`, `causaDeFallecimiento`.
– Irregularities in prepositions: e.g., `causaDeFallecimiento`, `causaFallecimiento`, `causaDelFallecimiento`.
– Spelling mistakes: e.g., `apeliido`, `apelldio`, `apellid`.
– Singular/plural irregularities: e.g., `apellido`, `apellidos`.
– Gender irregularities: e.g., `administrador`, `administradora`.
– Accent usage irregularities: e.g., `administracion`, `administración`.
– Parsing irregularities[13]: e.g., `altitudMin/máx`, `residencia/trabajo`, `idioma/s`.

Once the causes for duplicate properties were identified, we used more systematic approaches for analyzing the frequency of their occurrences. For identifying capitalization irregularities, we normalized all the property local names to

---

simple letters and identified the properties that only differ due to inconsistent capitalization. There were 857 properties under this category[14]. Similarly, we used a normalizer[15] that decomposes unicode text into their main characters and accents and then removed the accents from the property names. With this, we identified 1,252 properties[16] that differ only because of the inconsistent usage of accents. For identifying spelling mistakes, we used the Levenshtein string similarity measure that calculates the minimum number of single-character edits (i.e., insertions, deletions or substitutions) required to change one word into the other. With a threshold of 0.85 on a normalized scale, we found 7,495 similar properties[17]. However, manual inspection was required to remove false positives, *i.e.*, the properties which are similar but still have a unique meaning (e.g., año1dato and año2dato). We found 30 parsing irregularities with the "http://es.dbpedia.org/property/" prefix (when an infobox attribute has a slash, *e.g.*, idioma/s) and 77 with "http://dbpedia.org/property/" prefix. Other irregularities require advanced linguistic support (e.g., gender or singular/plural irregularities) and those are planned as future work.

3.2 Consistency

Under consistency, we first looked at the triples containing a given property that have both IRIs/blank nodes and literals as objects, *i.e.*, being both object and datatype properties at the same time. There are 3,380 properties that show this inconsistency. One common root cause for such inconsistencies is the fact that people uses links to pages in some pages and strings in some other pages. For example, when using a property such as esdbpedia:lugarDeEntierro (meaning burial place), both the label "Madrid"@es and the link to the corresponding resource http://es.dbpedia.org/resource/Madrid were used in different instances.

Further, we analyzed the extracted domain and range types of a given property (see Table 2) to identify domain and range classes which are defined in less than 1 % of the triples that contain the given property. We found 2,821 properties which contain at least one domain or range class that fits the aforementioned criterion. We manually inspected a sample of those less frequent domain and range classes to check whether those classes match with the semantics of the property. According to the analysis, we found that most cases are false positives, *i.e.*, even though those classes have a lower percentage than the rest they matched the semantics of the property (e.g., subclasses or similar classes defined in other ontologies). However, we also found cases in which they are different from the majority of the triples and can potentially be erroneous data. For instance, in the example shown in Table 2, it is suspicious that the property "edad" (meaning age) has instances of the "Place" class as objects in two triples. In future work, we plan to explore techniques for automatically detecting classes that are

---

[14] http://dx.doi.org/10.6084/m9.figshare.1491367.
[15] http://docs.oracle.com/javase/7/docs/api/java/text/Normalizer.html.
[16] http://dx.doi.org/10.6084/m9.figshare.1491372.
[17] http://dx.doi.org/10.6084/m9.figshare.1491432.

not consistent using the patterns in data through clustering techniques, even though ontology axioms defining the domain and range of the properties are not available.

3.3 Syntactic Validity

In the serialization level (*i.e.*, RDF/XML, Turtle, etc.), the Spanish DBpedia generates valid RDF for the resources. Thus, we decided to look at the syntactic accuracy at the datatype level within RDF. When an ontology that provides the explicit domain and range of the property is present, the data type ranges of the properties are known and validations can be performed to ensure that values have syntactic accuracy for a given type. However, in the case of infobox-properties there is no such information available about the valid range of a property.

In this analysis, we placed a special attention to numerical values because numerical values were more feasible to be analyzed automatically. Thus, we filtered the properties that contain numeric values and looked at numerical types which are uncommon compared to the rest of data of the same property. For instance, there are 3,675 properties that have more than 99 % integer objects and a very few string literals. When we manually inspected those string literals, we found that they are numerical values represented as strings (e.g., 2^^xsd:integer) due to an error in the mappings. Besides, another common error that we found is that IRIs are represented as strings (e.g., "http://...").

3.4 Semantic Accuracy

Semantic accuracy is harder to automatically analyze compared to the other dimensions because values have to be checked against real world facts to validate their accuracy. We again chose to analyze the numerical values due to the feasibility of automatic analysis and focused on outlier detection. For instance, when we looked at the minimum values we could identify negative values that do not match with the property semantics. For instance, in properties such as diameter we could see one negative value out of 326 values. Similarly, the property height had two negative values out of 25,137 distinct values.

In the future, we plan to use data fusion approaches by comparing the values from one dataset with several other datasets (e.g., the different local DBpedia chapters) to evaluate semantic accuracy.

4   Related Work

Zaveri *et al.* performed a survey of quality assessment metrics for Linked Data [9] and identified 69 quality metrics across 18 quality dimensions. In this work, we focus on four quality dimensions we find relevant for properties in the Spanish DBpedia dataset.

Databugger [6] is a framework for test-driven quality assessment of Linked Data and it generates a set of test cases using accompanying vocabularies, ontologies and knowledge bases. But these tests are mostly suitable when a vocabulary or ontology already exits. Wienand and Paulheim [8] apply unsupervised numerical outlier detection methods, using Interquantile Range (IQR), Kernel Density Estimation (KDE), and dispersion estimators for detecting incorrect numerical data in DBpedia. Their results have led to the identification of 11 systematic errors in the DBpedia extraction framework. Our work follows a similar approach but with a wider scope looking at the property characteristics in general. In addition to the identification of errors, we provide a web site that will make it easier to use such data.

Acosta *et al.* [1] present a tool that uses crowdsourcing as a means to handle Linked Data quality problems that are challenging to be solved automatically. This tool presents the Linked Data resources to the users and gets their feedback. Our approach can be used to increase the efficiency of such tools so that rather than presenting all resource data for the review, the tool can present a potential error list with data that have high probability to have quality problems.

LOD Laundromat [3] is a tool that cleans several quality defects in a dataset such as duplicate RDF statements and syntax errors automatically without any human intervention and provides a uniform entry point for the cleaned data. However, LOD Laundromat still does not handle the type of quality problems that we discussed in this paper.

5   Conclusions and Future Work

DBpedia plays a central role in the LOD cloud, and the local DBpedias provide valuable data that cannot be found in the English DBpedia. In this work we analyze the properties used in the Spanish DBpedia to identify quality issues focused in their conciseness, consistency, syntactic validity, and semantic accuracy. Furthermore, the data used for the analysis is available online[18].

In this study, we show that 97.93 % of the properties used in the Spanish DBpedia are auto-generated properties (not using the mappings in the DBpedia extraction process). Our results show that they suffer from conciseness quality issues due to several causes such as inconsistent capitalization (857 properties), inconsistent usage of accents (1,252 properties), slashes in infobox labels (107 properties), spelling mistakes, etc. We also found inconsistencies such as properties simultaneously being object and datatype properties (3,380 properties) or wrong domain/range values (2,821 properties). Syntactic validity problems were found in 3,675 properties.

The results of this analysis can be a valuable feedback to the DBpedia community to understand the current quality issues in DBpedia and to improve the extraction process to eliminate some of the identified quality issues. Specially some of the issues found in the conciseness dimension can be eliminated by performing some pre-processing and cleaning of the infobox attributes before converting them into properties.

As future work, the authors plan to perform an analysis of other DBpedia instances, *i.e.*, the English DBpedia and other local chapters. Such analysis will

---

[18] http://loupe.linkeddata.es/loupe/.

provide insights on which quality issues found in this paper are common to all DBpedia instances and which are specific to the Spanish DBpedia. It will also help to identify new language-specific quality problems in other DBpedia datasets. The method and the techniques used in this paper can be easily applied to the other DBpedia instances to find similar quality issues.

Further, in the analysis of quality issues, several tasks were not automated due to lack of tool support and time/effort constraints. Tasks such as the identification of property duplicates that use synonyms or words that only differ from gender/number require tools that provide linguistic support for the Spanish language. The authors plan to implement those linguistic services for detection of gender/number of nouns, generation of corresponding male/female nouns, or generation of corresponding singular/plural nouns, so that such irregularities in properties can be detected automatically. Furthermore, authors plan to improve the used methods with the usage of additional outlier detection and clustering techniques.

In this study, the authors only considered the property characteristics that were extracted from data because the majority of the properties used in the Spanish DBpedia were auto-generated infobox properties. However, there are properties from existing ontologies used in the dataset and the axioms of those ontologies can be used for detecting quality problems in such properties. This is also planned as future work.

Acknowledgments. This work was funded by the BES-2014-068449 grant under the 4V project (TIN2013-46238-C4-2-R), the LIDER project (EU FP7 610782), and the JCI-2012-12719 contract.

References

1. Acosta, M., Zaveri, A., Simperl, E., Kontokostas, D., Auer, S., Lehmann, J.: Crowd-sourcing linked data quality assessment. In: Alani, H., et al. (eds.) ISWC 2013, Part II. LNCS, vol. 8219, pp. 260–276. Springer, Heidelberg (2013)
2. Auer, S., Bizer, C., Kobilarov, G., Lehmann, J., Cyganiak, R., Ives, Z.: DBpedia: a nucleus for a web of open data. In: Aberer, K., et al. (eds.) ASWC/ISWC 2007. LNCS, vol. 4825, pp. 722–735. Springer, Heidelberg (2007)
3. Beek, W., Rietveld, L., Bazoobandi, H.R., Wielemaker, J., Schlobach, S.: LOD laundromat: a uniform way of publishing other people's dirty data. In: Mika, P., et al. (eds.) ISWC 2014, Part I. LNCS, vol. 8796, pp. 213–228. Springer, Heidelberg (2014)
4. Fürber, C., Hepp, M.: SWIQA a semantic web information quality assessment framework. In: Proceeding of the 19th European Conference on Information Systems (ECIS 2011), vol. 15, p. 19 (2011)
5. Hogan, A., Harth, A., Passant, A., Decker, S., Polleres, A.: Weaving the pedantic web. In: Proceedings of the Linked Data on the Web (LDOW 2010), CEUR Workshop Proceedings, vol. 628 (2010)
6. Kontokostas, D., Westphal, P., Auer, S., Hellmann, S., Lehmann, J., Cornelissen, R.: Databugger: a test-driven framework for debugging the web of data. In: Proceedings of the Companion Publication of the 23rd International Conference on World Wide Web Companion, pp. 115–118 (2014)

7. Mendes, P.N., Mühleisen, H., Bizer, C.: Sieve: linked data quality assessment and fusion. In: Proceedings of the 2012 Joint EDBT/ICDT Workshops, pp. 116–123. ACM (2012)
8. Wienand, D., Paulheim, H.: Detecting incorrect numerical data in DBpedia. In: Presutti, V., d'Amato, C., Gandon, F., d'Aquin, M., Staab, S., Tordai, A. (eds.) ESWC 2014. LNCS, vol. 8465, pp. 504–518. Springer, Heidelberg (2014)
9. Zaveri, A., Rula, A., Maurinob, A., Pietrobonc, R., Lehmanna, J., Auer, S.: Quality assessment for linked data: a survey. Semant. Web J. (2015)

Machine Learning and Data Mining

Measuring Data Imperfection in a Neighborhood Based Method

José M. Cadenas[1], M. Carmen Garrido[1], and Raquel Martínez[2(✉)]

[1] Department of Information Engineering and Communication,
University of Murcia, Murcia, Spain
{jcadenas,carmengarrido}@um.es
[2] Department of Computer Engineering,
Catholic University of San Antonio, Murcia, Spain
rmartinez@ucam.edu

Abstract. In this paper, we present an extension of k nearest neighbors method so it can perform imputation/classification from datasets with low quality data. The method performs a weighting of neighbors based on their imperfection and distance of classes. Thus the method allows us explicitly to indicate the average degree of imperfection of the neighbors that it is accepted to carry out the imputation/classification and the average distance of classes to the class of example to impute/classify that it is allowed. We carry out several experiments with both real-world and synthetic datasets with low quality data to test the proposed method.

Keywords: Classification · k-nearest neighbors · Low quality data · Measures distance

1 Introduction

Within the data mining phase of the Intelligent Data Analysis process, one of the best known methods for classification is the k nearest neighbors (kNN), where k is the number of neighbors considered, [9]. The kNN is a non-parametric method used for classification and regression. This method has the following advantages: It infers both nominal attributes (the most common attribute value between the k nearest neighbors) and numerical attributes (the average of the values of the k nearest neighbors); It allows missing values in the data; Does not create explicit models since the own training dataset is used as a "vague model". Thus, the method can be adapted easily to predict any attribute; etc.

The kNN method has been analyzed extensively by the research community and many approaches have been proposed, for example, the computation of similarity measures, the optimum choice of the k parameter, the definition of weighting schemes for patterns and attributes. Fuzzy sets theory has been the basis of a remarkable number of these approaches. All these approaches have been proposed with a clear objective: improving the accuracy of the kNN method. In [4], Derrac et al. discuss different k nearest neighbor algorithms.

© Springer International Publishing Switzerland 2015
J.M. Puerta et al. (Eds.): CAEPIA 2015, LNAI 9422, pp. 213–223, 2015.
DOI: 10.1007/978-3-319-24598-0_19

But, the kNN method, like many conventional methods of Intelligent Data Analysis, does not consider potential sources of imperfect information that may affect the input data. As a result, incomplete, imprecise and uncertain data are usually discarded and ignored of the input dataset and subsequently in the imputation/classification process. Nevertheless, these data inevitably appear in real world applications: the errors in the instruments and/or the corruption due to noise during experiments may lead to the obtaining of information with incomplete data when a value of a specific attribute is being obtained; the extraction of accurate information can be excessively expensive or unfeasible, moreover, it could be useful to complement the available data with additional information from an expert; etc. This information is normally obtained by imprecise data values such as: interval data, fuzzy concepts, etc. (called imperfect data or low quality data).

In this paper, an extension of kNN method to impute/classify from low quality data (denoted by kNN_{LQD} method) is presented. The method weights the importance of each neighbor in the final decision according to its imperfection (the more imperfect a neighbor is, the less weight it has in the final decision) and according to the distance of classes (the higher the distance of classes to example is, the less weight it has). Thus, in Sect. 2 the kNN_{LQD} method to impute/classify from a dataset with low quality values is exposed, describing all its components (distance measures, weighting schemes for neighbors, decision rules, etc.). In Sect. 3, some experiments are performed in order to measure the effectiveness of the proposal with a number of datasets with low quality values. In these experiments, we will focus on the classification task. Finally, the conclusions are presented.

2   K-Nearest Neighbors Method from Low Quality Data

2.1   Introduction

Suppose the set of examples E described by n attributes $x = \{x_1, x_2, \ldots, x_n\}$ with domains $\Omega_{x_1}, \Omega_{x_2}, \ldots, \Omega_{x_n}$ where we consider, without loss of generality, that n-th attribute is the class attribute. Domains Ω_{x_i}, $1 \le i \le n-1$, can be nominal and numerical and the domain Ω_{x_n} is composed of I classes represented by $\{\omega_1, \omega_2, \ldots, \omega_I\}$. The attributes are expressed using low quality values of different types:

- The numerical attributes may be defined by crisp, fuzzy, interval and missing values. To homogenize their representation, these values are described internally by a quadruple (a, b, c, d).

  For fuzzy values, quadruple defines a trapezoidal fuzzy membership function:

$$\mu(x) = \begin{cases} 0 & x < a \text{ or } x > d \\ \frac{x-a}{b-a} & a \le x < b \\ 1 & b \le x < c \\ \frac{d-x}{d-c} & c \le x < d \end{cases}$$

For interval and missing values, quadruple defines an interval where $a = b$ and $c = d$. In particular, for missing values, $a = b = min$ and $c = d = max$ where min and max correspond to the minimum/maximum values for this attribute in the dataset when the example class is missing or correspond to the minimum/maximum values, for this attribute, in the examples with equal class to the known class of the example. In addition, a numerical crisp value is represented by a quadruple (a, a, a, a).

- Nominal attributes can be defined by crisp values, crisp/fuzzy subsets and missing values. Again, to unify their representation, the crisp/fuzzy subsets and missing values are represented internally by subsets.
  The fuzzy subsets will be represented by $\{\mu(h_1)/h_1, \mu(h_2)/h_2, \ldots, \mu(h_n)/h_s\}$ and the crisp subsets and missing values by $\{h_1, h_2, \ldots, h_s\}$, where h_i are domain values. In particular, a missing value is represented by a crisp subset containing all the possible values of the attribute domain. In addition, a nominal crisp value is represented by a crisp subset composed of a simple domain value.

In the following subsections, we describe in detail each element that defines the kNN_{LQD} method.

2.2   Contribution from Neighbors for the Imputation/Classification

To perform the imputation/classification based on neighborhood, it is necessary to obtain the nearest neighbors using a distance function $d_{LQD}(\cdot, \cdot)$. We define the distance between two examples x and x', $d_{LQD}(x, x')$, as a heterogeneous distance function that can work with numerical and nominal attributes defined by low quality data. The $d_{LQD}(\cdot, \cdot)$ function is defined as follows:

$$d_{LQD}(x, x') = \sqrt{\frac{\sum_{i=1}^{n-1} f(x_i, x'_i)^2}{n-1}} \quad \text{with } f(x_i, x'_i) = \begin{cases} f_1(x_i, x'_i) & \text{if i is numerical} \\ f_2(x_i, x'_i) & \text{if i is nominal} \end{cases}$$

Function $f(\cdot, \cdot)$ is a heterogeneous measure of the distance between two attributes that could be defined by low quality values. Each of the functions $f_1(\cdot, \cdot)$ and $f_2(\cdot, \cdot)$ take values in the interval $[0, 1]$.

Using the $d_{LQD}(\cdot, \cdot)$ function, we obtain the set of k nearest neighbors to a given example z (this set will be denoted by $KLQD$). From this set we perform the imputation of missing values in z or its classification.

Weight of Each Neighbor Based on the Class Similarity. In the case of classical kNN method from crisp data, the known class of z causes that in the imputation the only neighbors considered are those belong to that class. Now, in the kNN_{LQD} method, the contribution of each neighbor to the imputation is weighted in proportion to the similarity of their class to the class of z. The contribution of each neighbor $x \in KLQD$ is defined in kNN_{LQD} method by

$p_1(x) = 1 - f_2(x_n, z_n)$ where $f_2(\cdot, \cdot)$ is the distance measure between nominal attributes of the function $d_{LQD}(\cdot, \cdot)$. In this way, in the extreme values of f_2, if $f_2(x_n, z_n) = 0$, the classes are equal and $p_1(x) = 1$ so the neighbor x contributes with maximum weight in the imputation of values of z; however, if $f_2(x_n, z_n) = 1$ then $p_1(x) = 0$ and the neighbor x is not considered in the imputation.

Weight of Each Neighbor Based on its Imperfection. Due to the fact that $KLQD$ examples can be defined by low quality values, the proposed method incorporates in the imputation/classification a second weighting of each neighbor based on its imperfection, so that the more low quality a neighbor is, the less influence it has in the imputation/classification. This value is defined by $p_2(x) = 1 - imp(x)$, where the $imp(x)$ function is as follows:

$$imp(x) = \left(\sum_{i=1}^{n} g(x_i) \right) / n$$

where function $g(\cdot)$ is a proper imperfection measure function for each attribute type x_i. We define the following functions.
For numerical attributes:

$$g(x_i) = \frac{entropy(x_i) + width(x_i)}{2}$$

where $entropy(x_i)$ is an entropy function which measures the fuzziness of fuzzy set value x_i (such measures characterize the sharpness of the membership functions, [7], in order to obtain global measures of the indefiniteness described by fuzzy sets, [6]) and $width(x_i)$ is the interval width or support of the fuzzy set.
For a nominal attribute x_i with value $= h$,

$$g(x_i) = \begin{cases} \left[entropy(h) + \frac{Card(h)}{Card(\Omega_{x_i})} \right] / 2 & \text{if } Card(h) > 1 \\ entropy(h) / 2 & \text{if } Card(h) = 1 \end{cases}$$

where $Card(\cdot)$ is the cardinality of set.

The Weight of the Neighbors in the Imputation/Classification. To indicate the degree with which each of the above weights $(p_1(x), p_2(x))$ are applied, the parameters $0 \leq F_1 \leq 1$ and $0 \leq F_2 \leq 1$ are used ($F_1 + F_2 = 1$). The imputed value in a numerical attribute or the degree of the domain value in a nominal attribute is the average of the values/degrees of these attributes in the k neighbors weighted by the similarity of classes, $p_1(\cdot)$, and by the imperfection of the examples, $p_2(\cdot)$. These values will be weighted by F_1 and F_2 values to indicate the importance that we want to give to each part.

When the method is used to classify, automatically these values are set as $F_1 = 0$ and $F_2 = 1$ since as the class of input examples is unknown and therefore it can not be used as weighting the distance of classes of the nearest neighbors. In this case, the contribution of each neighbor, in the classification of a new example, will be proportional to their "perfection degree".

2.3   Controlling the kNN$_{\mathrm{LQD}}$ Method

The kNN$_{\mathrm{LQD}}$ method allows us to define a similarity average value to be reached in order to carry out the imputation in an example. This value is defined by the threshold $0 \leq U_S \leq 1$. Thus, if the average similarity between classes of the nearest neighbors and the example z is below this threshold, the imputation is not performed. This threshold can be interpreted as the minimum average grade of belief with which the user wants to perform imputations. When $U_S = 0$ all imputations will be performed regardless of belief that supports them, and when $U_S = 1$, it is only carried out an imputation when it is based on examples with the same class value as the imputed example. In this last case, the method works as the classical method.

Likewise, the kNN$_{\mathrm{LQD}}$ method allows us to define a degree of maximum average imperfection (defined by the threshold $0 \leq U_I \leq 1$) between the nearest neighbors to perform the imputation/classification. Thus, if the imperfection degree of the nearest neighbors were very high, we could indicate that the imputation/classification was not carried out. When $U_I = 0$ the imputation/classification is only carried out when the neighbors are defined by crisp values and when $U_I = 1$ all imputations are carried out regardless of the quality of the neighbors.

2.4   The Process of the kNN$_{\mathrm{LQD}}$ Method

The process of the kNN$_{\mathrm{LQD}}$ method is described in Algorithm kNN$_{\mathrm{LQD}}$.

Algorithm – kNN$_{\mathrm{LQD}}$ - k Nearest neighbor applied to low quality data

---

Introduce z; k, $1 \leq k \leq |E|$; U_S, U_I;

if the class of z is missing **then** $F_1 = 0$; $F_2 = 1$ **else** Introduce F_1 ($F_2 = 1 - F_1$)

Obtain the set $KLQD$ with the k nearest examples to z according to $d_{LQD}(x, z)$;

if $F_1 \neq 0$ **then**

    for all x in $KLQD$ **do** $p_1(x) = 1 - f_2(x_n, z_n)$ **end for**

  $P1_{KLQD} = \sum_{x \in KLQD} p_1(x)$

else $P1_{KLQD} = 1$

end if

if $F_2 \neq 0$ **then**

    for all x in $KLQD$ **do** $p_2(x) = 1 - imp(x)$ **end for**

  $P2_{KLQD} = \sum_{x \in KLQD} p_2(x)$

else $P2_{KLQD} = 1$

end if

$IMP_{average} = \frac{P2_{KLQD}}{k}$; $SIM_{average} = \frac{P1_{KLQD}}{k}$

if ($((SIM_{average} \geq U_S$ and $P1_{KLQD} \neq 0)$ or $F_1 = 0)$ and

    $(IMP_{average} \leq U_I$ and $P2_{KLQD} \neq 0)$ or $F_2 = 0)$] **then**

    for all z_j missing in z **do**

      if z_j is numerical **then** $z_j = F_1 \cdot \frac{\sum\limits_{x \in KLQD} p_1(x) \cdot x_j}{P1_{KLQD}} + F_2 \cdot \frac{\sum\limits_{x \in KLQD} p_2(x) \cdot x_j}{P2_{KLQD}}$;

      else if z_j is nominal **then**

$$z_j = \{\frac{F_1 \cdot \sum\limits_{x \in KLQD} p_1(x) \cdot \mu_{x_j}(h) + F_2 \cdot \sum\limits_{x \in KLQD} p_2(x) \cdot \mu_{x_j}(h)}{k} /h\}; \ \forall h \in \Omega_j.$$

    end if
  end for
else Imputation/classification is not realized;
end if

3   Experimental Results

In this section we perform experiments based on real and synthetic datasets with low quality values. To do this, we define the distance measure used $d_{LQD}(\cdot, \cdot)$, the fuzzy entropy function used to define the imperfection measure $imp(\cdot)$, and in each case the experimental framework.

3.1 Fuzzy Distance Measure

To define the distance measure between examples with low quality values, we can use different measures of literature, [5,8,15,16], or we can define our own measure. We use the following measures:

- The distance of Diamond, [5], is defined between the numerical values of the i-th attribute of two examples u and v as:

$$f_1(u_i, v_i) = \frac{\sqrt{\frac{(a-a')^2 + (b-b')^2 + (c-c')^2 + (d-d')^2}{4}}}{max_i - min_i}$$

where u_i and v_i are numerical values defined by quadruples (a,b,c,d) and (a',b',c',d') respectively and max_i, min_i are the maximum and minimum values of attribute i in the dataset.

- The dissimilarity measure of Dubois and Prade, [8], is defined between two nominal values of the i-th attribute of two examples u and v as:

$$f_2(u_i, v_i) = 1 - \frac{Card(u_i \bigcap v_i)}{Card(u_i \bigcup v_i)}$$

where u_i and v_i are fuzzy sets and $Card(u_i \bigcap v_i)$ and $Card(u_i \bigcup v_i)$ are defined as the cardinality of fuzzy sets resulting from the union and intersection of u_i and v_i respectively.

3.2 Fuzzy Entropy Function

Among possible entropy functions, $entropy(\cdot)$, we can use different functions of literature, [6,12], etc., or we can define our own function. We use the Kaufmann function based on Hamming distance, [12]:

$$entropy(u_i) = \frac{2}{Card(\Omega_i)} \sum_{h \in \Omega_i} |\mu_{u_i}(h) - \mu_{\frac{1}{2}, u_i}(h)|$$

where $\mu_{\frac{1}{2}, u_i}(h) = \begin{cases} 0 \text{ if } \mu_{u_i}(h) < \frac{1}{2} \\ 1 \text{ if } \mu_{u_i}(h) \geq \frac{1}{2}. \end{cases}$

3.3 Classification Accuracy

Since the class value assigned to an example z by the method can be a fuzzy set $\{\mu_{z_n}(\omega_1)/\omega_1, \mu_{z_n}(\omega_2)/\omega_2, \ldots, \mu_{z_n}(\omega_I)/\omega_I\}$, this value is transformed to a crisp set $\{\omega_1, \ldots, \omega_j\}$ as follows. Let ω_m be the class with the highest membership degree in the previous fuzzy set, the crisp set is obtained as:

$$class_{KNN_{LQD}}(z) = \{\omega_m\} \bigcup \left\{ \omega_c \mid \frac{\mu_{z_n}(\omega_m) - \mu_{z_n}(\omega_c)}{\mu_{z_n}(\omega_m)} \leq \gamma \right\}$$

where γ is an external parameter to indicate how close to the majority class of the output set, ω_m, should be a class ω_c to be considered a final class. With $\gamma = 0$ the final class tends to be a set composed of a single class, the majority class, but it can be a set composed by more than one class in case of a tie between majority classes. With $\gamma = 1$, the final class is the one obtained by the algorithm. Therefore, to obtain the results of classification accuracy, we apply the decision process shown in Algorithm "Decision in Classification".

Algorithm – Decision in classification

---

success=0; error=0; success_error=0;
for all z in E_{test} **do**
    if $(class(z) = class_{kNN_{LQD}}(z))$ **then** success=success+1;
    else
        if $(class(z) \bigcap class_{kNN_{LQD}}(z) \neq \emptyset)$ **then** success_error=success_error+1;
        else error=error+1
    end if
end for

An interval $[Acc_{min}, Acc_{max}]$ of classification accuracy is constructed, where Acc_{min} is calculated as the percentage of success considering only the variable *success* and Acc_{max} is calculated as the percentage of success considering the sum of the variables *success + success_error*. We can interpret the lower bound of the interval as a pessimistic percentage of accuracy and the upper bound as an optimistic percentage of classification accuracy considering those cases where the real class is contained in the inferred class as success.

3.4 Synthetic Datasets with Low Quality Data

In this section we perform the testing of the kNN$_{LQD}$ method using synthetic datasets to which we have added different percentages of imperfection.

Datasets Description. In this experiment we have used several datasets from the UCI repository [13] (Table 1).

This Table 1 shows the number of examples $|E|$, the number of attributes (numerical Nu, nominal No), the number of classes (I) and if it contains missing values (M). "Abbr" indicates the abbreviation of the dataset. We have included explicitly low quality values in these datasets using the NIPip tool [3]. We include

Table 1. Datasets description

Datasets	Abbr	|E|	Nu	No	I	M
Australian	**AUS**	690	6	8	2	N
Credit screen	**CRX**	690	6	9	2	N
Glass	**GLA**	214	9	0	6	N
Hepatitis	**HEP**	155	6	13	2	Y
Horse-colic	**HOR**	368	7	15	2	Y
Zoo	**ZOO**	101	1	16	7	N

10 %–20 % of imperfect values divided between the following types of low quality values: interval values, fuzzy values, crisp subsets and fuzzy subsets. These percentages do not affect the class attribute.

Experimental Framework. We have used a tenfold cross-validation for all datasets. The kNN$_{\text{LQD}}$ method is executed for each dataset using $F_1 = 0$ ($F_2 = 1$), $\gamma = 0$ and changing U_I ($U_I = 1$, $U_I = 0.35$, $U_I = 0.15$). The best average accuracy value per dataset has been chosen considering k={1, 3, 5, 7, ... }.

Results. In Table 2 the percentages of average accuracy in classification are shown. These results are obtained with $U_I = 1$, i.e., all examples are classified. The results in column "Without Imperfection" are competitive with regard to those shown in literature, and the results in columns "With imperfection" show the stability of the kNN$_{\text{LQD}}$ method.

Table 2. Results with datasets of Table 1 with low quality data

	Without imperfection		With imperfection			
			10 %		20 %	
	Accuracy	k	Accuracy	k	Accuracy	k
AUS	87.10	9	84.93	9	82.75	5
CRX	87.10	5	84.64	9	83.33	9
GLA	71.92	1	64.59	1	63.64	1
HEP	85.78	9	84.61	7	84.37	7
HOR	84.24	17	80.51	13	80.20	17
ZOO	97.00	1	93.09	1	94.18	1

In Table 3 the percentages of average accuracy in classification are shown using values $U_I = 0.35$ and $U_I = 0.15$, i.e., examples will be classified according to the imprecision of its k nearest neighbors. Values shown as subscripts indicate the percentage of examples unclassified according to U value. In addition, we can see some results expressed as intervals due to the classification decision of

kNN_{LQD} method commented in SubSect. 3.3. When using $\gamma = 0$, these intervals indicate that the crisp subset inferred by the method consists of several majoritarian classes. The accuracy obtained with HOR dataset with 10 % and 20 % of imperfection it is very low because a very high percentage of examples are not classified due to the nearest neighbors contain a high imperfection.

3.5   Real-World Dataset with Low Quality Data

These experiments are conducted to test the accuracy of kNN_{LQD} applied to real-world datasets with imperfect values and compare the results with the ones obtained by the GFS classifier proposed in [14] and the FRF ensemble proposed in [1,2]. GFS classifier is an extension of a Genetic Fuzzy System to handle imperfect data based on the use of a interval or fuzzy valued fitness function, and FRF ensemble is a classification technique based on multiple classifier systems (this technique uses a fuzzy decision tree as base classifier and allows the treatment of imperfect information). In these experiments we used the datasets available in "http://sci2s.ugr.es/keel/" and the results available in [1,2,14].

Table 3. Results with datasets of Table 1 with low quality data

	10 %		20 %		10 %		20 %	
	U = 0.35				U = 0.15			
	Accuracy	k	Accuracy	k	Accuracy	k	Accuracy	k
AUS	84.93	9	82.75	5	84.93	9	$82.32_{0.14}$	9
CRX	84.64	9	83.33	9	84.64	9	$83.33_{0.14}$	9
GLA	64.59	1	63.64	1	64.59	1	63.64	1
	[60.25,68.13]	5	[61.67,66.37]	7	[60.25,68.13]	5	[61.67,66.37]	7
HEP	84.61	7	84.37	7	84.61	7	$72.11_{14.87}$	7
HOR	80.72	27	79.68	27	$48.93_{41.56}$	7	$23.90_{69.01}$	3
ZOO	93.09	1	94.98	1	93.09	1	$91.18_{5.82}$	1
	–		[93.18,95.18]	3	–		$[90.18,93.09]_{2.0}$	7

Datasets Description. In this experiment we have used three dataset collect of the Spanish women's athletic club championship whose description is as follows (all datasets have 25 examples, 4 attributes, 2 classes and no missing values, and all attributes are interval-valued and the output attribute is a crisp subset - a more detailed description may be found in [14]):

– "Long-4": Dataset used to predict whether an athlete will improve certain threshold in the long jump, given a set of indicators.
– "100 ml-4-I": Used for predicting whether a mark in the 100 m sprint race is being achieved.
– "100 ml-4-P": Same dataset as "100 ml-4-I", but the measurements have been replaced by the subjective grade the trainer has assigned to each indicator (i.e. "reaction time is low" instead of "reaction time is 0.1 s").

Experimental Framework. As in [2,14], we have used a tenfold cross-validation for all datasets. kNN_{LQD} method is executed with $F_1 = 0$ ($F_2 = 1$), $\gamma = 0$ and changing U_I ($U_I = 1, U_I = 0.1$) and $k = 1$.

Results. Table 4 shows the average accuracy percentages obtained in [14], the ones obtained by the FRF ensemble [2] and the ones obtained by kNN_{LQD}. We can see that the results obtained with the kNN_{LQD} method with the two parameter configurations are very competitive when compared with those obtained by other methods. When $U_I = 0.1$ some examples are not classified.

Table 4. Average accuracy percentage in classification

Technique	100 ml-4-I	100 ml-4-P	Long-4
kNN_{LQD}, $U_I = 1$	[75.00,96.00]	[78.33,94.00]	[55.00,61.67]
kNN_{LQD}, $U_I = 0.1$	[75.00,75.00]$_{21.0}$	[78.33,78.33]$_{15.7}$	[55.00,55.00]$_{6.7}$
FRFSM2 [2]	[57.30,76.70]	[70.30,90.00]	[51.70,78.30]
FRFMIWLF1 [2]	[53.30,72.70]	[70.30,90.00]	[55.00,81.70]
Crisp [14]	61.60	58.10	45.60
GGFS [14]	[52.40,81.10]	[59.40,83.00]	[38.40,65.10]

To complete the experiment, we perform a statistical analysis. Following the methodology proposed in [10], we use non-parametric tests. We use the Friedman test and the Holm procedure as post-hoc test. By Friedman test, a rejection of null-hypothesis implies the existence of differences in the performance of all the methods. If differences are detected, then Holm's procedure is used to find whether the proposed method shows statistical differences with regard to the other methods. In order to carry it out, we have used R packet [11].

On the one hand, we obtain the average values of the accuracy intervals. We apply Friedman's test and we get a rejection of the null-hypothesis (p-value = 2.431e-4) with a $\alpha = 0.01$ (there are significant differences). Applying the Holm's procedure to the hypotheses of comparison between the kNN_{LQD} method and the others, we obtain their p-values: 0.03804, 0.02920, 0.00274, 0.02920. Holm's procedure rejects the hypotheses. Therefore, KNN_{LQD} is statistically better regarding accuracy than the rest of methods ($\alpha = 0.05$).

On the other hand, we obtain the average values subtracting the average values of the intervals from the amplitude of them. Following the above procedure, we accept that there are significant differences with a $\alpha = 0.01$ (p-value = 6.687e-3). Applying the Holm's procedure (without compare with the Crisp technique), we obtain their p values: 0.01195, 0.01195, 0.01200. Holm's procedure rejects the hypotheses. Also, KNN is statistically better than the rest of methods ($\alpha = 0.02$).

4   Conclusions

In this paper we have presented the neighborhood based method, kNN_{LQD}, which allows us to carry out the imputation/classification of examples from a dataset with low quality data. The method weighs the importance of each neighbor in the final decision based on its imperfection and the distance of its class. The method allows us to use a set of external parameters to limit the allowed imperfection and the allowed distance average of classes to perform the imputation/classification. As future work, a more detailed analysis of the influence of both the distance measure and imperfection measure should be performed.

Acknowledgements. Supported by the projects TIN2011-27696-C02-02, TIN2014-52099-R and TIN2014-56381-REDT ("Red de Lógica Difusa y Soft Computing (LODI SCO)") of the Ministry of Economy and Competitiveness of Spain.

References

1. Bonissone, P.P., Cadenas, J.M., Garrido, M.C., Díaz-Valladares, R.A.: A fuzzy random forest. Int. J. Approximate Reasoning **51**(7), 729–747 (2010)
2. Cadenas, J.M., Garrido, M.C., Martínez, R., Bonissone, P.P.: Extending information processing in a fuzzy random forest. Soft. Comput. **16**, 845–861 (2012)
3. Cadenas, J.M., Garrido, M.C., Martínez-España, R.: Software tool: NIP tool, Universidad de Murcia (2012). http://heurimind.inf.um.es
4. Derrac, J., García, S., Herrera, F.: Fuzzy nearest neighbor algorithms: taxonomy, experimental analysis and prospects. Inf. Sci. **260**, 98–119 (2014)
5. Diamon, P., Kloeden, P.: Metric Spaces of Fuzzy Sets: Theory and Application. World Scientific, Singapore (1994)
6. DeLuca, A., Termini, S.: A definition of a nonprobabilistic entropy in the setting of fuzzy sets theory. Inf. Control **20**(4), 301–312 (1972)
7. Dombi, J., Porkolab, L.: Measures fuzziness. Ann. Universitasis Scientiarium Budapestinensis Sect. Computatorica **12**, 69–78 (1991)
8. Dubois, D., Parde, H.: Fuzzy Sets and System, Theory and Applications. Academic Press, New York (1980)
9. Duda, R.O., Hart, P.E., Stork, D.G.: Pattern Classification. Wiley, New York (2001)
10. García, S., Fernández, A., Luengo, J., Herrera, F.: A study statistical techniques and performance measures for genetics-based machine learning: accuracy and interpretability. Soft. Comput. **13**(10), 959–977 (2009)
11. Ihaka, R., Gentleman, R.: R: a language for data analysis and graphics. J. Comput. Graph. Stat. **5**(3), 299–314 (1996)
12. Eickhoff, J.: Introduction to the theory of fuzzy subsets. In: Eickhoff, J. (ed.) Onboard Computers, Onboard Software and Satellite Operations. SAT, vol. 1, pp. 3–6. Springer, Heidelberg (2012)
13. Lichman, M.: UCI Machine Learning Repository. University of California, School of Information and Computer Science, Irvine (2013). http://archive.ics.uci.edu/ml
14. Palacios, A.M., Sánchez, L., Couso, I.: Extending a simple genetic cooperative-competitive learning fuzzy classifier to low quality datasets. Evol. Intel. **2**, 73–884 (2009)
15. Ralescu, A.L., Ralescu, D.A.: Probability and fuzziness. Information. Science **34**, 85–92 (1984)
16. Zsolt, C.J., Kovács, S.: Distance based similarity measures of fuzzy sets. In: Proceedings 3rd Symposium on Applied Machine Intelligence (SAMI 2005), Slovakia (2005)

An Ensemble-Based Classification Approach to Model Human-Machine Dialogs

David Griol$^{(\boxtimes)}$ and Araceli Sanchis de Miguel

Computer Science Department, Carlos III University of Madrid,
Avda. de la Universidad, 30, 28911 Leganés, Spain
{david.griol,araceli.sanchis}@uc3m.es

Abstract. One of the most demanding tasks when developing dialog systems consists of designing the dialog manager, which decides the next system response considering the user's actions and the dialog history. A previously developed statistical dialog management technique is adapted in this work to reduce the effort and time required to design the dialog manager. This technique allows not only an easy adaptation to new domains, but also to deal with the different subtasks by means of the fusion of classifiers adapted to each dialog objective in the application domain. The practical application of the proposed technique to develop a dialog system for a travel-planning domain shows that the use of these specific dialog models increases the quality and number of successful interactions with the system in comparison with developing a single dialog model for the complete domain.

Keywords: Human-agent interaction · Spoken dialog systems · Speech interaction · Classification techniques · Data fusion · Statistical methodologies

1 Introduction

Spoken dialog systems are computer programs that receive speech as input and generate as output synthesized speech, engaging the user in a dialog that aims to be similar to that between humans [8]. Thus, these interfaces make technologies more usable, as they ease interaction [6], allow integration in different environments [5], and make technologies more accessible, especially for disabled people and the elderly [10].

Usually, these systems carry out five main tasks: Automatic Speech Recognition (ASR), Spoken Language Understanding (SLU), Dialog Management (DM), Natural Language Generation (NLG), and Text-To-Speech Synthesis (TTS). These tasks are typically implemented in different modules of the system's architecture.

The dialog manager decides the next action of the system, interpreting the incoming semantic representation of the user input in the context of the dialog. In addition, it resolves ellipsis and anaphora, evaluates the relevance and completeness of user requests, identifies and recovers from recognition and understanding

© Springer International Publishing Switzerland 2015
J.M. Puerta et al. (Eds.): CAEPIA 2015, LNAI 9422, pp. 224–233, 2015.
DOI: 10.1007/978-3-319-24598-0_20

errors, retrieves information from data repositories, and decides about the next system's response.

Statistical approaches for dialog management enable automatic learning of dialog strategies, thus avoiding the time-consuming process that hand-crafted dialog design involves. Statistical models can be trained from real dialogs, modeling the variability in user behaviors. Although the construction and parameterization of these models depend on expert knowledge about the interaction domain, the objective is to develop systems that are more robust for real-world conditions, and easier to adapt to different users and tasks [9].

The most widespread methodology for machine-learning of dialog strategies consists of modeling human-computer interaction as an optimization problem using Partially Observable Markov Decision Processes (MDP) and reinforcement methods [7]. The main drawback of this approach is that the large state space of practical domains makes its direct representation intractable [11].

In this paper we propose a practical implementation of a recently developed statistical approach for the development of dialog managers [2], which is mainly based on the use of a classification process for the estimation of a statistical model from the sequences of the system and user dialog acts obtained from a set of training data. The paper is specially focused on the application and evaluation of an ensemble-based classification process learned for each dialog subtask, instead of learning a single dialog model for the complete dialog system. To do this, the training data is divided into different subsets, each covering a specific dialog objective or subtask. These specific dialog models are selected by the dialog manager once the objective of the dialog has been detected, using the generic dialog model until this condition has been fulfilled.

We have applied the proposed methodology to develop two versions of a dialog system providing travel-planning information in Spanish. The first one uses a generic classifier and the second one combines specific classifiers learned for each dialog objective. An in-depth comparative assessment of the developed systems has been completed using a user-agent simulation technique [3]. The results of the evaluation show that the specific dialog models allow a better selection of the next system responses, thus increasing the number and quality of successful interactions with the system.

The rest of the paper is organized as follows. Section 2 describes our proposal for developing statistical dialog managers with specific dialog models. Section 3 shows a practical implementation of our proposal to generate a specific system. In Sect. 4 we discuss the evaluation results obtained by comparing two baseline versions of the system with a context-aware version that adapts its behavior integrating our proposal. Finally, in Sect. 5 we present the conclusions and outline guidelines for future work.

2   Our Proposed Methodology for Dialog Management

This section summarizes the proposed dialog management technique and the practical implementation proposed in this paper by means of specific classifiers adapted to each dialog subtask.

2.1   Proposed Statistical Methodology

In order to control the interactions with the user, our dialog manager represents dialogs as a sequence of pairs (A_i, U_i), where A_i is the output of the dialog manager (the system answer) at time i, and U_i is the semantic representation of the user turn (the result of the understanding process of the user input) at time i; both expressed in terms of dialog acts [4]. Each dialog is represented by:

$$(A_1, U_1), \cdots, (A_i, U_i), \cdots, (A_n, U_n)$$

where A_1 is the greeting turn of the system, and U_n is the last user turn. We refer to a pair (A_i, U_i) as S_i, the state of the dialog sequence at time i.

In this framework, we consider that, at time i, the objective of the dialog manager is to find the best system answer A_i. This selection is a local process for each time i and takes into account the previous history of the dialog, that is to say, the sequence of states of the dialog preceding time i:

$$\hat{A}_i = \underset{A_i \in \mathcal{A}}{\operatorname{argmax}} P(A_i | S_1, \cdots, S_{i-1}) \qquad (1)$$

where set $\mathcal{A}$ contains all the possible system answers.

Following Eq. 1, the dialog manager selects the following system prompt by taking into account the sequence of previous pairs (A_i, U_i). The main problem to resolve this equation is regarding the number of possible sequences of states, which is usually very large. To solve the problem, we define a data structure in order to establish a partition in this space, i.e., in the history of the dialog preceding time i. This data structure, which we call *Dialog Register* (*DR*), contains the information provided by the user throughout the previous history of the dialog. After establishing the equivalence relation in the histories of dialogs, the selection of the best A_i is given by:

$$\hat{A}_i = \underset{A_i \in \mathcal{A}}{\operatorname{argmax}} P(A_i | DR_{i-1}, S_{i-1}) \qquad (2)$$

Each user turn supplies the system with information about the task; i.e., the user asks for a specific concept and/or provides specific values for certain attributes. However, a user turn can also provide other kinds of information, such as task-independent information (for instance, *Acceptance*, *Rejection*, and *Not-Understood* dialog acts). This kind of information implies some decisions which are different from simply updating the DR_{i-1}. Hence, for the selection of the best system response A_i, we take into account the DR that results from turn 1 to turn $i - 1$, and we explicitly consider the last state S_{i-1}.

As stated before, the DR contains information about concepts and values for the attributes provided by the user throughout the previous history of the dialog. For the dialog manager to determine the next answer, we have assumed that the exact values of the attributes are not significant. They are important for accessing databases and for constructing the output sentences of the system. However, the only information necessary to predict the next action by the system is the presence or absence of concepts and attributes. Therefore, the codification we use for each field in the DR is in terms of three values, $\{0, 1, 2\}$, according to the following criteria: (0) The concept is unknown or the value of the attribute is not given; (1) the concept or attribute is known with a confidence score that is higher than a given threshold; (2) the concept or attribute has a confidence score that is lower than the given threshold. To decide whether the state of a certain value in the DR is 1 or 2, the system employs confidence measures provided by the ASR and SLU modules.

2.2 Proposed Implementation by Means of Specific Dialog Models

As a practical implementation of this methodology, in this paper we propose the use of two modules. The first module deals with the detection of the specific dialog objective described by the user. This detection is based on the specific semantic information regarded to the task that is provided by the SLU module. This module also updates the *Dialog Register* that contains the complete list of features provided by the SLU module through the dialog history until the current moment. Until a specific problem is detected, a generic model learned with all the training dialogs is used for the selection of the next system response.

Once the objective of the dialog has been detected, a second module uses a specific dialog model learned for each subtask to select the next system response. To do this, we propose to solve Eq. 2 by means of a classification process. This way, every dialog situation (i.e., each possible sequence of dialog acts) is classified taking into account a set of classes $\mathcal{C}$, in which a class contains all the sequences that provide the same set of system actions (responses). The objective of the dialog manager at each moment is to select a class of this set $c \in \mathcal{C}$, so that the system response is the one associated with the selected class.

The classification function can be defined in several ways. We have previously evaluated six different definitions of such a function: a multinomial naive Bayes classifier, an n-gram based classifier, a decision tree classifier, a support vector machine classifier, a classifier based on grammatical inference techniques, and a classifier based on artificial neural networks [4]. The best results were obtained using a multilayer perceptron (MLP) [1] where the input layer holds the input pair (DR_{i-1}, S_{i-1}) corresponding to the dialog register and the state. The values of the output layer can be seen as an approximation of the a posteriori probability of the input belonging to the associated class $c \in \mathcal{C}$. Figure 1 shows the described scheme for the practical implementation of the proposed dialog management technique and its interaction with the rest of the modules in the dialog system.

3 Practical Application

We have applied our proposal to develop and evaluate an adaptive system for a travel-planning domain. The system provides context-aware information in natural language in Spanish about approaches to a city, flight schedules, weather forecast, car rental, hotel booking, sightseeing and places of interest for tourists,

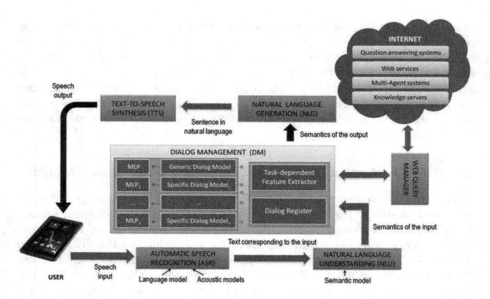

Fig. 1. Scheme of the complete architecture for the development of enhanced dialog systems

entertainment guide and theater listings, and movie showtimes. Different Postgress databases are used to store this information and automatically update the data that is included in the application. In addition, several functionalities are related to dynamic information (e.g., weather forecast, flight schedules) directly obtained from webpages and web services providing this information. This way, our system provides a speech access to facilitate this travel-planning information, which is adapted to each user taking into account context information.

Semantic knowledge is modeled in the system using the classical frame representation of the meaning of the utterance. We defined eight concepts to represent the different queries that the user can perform (*City-Approaches, Flight-Schedules, Weather-Forecast, Car-Rental,* and *Hotel-Booking, Sightseeing, Movie-Showtimes,* and *Theater-Listings*). Three task-independent concepts have also been defined for the task (*Affirmation, Negation,* and *Not-Understood*). A total of 101 system actions (DAs) were defined taking into account the information that the system provides, asks or confirms.

Using the *City_Approaches* functionality, it is possible to know how to get to a specific city using the different means of transport. If specific means are not provided by the user, then the system provides the complete information available for the required city. Users can optionally provide an origin city to try to obtain detailed information taking into account this origin. Context information taken into account to adapt this information includes user's current position, and preferred means of transport and city.

The *Flight_Schedules* functionality provides flight information considering the user's requirements. Users can provide the origin and destination cities, ticket class, departure and/or arrival dates, and departure and/or arrival hours. Using the *Weather_Forecast* it is possible to obtain the forecast for the required city and dates (for a maximum of 5 days from the current date). For both functionalities, this information is dynamically extracted from external webpages. Context information taken into account includes user's current location, preferred dates and/or hours, and preferred ticket class.

The *Car_Rental* functionality provides this information taking into account users' requisites including the city, pick-up and drop-off date, car type, name of the company, driver age, and office. The provided information is dynamically extracted from different webpages. The *Hotel_Booking* functionality provides hotels which fulfill the user's requirements (city, name, category, check-in and check-out dates, number of rooms, and number of people).

The *Sightseeing* functionality provides information about places of interest for a specific city, which is directly extracted from the webpage designed for the application. This information is mainly based on users recommendations that have been incorporated in this webpage. The *Theater_Listings* and *Movie_Showtimes* respectively provides information about theater performances and movie showtimes that takes into account the users requirements. These requirements can include the city, name of the theater/cinema, name of the show/movie, category, date, and hour. This information is also considered to adapt both functionalities and then provide context-aware information.

An example of the semantic interpretation of a user utterance is shown in Fig. 2. The *DR* defined for the task is a sequence of 57 fields, corresponding to the eight concepts defined for the dialog act representation (*City-Approaches, Flight-Schedules, Weather-Forecast, Car-Rental,* and *Hotel-Booking, Sightseeing, Theater-Listings,* and *Movie-Showtimes*), possible attributes defined for each one of them (a total of 45 attributes), the three task-independent concepts that users can provide (*Acceptance, Rejection* and *Not-Understood*), and a reference to the user profile.

A set of 25 scenarios were manually defined to cover the different queries to perform to the system including different user requirements and profiles. Basic scenarios defined only one objective for the dialog; it means, the user must obtain information about only one type of the possible queries to the system (e.g., to obtain flight schedules from an origin city to a destination for a specific date). More complex scenarios included more than one objective for the dialog (e.g., to obtain information about how to get to a specific city, car rental and hotel booking information). Two versions of the system have been developed. The first one (*Dialog System 1*) uses a generic dialog model for the task, which employs a single classifier to select the next system response. The second one (*Dialog System 2*) employs 25 specific dialog models, each one of them focused on the achievement of the objective(s) defined for a specific scenario.

Input sentence:
[SPANISH] *Sí, me gustaría conocer los accesos en coche y hoteles de cuatro estrellas disponibles en Valencia para mañana.*
[ENGLISH] *Yes, I would like to know how to get to Valencia by car and four stars hotels available for tomorrow.*

Semantic interpretation:
(*Affirmation*)
(*City Approaches*)
    City: Valencia
    Means Transport: Car
(*Hotel Booking*)
    City: Valencia
    Hotel Booking: Car
    Category: Four Stars
    Check in Date: Tomorrow

Fig. 2. An example of the labeling of a user turn in the travel-planning system

4   Results of the Evaluation

The dialog systems described in the previous section allow two operation modes. First, the system uses the ASR and the SLU modules for the normal interaction between the agent and the real users. Second, the system allows the automatic acquisition of dialogs by means of a recently developed user-agent simulator [3]. The evaluation of our proposal that we describe in this paper is focused on the latter technique.

4.1   Evaluation with a User Simulator

A total of 100 dialogs have been acquired for each of the 25 designed scenarios by means of the interaction of the dialog systems with the previously developed user-agent simulator. The following measures were defined to compare the two corpus acquired with the dialog systems: number of successful dialogs, average number of user turns, number of different dialogs (taking into account their labeling in terms of frames and not the exact values of the attributes), the number of repetitions and user turns of the most seen dialog (in term of frames), and the number of user turns of the shortest and longest dialogs. Table 1 shows the result of the evaluation.

    As it can be observed, the number of successfully simulated dialogs increases in most of the scenarios using the proposed technique with specific dialog models for each one of them (from a total of 1,305 successful dialogs acquired with the *Dialog System 1* to 1,543 successful dialogs acquired with the *Dialog System 2*). The user-agent simulator was developed to generate unsupervised dialogs, that is why a high amount of unsuccessful interactions were generated. In addition, there is a reduction in the average number of turns required to fulfill the objectives using the *Dialog System 2* (from an average of 4.7 turns using the *Dialog System*

Table 1. Results of the evaluation using a generic dialog model (top) or specific dialog models (bottom) and the user simulator

Dialog system 1		
	Basic scenarios	Complex scenarios
Number of successful dialogs	769	536
Average number of user turns	4.1	5.2
Number of different dialogs	378	303
Number of repetitions most seen dialog	11	6
Number of user turns most seen dialog	5	4
Number of user turns shortest dialog	2	2
Number of user turns longest dialog	8	11
Dialog system 2		
	Basic scenarios	Complex scenarios
Number of successful dialogs	911	632
Average number of user turns	3.7	4.9
Number of different dialogs	489	398
Number of repetitions most seen dialog	19	12
Number of user turns most seen dialog	4	4
Number of user turns shortest dialog	2	2
Number of user turns longest dialog	7	10

1 to 4.3 turns using the *Dialog System 2*). This general reduction in the number of turns is generalized also to the case of the longest, shortest and most seen dialogs for the *Dialog System 2*. Both results are specially remarkable for the most complicated subtasks, in which two objectives must be fulfilled and users must provide a large number of attributes.

On the other hand, the number of repetitions of the most seen dialog and the number of repeated dialogs is increased using the *Dialog System 2*. This can be explained due to the more reduced number of dialogs used to learn the specific dialog models, which reduces the space of dialog states in order to select the next system prompt. However, the *Dialog System 2* allows generating more different dialogs (from 681 different dialogs obtained with the *Dialog System 1* to 887 different dialogs with the *Dialog System 2*), then increasing the variability of the simulated corpus.

Additionally, we grouped all user and system actions into three categories: "goal directed" (actions to provide or request information), "grounding" (confirmations and negations), and "other". Table 2 shows a comparison between these categories. As can be observed, the dialogs provided by the *Dialog System 2* have a better quality, as the proportion of goal-directed actions is higher than the values obtained for the *Dialog System 1*.

Table 2. Proportions of dialog spent on-goal directed actions, ground actions and other possible actions

	Dialog system 1	Dialog system 2
Goal-directed actions	69.12 %	73.01 %
Grounding actions	29.82 %	26.01 %
Rest of actions	1.06 %	0.98 %

5   Conclusions and Future Work

In this paper, we have described a statistical methodology for the development of dialog systems and the optimization of dialog strategies. The methodology is based on the estimation of a statistical model from the sequences of system and user dialog acts obtained from a set of training data. The selection of the next system response is carried out by the dialog manager using two modules. The first module is used to detect the specific objective described by the user based on the specific task-dependent semantic information provided by the SLU module. The second module uses an ensemble-based classification process that takes into account the history of the dialog by means of a data structure and selects the specific dialog model generated by means of a MLP. We have defined a codification of this information to facilitate the correct operation of this classification function.

The results of the evaluation of our proposal for a dialog system providing travel-planning information show that the number of successful dialogs is increased in comparison with using a generic classification process for the task. Also, these dialogs are statistically shorter and present a better quality in the selection of the system responses. For future work, we want to consider the incorporation in the DR of additional information regarding the user, such as specific user profiles adapted to the each specific interaction domain. Finally, we want also to test fuzzy representations of the data in this register to evaluate the operation of the dialog manager.

Acknowledgements. This work has been supported in part by the Spanish Government under i-Support (Intelligent Agent Based Driver Decision Support) Project (TRA2011-29454-C03-03).

References

1. Borrajo, M., Baruque, B., Corchado, E., Bajo, J., Corchado, J.: Hybrid neural intelligent system to predict business failure in small-to-medium-size enterprises. Int. J. Neural Syst. **21**(4), 277–296 (2011)
2. Griol, D., Callejas, Z., López-Cózar, R., Riccardi, G.: A domain-independent statistical methodology for dialog management in spoken dialog systems. Comput. Speech Lang. **28**(3), 743–768 (2014)

3. Griol, D., Carbó, J., Molina, J.: An automatic dialog simulation technique to develop and evaluate interactive conversational agents. Appl. Artif. Intell. **27**(9), 759–780 (2013)
4. Griol, D., Molina, J.M., Callejas, Z.: Bringing together commercial and academic perspectives for the development of intelligent AmI interfaces. J. Ambient Intell. Smart Environ. **4**, 183–207 (2012)
5. Heinroth, T., Minker, W.: Introducing Spoken Dialogue Systems into Intelligent Environments. Kluwer Academic Publishers, New York (2012)
6. Hempel, T.: Usability of Speech Dialog Systems: Listening to the Target Audience. Springer, Heidelberg (2008)
7. Levin, E., Pieraccini, R., Eckert, W.: A stochastic model of human-machine interaction for learning dialog strategies. IEEE Trans. Speech Audio Process. **8**(1), 11–23 (2000)
8. Pieraccini, R.: The Voice in the Machine: Building Computers that Understand Speech. The MIT Press, Cambridge (2012)
9. Schatzmann, J., Weilhammer, K., Stuttle, M., Young, S.: A survey of statistical user simulation techniques for reinforcement-learning of dialogue management strategies. Knowl. Eng. Rev. **21**(2), 97–126 (2006)
10. Vipperla, R., Wolters, M., Renals, S.: Spoken dialogue interfaces for older people. Adv. Home Care Technol. **31**, 118–137 (2012)
11. Young, S., Schatzmann, J., Weilhammer, K., Ye, H.: The hidden information state approach to dialogue management. In: Proceedings of ICASSP 2007, pp. 149–152 (2007)

Pentaho + R: An Integral View
for Multidimensional Prediction Models

Adolfo Martínez-Usó[✉], José Hernández-Orallo, M. José Ramírez-Quintana,
and Fernando Martínez Plumed

Departament de Sistemes Informàtics i Computació,
Universitat Politècnica de València, Camí de Vera s/n, 46022 València, Spain
{admarus,jorallo,mramirez,fmartinez}@dsic.upv.es

Abstract. The integration of multidimensional data and machine learning seems to be natural in the area of business intelligence. On-Line Analytical Processing (OLAP) tools are frequent in this area where the data are usually represented in multidimensional datamarts and data mining tools are integrated in some of these tools. However, the efforts for a full integration of data mining and OLAP tools have not been as common as originally expected. Nowadays, this integration is mostly carried out on source code, implementing solutions that perform *(i)* all the operations on multidimensional data as well as *(ii)* the data mining algorithms to extract knowledge from these data. Hence, there now exists an important distinction between *implementation-based developments* where the entire solution is implemented on source code and *OLAP-tool-based developments* where (at least) the operations on multidimensional data are performed using an OLAP tool. This work analyses these two alternatives in cost-effective terms, performing an experimental analysis on a multidimensional problem and discussing when each approach seems to excel the other.

Keywords: Multidimensional data · OLAP cubes · OLAP tools · R · Pentaho · Business intelligence · XML

1 Introduction

On-Line Analytical Processing (OLAP) is a software tool in Business Intelligence (BI) that enables decision making based on the multidimensional analysis of summary data. OLAP manages multidimensional data and categorises the measurable facts (measures) and the hierarchical features (dimensions) that characterise the facts. Pentaho Business Analytics[1] is an OLAP tool for BI that performs data integration, business analysis and data mining (including Big Data support). Pentaho is very powerful, entirely open source (GNU), easy to use and it is able to handle almost any data source. Pentaho allows the user to perform many operations on cubes. Some of the key operations over OLAP cubes include, but are not limited to:

---

[1] http://www.pentaho.com/.

© Springer International Publishing Switzerland 2015
J.M. Puerta et al. (Eds.): CAEPIA 2015, LNAI 9422, pp. 234–244, 2015.
DOI: 10.1007/978-3-319-24598-0_21

- Roll-up which increases the aggregation level along one or more classification hierarchies.
- Drill-down which decreases the aggregation level (contrary to roll-up) giving more detail to the view.
- Slice or Dice which perform dimensionality reduction using selection or projection respectively.
- Pivoting or rotation which reorient the data view.
- Visualisation and data summarising with a significant number of statistics.

The R language [12] is a very popular trend in statistical programming with a widespread support within the statistical community. It is a free software project with many different libraries or packages and an extraordinary capacity for producing graphical results.

The integration of Pentaho and R is becoming popular for BI since it is seen as a powerful combination that provides versatility and efficiency. In order to carry out this integration, the *eXtensible Markup Language* (XML) meta language is becoming increasingly important as the communication channel between both parts [10].

The multidimensional model is a widely extended conceptual model originated in the database literature that can be used to properly capture the multiresolutional character of many datasets [4]. Multidimensional databases arrange data into fact tables and dimensions. Each row represents a fact, such as "The sales of product 'Tomato soup 500 ml' in store '123' on day '20/06/2014' totalled 25 units". The features (or fields) of a fact table are either measures (indicators such as units, Euros, volumes, etc.) or references to dimensions. In business terminology, an indicator is a quantifiable measurement used when a database is summarised, often for gauging business success. A dimension is here understood as a particular variable that has predefined (and hopefully meaningful) levels of aggregation, with a hierarchical structure. Figure 1 shows several examples of dimensions and hierarchies. Using the hierarchies, the data can be aggregated or disaggregated at different granularities. Each of this set of aggregation choices for all dimensions is known as a *data cube* or *OLAP cube*[2] [2]. This approach provides an easy understanding and offers flexibility for visualisation.

Two main processes take place when we want to obtain knowledge from multidimensional data: (1) the data must be in the desired level of granularity and (2) data mining algorithms should be applied on these data for extracting the important information. In the absence of a (free) tool that carries out both tasks, the former should be solved by means of an OLAP tool whereas the latter should be performed by a statistical programming language or any other data mining or machine learning tool, but the fact is that many researchers implement both tasks using only their own source code (e.g., using R or *python*). These two ways of facing the problem of dealing with multidimensional data has resulted in rather

---

[2] We use data cube independently from the number of dimensions, although we often find this term as *hypercube* when more than 3 dimensions are involved in the hierarchy.

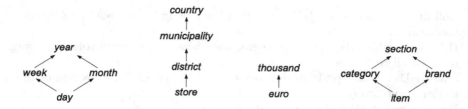

Fig. 1. Examples of dimensions and their hierarchies. Left: Time dimension, Middle Left: Location dimension, Middle Right: Money dimension, Right: Product dimension.

different solutions, that is, *implementation-based developments* (hereafter called Impl-Dev) and *OLAP-tool-based developments* (hereafter called OLAP-Dev).

Therefore, from a practical point of view, a system for the integration of multidimensional data jointly with an analytical tool able to extract usable statistical knowledge from the data is needed. A system like this, to the best of our knowledge, has not been fully developed so far. This is particularly interesting if we take into account that the problem of having several hierarchies, one for each dimension and seeing the problem (including predictions) at any possible resolution, is new [8].

This paper contributes with an OLAP-Dev integration of a comprehensive platform for business analytics such as Pentaho with the R statistical language. In addition, this integration is compared with an Impl-Dev solution in terms of memory consumption and time cost.

1.1 Related Work

There exist some commercial tools like SPSS[3] or ODM[4] that are often used by practitioners and where a solution for this integration is given as a whole. However, besides these major players, there have been only a few attempts of integrating OLAP tools with data mining approaches. A very well-ranked option when you look for an OLAP and R integration is the *X4R* package [3]. It is a package for R that executes an MDX query (via XMLA) and returns a dataset into a data frame. It is able to work with sources such as SAP BW, SAP HANA, SQL Server or Pentaho. However, we were unable to run this solution and there is not too much documentation about it. In addition, the testing sources provided by the author did not work either[5].

Another well-positioned resource is the *RPentaho* package [6] which is a R connector for Pentaho that obtains data in JSON format. The problem with *RPentaho* is that it really only works with Pentaho BI Server 4.8 since the necessary plugins for Pentaho 5.x have not been upgraded yet.

---

[3] http://www-01.ibm.com/software/de/analytics/spss.

[4] http://www.oracle.com/technetwork/database/options/advanced-analytics/odm/index.html.

[5] See https://github.com/overcoil/X4R/issues/ for a complete list of issues with this package.

A completely different option would be to use KNIME[6], which is a data mining and BI environment that offers support for R and *python*, multi-platform and free under a GPL license. The problem with KNIME is its sometimes poor applicability (ability to run a specific algorithm) and performance [13].

RapidMiner[7] is the most popular open-source for data mining[8]. However, it mostly depend on local machine memory and multidimensional developments using SQL sentences could be quite time-consuming.

Therefore, previous integration approaches have not addressed the special issues related to OLAP (e.g., dimensions with hierarchies), are thus not optimally suited for integrating data to be used for OLAP or they are too difficult to implement. The best option found as a solution for this integration is the one proposed in this paper, which will be described and analysed in the following sections in the framework of a multidimensional problem. More detailed reviews on data mining tools and libraries can be found in [5,11,15].

2 Experimental Setting

2.1 The Task

We consider a multidimensional data set D (or datamart) of schema $\langle X, Y \rangle$ where $X = \{X_1, \ldots, X_d\}$ is the set of d dimensions (used as predictor attributes or features) and Y, which is the *target attribute* (one measure or indicator that can be numeric or nominal). Each dimension has associated a hierarchy such that $X_i^{(j)}$ denotes the jth item in the hierarchy for dimension i. For instance, if $X_2 = $ location, as in Fig. 1 (middle left), we have $X_2^{(1)} = $ store, $X_2^{(2)} = $ district, $X_2^{(3)} = $ municipality and $X_2^{(4)} = $ country with store $<$ district $<$ municipality $<$ country as their transitive closure. We will consider that the top level for every hierarchy is All.

Given the above notation, now we consider a predictive problem from X to Y. For instance, how many tomatoes we expect to sell in Valencia next week? This is what we call *context* and it is directly associated with a data cube within the multidimensional data. Each time a cube is loaded, it is divided into training and test. The task consists of a simple prediction about which quantity of sales/money can be expected for our test set after training our baseline model.

In regression tasks, we usually look at a baseline method that consists of averaging the values for the training data and apply these values systematically during deployment. This is known as the *mean* or *constant* model (MEAN). Thus, given a training data T with measure Y and a deployment data D, we are going to use the MEAN model for measure Y at each *context* of the multidimensional lattice. The aggregation function used in our experiments has been the $sum(S) \triangleq \sum_{s \in S} s$.

Graphical results within this experimental section show the time cost (x-axis) and memory consumption (y-axis) for the described task, both for the Impl-Dev schema and the OLAP-Dev schema.

---

[6] http://www.knime.org.

[7] https://rapidminer.com/.

[8] http://www.kdnuggets.com/software/suites.html.

2.2   Multidimensional Data Description

Two datasets have been used in this experimental section. The first one (**TOY**) is a synthetic dataset created by us about sales, where the indicator is the quantity (units) sold. It has three dimensions and 9 different contexts or cubes (hierarchies in parenthesis): WHERE (City < Country < All), WHAT (Product < Category < All) and TIME (Year).

The second dataset (**AROMA**) is an artificial dataset constructed from IBM sales information. It contains sales data for coffee and tea products sold in stores across the United States [9]. The data is almost directly converted into a multidimensional datamart where each fact describes the sales of products using two measures (quantity and dollars, although we will only use quantity as the output variable in our experiments) according to five dimensions (hierarchies in parenthesis): PROMO (KeyPromo < PromoType < All), CLASS (KeyClass < All), PRODUCT (KeyProduct < All), STORE (KeyStore < KeyMKT < MKT-HQ-City < MKT-HQ-State < MKT-District < MKT-Region < All) and PERIOD (Year).

Note that as we use the TIME and PERIOD dimensions to split the data, we only consider one level here. Data goes from years 2004 to 2006 and the number of possible multidimensional contexts is $3 \times 2 \times 2 \times 7 \times 1 = 84$ (Fig. 2).

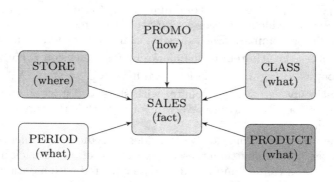

Fig. 2. AROMA hierarchies flow chart.

We split these datasets into training and test on the basis of a *split-year*, being particularly year 2006 for **AROMA** dataset (*split-year* included in the test set).

2.3   Implementation Details

In this experimental section we use the Pentaho open source Community Edition 5[9], which encompasses a great diversity of solutions for data integration, reporting, OLAP analysis, dashboarding and ETL.

---

[9] Concretely, we used biserver-ce-5.2.0.0-209 version of this software, which is not the last version but compatible. Visit http://community.pentaho.com/ for details.

Obviously, Pentaho is already running when we perform our experimentation (running on localhost:8080, Tomcat and MySQL also) and the datasets used in this section are already loaded into Pentaho by means of its *Manage Data Sources* utility that allows you to easily load a *csv* file.

In our implementation we have used RStudio 0.98.1091, with R version 3.1.2 on Windows 7. We have also used the R packages *RUnit*[1] and *RMDX*[7] which enable R to request data from an OLAP cube via XMLA by specifying an MDX query. The following code is used as a request for a multidimensional cube:

```
library(RUnit)
library(RMDX)
conn <- RMDX(connentaho='http://localhost:8080/pentaho/Xmla',
             userid='Admin', password='password')
#Pentaho changes '_' in attr names by spaces
myCUBE<-gsub("_"," ",myCUBE)
CurrentCube <- mdxquery(conn, 'Pentaho', DATAMART, myCUBE)
```

where function *RMDX* creates a connector with Pentaho, using in this case the local host and the *Admin* user (the users are provided by Pentaho). The following line of code transforms the underscore symbols to spaces[10]. Function *mdxquery* returns a R data frame on *CurrentCube* using in its call:

1. *DATAMART*, string with the name of the dataset in Pentaho (in our case **TOY** or **AROMA**) and
2. *myCUBE*, string with the MDX query. For instance, *myCUBE* could contain the following string for a cube request on **AROMA**:

```
"SELECT NON EMPTY {Hierarchize({{[Measures].[SAL_QUANTITY]}})} ON COLUMNS,
    NON EMPTY [KEY_PROMO].[KEY_PROMO].Members *
    [KEY_STORE].[KEY_STORE].Members * [KEY_CLASS].[KEY_CLASS].Members
    ON ROWS FROM [AROMA]".
```

2.4 Experiment 1: Cost-Benefit Analysis Across the Full Multidimensional Lattice

Multidimensional data is often shown as a lattice in the space of the all possible resolutions/granularities/cubes (9 for **TOY** and 84 for **AROMA**) that can be represented applying certain operations (roll-up, pivot, etc.) on the multidimensional data. In this first experiment, all the cubes in our multidimensional representation are visited. For each cube, data are divided into training and test, training the model and making the predictions on the test set by means of using the MEAN model (as Sect. 2.1 describes).

Figure 3 shows these results for the **TOY** dataset (top) and the **AROMA** dataset (bottom). For each dataset, the graph on the left shows the performance obtained under a Impl-Dev schema whereas the graph on the right shows the same result but using the OLAP-Dev schema. As it can be seen in both cases, being

---

[10] This is only necessary if, as often happens, you have attribute names written down using underscores.

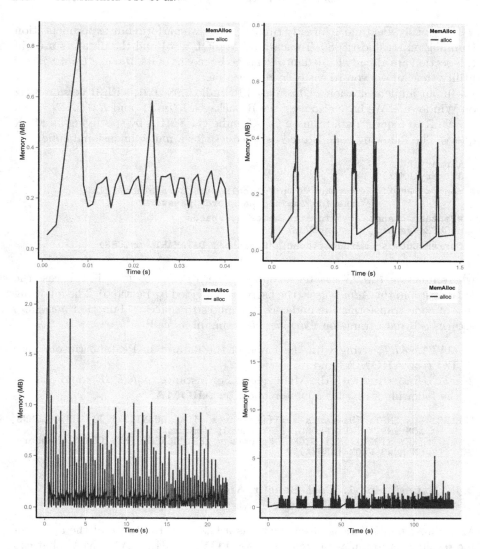

Fig. 3. Time cost (x-axis) and memory allocation (y-axis) performance for **TOY** (top) and **AROMA** (bottom) datasets. Graphs on the left column show the performance obtained under a Impl-Dev schema whereas the graphs on the right column show the same results but using the OLAP-Dev schema.

more remarkable with the **AROMA** dataset, the Impl-Dev solution requires much less resources in terms of time and memory.

Data flow (allocations and releases) for memory usage on R has been analysed using the *lineprof* package [14]. This analysis shows that, although the memory usage directly depends on the size of the cube, the OLAP-Dev approach performs 5 times more operations than the Impl-Dev approach on average. Moreover, if we measure the total memory usage accumulated during the whole process in this experiment, it is much higher for the OLAP-Dev approach than for the Impl-Dev approach. For instance, for the **TOY** dataset the accumulated memory allocations up to more than 60 MB for the OLAP-Dev approach in contrast to the almost 10 MB needed by the Impl-Dev approach.

2.5   Experiment 2: Cost-Benefit Analysis for a Single Cube Request

In this second experiment, a single request for a concrete cube is made, performing only in this cube the task described in Sect. 2.1. Since not all the cubes are equal, this single request has been done for two different cubes. Figure 4 shows the performance obtained by both approaches (Impl-Dev on the left and OLAP-Dev on the right) for cube number 1 (top) and cube number 84 (bottom). For cube number 1 no dimension is completely rolled-up whereas for cube number 84 all the dimensions but one are completely rolled-up; which means that the resulting data frame in each case is quite different, being the data frame for cube number 1 much larger than the data frame for cube number 84.

As it can be seen, for both cubes the memory consumption is much higher for the Impl-Dev approach since the whole dataset must be loaded in this approach, even if we are interested in just one cube. On the contrary, the OLAP-Dev approach only requests for the single cube we are interested in and only this memory usage is shown in the graph. As also expected, the memory used when the OLAP-Dev approach requests for the cube number 1 is higher than when the cube number 84 is requested.

Regarding the time cost, it is still higher when the cube number 1 is requested by the OLAP-Dev approach. Interestingly, it becomes lower (although quite similar) when the cube number 84 is requested, what again has to do with the influence of the XML files size in transactions between Pentaho and R.

3   Discussion and Conclusions

Multidimensional data is a rich and complex scenario where the same task can change significantly depending on the level of aggregation over some of the dimensions. Despite the success of multidimensional schemas and its widespread use for data warehouses for about two decades, a full integration of machine learning systems and multidimensional datasets has not taken place. When we analyse the problem more carefully, we see that the main issue for a successful integration is that we would like to use off-the-shelf machine learning techniques but taking full potential of the hierarchical information.

Nowadays, many data scientists are implementing their own solutions as a whole, living with their back to the OLAP tools, this is what we have called Impl-Dev. On the other hand, in business intelligence tools, which aim at integrating data warehouses, OLAP technology and data mining tools, the usual procedure is to select a cube using an OLAP query or operator, and derive a view from it. Next, this "minable view" is transferred to the data mining tool to apply

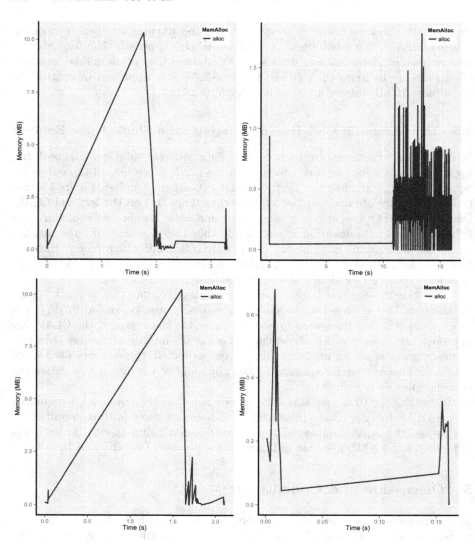

Fig. 4. AROMA dataset. Top graphs for the cube number 1 request, implemented (left) and Pentaho (right). Bottom graphs for the cube number 84 request, implemented (left) and Pentaho (right).

machine learning or statistical techniques to this flat/traditional view of the data. This is what we have called OLAP-Dev.

At this point, we found interesting to study the state of the art for the different possibilities for OLAP-Dev. Likewise, we have chosen the most desirable OLAP-Dev approach and shown what is its performance when compared to a traditional Impl-Dev implementation. The reasons for the different performances between both approaches have also been studied since, to the best of our knowledge, a comprehensive analysis of the cost-benefit of an integration solution has not been carried out yet.

From our experimental results, we see that the number of XML instructions needed in the OLAP-Dev schema are 5 times higher than the number of instructions needed by the Impl-Dev schema, on average. In addition, the data associated to these instructions are directly proportional to the size of the cube requested to the OLAP tool. Hence, an exhaustive navigation through the multidimensional lattice could be highly costly: the larger number of transactions, the higher the difference in memory consumption of the OLAP-Dev compared to Impl-Dev. On the contrary, memory consumption for a single request for the OLAP-Dev approach is much lower than the one needed for the Impl-Dev schema, since Impl-Dev must load the whole dataset before transforming the data to the desired granularity. Finally, time cost comparison between both approaches is more straightforward and the Impl-Dev approach is generally better in this regard, although the time cost for the OLAP-Dev approach varies a lot depending on the size of the cubes and the number of transactions. The take-home message is that, for an exhaustive navigation through the multidimensional lattice (multiple requests), the Impl-Dev approach is definitively better. This would also be the best alternative for a single request in terms of time cost. However, for a single request and from a memory consumption point of view, the OLAP-Dev approach performs much better, being this last case the most common one when we deal with very large datasets.

As a future work, we will consider more problems in order to reach more consolidated conclusions, for instance, justify whether the experiments could be extrapolated to more demanding machine learning methods. This demand not only is expected to be in terms of time and memory but we would also like to extend it to other factors such as extensibility, reliability or availability of proposed tools/packages. Likewise, a further comparison using those implementations that we have not been able to include in this work is also expected (*X4R*, *RPentaho*).

Finally, it is worth emphasising that the work presented provides valuable contributions in terms of how to implement and how should be the performance of a very demanded solution for integrating OLAP tools and machine learning methodologies.

Acknowledgements. We thank the anonymous reviewers for their comments, which have helped to improve this paper. This work was supported by the Spanish MINECO under grant TIN 2013-45732-C4-1-P and by Generalitat Valenciana PROMETEOII2015/013. This research has been developed within the REFRAME project, granted by the European Coordinated Research on Long-term Challenges in Information and Communication Sciences & Technologies ERA-Net (CHIST-ERA), and funded by the Ministerio de Economía y Competitividad in Spain (PCIN-2013-037).

References

1. Burger, M., Juenemann, K., Koenig, T.: RUnit: R Unit Test Framework. http://cran.r-project.org/web/packages/RUnit

2. Chaudhuri, S., Dayal, U.: An overview of data warehousing and OLAP technology. ACM Sigmod Rec. **26**(1), 65–74 (1997)
3. Chow, G., Lee, N.: X4R: XMLA/MDX cube tool for R (2013). https://github.com/overcoil/X4R
4. Golfarelli, M., Maio, D., Rizzi, S.: The dimensional fact model: a conceptual model for data warehouses. Intl. J. Coop. Inf. Syst. **7**, 215–247 (1998)
5. Han, J.: Data Mining: Concepts and Techniques. Morgan Kaufmann Publishers Inc., San Francisco (2005)
6. Harding, P.: RPentaho - R Connector for Pentaho via CTools CDA and CDB interface (2013). https://github.com/piersharding/RPentaho
7. Harding, P.: RMDX - An XML/A OLAP MDX interface (2015). https://github.com/piersharding/RMDX
8. Hernández-Orallo, J., Lachiche, N., Martínez-Usó, A.: Predictive models for multidimensional data when the resolution context changes. In: Ferri, C., Flach, P., Lachiche, N. (eds.) Workshop on Learning over Multiple Contexts at ECML 2014 (LMCE) (2014)
9. IBM Corporation: Introduction to Aroma and SQL (2006). http://www.ibm.com/developerworks/data/tutorials/dm0607cao/dm0607cao.html
10. Jensen, M., Moller, T., Pedersen, T.: Specifying OLAP cubes on XML data. In: Proceedings of the 13th International Conference on Scientific and Statistical Database Management (SSDBM), pp. 101–112 (2001)
11. Kováč, S.: Suitability analysis of data mining tools and methods. Ph.D. thesis (2012)
12. R Development Core Team.: R: A Language and Environment for Statistical Computing. R Foundation for Statistical Computing, Vienna, Austria (2012)
13. Wahbeh, A.H., Al-Radaideh, Q.A., Al-Kabi, M.N., Al-Shawakfa, E.M.: A comparison study between data mining tools over some classification methods. Int. J. Adv. Comput. Sci. Appl. **2**, 18–26 (2011)
14. Wickham, H.: Visualise line profiling results in R (2015). https://github.com/hadley/lineprof
15. Witten, I.H., Frank, E., Hall, M.A.: Data Mining: Practical Machine Learning Tools and Techniques, third edn. Morgan Kaufmann, Burlington (2011)

A Time Efficient Approach for Distributed Feature Selection Partitioning by Features

L. Morán-Fernández[✉], V. Bolón-Canedo, and A. Alonso-Betanzos

Laboratory for Research and Development in Artificial Intelligence (LIDIA),
Computer Science Department, University of A Coruña, 15071 A Coruña, Spain
laura.moranf@udc.es

Abstract. With the advent of high dimensionality, feature selection has
become indispensable in real-world scenarios. However, most of the traditional methods only work in a centralized manner, which —ironically—
increase the running time requirements when they are applied to this
type of data. For this reason, we propose a distributed filter approach
for vertically partitioned data. The idea is to split the data by features
and apply a filter at each partition performing several rounds to obtain
a final subset of features. Different than existing procedures to combine the partial outputs of the different partitions of data, we propose a
merging process according to the theoretical complexity of these feature
subsets instead of classification error. Experimental results tested in five
datasets show that the running time decreases considerably. Moreover,
regarding the classification accuracy, our approach was able to match,
and in some cases even improve, the standard algorithms applied to the
non-partitioned datasets.

1 Introduction

In the last few years, there has been an increase in the size of datasets in all fields
of application. The advent of this type of high dimensional datasets has posed a
big challenge for machine learning researchers, since it is difficult to deal with a
high number of input features due to the curse of dimensionality [14]. The scaling
up problem appears in any algorithm when the data size increases beyond the
capacity of the traditional data mining algorithms, damaging their classification
performance and efficiency. This problem can affect negatively in some other
aspects such as excessive storage requirements, increase of time complexity and,
finally, it affects generalization accuracy, introducing noise and overfitting. To
confront the problem of the high number of features it is natural —and perhaps essential— to investigate the effects of the application of feature selection.
Feature selection methods have received an important amount of attention in
the classification literature, where three kinds of algorithms have generally been
studied: *filter*, *wrapper* and *embedded* methods. The main difference between the
first two is that a wrapper makes use of the algorithm that will be employed to
build the final classifier, while a filter method does not. The embedded methods generally use classification learning models, and then an optimal subset of

© Springer International Publishing Switzerland 2015
J.M. Puerta et al. (Eds.): CAEPIA 2015, LNAI 9422, pp. 245–254, 2015.
DOI: 10.1007/978-3-319-24598-0_22

features is built by the classification algorithm. So, the interaction with the classifier required by wrapper and embedded methods comes with an important computational burden.

The use of an adequate feature selection method can lead to an improvement of the inductive learner, either in terms of learning speed, generalization capacity or simplicity of the induced model. However, we will have to deal with a scalability problem if we apply these techniques to large datasets. The advantages of feature selection come at a certain price, as the search for a subset of relevant features introduces an extra layer of complexity to the modeling task. This new layer increases the memory and running time requirements, making these algorithms very inefficient when applied to problems that involve very large datasets. Ironically, standard feature selection becomes impracticable on large datasets, which are the ones that would benefit most from its application.

Trying to overcome the drawbacks mentioned above, over the last years many distributed methods have been developed instead of the traditional centralized approaches. The first reason is that, with the advent of network technologies, data is being increasingly available already distributed in multiple locations, and it is not economic or legal to gather it in a single location. And, second, when dealing with large amounts of data, most existing feature selection methods are not expected to scale well, and their efficiency may significantly deteriorate or even become inapplicable. Therefore, a possible solution might be to distribute the data, run a feature selection method on each subset of data and then combine the results. There are two main techniques for partitioning and distributing data: by samples (horizontally), and by features (vertically). Most of the distributed feature selection methods have been used to scale up datasets that are too large for batch learning in terms of samples [2,6,7,18]. While not so common, there are some other developments which distribute the data by features [16,17].

In our previous work [5], we presented a methodology for distributing the data vertically which combined the partial feature subsets based on improvements in the classification accuracy. Although the experiments showed that the execution time was considerably shortened whereas the performance was maintained or even improved compared to the standard algorithms applied to the non-partitioned datasets, the drawback of this methodology was that it was dependent on the classifier. In order to overcome this issue, we proposed in [4] a new framework for distributing the feature selection process by samples which performed a merging procedure to update the final feature subset according to the theoretical complexity of these features, by using data complexity measures [13] instead of the classification error. In this way, we provided a framework for distributed feature selection which not only was independent of the classifier, but also reduced drastically the computational time needed by the algorithm, thus paving the way for its application in high dimensional datasets.

To examine the research problem in detail, this paper will be focused on the vertically distributed approach making use of data complexity measures. The experimental results from five different datasets demonstrate than our new proposal shows important savings in running times, as well as matching —and in some cases even improving— the classification accuracy.

2   Distributed Feature Selection

The methodology that we propose in this work consists in a distributed framework for feature selection by partitioning the data vertically, i.e., by features. Basically, the distributed algorithm adopts the following 3-step experimental framework: (1) partition of the training datasets, (2) application of the distributed algorithm to the subsets of features in several "rounds" and (3) combination of the results into a single subset of features. The repetition of the process in several rounds ensures that we have gathered enough information for the combination step to be useful, since each feature in the vector of votes can only take values 0 or 1 for each round, so we would not have enough data to decide which features form the final subset. The algorithm for the whole methodology is detailed in Algorithm 1.

For each round, we start by dividing the data D without replacement —as usually happens in real world when different features are collected on different locations— by randomly assigning groups of t features to each partition. Then, the chosen filter is applied to each partition separately and the features selected to be removed receive a vote. At this point, a new round is performed leading to a new partition of the dataset and another iteration of voting is accomplished until reaching the predefined number of rounds. Finally, the features that have received a number of votes above a certain threshold are removed. Notice that the maximum number of votes is the number of rounds r.

In order to calculate the threshold of votes to employ, an automatic method was used. In [9], the authors recommend that the selection of the number of votes must take into account two different aspects: the training classification error and the percentage of features retained. Both values must be minimized to the extent possible, by minimizing the fitness criterion $e[v]$:

$$e[v] \leftarrow \alpha \times error + (1 - \alpha) \times featPercentage, \qquad (1)$$

where α is a parameter with value in the interval $[0, 1]$. It measures the relative relevance of *error* and *featPercentage* values. Different values can be used if the researcher is more interested in reducing the storage requirements or the error. For this work, it was set to $\alpha = 0.75$, giving more influence to the classification error. At the end, the features with the number of votes above the obtained threshold are removed from the final subset of features S. This subset will be used in the training and test sets in order to obtain the final classification accuracy.

The problem with this approach is that, by involving a classifier in the process of selecting the optimal threshold, it makes our methodology dependent on the classifier chosen. Moreover, in some cases the time necessary for this task was higher than the time required by the feature selection process, even without distributing the data, which introduced an important overhead in the running time. Trying to overcome these issues, we propose to modify the function for calculating the threshold of votes by making use of data complexity measures. These measures are a recent proposal to represent characteristics of the data which are considered difficult in classification tasks beyond estimates of error rates [13]. The rationale for this decision is that we assume that good candidate features would contribute to decrease the complexity and must be maintained. Since our intention is to propose a framework that could be independent of the classifier and applicable to both binary and multiclass datasets, among the existing complexity measures, the Fisher discriminant ratio was chosen. Fisher's multiple discriminant ratio for C classes is defined as:

$$f = \frac{\sum_{i=1,j=1,i\neq j}^{c} p_i p_j (\mu_i - \mu_j)^2}{\sum_{i=1}^{c} p_i \sigma_i^2}, \tag{2}$$

where μ_i, σ_i^2, and p_i are the mean, variance, and proportion of the ith class, respectively. In this work we will use the inverse of the Fisher ratio, $1/f$, where a small complexity value represents an easier problem. Therefore, the new formula for calculating $e[v]$ is defined as:

$$e[v] \leftarrow \alpha \times 1/f + (1 - \alpha) \times featPercentage \tag{3}$$

Thus, the fundamental goals that we expect to achieve with the new formulation of Eq. (1) are a reduction in time to calculate the threshold and, also, a classifier-independent method.

3   Materials and Methods

In order to examine the effect of the proposed distributed framework for feature selection by partitioning the data vertically, we use five benchmark datasets, which are described in Table 1 depicting their main characteristics (number of features, number of training and test samples and number of classes). In this work the common partition 2/3 for training and 1/3 for testing was used.

Table 1. Summary of datasets' main characteristics

Dataset	Features	Samples		Classes	Download
		Training	Test		
Isolet	617	6238	1236	26	[3]
Madelon	500	1600	800	2	[3]
Mnist	717	40000	20000	2	[3]
Breast	24481	78	19	2	[1]
Lung	12600	136	68	5	[19]

It must be noted that the proposed framework explained above can be used with any feature selection method, although the use of filters is recommended since they are faster that other methods. In this work, five different filters were involved, all of them are implemented in the Weka [10] environment:

Algorithm 1. Pseudo-code for the proposed distributed methodology

Data: $\mathbf{D}_{(m \times n+1)}$ ← labeled training dataset with m samples and n input features

        X ← set of features, X=$\{x_1, ..., x_n\}$
        s ← number of submatrices of **D** with m samples and t features
        V ← vector of votes
        r ← number of rounds (5 in this experimentation)
        α ← 0.75

Result: S ← subset of features $\backslash$S $\subset$ X
//* Obtaining a vector of votes for discarding features *//

1. initialize the vector of votes V to 0, $|V|$=n
2. **for** each round **do**
3.   Split **D** into s disjoint submatrices with m samples and t features
4.   **for** *each submatrix* **do**
5.   apply a feature selection algorithm
6.   F ← features selected by the algorithm
7.   E ← features eliminated by the algorithm $\backslash$E $\cup$ F = X
8.   increment one vote in vector V for each feature in E
9.   **end**
10. **end**
    //* Obtaining a threshold of votes, *Th*, to remove a feature *//
11. *minVote* ← minimum threshold considered (1)
12. *maxVote* ← maximum threshold considered (number of rounds, r)
13. **for** v ← *minVote* to *maxVote with increment 1* **do**
14. F_{th} ← subset of selected features (number of votes $< v$)
15. $1/f$ ← inverse of Fisher ratio computed on training dataset **D** using only features in F_{th}
16.   *featPercentage* ← percentage of features retained $\left(\frac{|F_{th}|}{|X|} \times 100 \right)$
17. $e[v]$ ← $\alpha \times 1/f + (1-\alpha) \times$ *featPercentage*
18. **end**
19. Th ← *min(e)*, Th is the value which minimizes the function e
20. S ← subset of features after removing from X all features with a number of votes $\geq Th$

- **Correlation-based Feature Selection** (CFS) is a simple multivariate filter algorithm which measures the goodness of feature subsets according to the usefulness of individual features for predicting the class label along with the level of intercorrelation among them [11].
- The **Consistency-based Filter** (CONS) evaluates the worth of a subset of features by the level of consistency in the class values when the training samples are projected onto the subset of features [8].
- The **INTERACT** algorithm [20] is based on *symmetrical uncertainty* (SU). It consists of two major parts. In the first part, the features are ranked in

descending order based on their SU values. In the second part, features are evaluated one by one starting from the end of the ranked feature list. The authors stated that this method can effectively reduce the number of features, and maintain or improve predictive accuracy in dealing with interacting features.

- **Information Gain** [12] is one of the most common attribute evaluation methods. The univariate filter provides an ordered ranking of all the features which requires a threshold.
- **ReliefF** [15] is an extension of the original Relief algorithm that adds the ability of dealing with multiclass problems and is also more robust and capable of dealing with incomplete and noisy data. This method may be applied in all situations, has low bias, includes interaction among features and may capture local dependencies which other methods miss.

While the first three methods return a feature subset, the other two are ranker methods, so we need to establish the number of selected features. In this paper we have opted for retaining the p top features, being p the number of features selected by CFS, since it is a widely-used method and, among the three subset methods chosen, it is the one which usually selects the largest number of features. To test the adequacy of our proposal, four different classifiers, belonging to different families, were selected: C4.5, naive Bayes, kNN and SVM. Notice that two of them are linear (naive Bayes and SVM using a linear kernel) whilst the other two are non-linear (C4.5 and kNN).

4   Experiments and Analysis

This section presents the results over the datasets described in Table 1, comparing three different approaches: the centralized standard approach (C), the distributed approach which merges the partial subsets of features by taking classification error into account ("D-Clas") and, last, the distributed approach proposed in this work, which combines the partial outputs using data complexity measures ("D-Comp"). We will discuss the experimental results in terms of number of selected features, classification accuracy and runtime. In the case of the first three datasets (Isolet, Madelon and Mnist), we have opted for dividing the datasets in 5 packets, so that each packet will contain 20 % of features, without replacement. For the microarray datasets (Breast and Lung), the data is split by assigning groups of t features to each subset, where the number of features t in each subset is half the number of the samples, to avoid overfitting. In this manner, the considered datasets will have enough features to lead to a correct learning.

Figure 1(a) displays the average number of features selected by the five filters for the three different approaches. The full number of features for each dataset is shown in parenthesis. As we can see, the number of features selected by distributed methods is larger than those selected by the centralized approaches. This is caused by the fact that, with the vertical partition, the features are distributed

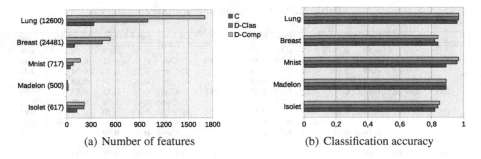

(a) Number of features

(b) Classification accuracy

Fig. 1. Number of features and classification accuracy for the different approaches

across the packets and it is more difficult to detect redundancy between features if they are in different partitions.

In terms of classification accuracy, Table 2 shows the best result for each dataset and classifier in bold face, whilst the best result for each dataset and approach is presented in Fig. 1(b). As we can see, the best results were obtained by our distributed approach ("D-Comp") for Isolet and Mnist, whilst for Mad elon, Breast and Lung it matches the best classification accuracy achieved by the other approaches. However, the important conclusion is that by distributing the data there is not a significant degradation in classification accuracy. It is worth mentioning the case of Mnist dataset, in which the test classification accuracy improves from 0.89 (centralized approach combined with kNN classifier and IG filter) to 0.97 ("D-Comp" approach with kNN classifier for both INT and CONS filters). This is probably due to the higher number of features selected by the filters in the "D-Comp" approach, which turn out to be more appropriate (see Fig. 1(a)).

Finally, Table 3 shows the runtime required by the feature selection methods for both centralized and distributed approaches. Notice that in the two distrib-uted approaches ("D-Clas" and "D-Comp"), the feature selection stage at each packet of data is the same, so the time required will be referred as "D" for both of them. Also, in the distributed approach, considering that all the subsets can be processed at the same time, the time displayed in the table is the maximum of the times required by the filter in each subset generated in the partitioning stage. In these experiments, all the subsets were processed in the same machine, but the proposed algorithm could be executed in multiple processors. The lowest time for each dataset is highlighted in bold face.

As expected, the time required by the distributed methods is drastically reduced for all datasets and filters if compared with that of the centralized approach, in some cases from 9434 s to 0.29 (Lung dataset with CFS filter). Notice that, the larger the dataset, the larger the reduction in time.

Moreover, for the distributed approaches, it is necessary to take into account the time required to calculate the threshold to combine the partial outputs of features. As was mentioned in Sect. 2, the distributed approach "D-Clas" makes

Table 2. Test classification accuracy

			Isolet	Madelon	Mnist	Breast	Lung				Isolet	Madelon	Mnist	Breast	Lung
	CFS	C	0.81	0.75	0.85	0.68	0.78		CFS	C	0.56	0.69	0.86	0.63	0.96
		D-Clas	0.81	0.75	0.86	0.59	0.81			D-Clas	0.58	0.72	0.91	0.57	0.96
		D-Comp	**0.83**	0.80	0.89	0.74	0.84			D-Comp	0.57	0.76	0.94	**0.79**	0.96
	INT	C	0.77	0.78	0.85	**0.79**	0.78		INT	C	0.47	0.73	0.85	0.53	0.94
		D-Clas	0.78	0.78	0.87	0.64	0.86			D-Clas	0.53	0.73	0.85	0.57	0.96
		D-Comp	0.80	0.79	**0.91**	0.74	0.75			D-Comp	0.45	0.78	**0.97**	0.86	0.96
C4.5	Cons	C	0.54	0.78	0.85	0.68	0.84	kNN	Cons	C	0.40	0.70	0.72	0.47	0.84
		D-Clas	0.75	0.77	0.85	0.65	0.81			D-Clas	0.57	0.74	0.96	0.59	0.93
		D-Comp	0.76	0.81	0.92	**0.79**	0.76			D-Comp	0.41	**0.89**	**0.97**	0.74	0.94
	IG	C	0.79	0.80	0.87	0.53	0.87		IG	C	0.54	0.78	0.89	0.68	0.96
		D-Clas	0.80	0.78	0.89	0.75	0.82			D-Clas	0.56	0.79	0.94	0.65	0.95
		D-Comp	0.82	0.72	0.88	0.74	0.82			D-Comp	0.53	0.66	0.94	**0.79**	**0.97**
	ReliefF	C	0.79	**0.83**	0.86	0.74	**0.88**		ReliefF	C	0.57	**0.89**	0.89	0.74	0.96
		D-Clas	0.80	0.81	0.89	0.64	**0.88**			D-Clas	**0.59**	**0.89**	0.96	0.74	0.94
		D-Comp	0.81	0.76	0.90	0.54	0.82			D-Comp	0.58	0.74	0.95	0.74	0.94
	CFS	C	0.72	0.70	0.72	0.37	0.93		CFS	C	0.82	0.65	0.80	0.68	0.94
		D-Clas	**0.74**	0.70	0.73	0.49	0.95			D-Clas	0.84	0.65	0.82	0.67	0.96
		D-Comp	**0.74**	**0.72**	0.74	0.37	**0.96**			D-Comp	**0.85**	0.66	0.83	**0.79**	0.99
	INT	C	0.67	0.70	0.70	0.37	0.94		INT	C	0.73	0.65	0.78	0.74	0.94
		D-Clas	0.65	0.69	**0.76**	0.52	0.94			D-Clas	0.80	0.65	0.78	0.67	0.94
		D-Comp	0.74	0.70	0.75	0.37	0.94			D-Comp	0.79	0.66	0.85	0.74	0.94
NB	Cons	C	0.40	0.70	0.72	0.37	0.85	SVM	Cons	C	0.30	0.65	0.74	0.32	0.79
		D-Clas	0.60	0.70	0.74	0.46	0.88			D-Clas	0.76	0.66	0.80	0.61	0.92
		D-Comp	0.64	0.70	0.73	0.37	0.91			D-Comp	0.69	0.66	**0.86**	**0.79**	**0.97**
	IG	C	0.70	0.70	0.69	0.37	0.88		IG	C	0.81	0.66	0.79	**0.79**	0.96
		D-Clas	0.71	0.70	0.71	0.39	0.88			D-Clas	0.83	0.65	0.80	0.73	0.96
		D-Comp	0.70	0.70	0.73	0.37	0.91			D-Comp	0.83	**0.68**	0.80	0.79	**0.97**
	ReliefF	C	0.65	0.70	0.70	**0.84**	0.88		ReliefF	C	0.82	0.66	0.75	0.63	**0.96**
		D-Clas	0.70	0.70	0.70	0.82	0.92			D-Clas	0.84	0.66	0.77	0.70	**0.97**
		D-Comp	0.69	0.67	0.60	**0.84**	0.91			D-Comp	**0.85**	**0.68**	0.80	0.68	**0.97**

Table 3. Runtime (seconds) for the feature selection methods tested

		Isolet	Madelon	Mnist	Breast	Lung
CFS	C	250	36	1787	7969	9434
	D	**40**	18	287	0.47	0.29
INT	C	196	40	3145	179	135
	D	46	16	**225**	0.68	1.12
Cons	C	368	52	6163	14.35	8.11
	D	58	16	**225**	**0.33**	0.45
IG	C	171	41	1451	1.88	1.99
	D	42	**15**	273	0.61	**0.24**
ReliefF	C	533	62	30413	3.95	5.05
	D	190	26	5522	0.70	0.26

use of a classifier to establish this threshold. Therefore, the time required by this method depends highly on the classifier, whilst with the distributed approach "D-Comp" the time is independent of the classifier. Table 4 depicts the average runtime on all datasets for each filter and distributed approach, as well as the speed up values, which indicate the performance improvement of the approach

Table 4. Runtime (seconds) for obtaining the threshold of votes

Method	D-Clas					D-Comp	SpeedUp
	C4.5	NB	kNN	SVM	Average		
CFS	149.67	85.2	171.3	641.41	261.90	2.33	**112.41**
INT	92.33	67.66	153.47	607.52	230.25	1.51	**152.48**
Cons	82.25	59.10	96.77	625.45	215.89	0.97	**222.57**
IG	101.10	76.23	132.54	576.87	222.44	2.19	**101.59**
ReliefF	114.20	101.45	149.76	989.75	338.79	2.27	**149.25**

"D-Comp" with respect to the average time of the four approaches "D-Clas". It is easy to notice that the time required to find the threshold in the proposed distributed approach "D-Comp" is notable lower than the approach "D-Clas", specially with the ReliefF filter, in which in some cases the time was reduced from 989.75 s to only 2.27.

5   Final Remarks

This paper presents a new methodology for distributed feature selection over vertically partitioned data. Typical procedures make use of classification algorithms to combine the partial outputs obtained from each partition. However, these approaches present two important drawbacks: (1) the method is dependent on the classifier and (2) it is necessary to add an extra running time in the process of merging the partial results from the different partitions. Trying to overcome these issues, we have designed a new approach based on a complexity data measure which is independent of the classifier and does not consume so much time in the merging stage.

In light of the results obtained using five datasets, we can conclude that the distributed approach proposed in this work ("D-Comp") performs successfully, since the classification accuracy matches and, in some cases, is even better than the use of the original feature selection algorithms over the whole datasets. In terms of execution time, we are able to reduce it significantly with respect to the distributed approach "D-Clas", being this fact (together with the independence from any classifier) the most important advantage of our method.

As future research, we plan to test the scalability properties of the proposed method by increasing the size of the datasets and modifying the number of packets. Moreover, another interesting line of research might be to deal with disjoint partitions, as well as the use of other complexity measures.

Acknowledgements. This research has been economically supported in part by the Ministerio de Economía y Competitividad of the Spanish Government through the research project TIN 2012-37954, partially funded by FEDER funds of the European Union; and by the Consellería de Industria of the Xunta de Galicia through the research project GRC2014/035. V. Bolón-Canedo acknowledges support of the Xunta de Galicia under postdoctoral Grant code ED481B 2014/164-0.

References

1. Technology agency for sciency and research. Kent ridge bio-medical dataset repository. http://datam.i2r.a-star.edu.sg/datasets/krbd/
2. Ananthanarayana, V.S., Subramanian, D.K., Murty, M.N.: Scalable, distributed and dynamic mining of association rules. In: Prasanna, V.K., Vajapeyam, S., Valero, M. (eds.) HiPC 2000. LNCS, vol. 1970, p. 559. Springer, Heidelberg (2000)
3. Bache, K., Linchman, M.: UCI machine learning repository. University of California, Irvine, School of Information and Computer Sciences (2013). http://archive.ics.uci.edu/ml/. Accessed January 2015
4. Bolón-Canedo, V., Sánchez-Maroño, N., Alonso-Betanzos, A.: A distributed feature selection approach based on a complexity measure. In: International Work Conference on Artificial Neural Networks (2015, in press)
5. Bolón-Canedo, V., Sánchez-Maroño, N., Cerviño-Rabuñal, J.: Toward parallel feature selection from vertically partitioned data. In: European Symposium on Artificial Neural Networks, Computacional Intelligence and Machine Learning (2014)
6. Chan, P.K., Stolfo, S.J.: Toward parallel and distributed learning by meta-learning. In: AAAI workshop in Knowledge Discovery in Databases, pp. 227–240 (1993)
7. Das, K., Bhaduri, K., Kargupta, H.: A local asynchronous distributed privacy preserving feature selection algorithm for large peer-to-peer networks. Knowl. Inf. Syst. 24(3), 341–367 (2010)
8. Dash, M., Liu, H.: Consistency-based search in feature selection. Artif. Intel. 151(1), 155–176 (2003)
9. de Haro García, A.: Scaling data mining algorithms. Application to instance and feature selection. Ph.D. thesis, Universidad de Granada (2011)
10. Hall, M., Frank, E., Holmes, G., Pfahringer, B., Reutemann, P., Witten, I.: The weka data mining software: an update. ACM SIGKDD Explor. Newsl. 11(1), 10–18 (2009)
11. Hall, M.A.: Correlation-based feature selection for machine learning. Ph.D. thesis, The University of Waikato (1999)
12. Hall, M.A., Smith, L.A.: Practical feature subset selection for machine learning. Comput. Sci. 98, 181–191 (1998)
13. Ho, T.K., Basu, M.: Data Complexity in Pattern Recognition. Springer, London (2006)
14. Jain, A., Zongker, D.: Feature selection: evaluation, application, and small sample performance. IEEE Trans. Patter Anal. Mach. Intel. 19(2), 153–158 (1997)
15. Kononenko, I.: Estimating attributes: analysis and extensions of RELIEF. In: Bergadano, F., De Raedt, L. (eds.) ECML 1994. LNCS, vol. 784, pp. 171–182. Springer, Heidelberg (1994)
16. McConnell, S., Skillicorn, D.B.: Building predictors from vertically partitioned data. In: Proceedings of the 2004 Conference of the Centre for Advanced Studies on Collaborative Research, pp. 150–162. IBM Press (2004)
17. Skillicorn, D.B., McConell, S.M.: Distributed prediction from vertically partitioned data. J. Parallel Distrib. Comput. 68(1), 16–36 (2008)
18. Tsoumakas, G., Vlahavas, I.: Distributed data mining of large classifier ensembles. In: Proceedings Companion Volume of the Second Hellenic Conference on Artificial Intelligence, pp. 249–256 (2002)
19. Vanderbilt University. Gene expression model selector. http://www.gems-system.org/
20. Zhao, Z., Liu, H.: Searching for interacting features. IJCAI 7, 1156–1161 (2007)

Analyzing Planning and Monitoring Skills of Users in a Multi-UAV Simulation Environment

Víctor Rodríguez-Fernández[1](✉), Héctor D. Menéndez[2], and David Camacho[1]

[1] Universidad Autónoma de Madrid (UAM), 28049 Madrid, Spain
victor.rodriguez@inv.uam.es, david.camacho@uam.es
http://aida.ii.uam.es
[2] University College London (UCL), London, UK
h.menendez@ucl.ac.uk

Abstract. The study of Unmanned Aerial Vehicles (UAVs) is currently a growing area. The accelerated expansion of these technologies is demanding the work of more and more qualified operators, able to supervise and control multiple UAVs at the same time. Unfortunately, the training process for this type of systems is still unstructured, and it is needed to define methods to assess and classify operators in the context of a specific skill, for both novice users and experts. This work is focused on analyzing the planning and monitoring skills of inexperienced users in a multi-UAV simulation environment, through the use of a set of metrics capturing the performance of a user and defining its profile. The user profiles will be clustered to extract shared behavioral patterns that help us to decide the planning and monitoring level for each group of users, and to select potential operators.

Keywords: UAVs · Human-Machine Interaction · Computer-based simulation · Planning · Performance metrics · Clustering · Behavioral patterns

1 Introduction

Unmanned Aerial Vehicles (UAVs) have been a growing field of study over the last few years. These new technologies offer many potential applications in multiple fields such as infrastructure inspection, monitoring coastal zones, traffic and disaster management, agriculture and forestry among others [9].

In recent years, two topics are emerging in relation to the study of UAVs and Unmanned Aircraft System (UASs). One is the effort to design systems such that the current many-to-one ratio of operators to vehicles can be inverted, so that a single operator can control multiple UAVs. The other is related to the fact that the fast evolution UAS has now outpaced current operator training regimens, leading to a shortage of qualified UAS pilots. Thus, it is necessary to re-design the current intensive training process to meet that demand, making UAV operations

© Springer International Publishing Switzerland 2015
J.M. Puerta et al. (Eds.): CAEPIA 2015, LNAI 9422, pp. 255–264, 2015.
DOI: 10.1007/978-3-319-24598-0_23

more accessible and available for a less limited pool of individuals, which may include, for example, high-skilled video-game players [10].

Unfortunately, the integration of the training science into UASs is still ineffective [14]. For this reason, Pavlas et al. establish a list of *Knowledges*, *Skills* and *Attitudes* (KSAs) that any "UAS-like" training system should take into account [11]. In this work, we will focus on capturing the performance of two specific skills of that list: **Mission Planning** and **Mission Monitoring** [4], both of them in the context of a multi-UAV simulation. This performance data will be used to extract behavioral patterns among users, and to rate them in terms of Planning and Monitoring skills, which could be used to select potential UAS operators.

The rest of the paper is structured as follows: In Sect. 2 we introduce different researches and topics related to this work. Section 3 gives a brief review of the simulation environment used to extract the data for this work. Section 4 details the set of measures developed to assess the user performance in the simulation environment used. Then, in Sect. 5 we make use of those metrics with the data extracted, and analyze the results using and validating some clustering techniques. Finally, Sect. 6 presents the conclusions and future work.

2 Related Work

The most common metrics used to assess performance on Human-Machine Interaction (HMI) systems focus on the user workload and its *Situational Awareness* [5]. However, it is also interesting to define some measures that collect the performance of a user in a direct way, as a type of global *score* indicating the quality of the performance. These metrics, which are also known as *Direct measures of performance quality*, are linked to the world of videogames, where these quality measurements create a *user profile* [1].

The information given by the different metrics and user interactions can help to recognize and extract some hidden information about the general use of the system. Here, *data mining and machine learning* techniques take much importance. Since multi-UAV systems are still futurist developments, there is still a high shortage of experts able to label data from this type of missions objectively, in order to develop a supervised analysis. Thus, we can only work in this field by using unsupervised learning techniques [2].

For this reason, the analysis made in this work is focused on *Clustering*, a popular unsupervised technique used to group together, in a blindly way, objects which are similar to one another. In order to assess the quality of a clusterization, and to compare and decide which clustering algorithm is better for a specific dataset, the data-mining literature provides a range of different *internal validation measures*, which take a clusterization and use information intrinsic to the data to evaluate the quality of the clustering [3].

Fig. 1. Screenshot of a multi-UAV mission in Drone Watch And Rescue (DWR).

3   DWR - A Multi-UAV Simulation Environment

The simulation environment used as the basis for this work has been designed following the criteria of availability and usability. It is known as Drone Watch And Rescue (DWR), and its description can be found in [12,13]. DWR might be considered as a serious game, since it gamifies the concept of a multi-UAV mission (See Fig. 1), challenging the user to capture all mission targets, while avoiding at the same time the possible incidents that may occur during a mission.

The usual settings of a simulation in DWR imply that the mission starts with a pre-loaded path plan for every UAV. However, in this work, as we intend to analyze the user planning skills, the simulator has been configured so that, before starting a simulation, the user must first assign a flying path to each available UAV, which is known as a **pre-planning** process.

Whenever an event occurs during a simulation, DWR stores the simulation status in that moment, as a *Simulation Snapshot*. This snapshot contains all relevant information of the current status of every element taking part in the simulation. The information stored by DWR allows to reproduce the entire simulation, which is helpful for the analysis process.

4   Measures of Planning and Monitoring Effectiveness

The main goal of this work is to analyze the user performance when designing and monitoring mission plans in the simulation environment introduced above.

That lead us to the need for defining a way to measure the performance of any user in a specific simulation, in the context of planning and monitoring skills.

To achieve this, four performance metrics have been defined: Score (S), Cooperation (C), Aggressiveness (A) and Initial Plan Complexity (IPC). All of them are numeric values in the range $[0, 1]$, where 0 represents the worst performance for that metric, and 1 represents the best. We can define, for a given user, his *performance profile* as the tuple (S, C, A, IPC), where each value represents an average on the set of simulations executed by the user.

4.1 Score

The *Score* (S) metric gives a global success/failure rate of a simulation. The main goal for a user planning and monitoring a mission in DWR is to capture the maximum number of targets, minimizing the resources consumed and returning all UAVs to an airport at the end of the mission. This goal can be divided into 3 sub-goals: detecting targets, minimizing resource loss and returning the UAVs to an airport to finish the mission.

Based on this description, we define the score of a simulation s as:

$$S(s) = \frac{1}{3} \left[\frac{|targetsDetected(s)|}{|T(s)|} + \left(1 - \frac{|destroyedUAVs(s)|}{|U(s)|} \right) + \frac{UAVsInBase(s, lSh(s))}{|U(s)|} \right], \tag{1}$$

where $U(s)$ is the set of UAVs participating in the mission, $T(s)$ is the set of mission targets and $destroyedUAVs(s)$ is the set of UAVs that were lost during the mission. Note that $UAVsInBase(s, lSh(s))$ queries how many UAVs were positioned on an airport at the last snapshot of the simulation *(lSh(s))*.

4.2 Cooperation

Cooperation (C) measures to what extent the user has interacted equally with all the available UAVs in a simulation. Let $I_U = \{|I_{u1}|, \ldots |I_{uN}|\}$ be the set containing the number of interactions performed to each of the N UAVs in the simulation, Cooperation is computed as follows:

$$C(s) = \frac{1}{1 + \sqrt{var(I_U)}},$$

i.e., it gets closer to 1 when the variance in the number of interactions per UAV is low, which means that the user interactions are well-balanced.

4.3 Aggressiveness

Aggressiveness (A) is related to how the user behaves when changing the path of a UAV. The simulation environment used in this work features three control modes (*Monitor*, *Add waypoints* and *Manual*), and each of them allows the user to change the waypoints of a UAV in a different way. In *Monitor* mode, the user is only allowed to move an existing waypoint, which is a "soft" interaction. Mode *Add waypoints* permits appending new waypoints to an existing path, while mode *Manual* allows the user to define a new path from scratch, which is an "aggressive" interaction.

Given the distinctions about waypoint handling in DWR, we can define $W_{MO}(s)$ as the set of waypoints interactions performed in mode *Monitor*, $W_A(s)$ as the corresponding to mode *Add waypoints*, and $W_{MA}(s)$ to mode *Manual*. Based on that, we compute the Aggressiveness of a simulation as:

$$A(s) = \frac{\alpha|W_{MA}(s)| + \beta|W_A(s)| + \gamma|W_{MO}(s)|}{|W(s)|}, \quad \alpha, \beta, \gamma < 1, \quad \alpha > \beta > \gamma,$$

where $W(s)$ is the set of all waypoint interactions in simulation s (Note that $W(s) = W_{MO}(s) \cup W_A(s) \cup W_{MA}(s)$). Parameters α, β, γ are the aggressiveness factors for each control mode. Obtaining values of this metric close to 1 indicates that the user has performed mostly aggressive interactions, i.e., path definitions. On the contrary, values close to 0 designate quick and soft waypoint handling.

4.4 Initial Plan Complexity (IPC)

Before starting a mission in the simulation environment used in this work, the user must define a path plan for each available UAV. The *Initial Plan Complexity* (*IPC*) metric rates the complexity of that initial plan, in terms of the time spent to design it and the number of waypoints comprising it. Let $t_p(s)$ be the time spent planning paths at the beginning of the simulation s, and $W_p(s)$ the set of waypoints added during that time interval, the *IPC* is defined as:

$$IPC(s) = \frac{1}{2}\left(\frac{t_p(s)}{t(s)} + \frac{|W_P(s)|}{|W(s)|}\right),$$

where $t(s)$ is the total simulation time and $W(s)$ is the set of all waypoints added during the whole simulation time. Note that a high value of this metric does not always refer to a high-quality path plan, it only indicates the effort put into designing it.

5 Experimentation

The purpose of the experiment carried out in this work consists in using the simulation environment DWR to analyze the performance of inexperienced users during a training session. Once we have a clean dataset, we will assess the performance of every user following the metrics defined above, and based on this evaluation, we will create and group user profiles in order to define **clusters** that indicate similar user performance. Finally, those clusters will be analyzed and classified in the context of planning and monitoring skills.

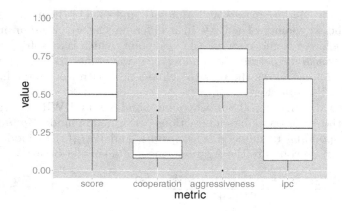

Fig. 2. Box-plots of the distribution of each metric in our dataset

5.1 Computing the Performance Metrics in a Simulations Dataset

In this experiment, the simulation environment (DWR) was tested using Computer Engineering students of the Autonomous University of Madrid (AUM), all of them inexperienced in "UAS-like" systems. All users received a brief tutorial before using the simulator, explaining the mission objectives and the basic controls. After that, they were told to plan and monitor a test mission designed for this experiment. That mission (See Fig. 1) featured a total of 3 UAVs performing 4 Surveillance Tasks in 2 different areas, in order to detect 4 mobile targets. The map also presented 4 No-Flight-Zones and 4 Refueling Stations. During the simulation, 4 mission incidents were triggered, affecting both the UAVs and the environment. For more information about these simulation elements see [13].

The dataset resulted from this experiment comprises **47 distinct simulations**, executed by a total of **16** users. To achieve a robust analysis of the data extracted, we must clean the dataset by removing those simulations which can be considered as useless. Taking into account difficulty level of the test missions, we have considered as useless those simulations aborted before 20 s of duration. From the 47 simulations composing our students dataset, only 33 of them are considered as useful, and will be used in the data analysis process.

Figure 2 shows the distribution of the metrics computed in the dataset of this experiment. From these plots two general behavior tendencies can be extracted right away: On the one hand, the Cooperation is in almost all the cases very low, which means that users tend to use only one of the three UAVs of the test mission to design a mission plan. On the other hand, Aggressiveness is generally high, which makes sense given that users were told to design a path plan from scratch before starting the simulations, resulting in aggressive interactions. The other two metrics (Score and IPC) present higher values of variance and well-balanced distribution functions.

5.2   Applying Clustering Algorithms to Group User Profiles

Computing the metrics for all users in our dataset results in a 4-dimensional metric space, on which we can apply **clustering** methods to group together users which have similar performance profiles. We make use of four clustering algorithms: *AGNES (Agglomerative Hierarchical), K-means, DIANA (Divisive hierarchical) and PAM* [6–8]. The Euclidean distance is used in all cases as similarity measure between the data. For the AGNES algorithm, the *average link* method is used to merge clusters.

For internal validation of the clusters, we selected three validation measures from the state of the art that reflect how good is the clusterization in terms of different properties: *Connectivity, Dunn Index and Silhouette width* [3]. While Connectivity assesses the connectedness of the cluster partitions, Dunn Index and Silhouette width combine compactness and separation measures into a single score. A good clusterization should minimize the Connectivity and maximize the Dunn Index and the Silhouette width.

All these clustering algorithms are tested fixing the number of clusters, k, with values from 2 to 6. To perform this iterative process, we make use of the R library *clValid* [3].

Table 1. Results for the Clustering Validation of user profiles in our dataset. Bolded cells represent the best results obtained for each cluster validation metric.

Clustering method	Validation metric	k = 2	k = 3	k = 4	k = 5	k = 6
AGNES	*Connectivity*	**6.341**	8.858	15.271	15.771	17.221
	Dunn	0.502	0.502	**0.523**	0.523	0.523
	Silhouette	**0.468**	0.395	0.276	0.220	0.162
K-Means	*Connectivity*	6.341	8.858	16.786	24.793	26.243
	Dunn	0.502	0.502	0.424	0.443	0.443
	Silhouette	0.468	0.395	0.276	0.225	0.201
DIANA	*Connectivity*	6.341	14.269	16.786	24.793	26.436
	Dunn	0.502	0.346	0.424	0.443	0.471
	Silhouette	0.468	0.299	0.276	0.225	0.230
PAM	*Connectivity*	6.341	14.269	16.786	23.112	25.112
	Dunn	0.502	0.346	0.424	0.382	0.382
	Silhouette	0.468	0.299	0.276	0.225	0.178

The numerical results for the clustering algorithms validation are given in Table 1. For $k = 2$, *Connectivity* and *Silhouette* reach the same optimal values for all the algorithms tested, which is a sign of a good clusterization, but does not help to discriminate which algorithm should be used. However, the *AGNES* clustering for $k = 4$ maximizes the *Dunn Index* and outperforms other algorithms, so, since it reaches optimal values for all metrics, we chose it as the most interesting algorithm to analyze.

5.3 Analyzing and Labeling the User Profile Clusters

Once we have validated and extracted the optimal algorithms to cluster our dataset, we must analyze the clusters obtained in order to interpret them, and to label them with classes in the context of planning and monitoring skills. Each skill can be categorized with the following rating labels: *[Very High, High, Normal, Low, Very Low]*. Due to the small number of users in this experiment, and given that we have designed the mission of this experiment and the simulation environment itself, we are able to do an expert cluster analysis manually by analyzing the profiles of each cluster.

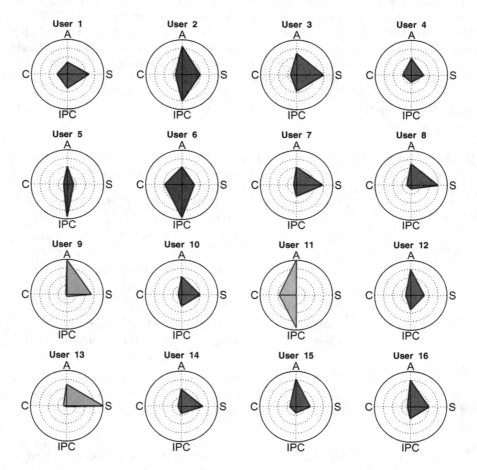

Fig. 3. User Profile Clusters, obtained from AGNES Clustering with k = 4 (Color figure online).

According to the clustering results, the best clusterizations for our dataset are obtained with values of $k = 2$ and $k = 4$. This means that two main patterns can be distinguished, and those can be broken down into four more specific patterns. Below is detailed the explanation of each of the clusters obtained by the *AGNES* algorithm with $k = 4$, along with the class with which it has been labeled, for both the *Planning* and the *Monitoring* skills (PS and MS). Figure 3 shows the clusterization results graphically.

1. *Users={1,3,4,7,8,10,12,14,15,16};[PS=Low];[MS=Normal]*: This cluster is the biggest, and therefore the most representative for describing users in our dataset. The profiles show the same tendencies as the distribution functions of Fig. 2, i.e., these users create simple plans at the beginning of the mission (low IPC) and adjust them during the simulation (high aggressiveness) (See Fig. 3, red profiles).

2. *Users={2,5,6};[PS=High];[MS=Low]*: This cluster contains planner profiles, typical from users that have put all their efforts into designing a complex initial plan (Very high IPC). Unfortunately, the low scores let guess that these users are not good at monitoring the mission status and tend to abort the simulation prematurely (See Fig. 3, blue profiles).

3. *Users={9,13};[PS=Very Low];[MS=High]*: This cluster is intriguing because it contains high-scored profiles, which means that the mission objectives have been accomplished successfully by the users. However, the extremely low values of Cooperation and IPC are saying that the user has completed the mission using only one UAV, without designing an initial plan, just doing an intense monitoring and a dynamic replanning (See Fig. 3, orange profiles).

4. *Users={11};[PS=Very High];[MS=Very Low]*: This cluster comprises only one user. It stands out for having maximum levels of Aggressiveness and IPC, good Cooperation values and extremely low scores. This means that the user has completely focused on designing complex and balanced plans for all the UAVs, and he scarcely spent time monitoring the mission (See Fig. 3, green profiles).

6 Conclusions and Future Work

This paper has presented a methodology for analyzing the planning and monitoring skills of a group of inexperienced users when interacting with a multi-UAV simulation environment. Four metrics have been defined in order to capture the performance of users in the context of those skills, and based on them, the profile of a user has been defined. User profiles are grouped by a clustering algorithm (selected after a validation process) to obtain shared profile patterns among users. Finally, each cluster is analyzed and classified in terms of the planning and monitoring levels deducted from the cluster members.

As future work, it is intended to take advantage of the web architecture on which the simulation environment is built upon, in order to extract large volumes of data and enrich the analysis carried out in this work. To achieve this, we must automate some manual processes made here as the cluster labeling and skill assignation. Also, the proposed metrics should be validated by expert users in the field and statistical tests should be applied. Finally, the results from this experiment will be contrasted with other unsupervised modelling techniques for HMI systems, as Hidden Markov (or Semi-Markov) Models.

Acknowledgments. This work is supported by the Spanish Ministry of Science and Education under Project Code TIN2014-56494-C4-4-P, Comunidad Autonoma de Madrid under project CIBERDINE S2013/ICE-3095, and Savier an Airbus Defense & Space project (FUAM-076914 and FUAM-076915). The authors would like to acknowledge the support obtained from Airbus Defence &Space, specially from Savier Open Innovation project members: José Insenser, Gemma Blasco, Juan Antonio Henríquez and César Castro.

References

1. Begis, G.: Adaptive gaming behavior based on player profiling. US Patent US6106395 A (2000)
2. Boussemart, Y., Cummings, M.L., Fargeas, J.L., Roy, N.: Supervised vs. unsupervised learning for operator state modeling in unmanned vehicle settings. J. Aerosp. Comput. Inf. Commun. **8**(3), 71–85 (2011)
3. Datta, S., Datta, S., Pihur, V., Brock, G.: clValid: an R package for cluster validation. J. Stat. Softw. **25**(4), (2008). American Statistical Association
4. Dixon, S.R., Wickens, C.D., Chang, D.: Unmanned aerial vehicle flight control: False alarms versus misses. In: Human Factors and Ergonomic Society 48th Annual Meeting (2004)
5. Drury, J.L., Scholtz, J., Yanco, H.A.: Awareness in human-robot interactions. In: IEEE International Conference on Systems, Man and Cybernetics, 2003, vol. 1, pp. 912–918. IEEE (2003)
6. Hartigan, J.A., Wong, M.A.: Algorithm as 136: A k-means clustering algorithm. Appl. Stat. **28**, 100–108 (1979)
7. Kaufman, L., Rousseeuw, P.: Clustering by means of medoids (1987)
8. Kaufman, L., Rousseeuw, P.J.: Finding Groups in Data: An Introduction to Cluster Analysis, vol. 344. Wiley, New York (2009)
9. Kendoul, F.: Survey of advances in guidance, navigation, and control of unmanned rotorcraft systems. J. Field Robot. **29**(2), 315–378 (2012)
10. McKinley, R.A., McIntire, L.K., Funke, M.A.: Operator selection for unmanned aerial systems: comparing video game players and pilots. Aviat. Space, Environ. Med. **82**(6), 635–642 (2011)
11. Pavlas, D., Burke, C.S., Fiore, S.M., Salas, E., Jensen, R., Fu, D.: Enhancing unmanned aerial system training: A taxonomy of knowledge, skills, attitudes, and methods. In: Proceedings of the Human Factors and Ergonomics Society Annual Meeting, vol. 53, pp. 1903–1907. SAGE Publications (2009)
12. Rodríguez-Fernández, V., Atencia, C.R., Camacho, D.: A Multi-UAV mission planning videogame-based framework for player analysis. In: 2015 IEEE Congress on Evolutionary Computation (CEC). IEEE (2015, in Press)
13. Rodríguez-Fernández, V., Menéndez, H.D., Camacho, D.: Design and development of a lightweight multi-UAV simulator. In: 2015 IEEE International Conference on Cybernetics (CYBCONF). IEEE (2015, in Press)
14. Stulberg, A.N.: Managing the unmanned revolution in the us air force. Orbis **51**(2), 251–265 (2007)

Metaheuristics and Evolutionary Computation

Learning Levels of Mario AI Using Genetic Algorithms

Alejandro Baldominos[(✉)], Yago Saez, Gustavo Recio, and Javier Calle

Universidad Carlos III de Madrid,
Avenida de la Universidad, 30, 28911 Leganes, Spain
{abaldomi,ysaez,grecio,fcalle}@inf.uc3m.es

Abstract. This paper introduces an approach based on Genetic Algorithms to learn levels from the Mario AI simulator, based on the Infinite Mario Bros. game (which is, at the same time, based on the Super Mario World game from Nintendo). In this approach, an autonomous agent playing Mario is able to learn a sequence of actions in order to maximize the score, not looking at the current state of the game at each time.

Different parameters for the Genetic Algorithm are explored, and two different stages are executed: in the first, domain independent genetic operators are used; while in the second knowledge about the domain is incorporated to these operators in order to improve the results.

Results are encouraging, as Mario is able to complete very difficult levels full of enemies, resembling the behavior of an expert human player.

Keywords: Mario AI · Games · Genetic algorithms · Learning

1 Introduction

Super Mario Bros. is a sidescroller platform videogame designed by Shigeru Miyamoto and released for the Nintendo Entertainment System three decades ago, in 1985. This game has become a great success, achieving over 40 million sales and making the fifth position in the list of best-selling videogames, the other four being released after 2005. Today, the Mario franchise has reaped significant success and Mario videogames and merchandising generate millions of dollars.

In 1990, another Mario game was released: Super Mario World. This game implied a technical improvement in graphics, audio and gameplay over the original sidescroller, and introduced new characters like Yoshi. In 2009, the Mario AI Championship was introduced [10], aiming at developing intelligent agents able to complete levels of increasing difficulty of a game based on Infinite Mario Bros., a game based at the same time on Super Mario World (but with pseudo-randomly generated levels). In 2010, the Mario AI Championship introduced a new track: the Learning track, where an agent was intended to learn the best strategy to obtain the maximum score in a fixed level of the game, being able to play a maximum of 10,000 games of that same level before the competition in order to learn it.

© Springer International Publishing Switzerland 2015
J.M. Puerta et al. (Eds.): CAEPIA 2015, LNAI 9422, pp. 267–277, 2015.
DOI: 10.1007/978-3-319-24598-0_24

While the competition is no longer organized (it was discontinued in 2013 in favour of the Platformer AI Competition), this paper aims at building an intelligent agent able to compete following the rules of the Mario AI Learning track. Genetic Algorithms will be used in order to learn the best strategy (i.e., sequence of actions performed by Mario) to maximize the score. This research work is an extension of a B.Sc. thesis published by Hector Valero [12].

This paper is structured as follows: Sect. 2 describes related work. Later, Sect. 3 describes the proposal, providing further details about how individuals are encoded and evaluated and how genetic operators are used. Experiments are conducted to validate and evaluate the proposal, and their setup and results are discussed in Sect. 4. Finally, Sect. 5 provides some conclusive remarks and proposes future lines of work.

2   State of the Art

Some work related to this paper can be found in the papers published by the organizers of the Mario AI Championship. For instance, the paper published by Togelius et al. summarizing the main results from the 2009 edition in the GamePlay track [10] describes the winner solution involving the use of the A* graph search algorithm, and briefly introduces other solutions using rule-based controllers, reactive controllers or finite state machines. Even when this paper referred to the Gameplay track, some solutions used learning algorithms such as genetic programming, stack-based virtual machines, and imitation or reinforcement learning; in some cases controllers are evolved using genetic algorithms. However, these approaches are not discussed in the paper, but rather mentioned.

Another work by Togelius et al. [11] discusses approaches using neural networks for learning controllers for the Super Mario game, involving multilayer perceptrons, simple recurrent networks and HyperGP for evolving the weights. Finally, a work by Karakovskiy and Togelius was published in 2012 [6] discussing the conclusions regarding the competition organization and summarizing the AI techniques used by contestants in the different tracks. Another approach using Q-learning imposing biological constraints for imitating the behavior of human players in the Infinite Mario Bros. is proposed by Fujii et al. [4,5].

Besides Super Mario, other authors have used AI techniques in order to learn controllers for videogame characters, imitating the behavior of a human player. It is specially outstanding a work published by Google DeepMind in Nature [8] describing the development of an agent to play several games for Atari 2600, using so-called deep Q-networks (neuron-based networks for reinforcement learning), where the inputs are the pixels in the screen. A framework for evaluating other agents in this same domain is provided by Bellemare et al. [2].

3   Proposal

This paper proposes the development of an agent able to maximize the score obtained in one specific Mario AI level. This agent is designed so that it could compete in the Learning Track of the Mario AI Championship, even when the last edition of this competition happened in 2012. The Learning track allows the agent to learn the level over N games, evaluating the agent in the game $N + 1$. The score is computed considering different aspects of the game, including the number of collected coins, killed enemies, remaining time after completing the level, etc. Details about how these aspects are weighted to compute the score are provided later, when the fitness function is described.

There are two constraints which must be considered when training the agent: (a) the agent is limited to 10,000 games ($N = 10000$) in order to be able to learn the level; and (b) the response time to decide the next action to be performed by the agent must not exceed 42 ms.

In order to generate the agent who will optimize the obtained score during a Mario AI game, genetic algorithms will be used. In this approach, the learning algorithm will not consider the current state of the game (i.e., how Mario is placed in the environment in a certain point in time), but rather will compute a predefined sequence of actions (the same actions that could be performed by a human player) and evaluate it over the game level. This sequence will be evolved in order to maximize the final score obtained when the level is finished, either because it is successfully completed or because the character dies.

3.1   Encoding

As described above, an agent is defined as a sequence of actions to be performed in a specific level of Mario AI. The chromosome must be able to represent a sequence of all possible actions performed by the agent in the game. In order to control the character, the player can use a D-Pad with four positions (up, left, down, right) and two additional buttons, namely A (jump) and B (run and shoot). The system allows several buttons to be pressed at once, resulting in a space of $2^6 = 64$ possible actions. However, this set of actions can be significantly reduced by introducing some domain knowledge: (a) the button *up* performs no action in the game; and (b) some combinations are not feasible, such as pressing *left* and *right* at the same time. With these considerations in mind, the number of actions can be reduced to 22, as pointed out in Table 1. For the genetic algorithm, we have encoded each gene as an integer in the range 0 to 21.

Once the definition of genes are formally described, the chromosome length must be determined. In this domain, there is not a fixed length for the sequence of actions. However, we can estimate a maximum length knowing that (a) the maximum time for completing a level are 200 s and (b) each second can be discretized in 15 ticks. As a result, we define sequences of actions of length 3,000, which implies chromosomes of 3,000 genes, even if not all the actions can be performed (i.e., if Mario completes the game or dies before performing 3,000 actions). This implies that there will be 22^{3000} combinations, so the search space is noticeably big. For this reason, in the first stage a reduced set of actions will be used where we assume that Mario is running everytime, i.e., we only consider actions where the button B is pressed, reducing the search space from 22 actions to 11 at the expense of imposing limits on the representation.

Table 1. List of actions along with the pressed buttons for each one.

0: ◁ ▼ ▷ Ⓐ Ⓑ	1: ◁ ▼ ▷ Ⓐ **B**	2: ◁ ▼ ▷ **A** Ⓑ
3: ◁ ▼ ▷ **A** **B**	4: ◁ **▼** ▷ Ⓐ Ⓑ	5: ◁ **▼** ▷ Ⓐ **B**
6: ◁ ▼ **▶** Ⓐ Ⓑ	7: ◁ ▼ **▶** Ⓐ **B**	8: ◁ ▼ **▶** **A** Ⓑ
9: ◁ ▼ **▶** **A** **B**	10: ◁ **▼** **▶** Ⓐ Ⓑ	11: ◁ **▼** **▶** Ⓐ **B**
12: ◁ **▼** **▶** **A** Ⓑ	13: ◁ **▼** **▶** **A** **B**	14: **◀** ▼ ▷ Ⓐ Ⓑ
15: **◀** ▼ ▷ Ⓐ **B**	16: **◀** ▼ ▷ **A** Ⓑ	17: **◀** ▼ ▷ **A** **B**
18: **◀** **▼** ▷ Ⓐ Ⓑ	19: **◀** **▼** ▷ Ⓐ **B**	20: **◀** **▼** ▷ **A** Ⓑ
	21: **◀** **▼** ▷ **A** **B**	

3.2 Fitness

The fitness function is defined to be the score function, and the genetic algorithm will look towards maximizing this value. The score function used is defined by the Mario AI Championship rules, and follows Eq. 1, where D is the physical distance traveled by Mario from the start to his final position; d_f, d_m and d_{gm} are the number of devoured flowers, mushrooms and green mushrooms respectively; k is the number of killed enemies; k_{st}, k_{sh} and k_f are the number of enemies killed by stomp (jumping), by throwing shells or by throwing fireballs respectively; s is the final status of the game, either won (1) or lost (0); m is the final status of Mario, either small (0), big (1) or fire (2); b_h is the total number of hidden blocks found; c is the total number of coins collected and t' is the time left.

$$S = D + 64d_f + 58d_m + 58d_{gm} + 42k + 12k_{st} + 17k_{sh}$$
$$+ 4k_f + 1024s + 32m + 24b_h + 16c + 8t'. \tag{1}$$

3.3 Genetic Operators

The Genetic Algorithm used performs tournament selection, crossover and mutation. When generating the new population, the offspring will replace their parents. Two different versions for each of these operators have been implemented, the first one being domain-independent and the second one introducing domain knowledge to optimize the behavior of the operator.

Initialization. In the first version, a naive initialization is used, where each action in the chromosome is randomly chosen. However, it is interesting to try a guided initialization, as the most frequent actions for completing the level are running to the right (*right* + B) or running to the right while jumping (*right* + A + B). For this reason, in the second version we introduce a hybrid initialization approach, where either one of the previous initialization methods (random or guided) is randomly for each action.

Selection. Tournament selection is performed, where T_s individuals are randomly selected from the population and face each other, and the one with highest fitness will be one of the parents used for generating the next population. The second version incorporates elitism.

Crossover. The first version uses single-point crossover, where a random point n is chosen, so that n is a number strictly smaller than the length of the chromosome ($n < l = 3000$). If the first parent is $p^1 = \langle b_1^1, b_2^1, \ldots, b_l^1 \rangle$ and the second is $p^2 = \langle b_1^2, b_2^2, \ldots, b_l^2 \rangle$, then the following two childs are begotten: $c^1 = \langle b_1^1, \ldots, b_n^1, b_{n+1}^2 \ldots, b_l^2 \rangle$ and $c^2 = \langle b_1^2, \ldots, b_n^2, b_{n+1}^1 \ldots, b_l^1 \rangle$.

The second version incorporates domain knowledge into the crossover operator. In particular, the crossover is guaranteed to be performed in a point where the absolute position of Mario in the game is similar, i.e. a value of n is pursued so that the position of Mario in both games is close (the euclidean distance between the pairs $[x_1, y_1]$ and $[x_2, y_2]$ falls below a threshold Δ). This ensures continuity in the game, for instance, if one parent had a good start but fails to keep playing well after a certain point $n^+ > n$ and the other parent starts playing bad but improves after a point $n^- < n$, then finding point n will generate offspring in which one child would be better than both parents.

Mutation. In the first version, mutation is performed randomly in M genes in the chromosome. In the second version, mutation is performed over the last w_t^i actions performed by the individual i in the last evaluation before the game ended. w_t^i is a value intrinsic to the individual and which may vary from one generation to another, and is computed as follows:

$$w_t^i = \begin{cases} 2 \times w_{t-1}^i & \text{if } S_t^i \leq S_{t-W}^i \\ w_0 & \text{if } S_t^i > S_{t-1}^i \end{cases}$$

where S_t^i is the fitness for individual i at iteration t and W is defined as a mutation window, which is variable over time.

The fact that the mutated actions are those before the game ended will mostly change the behavior of the character before he dies, at least in the first generations where it is likely to encounter bad individuals which will rarely complete the game. The size of the mutation window (the number of mutated actions) will double every W generations until the individual improves its fitness (S^i), and at this time its size will be reset to the default value w_0.

4   Evaluation

This section describes the parametrization and results for the two stages, the first using domain-independent genetic operators and a reduced set of 11 actions; and the second incorporating specific domain knowledge and all 22 actions.

4.1   1st Stage Experimental Setup

In order to execute the Genetic Algorithm, JGAP library [7] has been used. Regarding the parametrization of the experiments, the tested values are described below. In some cases, different values have been assigned to the same parameter:

Selection. The tournament size (T_s) is defined as a fraction over the population size (P). In the experiments, it is defined as $T_s = 15\%$ and forced to be $T_s \geq 3$.

Crossover. Different values are tried for the crossover rate: $C = 0.1\%$, $C = 0.2\%$, $C = 0.3\%$, $C = 0.4\%$ and $C = 0.5\%$.

Mutation. Different values are tried for the mutation rate: $M = 5\%$, $M = 3.3\%$, $M = 2.5\%$, $M = 2\%$, $M = 1.3\%$ and $M = 1\%$.

Population. Two values have been tested for the population size: $P = 20$ and $P = 50$.

Generations. The maximum number of evaluations is fixed by the Mario AI Championship rules to be $E_M = N = 10000$. The number of generations (G) must be defined as $G = E_M/P$.

Granularity. This parameter tries to resemble human behavior, as it is often the case that the time that happens since players press a button until they release it exceeds one tick. Granularity indicates how many ticks involve each action. Three different values are tested: $g = 1$, $g = 2$ and $g = 5$.

Besides the previous parameters, Mario AI accepts additional arguments in order to generate a level. The next arguments have been used:

- Visualization of the game is disabled (`-vis off`) as otherwise fitness evaluation time would increase significantly.
- Hidden blocks are enabled (`-lhb on`), so they can appear in the level.
- Enemies are enabled (`-lt on`), so they can appear in the level.
- Ladders are disabled (`-lla off`), so they cannot appear in the level.
- Dead ends are enabled (`-lde on`), so they can appear in the level.
- The level type is set to overground (`-lt 0`), other options being underground (1), castle (2) or random (3).
- The level difficulty is set to 1 (`-ld 1`) in a scale from 1 to 12.
- The level length is defined as 300 (`-ll 300`), in a scale from 50 to $2^{31} - 1$. While the maximum value is quite high, we have selected an average length based on the maps of the real game.
- The level PRNG seed is set to 20002.

In the first stage, where only domain-independent definitions of the generic operators are used, a total of 180 experiments have been executed, this number resulting from all the possible combinations for the previous parametrization.

Table 2. Fitness (average and max.) and completed games for each value of P

Average fitness		Maximum fitness		Completed games	
P = 20	P = 50	P = 20	P = 50	P = 20	P = 50
5,513.36	5,622.30	8,773.07	8,551.13	61,921	89,842

Table 3. Average fitness and completed games for each value of P vs. g

	Average fitness		Completed games	
	P = 20	P = 50	P = 20	P = 50
g = 1	4,917.90	4,770.22	4,796	0
g = 2	5,391.58	5,438.07	20,101	23,678
g = 5	6,230.61	6,658.62	38,024	66,164

4.2 Sensitivity Analysis of the Parameters

The high combination of parameters makes it impossible to describe all the results, for that reason, this section provides the main conclusions on how each parameter affects the score. Results are computed as the average of 10 different executions.

Population size (P). Table 2 shows the average fitness, the maximum fitness and the number of completed games for each value of the population size. It can be seen that there are no significant differences in the score (neither average nor maximum), but still a higher population size leads to a higher number of completed games.

Granularity (g). The impact of the granularity in the average fitness and completed games is shown in Table 3. It can be clearly seen that the value $g = 5$ provides better results for both metrics.

Table 4. Average fitness and completed games for each value of P vs. M and C

P vs. M					P vs. C				
	Avg. F.		Compl. G.			Avg. F.		Compl. G.	
	P = 20	P = 50	P = 20	P = 50		P = 20	P = 50	P = 20	P = 50
5%	4,468.19	4,577.51	0	0	0.1	5,718.19	5,571.73	17,059	13,341
3.3%	4,906.72	5,024.67	73	1,277	0.2	5,511.82	5,669.82	13,594	18,903
2.5%	4,866.14	5,519.18	0	3,887	0.3	5,565.07	5,684.42	17,184	19,991
2%	5,596.04	5,567.10	6,631	4,350	0.4	5,317.70	5,586.35	8,791	20,090
1.3%	6,213.64	6,120.62	11,081	30,569	0.5	5,454.03	5,599.19	5,293	17,517
1%	7,029.44	6,924.71	44,136	49,758					

Mutation rate (M). As it can be seen in Table 4, both the average fitness and the completed games increases when the mutation rate is decreased. This may be due to the fact that high mutation rates are promoting exploration, but not the exploitation of good solutions.

Crossover rate (C). As shown in Table 4, it is difficult to extract conclusions regarding the impact of the crossover rate: there are not significant differences in the average fitness, and while there are differences in the number of completed games, these changes do not adhere to any clear pattern.

4.3   2nd Stage Experimental Setup

After obtaining the results described in the previous section, the second phase starts. This phase incorporates domain-specific knowledge into the genetic operators and uses the full set of actions; and also the total number of experiments is reduced by removing some parameters assignations which have not performed well. In particular, the next parameters are affected:

Mutation. The only value left for the mutation rate is $M = 1\%$. The initial mutation window is set to $w_0 = 2$, and the values tested for W are $W = 2$, $W = 3$ and $W = 5$.

Granularity. The value $g = 1$ is removed because it was outperformed by the others, thus leading to values $g = 2$ and $g = 5$.

Moreover, new Mario AI combinations have been tested, all of them having visualization disabled (`-vis off`), hidden blocks enabled (`-lhb on`), dead ends enabled (`-lde on`), and level length of 300 (`-ll 300`):

- **Scenario 1**: level difficulty 4 (`-ld 4`), ladders disabled (`-lda off`), enemies enabled (`-le on`) and seed 01121987 (`-ls 01121987`).
- **Scenario 2**: level difficulty 4 (`-ld 4`), ladders enabled (`-lda on`), enemies enabled (`-le on`) and seed 201183 (`-ls 201183`).
- **Scenario 3**: level difficulty 4 (`-ld 4`), ladders enabled (`-lda on`), enemies disabled (`-le off`) and seed 334 (`-ls 334`).
- **Scenario 4**: level difficulty 4 (`-ld 4`), ladders enabled (`-lda on`), enemies enabled (`-le on`) and seed 333 (`-ls 333`).
- **Scenario 5**: level difficulty 4 (`-ld 4`), ladders disabled (`-lda off`), enemies enabled (`-le on`) and seed 11062011 (`-ls 11062011`).
- **Scenario 6**: level difficulty 4 (`-ld 4`), ladders enabled (`-lda on`), enemies enabled (`-le on`) and seed 444 (`-ls 444`).

4.4   2nd Stage Results

Again, the number of combinations is too big to describe the results thoroughly. Still, this section shows the evolution of the average fitness along each generation, which is displayed in Fig. 1. It can be noticed that the best configuration always involves the highest granularity ($g = 5$) and the lowest mutation rate ($M = 0.1\%$) with $W = 2$. However, best crossover rate varies across scenarios. Results are computed as the average of 10 executions.

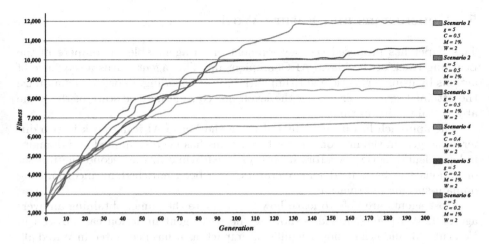

Fig. 1. Fitness evolution for the best configuration of each scenario.

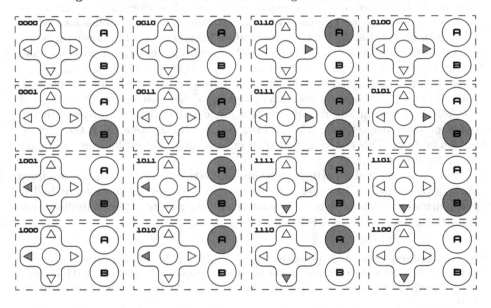

Fig. 2. Proposed new set of feasible actions, along with their encoding (4 bits).

4.5   Discussion

Results clearly show how agents evolve by learning the best strategy to complete the game and maximize the score they obtain. In the 2010 Mario AI Championship celebrated during CIG in Copenhagen [1] the winner obtained 45,017 points for five different games, i.e., an average score of 9,003.4 points per level. If we average the fitness of our best agent for each scenario, we obtain an average score of 12,059, outperforming the winner of that year.

5 Conclusions and Future Work

This paper has proposed the development of an agent able to compete in the Learning track of the Mario AI Championship. This agent learns a sequence of actions by using a genetic algorithm with integer encoding, in order to maximize the attained score after ending the level, not considering the state of the game at a certain point in time.

The approach has been evaluated using the Mario AI framework in two different stages: in the first one, the set of actions has been simplified and domain-independent genetic operators have been used; while in the second the full set of actions has been used and operators have been enriched by incorporating domain-specific information.

Most agents are able to learn how to complete the game, obtaining an average of 12,059 points. A video showing the best agent in action can be seen in YouTube [3] and it has shown significant impact, as it has been cited in Wired [9].

However, there is still room for improvements. For instance, we have noticed that while the button *down* is pressed, *right* and *left* perform no action; so the space of actions can be reduced even more, resulting in 16 combinations which are shown in Fig. 2 along with their encoding using 4 bits. The chosen encoding resembles Gray code as small changes in the genotype are translated into small changes in the phenotype, and it consists of the sequence of bits $\langle b_{ld}, b_{dr}, b_a, b_b \rangle$; where b_a and b_b respectively determine whether the A and B buttons are pressed, while b_{ld} and b_{dr} indicate whether *left*, *right* or *down* buttons are pressed using the following convention: if only one of b_{ld} or b_{dr} is 1, then the pressed button is *left* or *right* respectively, while if both b_{ld} and b_{dr} are one, then the pressed button is *down*. This encoding has been implemented and evaluating its quality is left for future work.

Finally, additional experimental setups can be tried in order to further improve Mario's performance. However, experiments with bigger populations or higher granularities are expensive to be evaluated, and the results obtained in this paper are satisfactory, so this task is left for future work.

Acknowledgements. This research work is co-funded by the Spanish Ministry of Industry, Tourism and Commerce under grant agreement no. TSI-090302-2011-11. Special acknowledgements are addressed at Hector Valero due to his contributions to the work.

References

1. Mario AI Championship 2010: Results (2010). https://sites.google.com/a/marioai. com/www/results. Accessed 24 May 2015
2. Bellemare, M.G., Naddaf, Y., Veness, J., Bowling, M.: The arcade learning environment: an evaluation platform for general agents. JAIR **47**, 253–279 (2013)
3. Emgallar: Intelligent NPC for Mario AI Championship (2011). https://www. youtube.com/watch?v=u_0pgFQ8HcM. Accessed 22 May 2015

4. Fujii, N., Sato, Y., Wakama, H., Katayose, H.: Autonomously acquiring a video game agent's behavior: letting players feel like playing with a human player. In: Nijholt, A., Romão, T., Reidsma, D. (eds.) ACE 2012. LNCS, vol. 7624, pp. 490–493. Springer, Heidelberg (2012)

5. Fujii, N., Sato, Y., Wakama, H., Kazai, K., Katayose, H.: Evaluating human-like behaviors of video-game agents autonomously acquired with biological constraints. In: Reidsma, D., Katayose, H., Nijholt, A. (eds.) ACE 2013. LNCS, vol. 8253, pp. 61–76. Springer, Heidelberg (2013)

6. Karakovskiy, S., Togelius, J.: The Mario AI benchmark and competitions. IEEE Trans. Comput. Intell. AI Games 4(1), 55–67 (2012)

7. Meffert, K., Rotstan, N.: JGAP: Java Genetic Algorithms Package (2015). http://jgap.sourceforge.com. Accessed 6 July 2015

8. Mnih, V., Kavukcuoglu, K., Silver, D., Rusu, A., Veness, J., Graves, A., Riedmiller, M., Fidjeland, A., Ostrovski, G., Petersen, S., Beattie, C., Sadik, A., Antonoglou, I., King, H., Kumaran, D., Wierstra, D., Legg, S., Hassabis, D.: Human-level control through deep reinforcement learning. Nature **518**, 529–533 (2015)

9. Steadman, I.: This AI 'Solves' Super Mario Bros. and Other Classic NES Games (2013). http://www.wired.co.uk/news/archive/2013-04/12/super-mario-solved. Accessed 22 May 2015

10. Togelius, J., Karakovskiy, S., Baumgarten, R.: The 2009 Mario AI competition. In: 2010 IEEE Congress on Evolutionary Computation, pp. 1–8 (2010)

11. Togelius, J., Karakovskiy, S., Koutnik, J., Schmidhuber, J.: Super Mario evolution. In: 2009 IEEE Symposium on Computational Intelligence and Games, pp. 156–161 (2009)

12. Valero, H., Saez, Y., Recio, G.: Computacin Evolutiva Aplicada al Desarrollo de Videojuegos: Mario AI (2011). http://e-archivo.uc3m.es/handle/10016/13308

GRASP Approach to a Min-Max Problem of Ergonomic Risk in Restricted Assembly Lines

Joaquín Bautista[✉], Rocío Alfaro-Pozo, and Cristina Batalla-García

Research Group OPE-PROTHIUS, Universitat Politècnica de Catalunya,
Avda. Diagonal, 647, 7th floor, 08028 Barcelona, Spain
{joaquin.bautista, rocio.alfaro,
cristina.batalla}@upc.edu

Abstract. A Greedy Randomized Adaptive Search Procedure (GRASP) is proposed to solve an extension of the assembly line balancing problem. The problem focuses on minimizing the maximum ergonomic risk of the assembly line when the space required by workstations, the cycle time, and the number of workstations of the line are given. To evaluate the GRASP procedure a case study linked to Nissan's engine plant in Barcelona is used and the obtained results are compared with those obtained by Linear Programming.

Keywords: GRASP · Assembly line balancing · Ergonomic risk · Linear area

1 Introduction

The design of assembly line workstations must consider social aspects, in order to meet the general principle of adaptation of work for the person; the necessary space required by the worker to perform their workload appropriately and the ergonomic risk associated to this workload are some of these issues. In this way, the job positions will be able to adapt to the workers' physical conditions, to movements and to the tools or machines and, therefore the workers may carry out the assigned workload naturally and without harming their health.

Indeed, some studies, where the above social aspects have been considered, can be found in the literature.

On one hand, Salvenson [1] and Battaïa and Dolgui [2] introduced the general aspects within the Simple Assembly Line Balancing Problems (SALBP) classified by Baybars [3].

On the other hand, Bautista and Pereira [4] extended the SALPB family via the incorporation of the spatial attribute, leading to the Time and Space Assembly Line Problems (TSALBP) [4]. Afterwards the ergonomic risk was also introduced into the balancing problems. First as a new constraint that limits maximum and minimum ergonomic risks in the TSALBP models [5, 6]. Secondly, as a new objective function that aims the minimization of the maximum ergonomic risk associated with the workload of workstations [7, 8]. These last studies do not consider the space limitation in their case studies, although their proposed models incorporate such limitation.

© Springer International Publishing Switzerland 2015
J.M. Puerta et al. (Eds.): CAEPIA 2015, LNAI 9422, pp. 278–288, 2015.
DOI: 10.1007/978-3-319-24598-0_25

Finally, Bautista, Batalla-García and Alfaro-Pozo [9] analyzed simultaneously the impact of both attributes into the balancing problem by means of a computational experience linked to a Nissan's engine plant in Barcelona (NMISA: Nissan Motor Ibérica - BCN). Specifically, they evaluated the impact of both, the available space, or linear area assigned to each workstation, and the number of workstations of the line over the maximum ergonomic risk of workstations.

Therefore, taking into account authors [9] used only the Mixed Integer Linear Programming (MILP) for solving the problem, and with reference to the procedure proposed by Bautista et al. [8], a new Greedy Randomized Adaptive Search Procedure (GRASP) is proposed to evaluate the impact of limited space for the workstations over the maximum ergonomic risk.

Specifically, in this work, starting from the mathematical model proposed in [9] and the case study from Nissan, two resolution procedures are compared: the MILP together with the here proposed non-exact procedure, the GRASP algorithm.

Accordingly the present document is structured as follows: Sect. 2 presents the mathematical model for the assembly line balancing problem with limited linear area and available time per station and with the objective of minimizing the maximum ergonomic risk. In this section, the ergonomic aspects are also presented. Section 3 contains the proposed GRASP procedure for the problem. Section 4 shows the computational experience based on real-world problem and the results given by both, MILP and GRASP algorithm, are compared. Finally, Sect. 5 is used to expose the conclusions of this research.

2   The TSALBP-R_erg

The problem under study in this research consists of the following: given a set of elementary tasks or operations $j(J = 1, \ldots, |J|)$, whose times, $t_j(j = 1, \ldots, |J|)$, required space, $a_j(j = 1, \ldots, |J|)$, ergonomic risk associated with the risk factors, $R_{\phi j}(\phi = 1, \ldots, |\Phi|; j = 1, \ldots, |J|)$, and the direct precedence tasks, $P_j(j = 1, \ldots, |J|)$, are known; the problem focuses on minimizing the ergonomic risk of the line while the tasks are assigned into a known set of workstations, $K(k = 1, \ldots, |K|)$, respecting the given values for the cycle time, c, and the maximum available space, A.

Thus, a prerequisite for the task assignment on workstations is to determine the values of temporal, spatial and ergonomic attributes for each one of the operations.

On one hand, the operation processing times must be determined in line with the demand plan, i.e., each production program must correspond to a set of average operation times weighted by the demand of the different products [4]. Consequently, the change in production mix may affect the weighted duration and ergonomic risk of operations and, therefore, may require a rebalancing of the line.

On other hand, the incorporation of ergonomic attributes into the balancing problems makes necessary to determine previously the ergonomic risk level of tasks by means of specialists in the field [10].

Thus, in order to determine the overall risk level to which workers will be subjected throughout their workday, we propose a unified risk level classification, which considers at once different methods to assess ergonomic risks. This classification allows us to determine the risk level of tasks, in regard with the somatic comfort, considering simultaneously the ergonomic levels defined by the Rapid Upper Limb Assessment (RULA), Occupational Repetitive Action (OCRA) and The National Institute for Occupational Safety and Health (NIOSH) methods, which assess postural loads, repetitive movements and manual handling, respectively [11]. Specifically, the defined risk levels are the following: 1 $\rightarrow$ acceptable; 2 $\rightarrow$ moderate; 3 $\rightarrow$ high; 4 $\rightarrow$ unacceptable.

Hence, considering the above and the aim of this research, we use the mathematical model proposed by [9], whose parameters and variables are the following:

Parameters	
J	Set of elemental tasks $(j = 1, \ldots, |J|)$
K	Set of workstations $(k = 1, \ldots, |K|)$
Φ	Set of ergonomic risk factors $(\phi = 1, \ldots, |\Phi|)$
t_j	Processing time of task $j(j = 1, \ldots, |J|)$ at normal activity
a_j	Linear area required by the elemental task $j(j = 1, \ldots, |J|)$
$\chi_{\phi,j}$	Category of task $j(j = 1, \ldots, |J|)$ associated to the risk factor $\phi(\phi = 1, \ldots, |\Phi|)$
$R_{\phi,j}$	Ergonomic risk of task $j(j = 1, \ldots, |J|)$ associated to the risk factor $\phi(\phi = 1, \ldots, |\Phi|)$. Here: $R_{\phi,j} = t_j \cdot \chi_{\phi,j}$
P_j	Set of direct precedent tasks of task $j(j = 1, \ldots, |J|)$
c	Cycle time. Standard time assigned to each workstation to process its workload (S_k)
m	Number of workstations. In this case: $m = |K|$
A	Available space or linear area assigned to each workstation

Variables	
$x_{j,k}$	Binary variable equal to 1 if the elemental task $j(j = 1, \ldots, |J|)$ is assigned to the workstation $k(k = 1, \ldots, |K|)$, and to 0 otherwise
R_ϕ	Maximum ergonomic risk for the risk factor $\phi(\phi = 1, \ldots, |\Phi|)$
$\bar{R}(\Phi)$	Average maximum ergonomic risk associated with the set of factors Φ

TSALBP-R_erg model:

$$\min \bar{R}(\Phi) = \frac{1}{|\Phi|} \cdot \sum\nolimits_{\phi=1}^{\Phi} R_\phi \tag{1}$$

Subject to:

$$\sum\nolimits_{k=1}^{K} x_{j,k} = 1 \quad (j = 1, \ldots, |J|) \tag{2}$$

$$\sum\nolimits_{j=1}^{J} t_j \cdot x_{j,k} \leq c \quad (k = 1, \ldots, |K|) \tag{3}$$

$$\sum_{j=1}^{J} a_j \cdot x_{j,k} \leq A \quad (k = 1, \ldots, |K|) \tag{4}$$

$$R_{\phi} - \sum_{j=1}^{|J|} R_{\phi j} \cdot x_{j,k} \geq 0 \quad (k = 1, \ldots, |K|), (\phi = 1, \ldots, |\Phi|) \tag{5}$$

$$\sum_{k=1}^{K} k(x_{i,k} - x_{j,k}) \leq 0 \quad (1 \leq i, j \leq |J| : i \in P_j) \tag{6}$$

$$\sum_{k=1}^{|K|} k \cdot x_{j,k} \leq m \quad (j = 1, \ldots, |J|) \tag{7}$$

$$\sum_{j=1}^{J} x_{j,k} \geq 1 \quad (k = 1, \ldots, |K|) \tag{8}$$

$$x_{j,k} \in \{0, 1\} \quad (j = 1, \ldots, |J|), (k = 1, \ldots, |K|) \tag{9}$$

The objective function (1) expresses the minimization of the maximum ergonomic risk of the line. This risk is measured as the average ergonomic risk due to the set Φ of risk factors. Constraints (2) indicate that each task can only be assigned to one workstation. Constraints (3) and (4) impose the maximum limitation of the workload time and the maximum linear area allowed by workstation. Constraints (5) determine the maximum ergonomic risk associated to the factor $\phi \in \Phi$ at workstations. Constraints (6) correspond to the precedence task bindings. Constraints (7) and (8) limit the number of workstations and force that there is no empty workstation, respectively. Finally, constraints (9) require the assignment variables be binary.

3   GRASP Algorithm

Due to the complexity of the balancing problems, the exact procedures may be ineffective if we consider the computational time required. For this reason it is normal to find, in the specialized literature, numerous heuristic applications with the aim of solving single [2] and multi-objective [12, 13] balancing problems. Thus, in this study the results obtained by linear programming [9] are compared with those obtained by a GRASP algorithm.

GRASP is a multi-start metaheuristic algorithm [14, 15] with two phases: (1) the construction phase where an initial feasible solution is built through a non-deterministic Greedy procedure; and (2) the improvement phase in which a local optimum, in the neighborhood of the constructed solution, is sought. These phases are consecutively applied until GRASP gives a solution which obviously is the best solution between all the iterations.

The construction phase requires a generator process of solutions, which gives acceptable solutions regarding the objective function and representative solutions of various regions of space to explore.

To ensure the diversity of solutions, given a sequence of decisions linked to a partial solution, the possible alternatives are randomly selected among the restricted candidate list (RCL). This RCL may contain all possible alternatives or a set of them on the basis of the best values for a function (bound, index, etc.) in line with the overall objective function of the problem to solve.

In brief, an optimization problem solved through GRASP implies the following:

1. To define the Greedy and the randomization procedure used for selecting a solution among the candidate alternatives.
2. To define the neighborhood of a solution and how to explore it.
3. To define the stopping criterion based on runtime or number of iterations.

3.1 Constructive Phase: Greedy Procedure

The construction phase consists of building progressively a sequence of tasks $\pi(N) = (\pi_1, \ldots, \pi_N)$. Indeed, at each stage associated to the position $n(n = 1, \ldots, N)$ of the sequence $\pi(N)$ it is added a candidate task from the $RCL(n)$.

Initially, the $RCL(n)$ is made up of tasks that: (1) are not assigned, i.e. tasks that are not in the sequence $\pi(n - 1) = (\pi_1, \ldots, \pi_{n-1})$; and (2) that have their precedent tasks assigned and therefore all precedent tasks are inserted in $\pi(n - 1) = (\pi_1, \ldots, \pi_{n-1})$. In short, all task in the $RCL(n)$ must satisfy the following: $\forall j \in RCL(n) \Rightarrow P_j \subseteq \pi(n - 1)$.

Afterwards, at each stage, the tasks in $RCL(n)$ are ranked according two hierarchical priority indices. The first index denotes the ergonomic risk generated by the task $j \in RCL(n)$ and the set of its following tasks, F_j^*, i.e.:

$$f_j^{(n)} = \sum_{\phi \in \Phi} t_j \cdot \chi_{\phi,j} + \sum_{\phi \in \Phi} \sum_{h \in F_j^*} t_h \cdot \chi_{\phi,h} \tag{10}$$
$$(\forall j \notin \pi(n - 1) \wedge P_j \subseteq \pi(n - 1))$$

The second index (for draws) serves to get regular task sequences in terms of ergonomic risk. The non-regularity index for the set of risk factors is defined as follows:

$$g_j^{(n)} = \sum_{\phi \in \Phi} \left(t_j \cdot \chi_{\phi,j} + \sum_{h=1}^{n-1} t_{\pi_h} \cdot \chi_{\phi,\pi_h} - n \cdot r_\phi(J) \right)^2 \tag{11}$$
$$(\forall j \notin \pi(n - 1) \wedge P_j \subseteq \pi(n - 1))$$

Where $r_\phi(J)$ is the ergonomic risk rate of factor $\phi \in \Phi$ for the set of tasks J, i.e.:

$$r_\phi(J) = \frac{1}{|J|} \cdot \sum_{j=1}^{J} t_j \cdot \chi_{\phi,j} \quad (\forall \phi \in \Phi) \tag{12}$$

After ranking the $RCL(n)$, in descending order, according to the $f_j^{(n)}$ (and only in draw cases, in ascending order according to $g_j^{(n)}$), the list is reduced by the admission factor Λ. This factor is defined as the percentage of candidate tasks that will be sorted

Table 1. Construction Phase Scheme of the task sequence with regular ergonomic risk.

---

0. Initialization:

   Input: $\Lambda, J, r_\phi(J), (t_j, a_j, \chi_{\phi,j}) \; \forall j \in J, \forall \phi \in \Phi$

   Initialize: $n = 0, \pi(n) = \{\emptyset\}, N = |J|$

1. Create the candidate set:

   $n \leftarrow n + 1$

   Let $RCL(n) = \{j \in J : j \notin \pi(n-1) \wedge P_j \subseteq \pi(n-1)\}$ be the set of candidate tasks.

2. Evaluate alternatives:

   $\forall j \in RCL(n)$ determine:

   $$f_j^{(n)} = \sum_{\phi \in \Phi} t_j \cdot \chi_{\phi,j} + \sum_{\phi \in \Phi} \sum_{h \in F_j^*} t_h \cdot \chi_{\phi,h}$$

   $$g_j^{(n)} = \sum_{\phi \in \Phi} \left(t_j \cdot \chi_{\phi,j} + \sum_{h=1}^{n-1} t_{\pi_h} \cdot \chi_{\phi,\pi_h} - n \cdot r_\phi(J) \right)^2$$

3. Sort alternatives:

   Let $\overline{RCL}(n) = (j_1, \ldots, j_{|RCL(n)|})$ be the sorted list, it is satisfied:

   $$\left(f_j^{(n)} > f_{j'}^{(n)} \right) \vee \left[\left(f_j^{(n)} = f_{j'}^{(n)} \right) \wedge \left(g_j^{(n)} < g_{j'}^{(n)} \right) \right] \Rightarrow$$
   $$\Rightarrow pos\left(j, \overline{RCL}(n)\right) < pos\left(j', \overline{RCL}(n)\right) \qquad \forall \{j, j'\} \subseteq RCL(n)$$

4. Select alternative:

   Let $pos^* = -int(-\Lambda \cdot |\overline{RCL}(n)| \cdot RND)$ be the selected position

   Then: $j^* = j_{pos^*} \in \overline{RCL}(n) = (j_1, \ldots, j_{|RCL(n)|})$ is the selected task

5. Update: $\pi(n) \equiv \pi(n-1) \cup \{j^*\}$

6. Finalization test

   If $n < N$ go to step 1

   Else END

---

among the best. In this way the list $\overline{RCL}(n, \Lambda)$ is obtained for the selection process; obviously, if $\Lambda = 100\%$, then $\overline{RCL}(n, 100) = \overline{RCL}(n)$.

Table 1 shows the GRASP constructive phase to generate a sequence without delays and with regular ergonomic risk.

This phase makes sure the final task sequence, $\pi(N)$, is consistent with both precedent and succession constraints and does not accumulate the ergonomic risk rate at the end of the line. Furthermore, the minimization of ergonomic risk rate variation for a line with only one workstation is added to the above criterion, in order to decide in case of draw.

From this sequence $\pi(N)$, the following stage consists of designing the assembly line imposing a fixed number of workstations, $m > 1$.

Given a number $m(m > 1)$ of workstations, the sequence $\pi(N)$ is broken up into m segments. These segments are compatible with the constraints (3) and (4), i.e. with the cycle time, c, of the line, and the maximum linear area, A, are constituted by adjacent tasks of the sequence, are not empty, are disjoint between them, and their union corresponds with the set J of tasks.

3.2 Local Improvement Phase

This improvement phase has four stages which are repeated consecutively until the solution reached does not improve at none stage. Between two solutions compatible with constraints (3) and (4), the solution with lower maximum ergonomic risk will be considered the best and, in case draw, the solution, with the greater minimum ergonomic risk, will win.

Specifically, the stages of the improvement phase are the following:

1. Download: This stage consists of selecting the workstation with greater ergonomic risk and then, moving the last task to the next station and the first one to the above station without altering the initial sequence and whenever the solution improves. Obviously constraints, such as cycle time and linear area must be always satisfied, and the maximum ergonomic risk can never get worse.
2. Reload: Whenever there is an improvement in the initial solution and while the task sequence is not altered, the station with the lower ergonomic risk will increase its load with the last task from the previous station and/or the first task from the next station. As in the previous stage, the cycle time and linear area constraints must be fulfilled and the maximum and minimum ergonomic risk must not get worse.
3. Insertion: The workstation with greater ergonomic risk inserts all its tasks, one by one, into any previous station and then into any next station. The constraints linked to the cycle time, the linear area and the precedence rules must be satisfied and the maximum ergonomic risk of the line must improve.
4. Exchange: This stage consists of performing exchanges between the tasks from the workstation with greater ergonomic risk, one by one, and the first task from the following workstations and, after, the last task from previous stations. As in the others stages, the exchanges must meet the cycle time, linear area and precedence constraints and obviously no exchange can suppose the increase of maximum ergonomic risk.

4 Computational Experience

In order to compare the results given by linear programming [9] and the proposed GRASP algorithm, we perform a computational experience linked to a case study from Nissan's engine plant in Barcelona (NMISA, Nissan Motor Ibérica – BCN).

Specifically, we use an instance that corresponds with a daily production plan. The production plan has 270 engines, divided equally into nine types, which are grouped into three families: p_1, p_2 and p_3 are engines for crossovers and SUVs; p_4 and p_5 are for vans; and p_6, p_7, p_8 and p_9 are intended for medium tonnage trucks. The assembly of any engine supposes 140 tasks with a cycle time of 180 s.

This experience allows us to evaluate the impact of both, the number of workstations of the line and the maximum available space per station, on the maximum ergonomic risk of the line whose minimization is the focus of the problem.

For that purpose we carry out a parametric sweep of number of workstations and maximum linear area per station. Indeed, we execute the algorithm for the following parameter values:

- Number of workstations: $m = \{19, 20, 21, 22, 23, 24, 25\}$.
- Maximum linear area allowed (in meters): $A = \{4, 5, 10\}$.
- Number of iterations: $Iter_{max} = 10000$.
- Admission factor: $\Lambda = \{25\%, 50\%, 100\%\}$.

Therefore, we have execute the GRASP algorithm 63 times on a iMac (Intel Core i7 2.93 Ghz, 8 GB de RAM, MAC OS X 10.6.8) and we have obtained the following results (Table 2):

Table 2. Best results, in regard with the maximum ergonomic risk of the line, given by GRASP algorithm, considering all possible values of the admission factor $\Lambda = \{25\%, 50\%, 100\%\}$. The '-' symbol means that not solution has been found.

A(meters)	m (Number of workstations)						
	19	20	21	22	23	24	25
4	-	-	495	360	315	295	270
5	-	-	315	300	285	270	260
10	350	330	305	295	278	270	255

On the other hand, we have solved the mathematical model with the CPLEX (v11.0) software, running on a Mac Pro computer with an Intel Xeon, 3.0 GHz CPU and 2 GB RAM memory under the Windows XP operating system, given a CPU time limit of 2 h. Briefly the results obtained are the following (Table 3).

Table 3. Maximum ergonomic risk of the line obtained by the CPLEX solver.

A(meters)	m (Number of workstations)						
	19	20	21	22	23	24	25
4	-	-	375	330	310	280	275
5	-	-	310	300	280	280	275
10	350	315	300	285	275	270	255

As we can see in the above tables, both procedures find solution for all cases, except when the number of workstations is 19 and 20 and the maximum linear area is 4 and 5 m.

Regarding found solutions, the GRASP algorithm uses a CPU time of 68.52 seconds on average, while the linear programming reaches the CPU limit (2 h). However, if we compare the results obtained by both methods, evaluating the gains of one procedure in faced of the other (13), we can see (Table 4) how linear programming gives better results than the GRASP algorithm in cases where the number of stations is more restricted.

Table 4. GRASP improvement versus MILP (ΔGvM).

A(meters)	m (Number of workstations)						
	19	20	21	22	23	24	25
4	-	-	−0.32	−0.09	−0.02	−0.05	0.02
5	-	-	−0.02	0.00	−0.02	0.04	0.06
10	0.00	−0.05	−0.02	−0.04	−0.01	0.00	0.00

$$\Delta GvM = \frac{S_{MILP}(m,A) - S_{GRASP}(m,A)}{\min\{S_{MILP}(m,A), S_{GRASP}(m,A)\}} (m = 19,\ldots,25), (A = 4, 5, 10) \quad (13)$$

In formula (13) S_{MILP} is the solution obtained by MILP procedure (given a number of workstations, m, and linear area, A). And S_{GRASP} is the solution obtained by the GRASP algorithm, given the same values of m and A.

5 Conclusions

A GRASP algorithm for solving the assembly line balancing problem given a fixed number of stations, constraints in regard with the time and space for the workstations and whose objective is to minimize the average of the maximum ergonomic risk of the line, has been proposed in this study.

The procedure builds task sequences that are consistent with the precedence sets and according two hierarchical priority indices in the task selection: (1) select the task with greater remaining ergonomic risk considering the set of all its following tasks; (2) select the task that minimizes the variation of the ergonomic risk rate. Given a sequence, this is segmented in the number of workstations of the line and then, the initial solution is improved by means of four stages: (1) Download of the workstation with the highest risk; (2) Reload of the workstation with lower risk; (3) Task insertion from the station with highest risk to the rest; and (4) Task exchange from workstation with greater ergonomic risk to the rest.

In order to evaluate the proposed GRASP, a computational experience has been carried out to compare the results of the GRASP with those obtained with MILP (Table 5). In addition, different values for both the number of workstations and the maximum available linear area have been used. This sweep of values has allowed us to conclude the following:

Table 5. Winner procedure in regard with the values of m and A.

A(meters)	m (Number of workstations)						
	19	20	21	22	23	24	25
4	-	-	MILP	MILP	MILP	MILP	GRASP
5	-	-	MILP	Idem	MILP	GRASP	GRASP
10	Idem	MILP	MILP	MILP	MILP	Idem	Idem

- In the instances severely restricted in the number of stations, m, and the area, A, MILP offers better results than GRASP.
- For instances relaxed in m and A, GRASP is better than MILP.
- In regard with CPU times, GRASP is more competent than MILP (69 s vs 2 h).
- On average, the gain, ΔGvM, of MILP in the face of GRASP is 0.06; while the gain of GRASP vs MILP is 0.04.

On average, the solutions offered by MILP are best in ergonomic risk by 3 %, while the CPU time used by MILP is 105 times that used by GRASP.

This small difference in ergonomic risk contrasted with CPU times for both procedures, suggest that GRASP is highly competitive for the problem under study.

Acknowledgments. This work is supported by Spanish Ministerio de Economía y Competitividad, under PROTHIUS-III (DPI2010-16759) and FHI-SELM2 (TIN2014-57497), both including EDRF funding.

References

1. Salvenson, M.E.: The assembly line balancing problem. J. Ind. Eng. **6**(3), 18–25 (1955)
2. Battaïa, O., Dolgui, A.: A taxonomy of line balancing problems and their solution approaches. Int. J. Prod. Econ. **142**(2), 259–277 (2013)
3. Baybars, I.: A survey of exact algorithms for the simple assembly line balancing problem. Manag. Sci. **32**(8), 909–932 (1986)
4. Bautista, J., Pereira, J.: Ant algorithms for a time and space constrained assembly line balancing problem. Eur. J. Oper. Res. **177**(3), 2016–2032 (2007)
5. Bautista, J., Batalla, C., Alfaro, R.: Incorporating ergonomics factors into the TSALBP. In: Emmanouilidis, C., Taisch, M., Kiritsis, D. (eds.) APMS 2012. IFIP AICT, vol. 397, pp. 413–420. Springer, Heidelberg (2013)
6. Bautista, J., Batalla, C. Alfaro, R., Cano, A.: Impact of ergonomic risk reduction in the TSALBP-1. In: Industrial Engineering and Complexity Management. Book of Proceedings of the 7th International Conference on Industrial Engineering and Industrial Management - XVII Congreso de Ingeniería de Organización, pp. 436–444 (2013). ISBN: 978-84-616-5410-9 doi:10.13140/2.1.2687.9041
7. Bautista, J., Batalla-García, C., Alfaro-Pozo, R.: Ergonomic risk minimisation in assembly line balancing. In: Cortés, P., Maeso-González, E., Escudero-Santana, A. (eds.) Ergonomic Risk Minimisation in Assembly Line Balancing, LNMIE, pp. 85–93. Springer International Publishing, Switzerland (2015)
8. Bautista, J., Batalla, C., Alfaro, R., Llovera, S.: Algoritmos GRASP para el equilibrado de líneas con riesgo ergonómico mínimo. In: Actas del X Congreso Español sobre Metaheurísticas, Algoritmos Evolutivos y Bioinspirados, MAEB 2015, pp. 249–256 (2015). ISBN: 978-84-697-2150-6 http://hdl.handle.net/2117/26249
9. Bautista, J., Batalla-García, C. Alfaro-Pozo, R.: Delimiting the linear area on the problems of assembly line balancing with minimal ergonomic risk. In: 9th International Conference on Industrial Engineering and Industrial Management, XXI International Conference on Industrial Engineering and Operations Management, International IIE Conference 2015. Aveiro, Portugal, 6–8 July 2015. http://hdl.handle.net/2117/28548

10. Otto, A., Scholl, A.: Incorporating ergonomic risks into assembly line balancing. Eur. J. Oper. Res. **212**(2), 277–286 (2011)
11. Batalla, C., Bautista, J., Alfaro, R.: Ergonomía y evaluación del riesgo ergonómico. OPE-wp.2015/01 (20150117) (2015). http://hdl.handle.net/2117/2607
12. Chica, M., Cordón, O., Damas, S., Bautista, J.: Multiobjective constructive heuristics for the 1/3 variant of the time and space assembly line balancing problem: ACO and random greedy search. Inf. Sci. **180**(18), 3465–3487 (2010)
13. Chica, M., Cordón, O., Damas, S., Bautista, J.: A Multiobjective GRASP for the 1/3 variant of the time and space assembly line balancing problem. In: García-Pedrajas, N., Herrera, F., Fyfe, C., Benítez, J.M., Ali, M. (eds.) IEA/AIE 2010, Part III. LNCS, vol. 6098, pp. 656–665. Springer, Heidelberg (2010)
14. Feo, T.A., Resende, M.G.C.: Greedy randomized adaptive search procedures. J. Glob. Optim. **6**(2), 109–133 (1995)
15. Resende, M.G.C., Ribeiro, C.C.: Greedy randomized adaptive search procedures: Advances, hybridizations, and applications. In: Gendreau, M., Potvin, J.-Y. (eds.) Handbook of Metaheuristics, pp. 283–319. Springer, New York (2010)

Multi-objectivising the Quadratic Assignment Problem by Means of an Elementary Landscape Decomposition

Josu Ceberio[✉], Borja Calvo, Alexander Mendiburu, and Jose A. Lozano

Intelligent Systems Group, Faculty of Computer Science,
University of the Basque Country UPV/EHU, 20018 Donostia, Gipuzkoa, Spain
{josu.ceberio,borja.calvo,alexander.mendiburu,ja.lozano}@ehu.es

Abstract. In the last decade, many works in combinatorial optimisation have shown that, due to the advances in multi-objective optimisation, the algorithms in this field could be used for solving single-objective problems. In this sense, a number of papers have proposed *multi-objectivising* single-objective problems in order to apply multi-objectivisation schemes in their optimisation. In this paper, we follow this idea by presenting a method to *multi-objectivise* single-objective problems based on an *elementary landscape decomposition* of their objective function. In order to illustrate this procedure, we consider the elementary landscape decomposition of the Quadratic Assignment Problem under the *interchange* neighbourhood. In particular, we propose reformulating the QAP as a multi-objective problem, where each elementary landscape in the decomposition is an independent function to be optimised. In order to validate this multi-objectivisation scheme, we implement a version of NSGA-II for solving the multi-objective QAP, and compare its performance with that of a GA on the single-objective QAP. Conducted experiments show that the multi-objective approach is better than the single-objective approach for some types of instances.

Keywords: Multi-objectivisation · Quadratic assignment problem · Elementary landscape decomposition · Interchange neighbourhood

1 Introduction

A combinatorial optimisation problem consists of finding an optimal solution of a function,

$$f : X \longrightarrow \mathbb{R}$$
$$x \longmapsto f(x)$$

such that the search space X is a finite or countable infinite set. Usually f is considered as a single-objective function. However, in many real-world problems, the optimisation process may involve multiple objectives (functions) simultaneously.

© Springer International Publishing Switzerland 2015
J.M. Puerta et al. (Eds.): CAEPIA 2015, LNAI 9422, pp. 289–300, 2015.
DOI: 10.1007/978-3-319-24598-0_26

These problems are known as multi-objective optimisation problems (MOPs). Formally, MOPs can be formulated as [21]:

$$\text{maximize} \quad F(x) = [f_1(x), \ldots, f_m(x)], \quad x \in X$$

where $F : X \longrightarrow \mathbb{R}^m$ consists of m real-valued objective (fitness) functions and $\mathbb{R}^m$ denotes the *objective space*.

During the last decades, multi-objective evolutionary algorithms (MOEAs), such as *Non-Dominated Sorting Genetic Algorithm II* (NSGA-II) [6] or *Multi-objective Evolutionary Algorithm based on Decomposition* (MOEA/D) [21], have shown their competitiveness when solving MOPs. Considering the unique ability of MOEAs to enhance the diversity of the population, authors have claimed that multi-objective algorithms might be helpful for single-objective optimisation as well [1]. In fact, according to a recent survey on MOEAs for single-objective optimisation [16], a number of papers [10, 13, 15] have proposed transforming single-objective problems into MOPs by transforming their fitness landscapes. This procedure, known as *multi-objectivisation*, was first used by Knowles *et al.* [10], where the authors distinguished between two types of schemes: *decomposition* and *aggregation*. The first scheme proposes decomposing the original function f into several components in such a way that the original optimum is in the Pareto optimum in the new formulation. The second scheme, instead, considers some additional objectives that are used in combination with the original function f.

Papers on this topic [9, 10] have demonstrated that the multi-objectivisation by decomposition increases the plateau regions of incomparable solutions in number and size, which might negatively influence the search. Contrarily, they have also showed that the introduction of plateaus reduces the number of local optima, which should ease the search in some cases.

Motivated by these results, in this paper, we present a novel scheme to multi-objectivise single-objective problems by means of the decomposition of the fitness function. Particularly, we propose using *elementary landscape decomposition* techniques in order to decompose the fitness function f as a sum of a set of elementary functions.

In landscape theory, *elementary landscapes* [18] are a class of landscapes whose main characteristic is that they can be modelled using the Groover's [8] *wave equation* (see Eq. 2). Among its multiple properties, it is possible to compute the average value of the fitness function in the neighbourhood of a solution with a closed form expression. Unfortunately, there are few combinatorial optimisation problems in the literature that generate elementary landscapes.

For most of the combinatorial optimisation problems, we do not know a neighbourhood system that is able to produce an elementary landscape, however, Stadler [17] proved that, for any fitness landscape, if the neighbourhood system has certain characteristics, then it is possible to decompose f as a sum of some elementary landscapes. And thus, f can be expressed as follows:

$$f(x) = \sum_{i=1}^{t} f_i(x)$$

where t is the number of landscapes in the decomposition, and f_i is the function related to the i-th landscape.

Works on elementary landscape decomposition have shown that the landscape produced by the MAX-k-SAT under the Hamming neighbourhood is a superposition of k elementary landscapes [19], and a superposition of two when considering the subset sum problem [4]. In addition, Chicano et al. [4] decomposed the general case of the Quadratic Assignment Problem (QAP) under the interchange neighbourhood[1], at most, as the superposition of three elementary landscapes.

In order to illustrate the multi-objectivisation scheme proposed in this paper, we will consider the QAP as a case study. As aforementioned, the landscape produced by the general formulation of the QAP (see Eq. 4) under the interchange neighbourhood can be decomposed at most as a sum of three elementary landscapes. Therefore, we reformulate the QAP as a multi-objective problem in which there is one objective for each elementary landscape in the decomposition.

For the sake of demonstrating the validity of the proposed method, we compare the performance of the NSGA-II on the multi-objectivised QAP, with the performance of its single-objective version genetic algorithm (SGA). The performed experiments on two different benchmarks (random and real-life like) show that solving the QAP in its multi-objective form is able to obtain better results than in the single-objective approach.

The remainder of the paper is organised as follows: in Sect. 2, the definition of the QAP is introduced. Next, in Sect. 3, the elementary landscape decomposition of the QAP is described. Section 4 presents a modified version of the NSGA-II for the multi-objective approach of the QAP. In Sect. 5, we compare the performance of NSGA-II and SGA on two benchmarks: random and real-life like. Finally, general conclusions and ideas for future work are summarised in Sect. 6.

2 The Quadratic Assignment Problem

The Quadratic Assignment Problem (QAP) [11] is the problem of allocating a set of facilities to a set of locations, with a cost function associated to the distance and flow between the facilities. The objective is to assign each facility to a location such that the total cost is minimised. Specifically, we are given two matrices with real elements $\mathbf{D} = [d_{i,j}]_{n \times n}$ and $\mathbf{H} = [h_{k,l}]_{n \times n}$, where $d_{i,j}$ stands for the distance between location i and location j, and $h_{k,l}$ denotes the flow between facility k and facility l. Given n facilities, the solution of the QAP is codified as a permutation $\sigma = (\sigma(1) \ldots \sigma(n))$ where $\sigma(i)$ $(i = 1, \ldots, n)$ represents the facility that is allocated to the i-th location. The fitness of any given permutation is calculated by the following function:

$$f(\sigma) = \sum_{i=1}^{n} \sum_{j=1}^{n} d_{i,j} h_{\sigma(i),\sigma(j)} \tag{1}$$

---

[1] The interchange neighbourhood considers that two solutions (permutations) are neighbours if one is obtained by interchanging two elements in the other.

Since the QAP belongs to the class of permutation problems, we will adopt the mathematical notation used for the *symmetric group*. Instead of x and Ω, we will use, from now on, σ and π to denote the solutions, and $\mathbb{S}_n$ to denote the search space.

3   Elementary Landscape Decomposition of the QAP

In combinatorial optimisation, a *fitness landscape* is understood as a triple $(\mathbb{S}_n, N, f)$ where $\mathbb{S}_n$ denotes the search space of solutions, $f : \mathbb{S}_n \to \mathbb{R}$ defines the fitness function, and the neighbourhood operator N assigns a set of neighbouring solutions $N(\sigma) \in \mathbb{S}_n$ to each solution σ.

In 1992, Grover [8], demonstrated that some fitness landscapes arising from certain classes of combinatorial optimisation problems could be modelled using the so-called Groover's *wave equation*:

$$\underset{\pi \in N(\sigma)}{avg} \{f(\pi)\} = f(\sigma) + \frac{k}{|N(\sigma)|}(\bar{f} - f(\sigma)) \tag{2}$$

where $\bar{f}$ denotes the average fitness value of all the solutions in the search space, $|N(\sigma)|$ is the size of the neighbourhood, and k is a constant value. Furthermore, Groover proved that, if a landscape satisfies Eq. 2, then all the local maxima solutions are greater than $\bar{f}$ and all the local minima are lower than $\bar{f}$. This class of landscapes was called *elementary landscapes* by Stadler [18]. According to Stadler, a landscape $(\mathbb{S}_n, N, f)$ is elementary if the function f is an eigenvector of the Laplacian matrix Δ that describes the neighbourhood N up to an additive constant c.

In general, an arbitrary landscape is not elementary. However, Chicano *et al.* [4] proved that any landscape can be decomposed as a sum of elementary landscapes if the neighbourhood system considered is *regular* ($|N(\sigma)| = d > 0$, for all $\sigma \in \mathbb{S}_n$) and *symmetric* (for all $\sigma, \pi \in \mathbb{S}_n, \pi \in N(\sigma) \iff \sigma \in N(\pi)$). As the authors stated, we know that, if a square matrix Q (with real entries) of size l is symmetric, then there exists an orthogonal basis in the vector space $\mathbb{R}^l$ that is composed of eigenvectors of Q. And thus, every vector of $\mathbb{R}^l$ can be written as the weighted sum of the vectors in the orthogonal basis. Since the Laplacian matrix Δ is defined as a symmetric square matrix with real entries, then it can be deduced that there exists an orthogonal basis of eigenvectors associated to it. As a consequence, f can be decomposed as the weighted sum of a set of elementary functions.

Rockmore *et al.* [14] showed that the landscape produced by the general formulation of the QAP (see Eq. 4) under the interchange neighbourhood can be written as a superposition of three elementary landscapes. And later, Chicano *et al.* [4] gave the exact expression of this decomposition. Since this point is an essential part of this work, in this section we provide a general overview of the decomposition. The explanation below has been summarised from [4], and thus, for extended descriptions, we recommend the interested readers to address the original works.

In order to analyse the elementary components of the fitness function of the QAP, it is useful to separate the instance-related part and the problem-related part. Therefore, we start the decomposition procedure by rewriting the fitness function of the QAP as:

$$f(\sigma) = \sum_{i,j=1}^{n} \sum_{p,q=1}^{n} d_{i,j} h_{p,q} \delta_{\sigma(i)}^{p} \delta_{\sigma(j)}^{q} \tag{3}$$

where $\delta_{\sigma(i)}^{p}$ denotes the Kronecker's delta and returns 1 if $\sigma(i) = p$, and 0 otherwise. At this point, we extend the decomposition of f to a more general function g in which the instance-related part of Eq. 3, the product $d_{i,j} h_{p,q}$, is replaced with a new variable ψ_{ijpq}. Alternatively, the problem-related part, $\delta_{\sigma(i)}^{p} \delta_{\sigma(j)}^{q}$, is rewritten as the parameterised function $\varphi_{(i,j)(p,q)}(\sigma)$. Thus, the generalised QAP function is defined as:

$$g(\sigma) = \sum_{i,j,p,q=1}^{n} \psi_{ijpq} \varphi_{(i,j)(p,q)}(\sigma) \tag{4}$$

where Eq. 3 is a particular case in which $\psi_{ijpq} = d_{i,j} h_{p,q}$.

As far as we know, g does not produce elementary landscapes. However, as the interchange neighbourhood is regular and symmetric, then it is possible to find an orthogonal basis composed of elementary functions in which to decompose g. To this end, Chicano et al. [4] focus exclusively on the decomposition of the problem-related part, since any result on $\varphi_{(i,j)(p,q)}$ can be extended to any linear combination of it, and subsequently to g.

First, we distinguish two cases of the function φ under the interchange neighbourhood: (1) $i = j \wedge p = q$ and (2) $i \neq j \wedge p \neq q$[2]. So, we rewrite Eq. 4 as follows:

$$g(\sigma) = \sum_{i,p=1}^{n} \psi_{iipp} \varphi_{(i,i)(p,p)}(\sigma) + \sum_{\substack{i,j,p,q=1 \\ i \neq j, p \neq q}}^{n} \psi_{ijpq} \varphi_{(i,j)(p,q)}(\sigma) \tag{5}$$

When $i = j \wedge p = q$, we can easily prove that the function φ is elementary and complies with Eq. 2 (when $k = n$) by demonstrating that the equation below holds for two constants a and b:

$$\underset{\pi \in N(\sigma)}{avg} \{\varphi(\pi)\} = a\varphi(\sigma) + b \tag{6}$$

Nonetheless, it is not elementary when $i \neq j \wedge p \neq q$. In order to decompose it as a sum of elementary functions, in [4] the authors introduced a set of auxiliary functions that provide the required orthogonal basis in the decomposition. Particularly, the authors prove that the right-hand term $\varphi_{(i,j)(p,q)}$ (see Eq. 5) can be decomposed as the sum of three elementary functions. As a result, the fitness function of the general QAP, g, is finally decomposed as follows:

---

[2] Note that cases of φ such as $i = j \wedge p \neq q$ are impossible ($\sigma(i) = \sigma(j) = p = q$), since under the interchange neighbourhood $i = j \iff p = q$, and also $i \neq j \iff p \neq q$.

$$g(\sigma) = \sum_{i,p=1}^{n} \psi_{iipp}\varphi_{(i,i)(p,p)}(\sigma)$$

$$+ \sum_{\substack{i,j,p,q=1 \\ i \neq j, p \neq q}}^{n} \psi_{ijpq} \left(\frac{\Omega^1_{(i,j)(p,q)}(\sigma)}{2n} + \frac{\Omega^2_{(i,j)(p,q)}(\sigma)}{2(n-2)} + \frac{\Omega^3_{(i,j)(p,q)}(\sigma)}{n(n-2)} \right) \quad (7)$$

where $\Omega^1_{(i,j)(p,q)}$, $\Omega^2_{(i,j)(p,q)}$ and $\Omega^3_{(i,j)(p,q)}$ stand for the elementary functions.

The decomposition above is for the general form of the QAP (Eq. 4), denoted as g. However, if we focus on the standard formulation of the QAP, i.e. $\psi_{ijpq} = d_{i,j}h_{p,q}$, and take into account that in the classical QAP instances:

- the diagonal values in $\mathbf{D} = [d_{i,j}]_{n \times n}$ and $\mathbf{H} = [h_{k,l}]_{n \times n}$ are 0 by default,
- and the entries in $\mathbf{D} = [d_{i,j}]_{n \times n}$ are symmetric with respect to the main diagonal,

then, variable ψ_{iipp} is 0, and the first function of the decomposition, $\Omega^1_{(i,j)(p,q)}(\sigma)$, is constant. As a consequence, g can be transformed as:

$$f(\sigma) = \lambda + \sum_{\substack{i,j,p,q=1 \\ i \neq j, p \neq q}}^{n} \psi_{ijpq} \frac{\Omega^2_{(i,j)(p,q)}(\sigma)}{2(n-2)} + \sum_{\substack{i,j,p,q=1 \\ i \neq j, p \neq q}}^{n} \psi_{ijpq} \frac{\Omega^3_{(i,j)(p,q)}(\sigma)}{n(n-2)} \quad (8)$$

where λ is the constant value associated to the first elementary landscape.

The time complexity of calculating the decomposition of any solution in the search space is $O(n^4)$. However, taking into account the symmetry of the matrix $\mathbf{D}$, we compute it in $O(n^3)$. Nonetheless, in [5] the authors report that it is possible to compute it in $O(n^2)$.

4   A Non-Dominated Sorting Genetic Algorithm for the Multi-objectivised QAP

In the previous section, we showed that the QAP function can be decomposed as the sum of two elementary landscapes and a constant value. Taking this decomposition as a basis, we reformulate the standard QAP as a problem with two objectives, where each component of the sum is a function to optimise (except λ).

In order to solve the multi-objectivised QAP, we propose a modified version of the Non-Dominated Sorting Algorithm II (NSGA-II) [6]. As stated in the introduction, NSGA-II is one of the most referenced algorithms for multi-objective optimisation. Presented as an improvement of NSGA, this algorithm introduces two innovations in the selection of the solutions that survive at each generation. Firstly, at every generation t, NSGA-II combines the population of the parents and offspring in a population P_t, and ranks the solutions according to a fast *non-dominance* sorting algorithm. This algorithm is an iterative scheme that, at each step, finds the set of non-dominated solutions in the population P_t, also known as *front*, and moves them into the next generation population P_{t+1}[3]. If the size of the front is smaller than the empty space in P_{t+1}, all the members of the front are chosen. The remaining members of the new population will be chosen from the subsequent non-dominated fronts. This procedure is continued until no more fronts can be accommodated. In general, the last front accommodated will be partially chosen, since, presumably, it will be larger than the empty space in P_{t+1}. In order to choose the solutions that will survive from that last front, NSGA-II implements the *crowded*-comparison operator which, based on the density estimation metric called *crowding* distance, selects the solutions that are spread out in that front.

In a standard MOP, all the solutions within a front are considered equally *fit*. However, the proposed formulation of the QAP is not purely a MOP, since, ultimately, f measures the fitness of a solution. Therefore, we adapt the original design of NSGA-II to use on the multi-objectivised QAP. Particularly, we replace the diversity preservation algorithm applied to the last accommodated front with a simple sorting algorithm, which ranks the solutions from best to worst.

Regarding the other operators of the NSGA-II, we have set an adapted version of the one-point crossover (OPX) for permutations [12], and the one-interchange mutation scheme. Both operators have been selected without performing previous experiments.

5   Experiments

In order to demonstrate the validity of the multi-objectivisation scheme proposed in this paper, we compare the performance of the adapted NSGA-II for the multi-objectivised QAP, with a simple genetic algorithm (SGA) for the standard QAP. The SGA is a simplified version of the adapted NSGA-II where the non-dominance sorting procedure has been replaced by a standard sorting algorithm that ranks the solutions in the population with respect to f (from best to worst).

We have selected 48 instances from the Taillard's QAP benchmark [20] (36 random instances, denoted as 'a', and 12 real-life like instances, denoted as 'b'), and 60 real-life like instances from the *Taixxeyy* benchmark [7].

5.1   Parameter Settings

In relation to the parameter settings, the size of the population has been set to $8n$, and all the solutions are selected for the *non-dominance* sorting algorithm. As regards the stopping criterion, a maximum number of $1000n^2$ evaluations has been set. The crossover and mutation operator probabilities are set to 1.0 (they are systematically applied to the whole pool of selected solutions).

Both algorithms, NSGA-II and SGA, have been implemented in the C++ programming language. The experimentation was performed on a cluster of 20 nodes, each of them equipped with two Intel Xeon X5650 CPUs and 48 GB of memory.

---

[3] A solution x *dominates* a solution y when there is no objective in the MOP for which x has a worse value than y, and there is at least one function for which x has a better value than y.

Table 1. ARPD results of NSGA-II and SGA for the Taillard's benchmark.

Inst.	Best	NSGA-II	SGA	Sig.	Inst.	Best	NSGA-II	SGA	Sig.
10a	135028	**0.0113**	0.0165	=	29a	1669394	0.0344	**0.0328**	=
10b	1183760	**0.0081**	0.0144	+	30a	1818146	**0.0313**	0.0326	=
11a	188368	0.0200	**0.0159**	=	30b	637117113	**0.0391**	0.0451	=
12a	224416	0.0345	**0.0332**	=	31a	1945072	**0.0323**	0.0328	=
12b	39464925	0.0178	**0.0148**	=	32a	2033652	0.0324	**0.0322**	=
13a	270750	**0.0231**	0.0238	=	33a	2117042	**0.0376**	0.0415	+
14a	339524	**0.0182**	0.0282	+	34a	2254262	0.0332	**0.0331**	=
15a	388214	**0.0208**	0.0221	=	35a	2422002	**0.0349**	0.0364	=
15b	51765268	**0.0018**	0.0022	=	35b	283315445	**0.0232**	0.0310	=
16a	436316	**0.0277**	0.0286	=	36a	2626156	**0.0060**	0.0063	=
17a	491812	**0.0273**	0.0296	=	37a	2784656	**0.0089**	0.0108	=
18a	568250	**0.0273**	0.0287	=	38a	2920742	**0.0071**	0.0103	=
19a	646208	**0.0368**	0.0404	=	39a	3046888	**0.0138**	0.0142	=
20a	703482	**0.0334**	0.0359	=	40a	3139370	**0.0349**	0.0356	=
20b	122455319	**0.0062**	0.0316	=	40b	637250948	**0.0377**	0.0438	=
21a	781678	**0.0323**	0.0345	=	50a	4941410	**0.0348**	0.0361	=
22a	894546	**0.0320**	0.0325	=	50b	458821517	**0.0288**	0.0360	=
23a	1005738	0.0370	**0.0362**	=	60a	7208572	0.0362	**0.0347**	=
24a	1101310	0.0347	**0.0346**	=	60b	608215054	**0.0343**	0.0372	=
25a	1167256	**0.0362**	0.0369	=	64c	1855928	0.0037	**0.0031**	=
25b	344355646	**0.0149**	0.0267	=	80a	13557864	**0.0281**	0.0299	=
26a	1287596	0.0318	**0.0298**	=	80b	818415043	**0.0372**	0.0451	+
27a	1398568	**0.0307**	0.0344	=	100a	21125314	**0.0269**	0.0275	=
28a	1542998	**0.0310**	0.0327	=	100b	1185996137	**0.0279**	0.0383	+

5.2   Results

Each *algorithm - instance* pair was run 30 times. The results of the executions for the benchmarks of Taillard and *Taixxeyy* are summarised in Tables 1 and 2 respectively[4]. For the first benchmark, the performance measure employed in this study is the average relative percentage deviation (ARPD) [3]: $ARPD = \frac{|AvgRes - Best|}{Best}$, where $AvgRes$ denotes the average result obtained throughout 30 repetitions of the algorithm, and $Best$ stands for the best known solution of the instances. So, the lower the ARPD value, the better the performance. As regards the results on the Taixxeyy benchmark, in view of the bi-modal distribution of

---

[4] Source code, instances and further details about the experimental results can be downloaded from http://www.sc.ehu.es/ccwbayes/members/jceberio/home/ publications.html.

Table 2. Relative percentage deviation of the median results of NSGA-II and SGA for the *Taixxeyy* benchmark.

	$n = 27$				$n = 45$				$n = 75$			
ID	Best	NSGA-II	SGA	Sig.	Best	NSGA-II	SGA	Sig.	Best	NSGA-II	SGA	Sig.
1	2558	**0.202**	0.301	+	6412	**0.325**	0.414	+	14488	**0.284**	0.329	+
2	2850	**0.160**	0.328	+	5734	**0.412**	0.802	+	14444	**0.301**	0.751	=
3	3258	**0.255**	0.267	=	7438	**0.298**	0.453	+	14154	**0.290**	0.325	=
4	2822	**0.226**	0.330	+	6698	**0.353**	0.818	+	13694	**0.301**	0.761	+
5	3074	**0.185**	0.281	+	7274	**0.262**	0.825	+	12884	**0.308**	0.355	+
6	2814	**0.232**	0.263	=	6612	**0.324**	0.467	+	12534	**0.298**	0.405	+
7	3428	**0.154**	0.237	+	7526	**0.346**	0.467	+	13782	**0.274**	0.318	=
8	2430	**0.172**	0.292	+	6554	**0.283**	0.800	+	13948	**0.323**	0.648	+
9	2902	**0.214**	0.251	+	6648	**0.346**	0.837	+	12650	**0.291**	0.750	+
10	2994	**0.202**	0.332	+	8286	**0.354**	0.693	+	14192	**0.250**	0.752	+
11	2906	**0.208**	0.254	+	6510	**0.255**	0.412	+	15250	**0.285**	0.755	+
12	3070	**0.182**	0.260	+	7510	**0.356**	0.809	=	12760	**0.270**	0.643	+
13	2966	**0.149**	0.244	+	6120	**0.376**	0.410	=	13024	**0.256**	0.368	+
14	3568	**0.182**	0.233	+	6854	**0.369**	0.712	=	12604	**0.312**	0.755	+
15	2628	**0.203**	0.350	+	7394	**0.293**	0.810	+	14294	**0.259**	0.757	+
16	3124	**0.218**	0.255	=	6520	**0.371**	0.390	=	14204	**0.255**	0.641	+
17	3840	**0.169**	0.227	+	8806	**0.289**	0.312	=	13210	**0.290**	0.356	+
18	2758	**0.198**	0.228	=	6906	**0.242**	0.717	+	13500	**0.254**	0.347	+
19	2514	**0.193**	0.271	+	7170	**0.224**	0.397	+	12060	**0.289**	0.777	+
20	2638	**0.260**	0.353	+	6510	**0.282**	0.441	+	15260	**0.266**	0.337	+

the fitness results, the ARPD has been calculated with the median value obtained throughout the repetitions, which turns out to be more appropriated than the average. Results in bold highlight the algorithm that obtained the best result.

Results show that NSGA-II obtains lower error than SGA in 37 instances out of 48 in the Taillard's benchmark, and 60 out of 60 in the *Taixxeyy* instances.

5.3 Statistical Analysis

In order to assess whether there exist statistical differences among the results obtained, first we analyze whether statistical differences were obtained in each benchmark. To this end, we applied a non-parametric Wilcoxon paired-test to the average results obtained by NSGA-II and SGA[5]. A level of significance $\alpha = 0.05$ was set in both cases. The statistical test reported significant differences between

---

[5] The statistical tests in this work have been carried out with the **scmamp** package for R [2], and following the guidelines included in the documentation of the package.

the algorithms with p-values 0.0534 and 8.14×10^{-12}. The statistical analysis clearly detects two different scenarios. In the Taillard's benchmark very weak differences were found. Inversely, in the Taixxeyy benchmark, the test confirmed the good performance of NSGA-II seen in Table 2.

In order to obtain more detailed information, we applied the Mahn-Whitney test on each instance (Wilcoxon non-paired), and the p-values were adjusted with the method of Finner. Results have been summarized in Tables 1 and 2 under the 'Sig.' column. We used the symbols '+' and '=' to denote that NSGA-II is statistically better than SGA or that no differences were found. The analysis pointed out that solving the QAP in its 2-objective form is preferred to the single-objective form in 53 instances out of 108, being equally efficient in the rest of the cases.

6   Conclusions and Future Work

In this paper, we presented a novel method to multi-objectivise single-objective problems based on the elementary landscape decomposition of the fitness function. In order to illustrate this procedure, we considered the QAP, whose decomposition into three elementary landscapes was introduced in [4]. Based on the analysis of the elementary functions, we transformed the QAP into a 2-objective problem. In order to study the validity of the proposed multi-objectivisation scheme, we compared the performance of an adapted version of NSGA-II for the multi-objective QAP, with a simplified version of the algorithm, SGA, for the mono formulation of the QAP.

Experiments on two benchmarks of instances showed that NSGA-II is more competitive than SGA in some cases. In fact, the statistical test concluded that solving the QAP in its 2-objective form is preferred in 53 instances out of 108, being equally efficient in the rest of the cases. Particularly, most of the successful results were concentrated in the $Taixxeyy$ benchmark, which suggests that the characteristics of these instances make the multi-objectivisation approach more appropriated.

As future work, we think that it is essential to understand the underlying reason for which the multi-objectivization resulted so efficient on the $Taixxeyy$ instances, and inversely, in $Taillard$ obtained similar results when compared to the mono-objective proposal. In this sense, to study the shapes of the Ω^2 and Ω^3 elementary functions in relation to the real-life like instances is fundamental. In addition, in order to obtain a general view of the performance of the proposed multi-objectivisation scheme, we also find it interesting to extend the experimental study to instances from other benchmarks reported in the literature.

The obtained results suggest that the multi-objectivisation of single-objective problems by means of elementary landscape decomposition could be a promising scheme to take into account in problems for which the decomposition of the landscape is already known. In this sense, we find it interesting to extend the present work to other problems, such as the Linear Ordering Problem (LOP), the Travelling Salesman Problem (TSP) or the DNA Fragment Assembly Problem, special cases of the QAP, or to the MAX-k-SAT and the subset sum problem for which an elementary landscape decomposition is known.

Finally, in order to prove the validity of the proposed multi-objectivization scheme, it would be interesting to extend the experimental study to include other multi-objective evolutionary algorithms such as MOEA/D [21].

References

1. Abbass, H.A., Deb, K.: Searching under multi-evolutionary pressures. In: Fonseca, C.M., Fleming, P.J., Zitzler, E., Deb, K., Thiele, L. (eds.) EMO 2003. LNCS, vol. 2632, pp. 391–404. Springer, Heidelberg (2003)
2. Calvo, B., Santafe, G.: scmamp: Statistical Comparison of Multiple Algorithms in Multiple Problems (2015). R package version 2.0
3. Ceberio, J., Irurozki, E., Mendiburu, A., Lozano, J.A.: A distance-based ranking model estimation of distribution algorithm for the flowshop scheduling problem. IEEE Trans. Evol. Comput. **18**(2), 286–300 (2014)
4. Chicano, F., Whitley, L.D., Alba, E.: A methodology to find the elementary landscape decomposition of combinatorial optimization problems. Evol. Comput. **19**(4), 597–637 (2011)
5. Chicano, F., Luque, G., Alba, E.: Autocorrelation measures for the quadratic assignment problem. Appl. Math. Lett. **25**(4), 698–705 (2012)
6. Deb, K., Pratap, A., Agarwal, S., Meyarivan, T.: A fast and elitist multiobjective genetic algorithm: NSGA-II. IEEE Trans. Evol. Comp. **6**(2), 182–197 (2002)
7. Drezner, Z., Hahn, P., Taillard, É.: Recent advances for the quadratic assignment problem with special emphasis on instances that are difficult for meta-heuristic methods. Ann. Oper. Res. **139**(1), 65–94 (2005)
8. Grover, L.K.: Local search and the local structure of NP-complete problems. Oper. Res. Lett. **12**(4), 235–243 (1992)
9. Handl, J., Lovell, S.C., Knowles, J.D.: Multiobjectivization by decomposition of scalar cost functions. In: Rudolph, G., Jansen, T., Lucas, S., Poloni, C., Beume, N. (eds.) PPSN 2008. LNCS, vol. 5199, pp. 31–40. Springer, Heidelberg (2008)
10. Knowles, J.D., Watson, R.A., Corne, D.W.: Reducing local optima in single-objective problems by multi-objectivization. In: Zitzler, E., Deb, K., Thiele, L., Coello Coello, C.A., Corne, D.W. (eds.) EMO 2001. LNCS, vol. 1993, p. 269. Springer, Heidelberg (2001)
11. Koopmans, T.C., Beckmann, M.J.: Assignment Problems and the Location of Economic Activities. Cowles Foundation Discuss. Papers 4, Yale University (1955)
12. Lim, M.H., Yuan, Y., Omatu, S.: Efficient genetic algorithms using simple genes exchange localsearch policy for the quadratic assignment problem. Comput. Optim. Appl. **15**(3), 249–268 (2000)
13. Neumann, F., Wegener, I.: Minimum spanning trees made easier via multi-objective optimization. Nat. Comput. **5**(3), 305–319 (2006)
14. Rockmore, D., Kostelec, P., Hordijk, W., Stadler, P.: Fast fourier transforms for fitness landscapes. App. Comp. Harmonic Anal. **12**(1), 57–76 (2002)
15. Scharnow, J., Tinnefeld, K., Wegener, I.: The analysis of evolutionary algorithms on sorting and shortest paths problems. J. Math. Model. Algorithms **3**(4), 349–366 (2005)

16. Segura, C., Coello, C., Miranda, G., Leon, C.: Using multi-objective evolutionary algorithms for single-objective optimization. 4OR **11**(3), 201–228 (2013)
17. Stadler, P.F.: Landscapes and their correlation functions. J. Math. Chem. **20**, 1–45 (1996)
18. Stadler, P.F.: Fitness landscapes. Appl. Math. Comput. **117**, 187–207 (2002)
19. Sutton, A.M., Whitley, L.D., Howe, A.E.: A polynomial time computation of the exact correlation structure of k-satisfiability landscapes. In: GECCO 2009, New York, USA, pp. 365–372 (2009)
20. Taillard, É.D.: Comparison of iterative searches for the quadratic assignment problem. Location Sci. **3**(2), 87–105 (1995)
21. Zhang, Q., Li, H.: MOEA/D: a multiobjective evolutionary algorithm based on decomposition. IEEE Trans. Evol. Comput. **11**(6), 712–731 (2007)

Overcoming the Linearity of Ordinal Logistic Regression Adding Non-linear Covariates from Evolutionary Hybrid Neural Network Models

Manuel Dorado-Moreno[✉], Pedro Antonio Gutiérrez,
Javier Sánchez-Monedero, and César Hervás-Martínez

Department of Computer Science and Numerical Analysis, University of Cordoba,
Campus de Rabanales, Albert Einstein building, 14071 Cordoba, Spain
{i92domom,pagutierrez,jsanchezm,chervas}@uco.es

Abstract. This paper proposes a non-linear ordinal logistic regression method based on the combination of a linear regression model and an evolutionary neural network with hybrid basis functions, combining Sigmoidal Unit and Radial Basis Functions neural networks. The process for obtaining the coefficients is carried out in several steps. Firstly we use an evolutionary algorithm to determine the structure of the hybrid neural network model, in a second step we augment the initial feature space (covariate space) adding the non-linear transformations of the input variables given by the hybrid hidden layer of the best individual of the evolutionary algorithm. Finally, we apply an ordinal logistic regression in the new feature space. This methodology is tested using 10 benchmark problems from the UCI repository. The hybrid model outperforms both the RBF and the SU pure models obtaining a good compromise between them and better results in terms of accuracy and ordinal classification error.

Keywords: Artificial neural networks · Hybrid basis functions · Proportional odds model · Evolutionary algorithms · Ordinal classification · Ordinal regression

1 Introduction

Artificial Neural Networks (ANNs) are a very flexible modelling technique based on biological neural systems, whose computing power is developed using an adaptive learning process. Properties and characteristics of ANNs have made them a common tool when successfully solving high complexity problems from different areas, e.g. medical diagnosis, financial data modelling, predictive microbiology, remote sensing, analytical chemistry... For some of these problems, items have to be classified into naturally ordered classes. They are traditionally handled by conventional methods intended for classification of nominal classes, where the order relation is ignored. This kind of supervised learning problems are referred

© Springer International Publishing Switzerland 2015
J.M. Puerta et al. (Eds.): CAEPIA 2015, LNAI 9422, pp. 301–311, 2015.
DOI: 10.1007/978-3-319-24598-0_27

to as ordinal regression, where an ordinal scale is used to label the examples. Therefore, in ordinal classification problems, the goal is to learn how to classify examples in the correct class. But one should take into account that the higher distance between predicted and real labels is (with respect to the ordinal scale), the more the misclassification error should be penalised.

In general, Logistic Regression (LR) is a simple and useful classification procedure, although it poses problems when applied to real-problems, where, frequently, we cannot make the assumption of additive and purely linear effects of the covariates. As suggested by [13], an obvious way to generalise the linear logistic regression is to replace the linear predictors with structured non-parametric models such as an additive model of basis function. In this paper, we extend the ideas introduced in [12], where a combination of LR and Neural Networks models was used to solve nominal classification problems. We present an adaptation of the corresponding algorithm to tackle ordinal classification combined with an ordinal ANN model with hybrid basis functions.

As exposed in [19], the motivation for studying hybrid basis functions for neural networks comes from many different branches. Biological neural systems are built from a large diversity of neuron types. We can also think about computational efficiency; neural networks with high diversity performs better [7]. That leads us to a third motivation, the reduction of complexity in the neural network; adding diversity to a neural network allows the number of nodes (and links) to be reduced [25].

One of the first models specifically designed for ordinal classification, and the one our model is built on, is the Proportional Odds Model (POM) [20], which is basically an ordinal logistic regression. This model is based on the assumption of stochastic ordering in the input space, and the use of thresholds to split the projected input space into different ordered classes. We propose a hybrid neural network ordinal model using a combination of projection functions (sigmoidal unit, SU) and kernel functions (radial basis function, RBF) in the hidden layer of a feed-forward neural network [11]. An evolutionary algorithm is adapted to train this model and applied for learning the model architecture, link weights and node typology. In order to obtain further conclusions, the hybrid basis neural network proposed is compared to its corresponding pure models: SU and RBF neural networks. A mixture of different kinds of basis functions [11] is an interesting alternative, which could be able to take advantage from the benefits of each one. Our proposal follows the idea of augmenting the vector of inputs with non-linear covariates obtained by the neural network hybrid hidden layer, and then use the POM in this new space of derived input features.

The estimation of the coefficients is carried out in several steps. In a first step, an evolutionary algorithm [27] (EA) is applied to design the structure and train the weights of a hybrid SURBF neural network [5,15] (SURBFNN). Evolutionary computation has been widely used in the late years to evolve NN architectures and weights. There have been many applications for parametric learning [22] and for both parametric and structural learning [1,17,26]. This evolutionary process determines the number of neurons in the model and the corresponding variables, which will be the new covariates in the non-linear LR model. The best model in the last generation is used for that purpose. In a second step, we augment the input space adding the SURBF non-linear covariates to the linear ones. That led us to add a third step, where we perform a local optimization algorithm using the new input covariates, with a maximum likelihood method for ordinal LR, based on the structure of the POM.

The rest of the paper is organized as follows. Section 2 introduces the hybrid neural networks. In Sect. 3, the neural network model for ordinal regression is explained. Section 4 presents the algorithm developed in order to obtain the coefficients for the hybrid model. Section 5 includes the experiments: experimental design, information about the datasets and results of the experiments. Finally, in Sect. 6, we present the conclusions of the paper.

2 Hybrid Artificial Neural Networks

Different types of neural networks are being used today for classification purposes, including neural networks based on a sigmoidal basis (SU), radial basis function (RBF) [15] and a class of multiplicative basis functions, called the product unit (PU) [18,23]. The combination of different basis functions in the hidden layer of a neural network has been proposed as an alternative to traditional neural networks [16]. We use RBF neurons and SU neurons according to Cohen and Intrator insights [7], based on the duality and complementary properties of projection-based functions (SU and PU) and kernel typology (RBF). These models have also been theoretically justified by Donoho [8], who demonstrated that any continuous function can be decomposed into two mutually exclusive functions, such as radial (RBF) and crest ones (SU and PU). In this way, RBF neurons contribute to a local recognition model [4], while SU neurons contribute to a global recognition one [18]. Their combination results in a high degree of diversity because the submodels differ from one another.

3 Proposed Neural Network Model

The POM model [20], as the majority of existing ordinal regression models, can be represented in the following general form:

$$
C(\mathbf{x}) = \begin{cases} \mathcal{C}_1, & \text{if } f(\mathbf{x}, \boldsymbol{\theta}) \leq \beta_0^1 \\ \mathcal{C}_2, & \text{if } \beta_0^1 < f(\mathbf{x}, \boldsymbol{\theta}) \leq \beta_0^2 \\ \cdots \\ \mathcal{C}_J, & \text{if } f(\mathbf{x}, \boldsymbol{\theta}) > \beta_0^{J-1}, \end{cases} \tag{1}
$$

where $\beta_0^1 < \beta_0^2 < \cdots < \beta_0^{J-1}$ (this will be the most important constraint in order to adapt the nominal classification model to ordinal classification), J is the number of classes, $\mathbf{x}$ is the input pattern to be classified, $f(\mathbf{x}, \boldsymbol{\theta})$ is a ranking function and $\boldsymbol{\theta}$ is the vector of parameters of the model. Indeed, the analysis of

Eq. (1) uncovers the general idea presented in [20]: patterns, $\mathbf{x}$, are projected to a real line by using the ranking function, $f(\mathbf{x}, \boldsymbol{\theta})$, and the biases or thresholds, β_0^j, are separating the ordered classes.

We are using an adaptation of the POM to artificial neural networks. This adaptation is based on two elements: the first one is a second hidden linear layer with only one node whose inputs are the non-linear transformations of the first hidden layer. The task of this node is to project the values into a line, to make them have an order. After this one node linear layer, an output layer is included with one bias for each class, whose objective is to set the optimum thresholds to classify the patterns in the class they belong to.

The structure of our model is presented in Fig. 1 which has two main parts. The lower one shows the SURBFNN model, where $\mathbf{x} = (x_1, \dots, x_k)$, is the vector of input variables and k is the number of variables in the database. $\boldsymbol{\omega} = (\omega_{1,10}, \dots, \omega_{1,m_1 k}, \omega_{2,10}, \dots, \omega_{2,m_2 k})$ is the matrix of weights of the connections from the input nodes to the hidden layer SU nodes $(\omega_{1,10}, \dots, \omega_{1,m_1 k})$ and to the RBF ones $(\omega_{2,10}, \dots, \omega_{2,m_2 k})$ and B are the nodes in the hybrid hidden layer, m_1 is the number of nodes of the first type and m_2 is the number of nodes of the second type, SU and RBF respectively in our case, and "1" is the bias of the layer, which takes part in the calculations.

The upper part of the figure shows a single node in the second hidden layer of the model, which is the one that performs the linear transformation of the POM model. Its result, $f(\mathbf{x}, \boldsymbol{\theta})$, is connected, together with a second bias, to the output layer, where J is the number of classes, and $\beta_0^0, \dots, \beta_0^{J-1}$ are the thresholds for the different classes. These $J-1$ thresholds are able to separate the J classes, but they have to fulfil the order constraint shown in the figure. Finally, the output layer obtains the outputs of the model, $f_j(\mathbf{x}, \boldsymbol{\theta}, \beta_0^j)$, for $j \in \{1, \dots, J-1\}$. These outputs are transformed using the function of the POM model, which transforms them into a probability $(g_j(\mathbf{x}, \boldsymbol{\theta}, \beta_0^j))$. This is the probability that each pattern has to belong to the different classes, and the class with the greatest probability is the one selected by the NN to be the class of the pattern.

4   Estimation of the Coefficients

The methodology proposed is based on the combination of an EA and an ordinal maximum likelihood optimization method. Figure 2 represents the different steps of the algorithm and the models obtained for the experiments. The different steps of the algorithm are now explained:

Step 1: We apply and EA to find the basis functions (SUs and RBFs):

$$\mathbf{B}(\mathbf{x}, \mathbf{W}) = \{B_{1,1}(\mathbf{x}, \mathbf{w}_{m_1}), \dots, B_{1,m_1}(\mathbf{x}, \mathbf{w}_2), \dots, B_{2,1}(\mathbf{x}, \mathbf{w}_2), \dots, B_{2,m_2}(\mathbf{x}, \mathbf{w}_{m_2})\}$$

corresponding to the non-linear part of the hybrid logistic regression model presented in this paper. The NN model for the EA is presented in Fig. 1. The EA begins with a random initial population, and each iteration the population is updated using a population-update algorithm [9]. The population is subject to

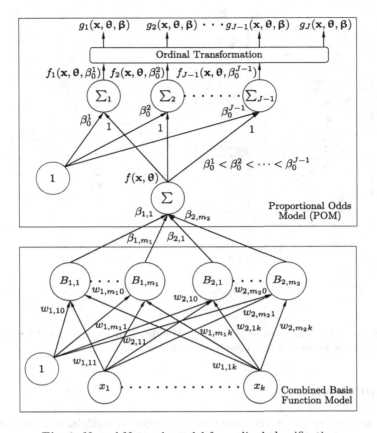

Fig. 1. Neural Network model for ordinal classification

operations of mutation and replication with ordinal constraints. Crossover is not used because of its disadvantages in evolving NNs [1].

Step 2: We perform a transformation of the input space, including the non-linear transformations of the inputs obtained by the EA in Step 1:

$$\mathbb{H} : \mathbb{R}^k \to \mathbb{R}^{k+m}$$
$$(x_1, x_2, \ldots, x_k) \to (x_1, x_2, x_k, \ldots, z_1, z_2, \ldots, z_m),$$

where $z_1 = B_1(\mathbf{x}, \mathbf{w}_1)$, $z_2 = B_2(\mathbf{x}, \mathbf{w}_2), \ldots, z_m = B_m(\mathbf{x}, \mathbf{w}_m)$.

Step 3: We apply an ordinal maximum likelihood optimization method in the new input space obtained in step 2. The optimization of the maximum likelihood is performed using a gradient descent algorithm called iRProp+ [14], which optimises the non-linear ordinal logistic regression for a defined number of epochs.

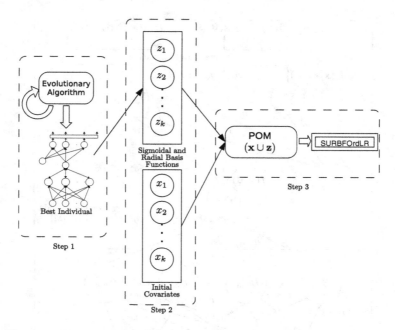

Fig. 2. Steps in the proposed methodology. The different models associated with this methodology are presented in a double squared box

5   Experiments

In order to analyse the performance of the proposed models, ten datasets have been tested, their characteristics being shown in Table 1. The collection of datasets is taken from the UCI [2] and the mldata.org [21] repositories. The experimental design was conducted using 10 random holdout procedures.

Three different neural networks have been compared: RBFOrdLR is the LR combined with the hidden nodes of an evolutionary RBFNN, SUOrdLR is the same model with SU functions on its hidden layer, finally SURBFOrdLR is the LR combined with both SU and RBF from the hybrid hidden layer of an evolutionary neural network. We also compare the results against the original POM model, SVOREX [6] and SVR [24], which is an ordinal regression transformed into an standard regression, changing the ordinal labels $(C_1, C_2, \ldots)$, for numbers $(0, 1/(Q-1), 2/(Q-1), \ldots, Q)$.

All the parameters of the algorithm are common to these ten problems. The main parameters of the algorithm are: number of generations: 100; population size: 250; mutation percentage: 10 %; minimum number of hidden nodes: 4; maximum number of hidden nodes: 14.

In order to set up the minimum number of hidden neurons, a preliminary experiment was done with one partition of each dataset. A 5-fold cross-validation (using only the training split) was done and repeated with the following minimum number of hidden nodes, $\{1, 2, 4, \ldots, 20\}$. We concluded that the optimum minimum number of hidden nodes was 4 and we added 10 nodes for the maximum, in order to give the EA some freedom to optimise the NN.

The idea of having a small population size and a small number of generations is to give less importance to the evolutionary algorithm because its computational time is much higher than the optimisation of the non-linear ordinal logistic regression. After finishing the EA, we took the SURBF hidden layer from the best model in the last generation to augment the input space and applied a gradient descent algorithm with 1000 epochs to optimise the non-linear ordinal logistic regression model.

Table 1. Characteristics of the ten datasets used for the experiments: number of instances (Size), inputs (#In.), classes (#Out.) and patterns per-class (#PPC)

Dataset	Size	#In.	#Out.	#PPC
Bondrate	57	37	5	(6,33,12,5,1)
Balance	625	4	3	(288,49,288)
Contact-lenses	24	6	3	(15,5,4)
Car	1728	21	4	(1210,384,69,65)
ESL	488	4	9	(2,12,38,100,116,135,62,19,4)
LEV	1000	4	5	(93,280,403,197,27)
Newthyroid	215	5	3	(30,150,35)
Pasture	36	25	3	(12,12,12)
Squash-stored	52	51	3	(24,24,4)
SWD	1000	10	4	(32,352,399,217)

The following two measures have been used for comparing the models:

- CCR: The Correct Classification Rate (CCR) is the rate of correctly classified patterns: $CCR = \frac{1}{n}\sum_{i=1}^{N} J y_i^* = y_i K$, where y_i is the true label, y_i^* is the predicted label and $J \cdot K$ is a Boolean test which is 1 if the inner condition is true and 0 otherwise.
- MAE: The Mean Absolute Error (MAE) is the average deviation (number of categories) in absolute value of the predicted class from the true class [3]: $MAE = \frac{1}{n}\sum_{i=1}^{N} e(\mathbf{x}_i)$, where $e(\mathbf{x}_i) = |\mathcal{O}(y_i) - \mathcal{O}(y_i^*)|$ is the distance between the true and the predicted ranks, $\mathcal{O}(\mathcal{C}_j) = j$. This is a way of evaluating the ordering performance of the classifier.

Table 2 shows the mean test value and standard deviation of the correct classified rate (CCR) and the mean absolute error (MAE) over the 10 models obtained.

To determine the statistical significance of the rank differences observed for each method in the different datasets, we have carried out a non-parametric Friedman test [10] with the ranking of CCR and MAE of the best models

Table 2. Generalization results obtained for benchmark datasets

Func	CCR(%) Mean ± SD	MAE Mean ± SD	CCR(%) Mean ± SD	MAE Mean ± SD
	Bondrate		Balance	
SURBFOrdLR	**56.66 ± 5.94**	**0.5467 ± 0.0883**	96.43 ± 1.87	0.0388 ± 0.0225
RBFOrdLR	54.00 ± 5.97	0.5667 ± 0.0864	95.09 ± 1.87	0.0535 ± 0.0217
SUOrdLR	52.66 ± 5.08	0.5600 ± 0.0922	96.17 ± 1.57	0.0414 ± 0.0314
POM	34.44 ± 1.94	0.9467 ± 0.6868	90.55 ± 1.85	0.1067 ± 0.0208
SVOREX	54.66 ± 8.04	0.6222 ± 0.1181	**99.78 ± 8.19**	**0.0021 ± 0.0081**
SVR	54.22 ± 9.20	0.5933 ± 0.1424	83.52 ± 1.47	0.1679 ± 0.0188
	Contact-lenses		Car	
SURBFOrdLR	65.00 ± 5.54	0.4800 ± 0.0883	93.12 ± 2.60	0.0721 ± 0.0307
RBFOrdLR	65.00 ± 5.97	0.4167 ± 0.0864	88.37 ± 2.72	0.1254 ± 0.0335
SUOrdLR	63.33 ± 5.08	0.4000 ± 0.0922	90.92 ± 1.72	0.0949 ± 0.0200
POM	61.66 ± 1.94	0.5333 ± 0.6868	15.74 ± 3.06	1.4505 ± 0.5482
SVOREX	64.44± 8.04	0.4833 ± 0.1181	**98.78 ± 2.24**	**0.0125 ± 0.0132**
SVR	**68.33 ± 9.20**	**0.3778 ± 0.1424**	97.30 ± 1.12	0.0270 ± 0.0110
	ESL		LEV	
SURBFOrdLR	**73.19 ± 2.39**	**0.2278 ± 0.0276**	62.49 ± 2.16	0.4032 ± 0.0295
RBFOrdLR	72.21 ± 2.74	0.2893 ± 0.0304	**64.40 ± 2.21**	0.4260 ± 0.0309
SUOrdLR	71.55 ± 2.32	0.2975 ± 0.0344	60.92 ± 3.73	0.4204 ± 0.0428
POM	70.54 ± 3.36	0.3103 ± 0.0380	62.33 ± 2.79	0.4093 ± 0.0303
SVOREX	70.98 ± 2.37	0.3019 ± 0.0209	62.45 ± 2.37	0.4105 ± 0.0227
SVR	70.38 ± 3.40	0.3117 ± 0.0298	62.48 ± 2.69	0.4086 ± 0.0288
	Newthyroid		Pasture	
SURBFOrdLR	**96.60 ± 1.30**	**0.0314 ± 0.0130**	**71.11 ± 5.94**	**0.2889 ± 0.0883**
RBFOrdLR	95.37 ± 1.57	0.0462 ± 0.1573	66.66 ± 5.97	0.3444 ± 0.0864
SUOrdLR	96.29 ± 2.76	0.0370 ± 0.0276	66.66 ± 5.08	0.3333 ± 0.0922
POM	96.22 ± 2.21	0.3277 ± 0.0221	49.62 ± 1.94	0.5818 ± 0.6868
SVOREX	96.48 ± 3.02	0.0351 ± 0.0462	65.18 ± 8.04	0.3333 ± 0.1181
SVR	95.55 ± 6.04	0.0322 ± 0.0604	66.29 ± 9.20	0.3222 ±
	Squash-stored		SWD	
SURBFOrdLR	**66.92 ± 5.94**	0.3604 ± 0.0883	**58.88 ± 1.40**	**0.4302 ± 0.0154**
RBFOrdLR	66.15 ± 5.97	**0.3584 ± 0.0864**	58.36 ± 1.23	0.4348 ± 0.0145
SUOrdLR	65.38 ± 5.08	0.3615 ± 0.0922	57.20 ± 1.80	0.4528 ± 0.0167
POM	38.20 ± 1.94	0.8121 ± 0.6868	56.78 ± 2.95	0.4501 ± 0.0304
SVOREX	62.56 ± 8.04	0.3667 ± 0.1181	56.78 ± 2.66	0.4464 ± 0.0339
SVR	61.28 ± 9.20	0.3692 ± 0.1424	56.52 ± 2.06	0.4513 ± 0.0316

The best result is shown in bold and the second best in italics

as the test variables. For CCR, the test shows that the effect of the method used for classification is statistically significant at a significance level of 10 %, as the confidence interval is $C_0(0, F_{0.10} = 1.97)$ and the F-distribution statistical value is $F^* = 6.78 \notin C_0$. For MAE, the test concludes the same, obtaining $C_0(0, F_{0.10} = 1.97)$ as confidence interval and $F^* = 4.73 \notin C_0$ as F-distribution variable. Consequently, we reject the null-hypothesis stating that all algorithms perform equally in mean ranking for both variables.

Based on this rejection, the Holm post-hoc test is used to compare all classifiers to each other using both CCR and MAE. The results of the Holm test for $\alpha = 0.10$ can be seen in Table 3, using the corresponding p and α'_{Holm} values. From the results of this test, it can be concluded that SURBFOrdLR obtains a significantly higher ranking of CCR and MAE when compared to the remaining methods, which justifies the proposed method in this paper. As MAE is a metric that needs to be minimised the best ranking is the higher one.

Table 3. Comparison of p-Value and α' for the Holm post-hoc non-parametric tests in CCR and MAE with a $\alpha = 0.1$ (SURBFOrdLR is the control method)

Algorithm	Mean CCR Rank	p-Value$_{CCR}$	α'_{CCR}	Mean MAE Rank	p-Value$_{MAE}$	α'_{MAE}
SURBFOrdLR	**1.60**	–	–	**5.20**	–	–
RBFOrdLR	*3.25*	0.04860	0.05000	*3.80*	0.01683	0.02500
SUOrdLR	3.45	0.02702	0.03333	3.30	0.02315	0.03333
POM	5.35	0.00001	0.02000	1.75	0.00004	0.02000
SVOREX	*3.25*	0.04860	0.10000	3.55	0.04860	0.10000
SVR	4.10	0.00281	0.02500	3.40	0.03144	0.05000

6   Conclusions

This work proposes to improve an ordinal linear logistic regression model and transform it into a non-linear one. To this end, the linear model is extended with non-linear covariates from the outputs of the hidden neurons of a hybrid SURBFNN. These neural network models are trained using an evolutionary algorithm that optimizes both its architecture and weights.

Moreover, the coefficients of the ordinal logistic regression model, consisting of the initial covariates and the SURBF non-linear outputs, are estimated by a gradient descent algorithm that tries to optimize the maximum likelihood.

Experiments show that this hybrid approach is promising and generally improves accuracy and order quality, performing better than the corresponding pure models. The model also obtains competitive results when compared to state-of-the-art ordinal classification algorithms.

Acknowledgements. This work has been partially subsidised by the TIN2014-54583-C2-1-R project of the Spanish MINECO, FEDER funds and P11-TIC-7508 project of the "Junta de Andalucía(Spain)".

References

1. Angeline, P.J., Sauders, G.M., Pollack, J.B.: An evolutionary algorithm that constructs recurrent neural networks. IEEE Trans. Neural Netw. **5**(1), 54–65 (1994)
2. Asuncion, A., Newman, D.: UCI machine learning repository (2007). http://www.ics.uci.edu/mlearn/MLRepository.html
3. Baccianella, S., Esuli, A., Sebastiani, F.: Evaluation measures for ordinal regression. In: Proceedings of the Ninth International Conference on Intelligent Systems Design and Applications (ISDA 09), Pisa, Italy, December 2009
4. Bishop, C.M.: Improving the generalization properties of radial basis function neural networks. Neural Comput. **8**, 579–581 (1991)
5. Buchtala, O., Klimek, M., Sick, B.: Evolutionary optimization of radial basis function classifiers for data mining applications. IEEE Trans. Neural Netw. Part B **35**(5), 928–947 (2005)
6. Chu, W., Keerthi, S.S.: Support vector ordinal regression. Neural Comput. **19**(3), 792–815 (2007)
7. Cohen, S., Intrator, N.: A hybrid projection-based and radial basis function architecture: initial values and global optimisation. Pattern Anal. Appl. **5**, 113–120 (2002)
8. Donoho, D.: Projection-based approximation and a duality with kernel methods. Ann. Stat. **5**, 58–106 (1989)
9. Dorado-Moreno, M., Gutiérrez, P.A., Hervás-Martínez, C.: Ordinal classification using hybrid artificial neural networks with projection and kernel basis functions. In: Corchado, E., Snášel, V., Abraham, A., Woźniak, M., Graña, M., Cho, S.-B. (eds.) HAIS 2012, Part II. LNCS, vol. 7209, pp. 319–330. Springer, Heidelberg (2012)
10. Friedman, M.: A comparison of alternative tests of significance for the problem of m rankings. Ann. Math. Stat. **11**, 86–92 (1940)
11. Gutiérrez, P.A., Hervás-Martínez, C., Carbonero-Ruz, M., Fernandez, J.C.: Combined projection and kernel basis functions for classification in evolutionary neural networks. Neurocomputing **27**(13–15), 2731–2742 (2009)
12. Gutiérrez, P.A., Hervás-Martínez, C., Martínez-Estudillo, F.J.: Logistic regression by means of evolutionary radial basis function neural networks. IEEE Trans. Neural Netw. **22**(2), 246–263 (2011)
13. Hastie, T., Tibshirani, R.: Generalized Additive Models. Chapman and Hall, London (1990)
14. Igel, C., Hüsken, M.: Empirical evaluation of the improved rprop learning algorithms. Neurocomputing **50**(6), 105–123 (2003)
15. Lee, S.H., Hou, C.L.: An art-based construction of RBF networks. IEEE Trans. Neural Netw. **13**(6), 1308–1321 (2002)
16. Lippmann, R.P.: Pattern classification using neural networks. IEEE Trans. Neural Netw. **27**, 47–64 (1989)
17. Maniezzo, V.: Genetic evolution of the topology and weight distribution of neural networks. IEEE Trans. Neural Netw. **5**, 39–53 (1994)

18. Martínez-Estudillo, A.C., Martínez-Estudillo, F.J., Hervás-Martínez, C., García, N.: Evolutionary product unit based neural networks for regression. Neural Netw. **19**(4), 477–486 (2006)
19. Maul, T.: Early experiments with neural diversity machines. Neurocomputing **113**, 136–48 (2013)
20. McCullagh, P.: Regression models for ordinal data (with discussion). J. Roy. Stat. Soc. **42**(2), 109–142 (1980)
21. PASCAL: Pascal (pattern analysis, statistical modelling and computational learning) machine learning benchmarks repository (2011). http://mldata.org/
22. van Rooij, A.J.F., Jain, L.C., Johnson, R.P.: Neural Networks Training Using Genetic Algorithms. Series in Machine Perception and Artificial Intelligence, vol. 26. World Scientific, Singapore (1996)
23. Schmitt, M.: On the complexity of computing and learning with multiplicative neural networks. Neural Comput. **14**, 241–301 (2001)
24. Smola, A., Scholkopf, B.: A tutorial on support vector regression. Stat. Comput. **14**(3), 199–222 (2004)
25. Soltesz, I.: Diversity in the Neuronal Machine: Order and Variability in Interneuronal Microcircuits. Oxford University Press, New York (2002)
26. Yao, X., Liu, Y.: A new evolutionary system for evolving artificial neural networks. IEEE Trans. Neural Netw. **8**, 694–713 (1997)
27. Yao, X.: Evolving artificial neural networks. Proc. IEEE **87**(9), 1423–1447 (1999)

On the Applicability of Ant Colony Optimization to Non-Intrusive Load Monitoring in Smart Grids

Antonio Gonzalez-Pardo[1,2]([⊠]), Javier Del Ser[2], and David Camacho[3]

[1] Basque Center for Applied Mathematics (BCAM), Alameda de Mazarredo,
14, 48009 Bilbao, Basque Country, Spain
agonzalezp@bcamath.org
[2] OPTIMA Area, TECNALIA, 48160 Derio, Spain
javier.delser@tecnalia.com
[3] Computer Science Department, Escuela Politécnica Superior,
Universidad Autónoma de Madrid, Madrid, Spain
david.camacho@uam.es

Abstract. Along with the proliferation of the Smart Grid, power load disaggregation is a research area that is lately gaining a lot of popularity due to the interest of energy distribution companies and customers in identifying consumption patterns towards improving the way the energy is produced and consumed (via e.g. demand side management strategies). Such data can be extracted by using *smart meters*, but the expensive cost of incorporating a monitoring device for each appliance jeopardizes significantly the massive implementation of any straightforward approach. When resorting to a single meter to monitor the global consumption of the house at hand, the identification of the different appliances giving rise to the recorded consumption profile renders a particular instance of the so-called source separation problem, for which a number of algorithmic proposals have been reported in the literature. This paper gravitates on the applicability of the Ant Colony Optimization (ACO) algorithm to perform this power disaggregation treating the problem as a Constraint Satisfaction Problem (CSP). The discussed experimental results utilize data contained in the REDD dataset, which corresponds to real power consumption traces of different households. Although the experiments carried out in this work reveal that the ACO solver can be successfully applied to the Non-Intrusive Load Monitoring problems, further work is needed towards assessing its performance when tackling more diverse appliance models and noisy power load traces.

Keywords: Non-intrusive load monitoring · Ant colony optimization · Power consumption disaggregation

1 Introduction

Smart meters lie at the core of the Smart Grid ecosystem by providing the distribution operator with fine-grained information about the energy consumption

© Springer International Publishing Switzerland 2015
J.M. Puerta et al. (Eds.): CAEPIA 2015, LNAI 9422, pp. 312–321, 2015.
DOI: 10.1007/978-3-319-24598-0_28

of the house, facility, industry or whatever energy consumer it monitors. The knowledge that can be extracted from these data can be used for a wide variety of purposes. As to mention, depending on the regulatory context power distribution companies or energy dealers could extract energy consumption patterns of their clients by analyzing their daily traces, and consequently propose personalized contracts taking into account these patterns. Moreover, companies could use these data to predict, or estimate, the future power demand of a specific area or building, which calls for inherent opportunities in short-term demand side management schemes. But benefits do not fall only on the side of the energy distributor. Customers could take advantage from the data extracted by the smart meters as well: this data allow users to timely know their power consumption and what appliances have generated this consumption, towards eventually changing their consumption habits.

The main problem underlying beneath this last hypothesized utility of disaggregating the power profile registered by the meter is the way these data can be obtained. One possible way consists of deploying a metering device per installed appliance. However, the costs associated with this approach are much higher than that incurred by using only one meter that captures the overall power consumption associated with the house, which makes the former a metering layout restricted to very particular scenarios.

When using this last approach (i.e. a single meter per house), a procedure for disaggregating the power signal is required in order to discriminates what appliances (model, number and on/off time instants) correspond to the observed consumption. This disaggregation is widely known as *Non-Intrusive Load Monitoring* (NILM) [13]. Unfortunately, the evergrowing variety of appliances and the different power consumption modes for a given appliance makes it extremely difficult to solve NILM problems from a generalistic standpoint, fact that has unchained a flurry of research on algorithmic approaches to this family of paradigms. As such, research works focused on NILM problems can be grouped in non-supervised and supervised methods. Non-supervised approaches exploit unlabeled data, hence there is no training process for the identification model. Most of the related work refer to *blind source separation* [10], *Hidden Markov Models* (HMM) [10,30], or *Factorial Hidden Markov Models* (FHMM) [6,16]. On the other hand, supervised approaches require a labeled dataset and a training process to adjust some of the parameters of the model. The application of supervised approaches to NILM problems mainly concentrates on pattern recognition and optimization tasks [17,22]. Pattern recognition relies mostly on *Neural Networks* (NN) [25] or *Support Vector Machines* (SVM) [18,25]. Likewise *hierarchical clustering* [3,14], *fuzzy C-means* [4], *Self-Organizing Maps* (SOM) [28,29] or *Hopfieldś networks* [19,20] are among the most popular clustering techniques used for NILM problems.

Notwithstanding the activity in this area, the application of computational intelligence algorithms for NILM problems has not been explored in depth yet. There are several works that instead of applying bio-inspired algorithms to disaggregate power consumption traces, such techniques optimize part of the parameters of the underlying model such as the weights of the NN, or the definition of the clusters that contains the consumption profiles of the different appliances. In this sense, *Particle Swarm Optimization* (PSO) [2], Genetic Algorithms (GA) [1,7], Ant Colony Optimization (ACO) algorithms [26] or *Honey Bee Mating Optimization* [9] have been used for this purposes.

In this work the application of ACO for NILM problems is studied from a different perspective. The disaggregation of power consumption can be viewed as a Constraint Satisfaction Problem (CSP), for whose resolution several ACO approaches are available. This paper presents an initial study about the performance of a new ACO model for complex graph-based problems, which was first proposed in [11]. The model is described in detail particularly in what regards to the formulation of the NILM problem as a variant of the CSP. Simulation results will preliminarily show that the proposed ACO solver excels at disaggregating power signatures corresponding to different appliances generated from real consumption traces.

This paper is structured as follows: first, Sect. 2 shows how CSP problems can be tackled via ACO, whereas Sect. 3 describes the new ACO model proposed for the CSP problem modeling the power disaggregation paradigm undertaken in this manuscript. Section 4 discusses the obtained simulation results over real datasets and, finally, Sect. 5 ends the paper by drawing concluding remarks and outlining lines of future research.

2   Solving CSP Problems Using ACO Algorihtms

Nowadays, there is a huge number of problems that can be modeled as Constraint Satisfaction Problems (CSP). This family of problems is defined by a triple $\{X, D, C\}$, where X is the set of variables that compose the problem, D contains the possible values for the variables described in X, and C is a set of constraints that relate the values of the different variables [8,27]. The NP-hard complexity featured by CSP problems motivates the widely reported use of heuristic algorithms for solving them efficiently, among which ACO schemes outstand prominently.

ACO algorithms are based on the foraging behaviour of ants [5]. Ants take different decisions during their execution that allow them to build their own solutions to the problem. The utilization of ACO algorithms to solve CSP problems requires the representation of the problem as a graph, over which the ACO is executed. This graph, called *construction graph*, is defined as $G = (V, E)$ where V represents the nodes of the graph and E is the set of edges that connect the nodes. Roli *et. al.* proposed this construction graph for solving CSP problems in [21], where they established a fully connected graph where nodes are pairs ⟨*variable, value*⟩. There are other different approaches from the one just described. Examples are the models proposed by Solnon [23,24] and Khan et. al. [15]. But in all of them, the resulting graph is extremely big due to the high number of nodes and edges created in the system.

In this work, a new model proposed in [11] is used to perform the disaggregation power consumption. This model has been used to solve the *N-Queens* [11] problem and the *Resource-Constraint Project Scheduling Problem* [12].

3 Description of the New Model for CSP Problems

This section describes the model proposed in [11] for solving CSP problems. This model is composed by three important aspects:

1. *Smaller Decision Graph*: in this model the decision graph is smaller than then ones generated in the approaches described in the previous section. This is due to the fact that in the new model the resulting graph contains a node per variable involved in the problem (independently of the different values that can be assigned to this variable).
2. *New Ants Behaviour*: the behaviour of the ants in the classical approaches (Roli et al., Solnon and Khan et al.) is simple: ants only travel through the graph. The action of visiting a node corresponds to an assignment of a value to a variable, because both (variable and value) are encoded in the node. In the new approach, ants have a slightly more complex behaviour, because when the ants arrive to a certain node, they have to select a value for the corresponding variable taking into account their own local solution and the different restrictions involved in the problem.
3. *The Oblivion Rate Meta-Heuristic*: the simplification in the size of the decision graph entails a fast growth in the number of pheromones created by the ants. For this reason, a new meta-heuristic has been included in the system for controlling the number of created pheromones.

This model can be used to solve any CSP problem as the one behind the NILM problem central to this paper. The rationale for formulating the NILM problem as a CSP instance lies on the triple $\langle X, D, C \rangle$ where, in the NILM case, X is the set of appliances contained in the house and D denotes the times of the day at which the different appliances can be turned on. Finally, C limits that the maximum consumption at an specific time can not exceed the power consumption registered by the smart meter or, for example, that two different ovens are not intuitively expected to be used at the same time. Taking into account this description of the NILM problem as a CSP, the resulting graph contains a node per appliance. The edges of the graph connects the different nodes to allow ants to explore the start of different appliances and its compliance with the metric. Note that by using the classical approach (i.e. to represent that a single appliance can be turned on at e.g. any minute of a day), a total of 1440 nodes per appliance would be obtained. Nowadays, smart meters that register the power consumption per seconds are available in the market, and tens of appliances can be easily found in domestic houses. Consequently, the size of the resulting graph would be unmanageable.

Ants selects randomly the node their going to visit taking into account their local solution built so far, the heuristic function of the problem, and the pheromones deposited in the graph. In this work, the heuristic function corresponds to the difference between the power registered by the smart meter and the power consumption generated by the solution built by the ant. More formally, given the power consumption registered by the smart meter at time t (denoted as $P(t)$) and the historic power consumption generated by the ants solution up to time t (denoted as $(S(t))$), the heuristic function used in this work favours those appliances whose power consumption at time t $(a(t))$ approximates $S(t)$ to $P(t)$, i.e. $P(t) - (S(t) + a(t))$ is minimum.

Regarding the *Oblivion Rate* meta-heuristic, in this initial work there is no need to control the number of pheromones because in the experimental phase controlled experiments have been carried out focused on the study about the applicability of ACO algorithm to solve NILM problems.

4   Experiments and Discussion

This section presents the different experiments carried out in this work. As previously highlighted, the goal of this work is to test whether the ACO model proposed in [11] can be applied to NILM problems. To this end, the first step is to obtain a valid dataset with real measurements. We have selected the REDD database [16] from the set of open databases available in the Internet. This database stores the power consumption of 6 different houses during 1 month. For each house, the database contains the power readings of the two power mains and the individual circuits for the house. The individual circuits (the ones used in this work) contains the apparent power logged once every three seconds. In this work, we have used the dataset corresponding to `house2`, from which we have identified the individual power consumption for some of the appliances, specifically the refrigerator, the stove, the dishwasher, the disposal and the kitchen outlets. Figure 1(a) exemplifies this set of extracted signatures by depicting that obtained for the dishwasher via a thresholded amplitude gain detection procedure.

Once these individual signatures have been extracted, we have combined them to create several artificially aggregated power consumption of 20 houses during 1 day (i.e. 28800 measurements). For the simplicity of this initial study, we have assumed that there is not more than 1 appliance of each class in the house. This means that, for example, two refrigerators are not allowed to turn on at the same time. Each appliance can be turned on a certain maximum number of times in a day: disposal (2), dishwasher (3), outlets (5) and stove (2). Note that the refrigerator is assumed to be always on. In this work, we have generated a synthetic consumption of 20 instead of using the real data provided in the REDD database, because the goal of this preliminary work is to test the applicability of the described ACO model to NILM problems. For this reason, we need some controlled and reduced experiments to understand the practical behaviour of the system. Figure 1(b) shows one of the produced daily power consumption profiles.

Once we have generated the global power consumption of the houses, the ACO model is built. As shown in Fig. 2 the decision graph is composed by 6 nodes, each representing one of the 5 different appliances taken into account

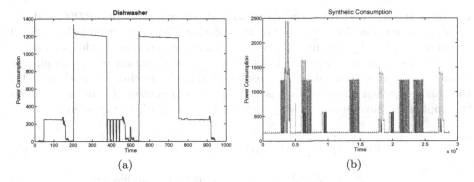

Fig. 1. (a) Evolution of the power consumption of the dishwasher; (b) One of the 20 synthetically generated power consumption profiles.

plus an additional appliance that stands for the initial status of the house when no appliance is on. Since we are dealing with 5 appliances and 28800 different timesteps (3 second sampling rate), by using the classical representation and the previous reasoning the resulting graph would amount up to 144000 nodes and 2.073×10^{10} edges.

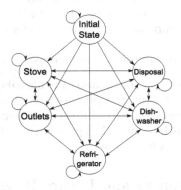

Fig. 2. Decision graph created in this work for the NILM problem using the approach described in [11].

Finally, the ACO algorithm is executed with 100 ants, 200 iterations, evaporation rate equal to 0.05, $\alpha = 1$, $\beta = 2$ and 10 repetitions. The evaporation rate defines the decrease speed of the pheromone values per step to permit bad solutions to disappear from the graph. Finally, α and β are parameters that measures the influence of the heuristic value (α) and the pheromones (β) on the decision process.

The evaluation of the quality of the produced solutions is given by the *mean square error* and the *precision* of the algorithm. The mean square error (MSE) measures the different between the registered power consumption $P(t)$ and the power consumption $S(t)$ furnished by the solution of the ant over the $N = 28800$ samples measured by the smart meter. The precision is defined as the percentage of appliances correctly identified. The correct identification of any appliance results in the identification of the appliance (i.e. the kitchen outlets) but also the timestep when the appliance is turned on. A precision of 1 means that all the appliances have been correctly identified. Mathematically speaking:

$$\text{MSE} \doteq \frac{1}{N} \sum_{i=1}^{N} |P(t) - S(t)|^2 \tag{1}$$

$$\text{Precision} \doteq \frac{\text{Number of correctly detected appliances}}{\text{Total number of appliances in the daily profile}} \tag{2}$$

The performed experimental results over the synthetically produced profiles revealed that the proposed ACO model was able to fully solve 18 out of the posed 20 disaggregation problems with MSE = 0 and Precision = 1. In general the system gets the true solution in the early phase of the algorithm (initial steps). This was expected due to the following conditions:

1. The system operates on a reduced dataset in terms of number of appliances.
2. The global power consumption is generated using the individual signatures of the appliances and we do not consider different consumption profiles for the same appliance, nor do we address any variable-length power signature.
3. The global power consumption is generated only for one day (28800 measurements).
4. The generated power consumption is not subject to background noise.

All these characteristics ease significantly the identification of the appliances, yet still permits to conclude that the proposed ACO model can be applied to the NILM problem. Furthermore, the obtained results shed light on the practical applicability of this approach to the NILM problem and its expected performance when the above assumptions are removed.

5   Concluding Remarks and Future Research

The disaggregation of power consumption profiles is a area that is gaining momentum in the research community due to the plethora of applications and benefits for companies and customers stemming from the identification of customers' behavioral profiles in terms of energy consumption. In particular this paper has focused on the so-called Non-Intrusive Load Monitoring problem, which can be casted as to find the set of appliances of a certain energy consumer and their on/off instants based exclusively on its overall measured consumption.

This paper has elaborated on the applicability of the ACO algorithm for NILM problems. First of all, the problem has been shown to yield a Constraint Satisfaction Problem (CSP) where the set of variables are the different appliances, the values corresponds to the timestep when the appliances can be turned on and the constraint limits the maximum power consumption per timestep. The ACO model for solving CSP proposed in [11] has been put to practice in this application scenario. This model creates a decision graph with a node per each appliance in the house being analyzed.

An individual power consumption signature for each appliance has been extracted from the selected REDD dataset, from which the power consumption of 20 different houses during one day has been artificially generated by taking into account the different appliances. Experimental results reveals that the ACO model can correctly disaggregate 18 out of 20 power consumptions.

Future work will be devoted to (1) the utilization of real power consumption during a longer time; and (2) the usage of Big Data functionalities (e.g. SPARK) to implement distributed, computationally efficient versions of the ACO algorithm aimed at accommodating the disaggregation of concurrently arriving meter data. Also will be of interest to assess the influence of measurement noise on the performance of the ACO algorithm and whether the Oblivion Rate meta-heuristic is needed.

Acknowledgements. This work is supported by the Spanish Ministry of Science and Education under grant number TIN2014-56494-C4-4-P, the Comunidad Autonoma de Madrid under the CIBERDINE project (S2013/ICE-3095), Airbus Defense & Space projects FUAM-076914 and FUAM-076915, and the Basque Government under the Etortek Programme.

References

1. Baranski, M., Voss, J.: Genetic algorithm for pattern detection in nialm systems. In: Proceedings of IEEE International Conference System, Man Cybernetics, vol. 4, pp. 3462–3468 (2004)
2. Chang, H.-H., Lin, L.-S., Chen, N., Lee, W.-J.: Particle-swarm-optimization-based nonintrusive demand monitoring and load identification in smart meters. IEEE Trans. Ind. Appl. **49**(5), 2229–2236 (2013)
3. Chicco, G., Napoli, R., Piglione, F.: Comparison among clustering techniques for eleelectric customer classification. IEEE Trans. Power Syst. **21**, 993–940 (2006)
4. Chicco, G., Napoli, R., Piglione, F., Postolache, P., Scutariu, M., Toader, C.: Emergent electricity customer classification. IEEE Gener. Trans. Distrib. **152**, 164–172 (2005)
5. Dorigo, M.: Optimization, Learning and Natural Algorithms (in Italian). Ph.D. thesis, Dipartimento di Elettronica, Politecnico di Milano, Milan, Italy (1992)
6. Egarter, D., Bhuvana, V.P., Elmenreich, W.: Paldi: online load disaggregation via particle filtering. IEEE Trans. Instrum. Meas. **64**(2), 467–477 (2015)
7. Egarter, D., Sobe, A., Elmenreich, W.: Evolving non-intrusive load monitoring. In: Esparcia-Alcázar, A.I. (ed.) EvoApplications 2013. LNCS, vol. 7835, pp. 182–191. Springer, Heidelberg (2013)
8. Eiben, A.E., Ruttkay, Z.S.: Constraint Satisfaction Problems. IOP Publishing Ltd. and Oxford University Press, New York (1997)

9. Gavrilas, M., Gavrilas, G., Sfintes, C.V.: Application of honey bee mating optimization algorithm to load profile clustering. In: 2010 IEEE International Conference on Computational Intelligence for Measurement Systems and Applications (CIMSA), pp 113–118, September 2010

10. Goncalves, H., Ocneanu, A., Berges, M., Fan, R.H.: Unsupervised disaggregation of appliances using aggregated consumption data. In: Proceedings of KDD Workshop Data Mining Applications Sustainability (SustKDD) (2011)

11. Gonzalez-Pardo, A., Camacho, D.: A new csp graph-based representation for ant colony optimization. In: 2013 IEEE Conference on Evolutionary Computation, 20–23 June 2013, vol. 1, pp. 689–696 (2013)

12. Gonzalez-Pardo, A., Camacho, D.: A new csp graph-based representation to resource-constrained project scheduling problem. In: 2014 IEEE Conference on Evolutionary Computation (2014, in press)

13. Hart, G.W.: Residential energy monitoring and compcomputer surveillance via utility power flow. IEEE Technol. Soci. Mag. **8**(2), 12–16 (1989)

14. Jota, P.R.S., Silva, V.R.B., Jota, F.G.: Building load management using cluster and statistical analyses. Int. J. Electr. Power Energ. Syst. **33**(8), 1498–1505 (2011)

15. Khan, S., Bilal, M., Sharif, M., Sajid, M., Baig, R.: Solution of n-queen problem using aco. In: IEEE 13th International Multitopic Conference, INMIC 2009 (2009)

16. Kolter, J.Z., Johnson, M.J.: Redd: a public data set for energy disaggregation research. In: SustKDD Workshop on Data Mining Applications in Sustainability (2011)

17. Liang, J., Ng, S.K.K., Kendall, G., Cheng, J.W.M.: Load signature study - part i: Basic concepts, structure, and methodology. IEEE Trans. Power Deliv. **25**(2), 551–560 (2010)

18. Lin, G.-Y., Lee, S.-C., Hsu, J.Y.-J., Jih, W.-R.: Applying power meters for appliance recognition on the electric panel. In: Proceedings of 5th IEEE Conference Industrial Electronics Applications (ICIEA), pp. 398–405 (2010)

19. López, J.J., Aguado, J.A., Martín, F., Munoz, F., Rodríguez, A., Ruiz, J.E.: Electric customer classification using hopfield recurrent ann. In: Proceedings of 5th International Conference on the European Electricity Market (EEM08) (2008)

20. López, J.J., Aguado, J.A., Martín, F., Munoz, F., Rodríguez, A., Ruiz, J.E.: Hopfield-k-means clustering algorithm: a proposal for the segmentation of electricity customers. Electr. Power Syst. Res. **81**(2), 716–724 (2011)

21. Roli, A., Blum, C., Dorigo, M.: ACO for maximal constraint satisfaction problems. In: Proceedings of MIC'2001 - Metaheuristics International Conference, vol. 1, pp. 187–191. Porto, Portugal (2001)

22. Shaw, S.R., Leeb, S.B., Norford, L.K., Cox, R.W.: Nonintrusive load monitoring and diagnosis in power systems. IEEE Trans. Instrum. Meas. **57**(7), 1445–1454 (2008)

23. Solnon, C.: Ants can solve constraint satisfaction problems. IEEE Trans. Evol. Comput. **6**, 347–357 (2002)

24. Solnon, C.: Ant Colony Optimization and Constraint Programming. Wiley-ISTE, UK (2010)

25. Srinivasan, D., Ng, W.S., Liew, A.C.: Neural-network-based signature recognition for harmonic source identification. IEEE Trans. Power Deliv. **21**(1), 2254–2259 (2010)

26. Sum, Y.M., Wang, C.L., Zhang, Z.S., Liu, S.: Clustering analysis of power systems load series based on ant colony optimization algorithm. In: Proceedings of the Csee, pp. 40–45 (2005)

27. Tsang, E.P.K.: Foundations of Constraint Satisfaction. Computation in Cognitive Science. Academic Press, London (1993)
28. Tsekouras, G.J., Kotoulas, P.B., Tsirekis, C.D., Dialynas, E.N., Hatziargyrou, N.D.: A pattern recognition methodology for evaluation of load profiles and typical days of large electricity customers. Electr. Power Syst. Res. **78**, 1494–1510 (2008)
29. Valero, S., Ortiz, M., Senabre, S., Gabaldón, A., García, F.: Classification, filtering and identification of electrical customer load patterns through the use of self-organizing maps. IEEE Trans. Power Syst. **21**, 1672–1682 (2006)
30. Zaidi, A.A., Kupzog, F., Zia, T., Palensky, P.: Load recognition for automated demand response in microgrids. In: Proceedings 36th Annual Conference IEEE Industrial Electronics Society (IECON), pp. 2242–2447 (2010)

Beyond Unfeasibility: Strategic Oscillation for the Maximum Leaf Spanning Tree Problem

Jesús Sánchez-Oro(✉) and Abraham Duarte

Universidad Rey Juan Carlos, Madrid, Spain
{jesus.sanchezoro,abraham.duarte}@urjc.es

Abstract. Given an undirected and connected graph, the maximum leaf spanning tree problem consists in finding a spanning tree with as many leaves as possible. This $\mathcal{NP}$-hard problem has practical applications in telecommunication networks, circuit layouts, and other graph-theoretic problems. An interesting application appears in the context of broadcasting in telecommunication networks, where it is interesting to reduce the number of broadcasting computers in the network. These components are relatively expensive and therefore its is desirable to deploy as few of them as possible in the network. This optimization problem is equivalent to maximize the number of non-broadcasting computers. We present a strategic oscillation approach for solving the maximum leaf spanning tree problem. The results obtained by the proposed algorithm are compared with the best previous algorithm found in the literature, showing the superiority of our proposal.

Keywords: Telecommunication networks · Broadcasting · Spanning tree · Strategic oscillation

1 Introduction

Soft Computing is a discipline with the aim of solving optimization problems using a set of techniques such fuzzy logic, neural networks, or evolutionary computing, among others. Most of real world problems can be formulated as optimization problems. These real-life optimization problems are usually hard to solve because they have many local optima, making traditional methods to fall in local optima traps, from where is hard to escape. Besides exact methods, that can be only used for moderate size problems, there exists many approximation techniques for obtaining high quality solutions. Metaheuristics emerge as a set of methodologies which provide near optimal solutions in reasonable computing time. Some of the most used metaheuristics are GRASP [5,6], Tabu Search [3,15], Variable Neighborhood Search [17,21], and Scatter Search with Path Relinking [18,20], among others. Metaheuristics have been successfully applied to a large variety of optimization problems, such as the bipartite unconstrained 0–1 quadratic programming problem [3], the differential dispersion minimization problem [4], or the maximally diverse grouping problem [11].

© Springer International Publishing Switzerland 2015
J.M. Puerta et al. (Eds.): CAEPIA 2015, LNAI 9422, pp. 322–331, 2015.
DOI: 10.1007/978-3-319-24598-0_29

In this paper we focus on the maximum leaf spanning tree problem (MLSTP), which can be theoretically described as follows. Given an undirected and connected graph $G = (V, E)$, where V is the set of vertices and E the set of edges, the MLSTP consists of finding a spanning tree with as many leaves as possible. MLSTP can be trivially solved for complete graphs, since any spanning tree has the same number of leaves. However, it is $\mathcal{NP}$-hard for the general case [12]. Several approximation algorithms for the MLSTP have been proposed, being two approximation algorithms of factor 3 and 2 [19,22], respectively, the most relevant approaches. The problem has also been studied from an exact perspective [10] with an algorithm based on an original formulation previously proposed [7]. Finally, a new formulation and polyhedral investigation has been proposed in [9].

The MLSTP has practical applications in telecommunication networks, circuit layouts, and other graph-theoretic problems [23]. An interesting application for the MLSTP emerges in the context of broadcasting in telecommunication networks. Given a communication network, each computer in it must be able to transmit information to any other connected computer. Since not all computers are connected among them, it is necessary to add a special component in some computers of the network which transform them in broadcasting computers. This component permits the communication among those computers that are directly connected to it. Figure 1 shows an example with four different computers (A, B, C, and D), where there are three physical links ($A - D$, $B - D$, and $C - D$) represented with solid black lines. If we consider that computer D hosts a broadcasting component, then three new connections (represented with dotted lines) are created ($A - B$, $A - C$, and $B - C$).

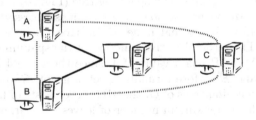

Fig. 1. The insertion of broadcasting computer D permits the communication between $A - B$, $A - C$ and $B - C$ (represented with dotted lines)

The price of these components is relatively expensive so it is important to reduce the number of broadcasting computers in a network in order to reduce its cost. This problem is equivalent to maximize the number of non-broadcasting computers in the network, which directly corresponds to MLSTP [8].

If we now analyze the problem from a theoretical point of view, the network can be represented with an undirected connected graph, where vertices and edges correspond to computers and physical links, respectively. If the graph is complete, then there is no need to add broadcasting computers. However, in the general case (sparse graphs), it is necessary to add one or more broadcasting

computers in order to communicate every pair of computers in the network. If
we construct a spanning tree of the corresponding graph, we can see that hosting
a broadcasting computer in each internal node, results in a fully communicated
network. Then, the main objective is to reduce the number of internal nodes of
the spanning tree, or equivalently, to maximize the number of leaves of the tree
(i.e., the maximum leaf spanning tree problem).

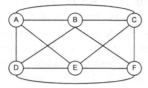   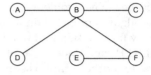

(a) Example of a possible
network represented as
an undirected connected
graph G

(b) Example of a spanning
tree of G with root in B

Fig. 2. Construction of a spanning tree over a network in order to select the broadcasting nodes

Figure 2 shows an example of a network modeled as a graph (Fig. 2a), where
the pairs of vertices that cannot directly communicate between them are (A, F)
(B, E), and (C, D). An example of a spanning tree (Fig. 2b) is constructed starting from vertex B. Analyzing the spanning tree, it is necessary to add a broadcasting computer in each internal node of the tree (i.e., those which are not
leaves, B and F). Then, the objective function of the spanning tree constructed
in Fig. 2b for the MLSTP has a value of 4, since there are 4 leaves in the tree
(vertices A, C, D, and E). More formally, given a graph G and being $\mathbb{T}(G)$ the
set of all possible spanning trees of G, the MLSTP consists of finding a spanning
tree $t^\star \in \mathbb{T}(G)$ with the maximum number of leaves. In mathematical terms,

$$t^\star \leftarrow \underset{t \in \mathbb{T}(G)}{\arg\max} |\{v \in V : \deg(v, t) = 1\}|.$$

where $\deg(v, t)$ represents the degree of the vertex v in tree t.

This problem is closely related to the Minimum Connected Dominating Set
Problem (MCDSP) [16]. Specifically, a subset of vertices of a graph is a dominating set if each edge of the graph has, at least, one endpoint in it. The MCDSP
consist in finding the connected dominating set of minimum cardinality. Notice
that given an optimal connected dominating set for the MCDSP, we can construct a tree over it resulting in an optimal solution for the MLSTP and vice
versa. The MCDSP was also proved to be $\mathcal{NP}$-hard in [12], and several approximation algorithms have been proposed [1,16]. Neither MLSTP nor MCDSP have
been extensively studied from a heuristic point of view.

In this paper, we focus on the maximum leaf spanning tree problem, proposing a heuristic algorithm that follows a strategic oscillation approach (Sect. 2). The computational results and comparisons with previous algorithms are reported in Sect. 3. Finally, the conclusions derived from the research are sketched in Sect. 4.

2 Algorithmic Proposal

The algorithm proposed in this work follows the strategic oscillation methodology (SO) [11,13,14], which is closely related to tabu search. SO focuses the search in relation to a critical level, which is commonly a boundary in which an algorithm would normally stop. However, when reaching that boundary, SO modifies the rules of the search, allowing the algorithm to surpass it and continue the exploration. In the context of MLSTP, we select the feasibility of the solution as the boundary for strategic oscillation. Specifically, the SO algorithm proposed in this paper is intended to explore solutions beyond the feasibility frontier.

2.1 Solution Representation

Given a graph $G = (V, E)$, and a spanning tree T of G, a solution S for the maximum leaf spanning tree problem is represented by the subset of vertices in V, which contains the leaves of the tree. More formally,

$$S \leftarrow \{v \in V : \deg(v, T) = 1\}$$

Alternatively, we define the subset $S' \leftarrow V \setminus S$ as the one that contains those vertices which are internal nodes of T. For example, the solution S for the spanning tree represented in Fig. 2b is $S = \{A, C, D, E\}$, while $S' = \{B, F\}$. Notice that the objective function for the MLSTP, which is the number of leaves in T, is evaluated as $|S| = 4$.

We now define the graph $G' = (S', E')$, as the subgraph derived from G which contains the vertices in S' and the edges among them. In mathematical terms, the set of edges is defined as,

$$E' \leftarrow \{(u, v) \in E : u, v \in S'\}$$

The feasibility of a solution S is determined by two conditions. First of all, since S' represents the internal nodes of the spanning tree, the graph $G' = (S', E')$ must be connected. The second condition assures that every vertex in S is connected, at least, to one vertex in S', in order to assure that S contains the leaves of the tree. More formally,

$$\forall v \in S \quad \exists u \in S' : (u, v) \in E.$$

2.2 Constructive Procedure

The constructive procedure is intended to create a promising starting point for a search procedure. Instead of starting from a random solution, this procedure tries to maximize the number of vertices in S, avoiding the exploration of low quality solutions. The constructive algorithm builds the corresponding solution in a greedy manner. The procedure starts by considering all vertices in S (i.e., $S = V$). The method then selects the vertex with the largest degree in G. It becomes the root of the spanning tree under construction and it is removed from S and inserted in S'. Then, a candidate list is created with the adjacent vertices of the root. The vertices in the candidate list are evaluated according to the greedy function, g, defined as:

$$g(v) \leftarrow |N(v) \cap S| - |N(v) \cap S'|$$

where $N(v) = \{u \in V : (v, u) \in E\}$ is the set of adjacent vertices to v.

In each iteration, the method selects the vertex $v^\star$ from the candidate list with the largest g-value updating accordingly sets S and S'. In the next iteration, the candidate list is updated with the adjacent vertices to $v^\star$ which belong to S. The method stops when the feasibility conditions defined in Sect. 2.1 are satisfied. Notice that the first feasibility condition is maintained during the construction, since the candidates are selected among the adjacency of vertices which are already in S'.

2.3 Strategic Oscillation

Before defining the strategic oscillation algorithm, it is necessary to define the type of moves used in the search. In particular, for the MLSTP, we propose two different moves. The first move, defined as $\mathrm{drop}(v, S)$, consists of removing a vertex v from S, inserting it in S'. The second one, defined as $\mathrm{add}(v, S)$, inserts the vertex v in the solution S, removing it from S'. In mathematical terms,

$$\mathrm{drop}(v, S) = \begin{cases} S & \leftarrow S \setminus \{v\} \\ S' & \leftarrow S' \cup \{v\} \end{cases} \quad \mathrm{add}(v, S) = \begin{cases} S & \leftarrow S \cup \{v\} \\ S' & \leftarrow S' \setminus \{v\} \end{cases}$$

The drop-move never results in an unfeasible solution, since removing a vertex from S (i.e., a leaf of the spanning tree) does not break any feasible condition. Specifically, if we drop a vertex from S, all vertices in S remain connected to at least one vertex in S', and subgraph $G' = (S', E')$ remains connected. On the other hand, it is difficult to perform an add-move without obtaining an unfeasible solution. In particular, adding a vertex to S (and removing it from S') can eventually disconnect the subgraph G'. Furthermore, the second condition of feasibility is broken if there is any vertex in S whose only adjacent in S' is the added vertex. Notwithstanding, only add moves are able to improve the quality of a solution, since they increase the size of S, which determines the value of the objective function. In other words, adding vertices to S increases the number of leaves of the corresponding tree. However, dropping vertices from S would only reduce the number of leaves in the tree, and, therefore, the quality of the solution is deteriorated. For that reason, the strategic oscillation takes on special significance, since traditional improving methods would quickly find a basin of attraction from which is difficult to scape.

The main idea behind strategic oscillation is based on giving the algorithm the opportunity to explore unfeasible solutions and then bring them back to feasibility. Specifically, the search performed by the SO algorithm is based on adding some vertices to S with add moves (which leads to unfeasible solutions), and then repair the solution by dropping new vertices until the incumbent solution becomes feasible. Then, a solution is improved if and only if the number of added vertices is larger than the number of dropped ones. The number of vertices that are added in each iteration is determined by the parameter k, which indicates how far a solution is from feasibleness. Specifically, the oscillation strategy allows the procedure to visit solutions close to the feasibility region (small values of k), when it finds improvement moves, or far away from the feasibility region (large values of k) when no improvement is found.

Algorithm 1. Strategic Oscillation$(G = (V, E), k_{\text{step}}, k_{\text{max}})$

1: $S \leftarrow \text{Construct}(G)$
2: $S' \leftarrow V \setminus S$
3: $k \leftarrow k_{\text{step}}$
4: **while** $k \leq k_{\text{max}}$ **do**
5:      $\Delta^+ \leftarrow \emptyset, \Delta^- \leftarrow \emptyset$
6:      **for** $i = 1$ to $k * |S'|$ **do**
7:          $v \leftarrow \text{SelectRandom}(S')$
8:          $\text{add}(v, S)$
9:          $\Delta^+ \leftarrow \Delta^+ \cup \{v\}$
10:     **end for**
11:     **while not** feasible(S) **do**
12:         $v^* \leftarrow \arg\max_{v \in S} |N(v) \cap S| - |N(v) \cap S'|$
13:         $\text{drop}(v^*, S)$
14:         $\Delta^- \leftarrow \Delta^- \cup \{v^*\}$
15:     **end while**
16:     **if** $|\Delta^+| > |\Delta^-|$ **then**
17:         $k \leftarrow k_{\text{step}}$
18:     **else**
19:         $k \leftarrow k + k_{\text{step}}$
20:         $S \leftarrow S \cup \Delta^- \setminus \Delta^+$
21:         $S' \leftarrow S' \cup \Delta^+ \setminus \Delta^-$
22:     **end if**
23: **end while**

Algorithm 1 depicts the pseudocode of the strategic oscillation method proposed in this paper. It starts by constructing the initial solution with the greedy procedure described in Sect. 2.2 (step 1). SO is parametrized by k_{max} and k_{step}. The former indicates the maximum distance to feasibility that the algorithm is allowed to reach, while the latter represents the increment of that distance in each iteration. Starting from $k = k_{\text{step}}$ (step 3), SO iterates until reaching the maximum value of k (steps 4–23). For each iteration, the algorithm adds k vertices at random to the current solution (steps 6–10). At this step of the algorithm, the solution has become unfeasible, so it needs to be repaired by dropping vertices until it becomes feasible again (steps 11–15). Notice that the selection of the next vertex to be dropped follows the same greedy criterion than the constructive procedure (step 12), which consists of selecting the vertex that maximizes the g-value (see Sect. 2.2). Finally, if the number of added vertices is lower than the number of dropped vertices, then an improved solution has been found, so the algorithm oscillates again closer to the feasibility by reducing k to the minimum value (step 17). On the other hand, if no improvement has been found, SO oscillates further from feasibility by increasing the value of k (step 19). In this case, the performed moves are undone by dropping the added vertices and vice versa (steps 20–21). The algorithm stops when reaching the furthest point from feasibility ($k_{\max}$) without finding an improvement, returning the best solution found.

3   Experimental Results

In this section we analyze the efficiency and effectiveness of the proposed algorithm when tackling the MLSTP. All the algorithms were coded in Java 8 and the experiments were conducted on an Intel Core i7 920 CPU (2.67 GHz) and 8GB RAM. The best previous work found in the literature [4] was originally proposed for solving a problem where the objective function is equivalent to minimize the number of internal nodes in a spanning tree, so the results can be directly adapted to the MLSTP [2].

In order to make a fair comparison, we have used in this work the publicly available instances[1] already used in previous works [2,4]. The instances correspond to 480 randomly generated networks. Each instance is generated based on two parameters: the number of nodes in the network (n) and the percentage of pairs which cannot share information in the network (p). Specifically, the values for n ranges from 40 to 500 and the values for p ranges from 10 % to 90 %. The computational experiments are divided into two parts: the preliminary experimentation and the final experimentation. The former is intended to select the best parameters for the proposed algorithm, and it uses a subset of 200 representative instances in order to avoid over-training, while the latter is devoted to compare the quality of our proposal against the best previous method [4]. The testbed is split into small instances ($k \leq 100$) and large instances ($k > 100$).

The preliminary experimentation is intended to set the best values for the parameters of the algorithm: k_{step} and $k_{\max}$. In particular, we performed a full-factorial design for a specific range of $k_{\text{step}} = \{0.01n, 0.05n, 0.10n\}$ and $k_{\max} = \{0.25n, 0.50n, 1.00n\}$ values, being n the number of vertices in the graph.

Table 1 shows the results obtained for the considered values of k_{step} and $k_{\max}$. The results are divided into small and large instances, reporting individual results for each n are shown, with the best value found highlighted in gray. The best results are consistently obtained when $k_{\max} = 1.00$. This value produces the furthest solutions from unfeasibility, which endorses the use of strategic

---

[1] http://homepage.univie.ac.at/ivana.ljubic/research/rlp/.

Table 1. Parameter tunning for the strategic oscillation algorithm over a subset of 200 representative instances. The best value for each n is highlighted in gray.

n		40		60		80		100		n		200		300		400		500	
k_{max}	k_{step}	MLSTP	Time (s)	MLSTP	Time (s)	MLSTP	Time (s)	MLSTP	Time (s)	k_{max}	k_{step}	MLSTP	Time (s)	MLSTP	Time (s)	MLSTP	Time (s)	MLSTP	Time (s)
	0.01	35.68	0.01	55.00	0.03	75.36	0.06	94.96	0.12		0.01	191.43	1.53	291.24	4.65	387.60	17.59	493.26	16.84
0.25	0.05	35.63	0.01	54.96	0.01	75.36	0.02	94.92	0.04	0.25	0.05	191.43	0.72	291.24	2.36	387.60	9.80	493.22	8.80
	0.10	35.63	0.01	54.96	0.01	75.36	0.02	94.92	0.03		0.10	191.43	0.57	291.24	1.84	387.60	8.17	493.22	7.76
	0.01	35.84	0.03	55.11	0.10	75.43	0.17	94.96	0.32		0.01	191.48	4.99	291.29	15.48	387.65	57.26	493.26	51.88
0.50	0.05	35.68	0.01	55.19	0.03	75.46	0.05	94.96	0.09	0.50	0.05	191.43	1.46	291.26	4.72	387.65	18.86	493.26	16.10
	0.10	35.68	0.01	55.00	0.02	75.43	0.03	94.96	0.06		0.10	191.43	0.99	291.24	3.17	387.60	13.21	493.26	11.82
	0.01	35.84	0.11	55.22	0.36	75.54	0.67	95.08	1.39		0.01	191.83	25.11	291.53	74.40	388.00	358.49	493.48	306.62
1.00	0.05	35.79	0.02	55.19	0.07	75.46	0.13	95.04	0.29	1.00	0.05	191.65	4.96	291.41	15.53	387.75	61.14	493.26	62.89
	0.10	35.79	0.01	55.15	0.05	75.46	0.08	95.04	0.17		0.10	191.61	2.98	291.38	9.72	387.75	39.57	493.26	37.47

oscillation for the MLSTP. Among the variants with $k_{max} = 1.00$, the best one is obtained when $k_{step} = 0.01$, which results in a fine-grained exploration of the solution space, since the distance from feasibility is increased in only 0.01 units in each iteration. As it can be seen in the results, the increment in the size of k_{step} results in a faster algorithm, but producing worse solutions. However, the computing time remains reasonable even for the lowest variant (which is the best one in quality), requiring on average less than one second per vertex in the graph. For that reason, we select $k_{step} = 0.01$ and $k_{max} = 1.00$ for the comparison with the best previous method.

The final experiment is intended to compare the efficiency and effectiveness of the proposed algorithm when compared with the best previously published method, which corresponds with the GRASP algorithm originally proposed for the RLP [4]. The complete set of instances used in this work is not publicly available, so we have executed the same original code over the whole set of instances in the same computer, in order to provide a fair comparison.

Table 2 shows the comparison between the proposed SO algorithm and the previous best method (GRASP). Again, results from small and large instances are reported independently. Additionally to the number of vertices, in this case we add the value of p for each subset of instances. Notice that for a given number

Table 2. Comparison between SO and GRASP algorithms in small (left) and large (right) set of instances

		SO		GRASP				SO		GRASP	
n	p	MLSTP	Time (s)	MLSTP	Time (s)	n	p	MLSTP	Time (s)	MLSTP	Time (s)
	10	38.60	0.02	38.60	0.19		10	58.10	0.06	58.10	0.68
	20	38.00	0.03	38.00	0.22		20	58.00	0.09	58.00	0.83
	30	38.00	0.04	38.00	0.26		30	58.00	0.13	58.00	0.95
	40	37.40	0.06	37.60	0.29		40	37.40	0.06	37.60	0.29
40	50	37.00	0.07	37.00	0.31	60	50	57.00	0.23	57.00	1.17
	60	36.40	0.09	36.60	0.32		60	56.00	0.27	56.00	1.21
	70	35.70	0.12	35.70	0.34		70	55.00	0.36	55.20	1.32
	80	34.40	0.14	34.40	0.36		80	53.20	0.46	53.60	1.48
	90	30.90	0.24	30.50	0.43		90	49.60	0.87	49.60	1.76
	10	78.10	0.13	78.10	1.64		10	98.00	0.23	98.00	3.21
	20	78.00	0.18	78.00	2.07		20	98.00	0.37	98.00	3.83
	30	77.40	0.30	77.70	2.55		30	97.20	0.53	97.30	4.66
	40	77.00	0.37	77.00	2.74		40	97.00	0.73	97.00	5.71
80	50	76.60	0.52	76.80	2.92	100	50	96.00	0.94	96.10	6.21
	60	76.00	0.69	76.00	3.18		60	95.20	1.25	96.00	6.54
	70	74.70	0.97	75.00	3.58		70	94.20	1.76	94.50	7.20
	80	73.00	1.44	73.00	3.88		80	92.60	2.76	92.60	7.95
	90	68.30	1.91	68.80	4.74		90	87.60	3.74	88.00	10.13

		SO		GRASP				SO		GRASP	
n	p	MLSTP	Time (s)	MLSTP	Time (s)	n	p	MLSTP	Time (s)	MLSTP	Time (s)
	10	198.00	1.77	198.00	39.92		10	298.00	5.08	298.00	152.44
	30	197.00	4.40	197.00	55.67		30	297.00	14.94	297.00	228.06
200	50	196.00	9.23	196.00	69.94	300	50	295.10	28.12	295.00	314.53
	70	193.10	15.75	193.00	96.54		70	292.70	64.22	292.40	369.05
	90	184.70	52.11	184.10	153.83		90	282.60	176.29	281.70	599.69
	10	398.00	11.51	398.00	424.57		10	498.00	21.81	498.00	843.94
	30	396.90	35.06	397.00	618.54		30	496.20	70.56	496.90	1258.29
400	50	395.00	71.14	395.00	808.05	500	50	495.00	158.68	495.00	1665.78
	70	392.00	152.25	391.40	1083.14		70	492.00	375.99	491.00	2763.23
	90	381.70	637.53	379.60	1809.32		90	480.10	1456.21	478.00	6240.43

of vertices n, the higher the value of p, the harder the instance, so it is interesting to compare the evolution of both algorithms when considering harder instances. As stated in Table 1, the best results for each n and p are highlighted in gray. The first conclusion we can derive from these results is that the GRASP algorithm is much slower than the SO procedure. Specifically, the time needed by GRASP is six times larger on average than the time required by SO, and this difference increases with the number of vertices of the instance. The GRASP method performs slightly better in small instances, while the superiority of SO is clearly exposed in the set of large instances, showing the scalability of the proposed method when increasing the size and difficulty of the instance. We have conducted the Wilcoxon test to perform a pair-wise comparison between the proposed algorithm and the best previous method. The resulting p-value of 0.002 indicates that there are statistically significant differences between both methods, emerging SO as the best algorithm.

4 Conclusions

In this paper we have presented an algorithm based on the strategic oscillation methodology for solving the maximum leaf spanning tree problem. In particular, we have studied the effect of exploring unfeasible solutions and then bring them back to feasibility through the use of two move operators: add and drop. The algorithm has been compared with a previous method for a problem that can be adapted to the MLSTP over a set of 480 instances of different size and density. The computational results have shown that the proposed SO algorithm outperforms the previous method, based on GRASP methodology, both in quality and computing time. The scalability of the proposal versus the previous method has also been proved when increasing the size of the problems.

Acknowledgments. This research was partially supported by the Ministerio de Economía y Competitividad of Spain (Project Number TIN2012-35632-C02) and the Comunidad de Madrid (Project Number S2013/ICE-2894).

References

1. Butenko, S., Cheng, X., Du, D., Pardalos, P.M.: On the constructionof virtual-backbone for ad hoc wireless network. In: Butenko, S., Murphey, R., Pardalos, P.M. (eds.) Cooperative Control: Models,Applications and Algorithms, Cooperative Systems, vol. 1, pp. 43–54. Springer, US (2003)
2. Chen, S., Ljubić, I., Raghavan, S.: The regenerator location problem. Networks **55**(3), 205–220 (2010)
3. Duarte, A., Laguna, M., Martí, R., Sánchez-Oro, J.: Optimization procedures for the bipartite unconstrained 0–1 quadratic programming problem. Comput. Operat. Res. **51**, 123–129 (2014)
4. Duarte, A., Martí, R., Resende, M., Silva, R.: Improved heuristics for the regenerator location problem. Int. Trans. Oper. Res. **21**(4), 541–558 (2014)

5. Duarte, A., Sánchez-Oro, J., Resende, M., Glover, F., Mart, R.: Greedy randomized adaptive search procedure with exterior path relinking for differential dispersion minimization. Inf. Sci. **296**, 46–60 (2015)
6. Feo, T.A., Resende, M., Smith, S.H.: A greedy randomized adaptive search procedure for maximum independent set. Oper. Res. **42**(5), 860–878 (1994)
7. Fernandes, L.M., Gouveia, L.: Minimal spanning trees with a constraint on the number of leaves. Eur. J. Oper. Res. **104**(1), 250–261 (1998)
8. Fernau, H., Kneis, J., Kratsch, D., Langer, A., Liedloff, M., Raible, D., Rossmanith, P.: An exact algorithm for the maximum leaf spanning tree problem. In: Chen, J., Fomin, F.V. (eds.) IWPEC 2009. LNCS, vol. 5917, pp. 161–172. Springer, Heidelberg (2009)
9. Fujie, T.: The maximum-leaf spanning tree problem: Formulations and facets. Networks **43**(4), 212–223 (2004)
10. Fujie, T.: An exact algorithm for the maximum leaf spanning tree problem. Comput. Oper. Res. **30**(13), 1931–1944 (2003)
11. Gallego, M., Laguna, M., Martí, R., Duarte, A.: Tabu search with strategic oscillation for the maximally diverse grouping problem. J. Oper. Res. Soc. **64**(5), 724–734 (2013)
12. Garey, M.R., Johnson, D.S.: Computers and Intractability: A Guide to the Theory of NP-Completeness. W. H. Freeman and Co., New York (1979)
13. Glover, F.: Heuristics for integer programming using surrogate constraints. Decis. Sci. **8**(1), 156–166 (1977)
14. Glover, F., Laguna, M.: Tabu Search. Kluwer Academic Publishers, Norwell (1997)
15. Glover, F., Laguna, M.: Tabu search. In: Du, D.-Z., Pardalos, P.M. (eds.) Handbook of Combinatorial Optimization, pp. 2093–2229. Springer, US (1999)
16. Guha, S., Khuller, S.: Approximation algorithms for connected dominating sets. Algorithmica **20**(4), 374–387 (1998)
17. Hansen, P., Mladenović, N., Moreno, J.A.: Variable neighbourhood search: methods and applications. Ann. Oper. Res. **175**(1), 367–407 (2010)
18. Laguna, M., Marti, R.: Scatter Search: Methodology and Implementations in C. Kluwer Academic Publishers, Norwell (2002)
19. Lu, H., Ravi, R.: Approximating maximum leaf spanning trees in almost linear time. J. Algorithms **29**(1), 132–141 (1998)
20. Sánchez-Oro, J., Laguna, M., Duarte, A., Martí, R.: Scatter search for the profile minimization problem. Networks **65**(1), 10–21 (2015)
21. Sánchez-Oro, J., Pantrigo, J.J.: Duarte: Combining intensification and diversification strategies in vns. an application to the vertex separation problem. Comput. Oper. Res. **52**(Pt. B(0)), 209–219 (2014)
22. Solis-Oba, R.: 2-approximation algorithm for finding a spanning tree with maximum number of leaves. In: Bilardi, G., Pietracaprina, A., Italiano, G.F., Pucci, G. (eds.) ESA 1998. LNCS, vol. 1461, pp. 441–452. Springer, Heidelberg (1998)
23. Storer, J.: Constructing full spanning trees for cubic graphs. Inf. Process. Lett. **13**(1), 8–11 (1981)

An Evolutionary Algorithm to Generate Real Urban Traffic Flows

Daniel H. Stolfi$^{(\boxtimes)}$ and Enrique Alba

LCC, University of Malaga, Málaga, Spain
{dhstolfi,eat}@lcc.uma.es

Abstract. In this article we present a strategy based on an evolutionary algorithm to calculate the real vehicle flows in cities according to data from sensors placed in the streets. We have worked with a map imported from OpenStreetMap into the SUMO traffic simulator so that the resulting scenarios can be used to perform different optimizations with the confidence of being able to work with a traffic distribution close to reality. We have compared the results of our algorithm to other competitors and achieved results that replicate the real traffic distribution with a precision higher than 90 %.

Keywords: Evolutionary algorithm · Traffic simulation · SUMO · Smart mobility · Smart city

1 Introduction

Road traffic related problems have been studied frequently in the last decades. Several published articles are based on traffic simulations and, if the city modeled is big enough, the need for not only real maps, but also real traffic distribution is obligatory in order to obtain valid conclusions.

Therefore, a traffic flow study is an important aspect to be taken into account when modeling scenarios based on real maps. These maps can later be used to optimize traffic light cycles [12], to study the placement of LED Panels throughout the city [14], to reroute vehicles with the aim of reducing travel times [13], and for many other uses in smart mobility [1,5,6,9].

Usually, local councils publish data about traffic (and other useful information about the city), under a smart city initiative: the so called *Open Data*. Within this information we can find origin-destination matrices, main vehicle flows, or the number of vehicles at specific measurement points. When these data are available they can be used to analyze drivers' habits, predict traffic congestion, or model a real traffic distribution consisting of traffic flows that match the real values.

The problem we are solving here consists in calculating the best vehicle flows on a real map so that the number of vehicles counted in several measurement points are as close as possible to the data available from the local council. Our proposal is a new strategy based on an evolutionary algorithm which is able to

© Springer International Publishing Switzerland 2015
J.M. Puerta et al. (Eds.): CAEPIA 2015, LNAI 9422, pp. 332–343, 2015.
DOI: 10.1007/978-3-319-24598-0_30

calculate several traffic flows based just on a few measurement points, so that it can reproduce the real traffic, which in addition to a real map imported from OpenStreetMap, achieves instances for traffic study which are close to reality.

2 Related Work

There are many studies (see survey in [2]) which focus on the estimation of origin-destination matrix based on traffic counting locations. They can be static [7,8] or dynamic [3,10]. However, these algorithms assume that all link costs are available, which may not be true in practical situations such as our case study. Unfortunately, authors do not usually detail the scalability of their algorithms for larger networks, which is a key issue for the interest in their solutions.

In [15] a Hopfield Neural Network (HNN) model is used to estimate the urban origin-destination distribution matrix. The author claims that due to the ability of quick computation, parallel distributed processing and hardware realization of neural networks, it is possible to overcome the difficulties of mathematical optimization models. He finds the global optimal solution to the problem and experiments on a graph made of just five nodes representing the same number of zones. To the contrary, our method focuses on individual streets rather than zones (finer grain, higher realism) and we need to route vehicles via individual streets. Consequently, there are several routes available between measurement points in which the vehicles are counted. Therefore, we need to use a different technique to calculate the flows.

An open-source software, called TrafficModeler, is presented in [11]. This program implements a traffic definition model describing traffic via a set of traffic layers placed over a road network. By using those layers it is possible to represent specific traffic patterns associated with different attributes. Additionally, traffic flows can be obtained from virtual populations based on demographic data (i.e. transportation between home, school and work). This tool for modeling traffic flows differs from our proposal in that it cannot be applied when the only source of data is the number of vehicles measured by sensors.

Finally, there are two utilities included in the SUMO [4] software package called ACTIVITYGEN and DFROUTER. The former computes the mobility wishes for a group of citizens matching a map, while the latter uses values from induction loops (sensors) to compute vehicle routes. ACTIVITYGEN is quite similar in some aspects to the aforementioned article, analyzed in this section, although it does not provide a graphic user interface. DFROUTER is a tool that may be used in the same way as the work we present in this article, however, it assumes that the map is completely covered by sensors, especially on its borders, and it requires the exact timestamp in which vehicles were detected and their speed in all the measurement points. None of these options are suitable for the problem we are solving as they cannot be applied to calculate the traffic flows in the city based on just the number of vehicles counted by each sensor.

3   Problem Description

The aim of this article is to present a new strategy to generate traffic distributions in a city by using the data previously collected from sensors which count vehicles in a few streets. It is based on an evolutionary algorithm especially adapted to work with the difficulties that are present in this problem, such as high complexity due to the high number of vehicles and large scenarios, long evaluation times, and the high probability of traffic jams occurring in an actual city scenario when the number of vehicles moving through its streets increases.

Furthermore, as is the case in many cities of the world, we do not have access to the actual vehicle flows, as this information is often not known (or not published) by the city traffic authorities. However, our algorithm is capable of dealing with this drawback by modifying the number of vehicles in each flow, in order to match the number counted by the sensors at several points of the simulated city, increasing the realism of the simulation.

Let $v^* = (v_1^*, \ldots, v_N^*)$ be a vector containing the values collected from N sensors in the real city, and $v = (v_1, \ldots, v_N)$ a vector containing the values obtained from the evaluation of the city map. Our objective is to minimize the error $e_i = |v_i^* - v_i|, i \in \{1, \ldots, N\}$ by modifying the vehicle flows $f = (f_1, \ldots, f_M)$ in the city.

In short, by looking for appropriate flows (decision variables) we compute estimated flows on a simulator with the goal that they match real measured ones in the city where they are available. Of course, the set of flows contain a subset of proposed ones for the streets where no measurements are available at all, thus allowing the researcher to further study the city by using existing and approximated flows for all streets.

4   Case Study

In order to evaluate our proposal we have selected the downtown of Malaga, Spain, where several vehicle sensors have been installed by the local council. The geographical area under study is delimited to the north by San Bartolomé Street and Ferrándiz Street, to the west by the Guadalmedina River, to the east by Keromnes Street, and to the south by the Mediterranean Sea, which encompasses an area of about $3\,\text{km}^2$.

We imported the selected area from OpenStreetMap into SUMO [4] traffic simulator by using the program NETCONVERT included in the SUMO package so that we could work with a real road distribution consisting of the actual streets, traffic lights, roundabouts, and junctions. Then, we added the measurement points provided by the city council by using SUMO's induction loops (logical resource) in order to collect the number of vehicles in each of these points and compare them to the real ones.

In Fig. 1 the map from OpenStreetMap and a snapshot of the same map imported into SUMO are depicted. Note that the traffic sensors are located at the original positions in which the vehicles are counted.

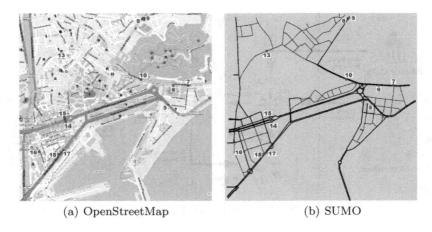

(a) OpenStreetMap   (b) SUMO

Fig. 1. Case study: Center of Malaga, Spain

Finally, we generated estimated flows between the input streets to the area, output streets, and local sources by using the DUAROUTE program included in SUMO to calculate routes by using the travel time as the weight function. All in all, we defined 63 flows, which determined the length of the status vector. Note that each flow consists in a sorted list of streets describing a route between the origin and destination points in the city

In all our results we analyzed the case study for one hour of traffic, as the values from the sensors correspond to this period of time. Additionally, we established a warm up period of 10 min so as not to start our analysis in an empty city, which is rather unrealistic.

5   Flow Generator Algorithm (FGA)

We propose here for the first time a Flow Generator Algorithm (FGA) to find the flows which minimize the differences between the vehicles measured in the city by the sensors and the values obtained after the simulation of the map.

Figure 2 shows the optimization process where we can see that FGA uses the available sensor data and the map from OpenStreetMap as inputs to evaluate individuals by using the SUMO traffic simulator. During the optimization process the algorithm generates and evaluates different individuals which represent the number of vehicles in each flow. Finally, when the optimization ends, the output produced is the number of vehicles in each flow plus the map of the city.

FGA is based on a (10+2)-EA, a steady state EA with a population of ten individuals generating two new individuals at each step. We used Binary Tournament as the selection operator, Uniform Crossover as the recombination operator, and an elitist replacement policy. We used local search instead of mutation after applying the recombination operator because it is necessary to provide extra information to the algorithm to avoid saturating the streets with a number of

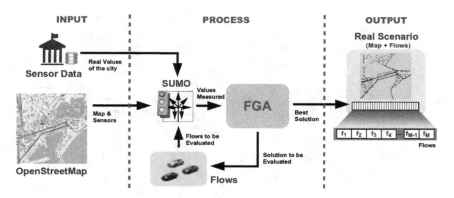

Fig. 2. Optimization Process.

vehicles so large that they will always provoke jams (not enough capacity in the streets). The local search is described later in Sect. 5.3.

5.1 Problem Representation

In Fig. 3 we can see the status vector containing flow values which are actually the number of vehicles that are following each flow. There are 63 flows ($M = 63$) in the case study we are optimizing, each one of the vector's values consists of an integer which can take values of between 10 and 500.

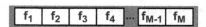

Fig. 3. Status vector containing the number of vehicles for the 63 flows.

5.2 Evaluation Function

Our evaluation function (Eq. 1) assigns a numeric value to a configuration representing the vehicle flows (an individual of the FGA). We calculate the absolute value of the difference between the real values ($v^\star$) measured in the city and the ones (v) collected during the simulation of the map using the flows represented by the individual under evaluation. The fitness value of an individual is calculated by applying the evaluation function so that the numeric value of F is the summation of the absolute values of the differences for all the N sensors. This only happens if $C(v) \leq 0.2$, otherwise, we apply a penalization of a large constant value in the algorithm (infinite) because we are minimizing, so the lower, the better.

$$F(v) = \begin{cases} \sum_{i=1}^{N} |\frac{v_i - v_i^*}{v_i^*}| & \text{if } C(v) \leq 0.2, \\ \infty & \text{if } C(v) > 0.2. \end{cases} \quad (1)$$

$$C(\boldsymbol{v}) = \max\left(\frac{\boldsymbol{v}_i - \boldsymbol{v}_i^*}{\boldsymbol{v}_i^*}\right), i \in \{1, \dots, N\} \tag{2}$$

As we want to avoid traffic jams, we need to keep the number of vehicles in each street low while we target the real value as much as possible by adding vehicles to different flows. To do this, we set a limit of 20 % ($C(\boldsymbol{v}) \leq 0.2$) as the maximum percentage each sensor can exceed the desired one (we have seen that bigger values lead to traffic jams which the algorithm cannot detect). In Eq. 2 we present the calculation of $C(\boldsymbol{v})$ as the maximum difference between the $\boldsymbol{v}_i$ value and the $\boldsymbol{v}_i^*$ one, so that if one of the values obtained from the simulation is higher than 20 % of the real one, the individual is invalidated. This threshold only affects high values while the lower ones are actually considered by the algorithm as we wish to match the desired number of vehicles by incrementing them progressively, preventing street congestions.

5.3 Operators

As we have said, we used Binary Tournament as the selection operator, Uniform Crossover as the recombination operator, and an elitist replacement policy. After applying the recombination operator we applied the local search operator whose pseudocode is shown in Algorithm 1.

Algorithm 1. Local Search

```
procedure LOCALSEARCH(individual,Δ(t))
    v ← calculateSensorValues(individual)
    f ← getFlows(individual)
    for all fᵢ ∈ f do
        if random() ≤ P_LS then
            sensors ← getRelatedSensors(fᵢ)
            s ← selectSensorRND(sensors)
            if v[s] − sensors[s] < 0 then
                incrementVehicles(fᵢ, Δ(t))
            else
                decrementVehicles(fᵢ, Δ(t))
            end if
        end if
    end for
    return individual
end procedure
```

First, the algorithm obtains the number of vehicles measured in each sensor by simulating the scenario with the flow configuration provided by the individual and stores the values in the vector v so that it is able to decide whether the number of vehicles measured by each sensor is under or over the real value. Second, it obtains all the flows from the individual and stores them in the vector f to iterate over it. Third, it selects which flows are modified according to the P_{LS}

parameter. Then, all the sensors which depend on the selected flow f_i are stored in the vector *sensors*, and just one of them is randomly selected and stored in s. This dependency data is available from the case study and depends on the positions of the sensors and the routes of the vehicles which do not change during the optimization process. If more vehicles are needed in the selected measurement point $v[s]$, the number of vehicles in the flow f_i is incremented by $\Delta(t)$, otherwise $v[s]$ is reduced by the same amount $\Delta(t)$. Note that we have set a minimum value of 10 vehicles and a maximum of 500 for each flow, the former, to be sure that all the flows are in use and the latter, as a value sufficiently higher than the maximum obtained in our initial experiments. Finally, after the loop, the local search ends and the individual is returned in order to be evaluated by the fitness function.

The value of $\Delta(t)$ is calculated based on the minimum fitness value of the population according to Eq. 3 so that the lower the fitness value, the lower the variation the algorithm makes to the individual. This mechanism allows us to make big changes when the optimization begins (exploration) and lower ones when the values from the simulation are close to the real ones (exploitation). We have set α equal to 20 as this is the lower bound of $\Delta(t)$ and β equal to 3 in order to control the reduction pace of $\Delta(t)$ as the FGA converges.

$$\Delta(t) = \lceil \alpha * e^{(\min Fitness_i(t))/\beta} \rceil, i \in [1, \lambda], \lambda = 10 \qquad (3)$$

In Fig. 4 we show and example of the local search performed on an individual. First, f_i is selected to be modified. Second, one of the sensors (s_j) whose value depends on the flow f_i is randomly selected. Finally, the number of vehicles in f_i is incremented or decremented according to the number of vehicles counted by s_j in order to be closer to the real value v_j.

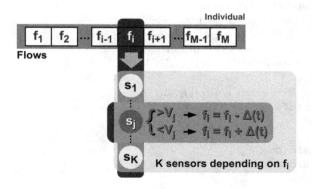

Fig. 4. Local search example.

We have experimentally found the values of the crossover probability ($P_C = 0.9$) and the local search probability ($P_{LS} = 1/L$). The maximum number of generations was set to 3000, however, if the best individual does not change for more than 500 generations, the FGA execution ends.

6   Competitors for Our FGA

In order to evaluate our local search operator, we propose two different alternatives to configure the traffic flows in our case study: (i) Random Search (RS) and (ii) an Evolutionary Algorithm (EA).

6.1   Random Search (RS)

We report the behavior of a pure random algorithm to perform a sanity check on the validity of our FGA. We have implemented Random Search (RS) to obtain configurations of the traffic flows by generating different random configurations, saving the best of them until a better one is found. We have set a limit of 3000 iterations for the search process, the same number as in the FGA.

6.2   Evolutionary Algorithm (EA)

The Evolutionary Algorithm (EA) is exactly the same algorithm as the FGA but for the mutation operator that is used instead of the local search. This operator randomly selects flows according to the mutation probability (P_M) and modifies them with a constant number of vehicles (Γ). However, unlike FGA, the current value of the flow is incremented or decremented with a probability of 0.5, as this operator does not have further knowledge of the sensors affected by each flow. The main idea here is to support our choice of local search operator instead of the mutation one, rather than compete against a basic EA which is clearly unfair. Moreover, the parameters of the EA are the same as the FGA, that is, $P_C = 0.9$, $P_M = 1/L$, $\Gamma = 50$, 3000 generations, and 500 generations as convergence criterion.

7   Results

First, we have conducted the comparison between algorithms in order to analyze the performance of our proposal (FGA). We carried out 30 independent runs of each algorithm optimizing the same scenario and then collected and processed the results which are shown in Table 1. There, we present the average fitness

Table 1. Comparison between algorithm.

Algorithm	Fitness			Friedman	Wilcoxon
	Average	StdDev	Minimum	Rank	*p-value*
RS	2.610	**7.01 %**	2.117	3.00	0.00
EA	0.775	20.22 %	0.541	2.00	0.00
FGA	**0.224**	32.53 %	**0.154**	**1.00**	—

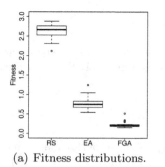

(a) Fitness distributions.

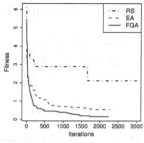

(b) Convergence curves.

Fig. 5. Comparison between the RS, EA, and FGA. We show in the box plot the fitness distribution of the 30 runs of each algorithm on the left, and the convergence curve of the best of those runs on the right.

value, the standard deviation, and the minimum (best) fitness solution. Additionally, we have calculated the Friedman Rank and the Wilcoxon *p-value* in order to know the statistical significance of our results.

We can see that FGA outperforms the rest of algorithms of this comparison as it achieves the lowest fitness (both absolute and on average). Moreover, FGA is the best ranked algorithm for this study, according to the Friedman Rank. Having calculated the Wilcoxon *p-value*, we can say that the values reported are statistically significant.

As was to be expected, RS produces the worst solution because it searches in the solution space without any information of the problem's characteristics. Additionally, the results achieved by EA indicate configurations of the flows far worse than the ones achieved by FGA, which better represents the real city traffic. This confirms that the local search operator proposed (FGA) performs much better than the ordinary mutation implemented in an EA as was expected.

Using the data from the 30 runs performed we have drawn a box plot, shown in Fig. 5(a), to represent the fitness distribution of the algorithms. This figure confirms the differences between the algorithms and how the fitness values of FGA are the lowest ones. Furthermore, in Fig. 5(b) we present the fitness evolution during the best run of each algorithm where the more appropriate behavior of the FGA is clearly depicted.

Second, we have tested the best solution achieved by the FGA by running the simulation of the city with the configuration of the flows according to that solution. In Table 2 we can see the names of the sensors, the same names as given by the local council of Malaga, the real number of vehicles (third four-month period of 2014), the number of vehicles measured in SUMO when we used the flow values calculated by the FGA, and the percentage difference.

We can observe that the differences are under 1 % except for sensor 16 (9.96 %). Moreover, the number of vehicles measured by sensors 7 and 8 in the simulation are exactly the same as in the real world. We have analyzed the anomaly observed in sensor 16 and found that the main source of vehicles for the street

Table 2. Very accurate results found by FGA (best individual) for our case study.

Sensor	Vehicles		Difference
	Real	FGA	
5	1088	1078	−0.92 %
6	349	351	0.57 %
7	289	289	**0.00 %**
8	265	265	**0.00 %**
9	263	265	0.76 %
10	653	648	−0.77 %
13	228	230	0.88 %
14	510	512	0.39 %
15	663	658	−0.75 %
16	522	470	−9.96 %
17	850	852	0.24 %
18	571	570	−0.18 %

in which sensor 16 is placed (see Fig. 1), includes a left-turn intersection controlled by a traffic light. We have observed that many vehicles are waiting at this traffic light so that they cannot reach the sensor during the simulation. We think that a modification of the light cycle of that traffic light is necessary in the simulated map to allow more vehicles to cross the junction and be detected. The analysis of previous optimization processes to be accomplished on the map before launching FGA is part of our future work. In this study we have used the traffic light cycles calculated by the experts from SUMO.

8   Conclusions and Future Work

In this article we have presented a strategy based on an evolutionary algorithm, called FGA, to add vehicle flows to maps imported from OpenStreetMap into the SUMO traffic simulator. As we use the real number of vehicles counted by sensors placed throughout the city, the resulting flows can be used to perform different types of optimizations with the confidence of being able to work with a traffic distribution close to reality.

We have tested our proposal against other competitor algorithms, obtaining results that show the best characteristics of our FGA. Furthermore, we have optimized the number of vehicles in measurement points and compared them against the real ones published by the mobility department of Malaga. Our results show that the number of vehicles in 11 out 12 sensors of the simulated map are under 1 % the real value, and 0.8 % on average if we consider all of them.

As a matter of future work we wish to study the previous optimizations process (traffic lights, routes, etc.) required before applying our solution, as well as extend the geographical area to be analyzed to include the entire city which represents not only more vehicles and analysis time, but also more sensors. It will be interesting to compare our FGA with other competitor algorithms which could be applied to our case study by using the available data (sensors) as inputs. However, at the moment they are hard to find.   /

Acknowledgments. This research has been partially funded by project number 8.06/ 5.47.4142 in collaboration with the VSB-Technical University of Ostrava and Universidad de Málaga UMA/FEDER FC14-TIC36, programa de fortalecimiento de las capacidades de I+D+i en las universidades 2014–2015, de la Consejería de Economía, Innovación, Ciencia y Empleo, cofinanciado por el fondo europeo de desarrollo regional (FEDER). Also, partially funded by the Spanish MINECO project TIN2014-57341-R (http://moveon.lcc.uma.es). The authors would like to thank the FEDER of European Union for financial support via project "Movilidad Inteligente: Wi-Fi, Rutas y Contaminación" (maxCT) of the "Programa Operativo FEDER de Andalucía 2014-2020". We also thank all Agency of Public Works of Andalusia Regional Government staff and researchers for their dedication and professionalism. Daniel H. Stolfi is supported by a FPU grant (FPU13/00954) from the Spanish Ministry of Education, Culture and Sports. University of Malaga. International Campus of Excellence Andalucia TECH.

References

1. Angius, F., Reineri, M., Chiasserini, C., Gerla, M., Pau, G.: Towards a realistic optimization of urban traffic flows. In: 2012 15th International IEEE Conference on Intelligent Transportation Systems (ITSC), pp. 1661–1668, Sep 2012
2. Bera, S., Rao, K.V.K.: Estimation of origin-destination matrix from traffic counts: The state of the art. European Transport - Trasporti Europei **49**(49), 3–23 (2011)
3. Hazelton, M.L.: Statistical inference for time varying origin-destination matrices. Transp. Res. Part B: Methodological **42**(6), 542–552 (2008)
4. Krajewicz, D., Erdmann, J., Behrisch, M., Bieker, L.: Recent development and applications of SUMO - Simulation of Urban MObility. Int. J. Adv. Syst. Meas. **5**(3), 128–138 (2012)
5. Krajewicz, D., Wagner, P.: Large-scale vehicle routing scenarios based on pollulant emissions. In: Meyer, G., Valldorf, J. (eds.) Advanced Microsystems for Automotive Applications, pp. 237–246. Springer, Heidelberg (2011)
6. Kwatirayo, S., Almhana, J., Liu, Z.: Adaptive traffic light control using VANET: A case study. In: 2013 9th International Wireless Communications and Mobile Computing Conference (IWCMC), pp. 752–757, Jul 2013
7. Li, B.: Bayesian inference for origin-destination matrices of transport networks using the EM algorithm. Technometrics **47**(4), 399–408 (2005)
8. Lo, H.P., Chan, C.P.: Simultaneous estimation of an origin-destination matrix and link choice proportions using traffic counts. Transp. Res. Part A: Policy Pract. **37**(9), 771–788 (2003)
9. Mckenney, D., White, T.: Distributed and adaptive traffic signal control within a realistic traffic simulation. Eng. Appl. Artif. Intell. **26**(1), 574–583 (2013)
10. Nie, Y.M., Zhang, H.M.: A variational inequality formulation for inferring dynamic origin-destination travel demands. Transp. Res. Part B: Methodological **42**(7), 635–662 (2008)

11. Papaleondiou, L.G., Dikaiakos, M.D.: TrafficModeler: a graphical tool for programming microscopic traffic simulators through high-level abstractions. In: IEEE 69th Vehicular Technology Conference, VTC Spring 2009, pp. 1–5, Apr 2009
12. Sánchez-Medina, J., Galán-Moreno, M., Rubio-Royo, E.: Traffic signal optimization in saragossa under congestion conditions, using genetic algorithms, traffic microsimulation, and cluster computing. IEEE Trans. Intell. Transp. Syst. **11**(1), 132–141 (2010)
13. Stolfi, D.H., Alba, E.: Red Swarm: Reducing travel times in smart cities by using bio-inspired algorithms. Appl. Soft Comput. **24**, 181–195 (2014)
14. Stolfi, D.H., Alba, E.: Smart mobility policies with evolutionary algorithms: the adapting info panel case. In: Proceedings of the 2015 Conference on Genetic and Evolutionary Computation Conference, GECCO 2015, Madrid (2015, in Press)
15. Gong, Z.: Estimating the urban OD matrix: A neural network approach. Eur. J. Oper. Res. **106**(1), 108–115 (1998)

Social Robotics

Social Navigation Restrictions for Interactive Robots Using Augmented Reality

Francisco J. Rodríguez Lera$^{(\boxtimes)}$, Fernando Casado, Camino Fernández, and Vicente Matellán

School of Industrial Engineering and Information Technology, University of León, León, Spain
{fjrodl,fcasag00,camino.fernandez,vmato}@unileon.es
http://robotica.unileon.es

Abstract. This paper describes the navigation mechanisms proposed for a mobile robot that uses augmented reality as interaction mechanism and laser scanners as main sensors. The peculiarities imposed by this interaction mechanism require continuous tracking of the person being escorted. The mechanism proposed for detecting and tracking people is based on a population of Kalman Filters and a basic association algorithm that matches past and new observations. The navigation system has been designed taking into account the special needs that an augmented reality interaction system imposes to a social navigation algorithm. This navigation system is integrated into a motivational control architecture that is also briefly described, as well as some preliminary experiments.

Keywords: Social navigation · Path planning · Augmented reality · Human-robot interaction

1 Introduction

Navigating in a socially acceptable way is an important ability for mobile robots in populated environments that requires efficiently detecting and tracking humans to negotiate the space with. In particular, walking side by side is not a trivial problem that involves relative positioning calculations to the accompanying person taking into account the environment limitations (narrow corridors, turnings, etc.) as well as keeping its track towards its destination.

Social robots also have to take into account their interaction mechanisms when navigating with humans. We have developed a low-cost mobile robot whose interaction abilities are based on augmented reality [9]. This makes "interactive navigation" even harder because the robot needs to orient the screen to the person at all times and the screen has a fixed position in the robot frame.

In this context, the problem that we want to solve can be summarized as walking side-by-side with a person while guiding it to a defined goal in an already mapped indoor environment.

© Springer International Publishing Switzerland 2015
J.M. Puerta et al. (Eds.): CAEPIA 2015, LNAI 9422, pp. 347–356, 2015.
DOI: 10.1007/978-3-319-24598-0_31

Navigation in peopled, mapped, indoor environments has been faced in the literature from different perspectives as reviewed in [14]. Many approaches just consider people as obstacles to be avoided or taking into account social conventions [10].

The problem of navigation for accompanying robots can be divided into three different sub-problems: guiding, following, and side by side navigation. Guiding a person [4] or a group of people [5] proposals usually assume that the robot leads and the people is able to follow it. Experiments [6] have shown that the direction-following behavior is significantly more human-like than when the robot follows the persons path in the following robot sub-problem.

Regarding side by side navigation, many proposals are related to wheelchair navigation. In this way, Prassler et al. [13] extended the velocity obstacle navigation algorithm to track a virtual target which allow them to vary the robot's heading and velocity according to the locomotion of the accompanied person and the environment. Kobayashi et al. [7] have used similar approaches incorporating the "comfort zone" concept from proxemics.

Morales et al. [12] proposed a utility function to approximate and predict the trajectory of the walking partner. We propose a similar approach, which implies that the robot has to be able to efficiently identify and track the person walking with it.

In our platform we will use a 2D laser range finder for tracking the people. This laser is place at 1.1 m height in the robot oriented perpendicularly to the robot front, which means that people is detected at chest level. The robot has additional range sensors at 0.3 m for obstacle detection, as well as an RGB-D camera used for scene recognition and navigation process.

One of the alternatives for locating and tracking people under these conditions is the use of a particle filter as [11]. In our proposal we used an approach similar to the one proposed in [2] were Kalman Filters are used.

The paper is organized as follows: Sect. 2 presents the basic social navigation system. Next section describes the different strategies involved in social robot navigation using AR. The design of the system along with first tests are presented in Sect. 4. Conclusions and further works are discussed in Sect. 5.

2   Control Architecture

The proposed navigation system is integrated in an hybrid architecture [8] based on motivational variables. The navigation module of the architecture is sketched in Fig. 1.

The motivational system can activate two different navigation mechanisms: individual or social navigation. The individual produces smooth and safe trajectories using a map, that will be executed by the local navigator. The local planner update the trajectories according the environment evolution.

When social navigation is activated, the trajectory is calculated according an interaction plan which can be verbal or non verbal. In a verbal interaction the user only needs an environmental noise-free area. In a non-verbal approach

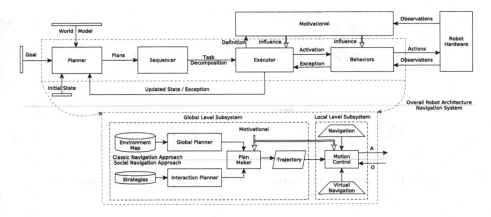

Fig. 1. Navigation architecture.

how the information is served to user is the key because it usually needs visual perception.

When a trajectory is generated the local planner uses the information from the sensors of the robot to navigate. In classic approaches obstacle avoidance is the main restriction for the local planner, but in social navigation the major restriction are proxemic requirements.

The "Global Level Subsystem" computes collision-free courses to a target position. The Interaction Planner computes paths that allow walking side-by-side with a person when the social approach is active, and also recalculates the pose at the final destination according to the interaction restrictions.

The "Local Level Subsystem" has three navigation units. The main unit named "motion control" which manages the velocity and position control of the platform, although only velocity control has been used in this work. The "navigation" unit which computes collision-free courses to a target position taking into account the stationary and moving obstacles using the Curvature Velocity method [15]. The "virtual navigation" unit which generates relative targets according to a defined relative position of the robot with respect to the person which is to be accompanied.

As perception in the robot takes place at discrete time steps (20 Hz), we can consider the problem of navigating side by side while showing the AR screen at a discrete time step t, as shown in Fig. 4, which requires a precise tracking of the accompanying person.

Our tracking system maintains a set S of tracked moving elements. From this set we extract a tracked person with whom the robot is going to navigate side by side.

We can define the perceptual space of the robot for tracking people around as a set of 2D points that represent the maximum distance without obstacles from the sensor up to 12 m. Given a view from above as in Fig. 2, what we get from the environment (left side of Fig. 2) is set of points at 20 Hz (right side).

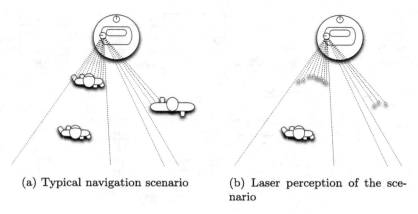

(a) Typical navigation scenario

(b) Laser perception of the scenario

Fig. 2. Display configurations in the platform.

These points are clustered if the euclidean distance between two successive points in the laser beam is lower than an heuristically established distance (D_{max}). Thus, each of the clusters are a set of points as shown in Fig. 3 that we called a "segment" as in [1].

For each of the clusters the tracking system calculates:

- *Segment*, the straight line from the first to the last point in the cluster.
- *Center*, the centroid of the points of the segments.
- *Length* of the cluster, defined as the sum of all distance of consecutive points (P_i, P_{i+1})
- *Width* of the cluster as the distance from the first point to the last point in the segment.
- *Depth* defined as the maximum distance from every point P_i to the segment.
- *Orientation* defined as the unit vector perpendicular to the segment that goes through the centroid.
- *Distance* to robot, defined as the distance from the centroid to the center of the robot.

Once the clusters have been characterized, they are classified as "potential persons" if the length, width, depth and distance values of the cluster meet some predefined thresholds. Then we use a Kalman Filter based multi-target tracker [3] to get updated predictions of people's positions and velocities. The main components of the tracker are:

- State prediction. Each person is represented as $x = (x, y, v_x, v_y)$, where $P = (x, y)$ are the center of the track and $V = (v_x, v_y)$ are the velocities, that are initialized to zero for each new track.
- Motion prediction. We have supposed a constant velocity model: $P_t = P_{t-1} + V * t$.
- Measurement prediction. (x, y) are directly observable, so H is 2×2 identity matrix for x and y and zero for v_x and v_y.

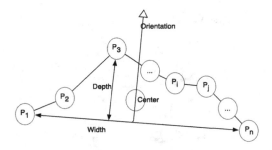

Fig. 3. Segment elements.

- Observation. We use the potential persons obtained from the clusters.
- Data association. The correspondence algorithm assigns the closest centroid from the new segments observed to the predicted position of the current existing trackers. If there were new segments no assigned to previously existing trackers, a new tracker is created.
- Estimation. The state and measurement prediction models are linear, so a non-extended Kalman filter is employed under the Gaussian assumption.

Each tracked element has an associated "confidence value" defined as the number of times the track has got a right association, versus the times it has not got one in the data association step. This value is used to choose the person to walk with (H). Its position and its velocity are incorporated into the control architecture described in next section. If a given person has not got an association from the observations in a given period, that person is removed from the S set.

Let us name H as the tracked human, and R the robot. $p_H(t)$ and $p_R(t)$ are their positions in instant t, and v_H and v_R the velocities, all of them calculated by the tracking system previously described. The desired relative position of the robot with respect to the human will be given by the vector $p_H - p_R$ as described in [13]. In the figure p^- and v^- represent the desired position and velocity for the robot, while $\hat{p}$ and $\hat{v}$ denote the predicted positions. The velocity $\hat{v}_R(t+1)$ will be the input generated by the "virtual navigation" layer for the "navigation" layer, and will be calculated taking into account the desired distance to maintain with the person d_L, the predicted position of the person $\hat{p}_H(t+1)$ and the error from the previously desired position of the robot ($p_R^-(t)$) and the real one $p_R(t)$.

3   Navigation with AR

The virtual navigation system described in the preceding section make up the basic social navigation system. Our interaction system is based on non-verbal communication using augmented reality (AR) which raises the question of how the navigation algorithm impacts in our interaction mechanism.

We have identified two main problems associated with the navigation system if we want to show augmented reality in our robot: the way the augmented

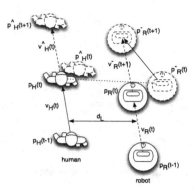

Fig. 4. Side by side navigation.

information is presented during the navigation, and the best pose of the robot to show the goal in a static scene using AR.

The first problem is related to the classic guide task and has associated the proxemics issue. The robot has to control the human position during navigation because we have to manage the social distance and the human territoriality space to offer a safe AR solution.

The second one is related to occlusion problems. Given a static goal, the planner should choose the best place to present the virtual information through its display. So the final pose will be given according screen setting. Instead of classic verbal messages as "this is the object" or "the object is here" we are going to present a virtual mark in the screen of the robot which marks the goal or the object. This will solve classical spacial deixis concerns associated with the absence of contextual information.

3.1 Proxemics Strategy

Augmented reality was used as a guiding tool during the navigation process, which requires specialized calculation of the orientation during navigation planning as previously described. The navigation system has also to take into account proxemics issues, in particular the relative distance to the human. Namely, if the robot gets closer than the "personal distance" (less than 1.2 m), then an action has to be done, such as increasing the speed or stopping the platform and ask to increase human distance. The local planner deals with these issues.

Figure 5 presents the proxemics space and motion control of our differential robot, showing both angular velocity ω, the linear velocity v decomposed into linear wheels velocity (v_r, v_l), and the Instantaneous Curvature Center (ICC) of a calculated radius R for generation the robot local trajectory. The kinematic model in the world frame is presented in Eqs. 1, 2, 3.

$$v(t) = w(t)R = \frac{1}{2}(v_r(t) + v_l(t)) \qquad w(t) = \frac{v_r(t) - v_l(t)}{L} \qquad (1)$$

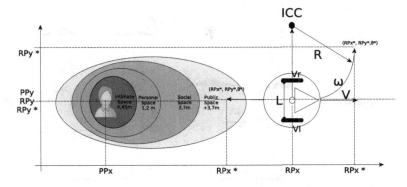

Fig. 5. Human proxemics space and motion control of a differential-drive robot.

$$\dot{x}(t) = v(t)cos\theta(t) \quad \dot{y}(t) = v(t)sin\theta(t) \quad \dot{\theta}(t) = w(t) \tag{2}$$

$$\begin{bmatrix} \dot{x}(t) \\ \dot{y}(t) \\ \dot{\theta}(t) \end{bmatrix} = \begin{bmatrix} cos\theta(t) & 0 \\ sen\theta(t) & 0 \\ 0 & 1 \end{bmatrix} \begin{bmatrix} v(t) \\ w(t) \end{bmatrix} \tag{3}$$

As previously explained, during the navigation process, the local navigation subsystem manages the velocity to maintain the right position and velocity according to the pose and velocity prediction of the "potential person".

3.2 Occlusion Strategy

The aim of this strategy is to correct the robot's final position. The motivational system would decide if the AR is going to be used or not, if so, the robot has to compute the final pose to be able to show the AR to the user, if not, the final pose just need to be the required position. The strategy database connected to interaction planner will contain the solutions available according to the robot morphology.

We have considered two solutions to this problem depending on the morphology of the robot. Figure 6 shows them and their associated solutions. In morphology 1 the display is situated on robot's back, while morphology 2 presents the display in the front of robot. Unfortunately, each morphology presents problems related to occlusions: the display may occlude the goal or the object to interact with.

We have depicted in Fig. 6 four situations that appears when considering the position of the display. Situations 1 and 3 correspond to morphology 1, where the human is looking the back of the robot which is looking to the object. Situations 2 and 4 correspond to morphology 2, where the robot and the person are looking at each other. Reciprocal situations make the non-verbal interaction through the AR unfeasible.

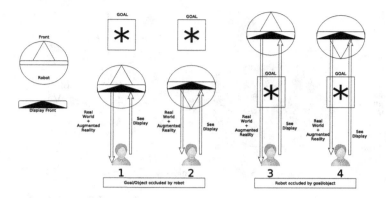

Fig. 6. The four solutions available depend on the position of the display.

4   Implementation and Test Design

In order to test our proposal we defined a simple task. Let us suppose that the user needs some item but he does not know where it is and that the robot knows the localization of the requested object. The user ask the robot for guiding to the object.

A classical task decomposition would be: (a) the human ask for the object verbally, (b) the robot calculates the route to the object, (c) the robot starts the navigation (d) the human follows the robot (e) the robot reach the position of the object and (f) robot says a verbal message.

The enhanced task using AR will be: (a) the human ask for the object, (b) the robot shows a message in the display (c) robot calculates the route to the object taking into account the orientation during the route, (d) the robot shows virtual arrows in the display while navigating to the goal, which means that the robot has to control the human position during navigation (e) the robot reach the position of the object (f) the robot choose the best place to notify the human with AR.

The aim of the experiments conducted so far were to validate the "potential person" system through the 2D LIDAR in a real environment and to test the first version of overall social navigation system under simulated conditions. All experiences were performed using ROS. Gazebo simulator was used in simulated environment.

The task was to reach an object that was on the table on a domestic environment as shown in Fig. 7. The robot had to navigate for the environment guiding the person until it reached the object and then it had to alert the user. The robot should show during the trajectory the AR on the screen and the human should be following it in safe conditions. The trajectory and the expected final pose (robot's back's staring at the table) are present in Fig. 7.

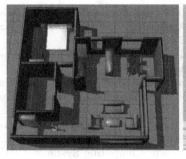

Fig. 7. Navigation in a simulated scenario

5 Conclusions and Further Work

We have presented an approach to improve the explicit HRI dialogue using augmented reality. Due to the robot morphology and the restrictions imposed by the dialogue using the AR, the path planning has to be modified to get not only the best trajectory, but the best point of view to human during the travel and at the final point.

The main contribution of this work is the proposal of a navigation control system oriented to augmented reality interaction that takes into account the social distance in the path planning phase, being able to reach a goal keeping the human distance and orientation.

The proposal has only been initially validated on the simulator, we are currently developing the quantitative evaluation of the proposal and then next we will try it in the real platform in order to validate the utility of the augmented reality in guidance assistance tasks.

Acknowledgments. This work has been partially funded by the Spanish Ministry of Economy and Competitiveness under grant DPI2013-40534-R.

References

1. Aguirre, E., Garcia-Silvente, M., Plata, J.: Leg detection and tracking for a mobile robot and based on a laser device, supervised learning and particle filtering. In: Armada, M.A., Sanfeliu, A., Ferre, M. (eds.) ROBOT 2013: First Iberian Robotics Conference. AISC, vol. 252, pp. 433–440. Springer, Heidelberg (2014)
2. Arras, K.O., Lau, B., Grzonka, S., Luber, M., Mozos, O.M., Meyer-Delius, D., Burgard, W.: Range-based people detection and tracking for socially enabled service robots. In: Prassler, E., et al. (eds.) Towards Service Robots for Everyday Environ. STAR, vol. 76, pp. 235–280. Springer, Heidelberg (2012)
3. Bar-Shalom, Y., Li, X.-R.: Multitarget-Multisensor Tracking: Principles and Techniques, vol. 19. YBS Publishing, Storrs (1995)

4. Cosgun, A., Florencio, D., Christensen, H.I., et al.: Autonomous person following for telepresence robots. In: 2013 IEEE International Conference on Robotics and Automation (ICRA), pp. 4335–4342. IEEE (2013)

5. Garrell, A., Sanfeliu, A.: Cooperative social robots to accompany groups of people. Int. J. Robot. Res. **31**(13), 1675–1701 (2012)

6. Gockley, R., Forlizzi, J., Simmons, R.: Natural person-following behavior for social robots. In: Proceedings of the ACM/IEEE International Conference on Human-Robot Interaction, pp. 17–24. ACM (2007)

7. Kobayashi, Y., Suzuki, R., Sato, Y., Arai, Kuno, M.Y., Yamazaki, A., Yamazaki, K.: Robotic wheelchair easy to move and communicate with companions. In: 2013 ACM SIGCHI Conference on Human Factors in Computing Systems, CHI 2013, Paris, France, 27 April–2 May, 2013, Extended Abstracts, pp. 3079–3082 (2013)

8. Rodríguez Lera, F.J., Matellán, V.: Hybrid architecture for human-robot interaction: Updating the classical three-layer solution. In: Actas del XV Workshop en Agentes Físicos (2013)

9. Rodríguez Lera, F.J., Rodríguez, V., Rodríguez, C., Matellán, V.: Augmented reality in robotic assistance for the elderly. In: Alonso, I.G. (ed.) International Technology Robotics Applications. Intelligent Systems, Control and Automation: Science and Engineering, vol. 70. Springer International Publishing, Switzerland (2014)

10. Matellán, V., Simmons, R.: Implementing human-acceptable navigational behavior and a fuzzy controller for an autonomous robot. In: Actas del Workshop en Agentes Físicos (2002)

11. Montemerlo, D., Thrun, S., Whittaker, W.: Conditional particle filters for simultaneous mobile robot localization and people-tracking. In: International Conference on Robotics and Automation ICRA 2002 (2002)

12. Morales, Y., Kanda, T., Hagita, N.: Walking together: Side-by-side walking model for an interacting robot. J. Human-Robot Interact. **3**, 50–73 (2014)

13. Prassler, E., Bank, D., Klunge, B.: Key technologies in robot assistants: Motion coordination between a human and a mobile robot. In: ICASE: Institute of Control, Automation adn Systems Engineering, KOREA (2002)

14. Rios-Martinez, J., Spalanzani, A., Laugier, C.: From proxemics theory to socially-aware navigation: A survey. Int. J. Soc. Robot. **7**, 137–153 (2015)

15. Simmons, R.: The curvature-velocity method for local obstacle avoidance. In: Proceedings of the 1996 IEEE International Conference on Robotics and Automation, vol. 4, pp. 3375–3382. IEEE (1996)

Author Index